Writing the Past,
Writing the Future

Writing the Past, Writing the Future

Time and Narrative
in Gothic and Sensation Fiction

Richard S. Albright

Lehigh
University
Press

Bethlehem: Lehigh University Press

Associated University Presses
2010 Eastpark Boulevard
Cranbury, NJ 08512

The paper used in this publication meets the requirements of the American National Standard for Permanence of Paper for Printed Library Materials Z39.48-1984.

Library of Congress Cataloging-in-Publication Data

Albright, Richard S., 1951–
    Writing the past, writing the future : time and narrative in gothic and sensation fiction / Richard S. Albright.
        p. cm.
    Includes bibliographical references and index.
    ISBN 978-0-9801496-4-7 (alk. paper)
    1. Gothic fiction (Literary genre), English—History and criticism.   2. Time in literature.   3. Narration (Rhetoric)—History.   4. Sensationalism in literature.   I. Title.
    PR408.G68A44   2009
    823′.087209384—dc22   2008048325

PRINTED IN THE UNITED STATES OF AMERICA

To my family

Contents

Acknowledgments   9

Introduction   13

1. No Time Like the Present: *The Mysteries of Udolpho*   31

2. The Clock is Ticking: *Melmoth the Wanderer*   68

3. Transcending Time: Mary Shelley and the Power of Narrative   118

4. Aporia in the House: Three Sensation Novels   165

5. Conclusion   215

Notes   218

Works Cited   252

Index   262

Acknowledgments

I AM GRATEFUL TO MY PARENTS FOR FIRST AWAKENING MY LOVE OF LITER-
ature, and for instilling in me the determination that I needed to
complete this project; and to my wife, Marcia, and our children,
Christopher and Courtney, for their unceasing love and support.

I am thankful to the authors whose works I explore in this book,
to theorists such as Paul Ricoeur and M. M. Bakhtin for giving me
so much to think about, and to Edmund Burke for such a richly
evocative metaphor about succession and continuity.

Cynthia Dilgard, Beverly Schneller, and Robert Carballo, of Millersville University, read an early version of chapter 3 and provided
many helpful suggestions. I owe a great deal to Lehigh University
and its English Department for inspiring me during my two so-
journs there, a generation apart. I have little doubt that my perception of "double vision," the sense of a past superimposed on the
present that I experienced when I returned to Lehigh, informed
this project, and particularly resonated with my readings of some of
the incidents that I describe in chapters 1 and 4. The comments
and suggestions of Rosemary Mundhenk, Addison Bross, and Michael Mendelson (the latter from the Philosophy Department),
who each read a number of versions of this manuscript as it
evolved, were invaluable. Barry Kroll, though not directly involved
in this book, taught me a great deal about writing and teaching and
remains an unseen, and otherwise unacknowledged, presence
throughout. I always benefitted from the countless stimulating discussions about Gothic and sensation fiction with my good friend
and former colleague, Albert Sears, along with his support and encouragement.

I offer my special thanks to Scott Gordon of Lehigh's English Department and the Lehigh University Press, because—despite the
cliché—this book literally would not exist were it not for him; he
probably read more versions of these chapters than anyone else and
he always had an uncanny ability to pinpoint what I was trying to
say and what I needed to do to get myself back on track. Moreover,
he provided the nudge that prompted me to pursue this project to

its completion, as well as much advice and encouragement along the way.

I gratefully acknowledge the members of the North American Society for the Study of Romanticism (NASSR-L) and Victoria Nineteenth Century British Culture and Society (Victoria-L) Listservs, an extraordinary community of scholars, and John Rethorst of the WordPerfect Mac user group for his encyclopedic knowledge and unfailing willingness to offer assistance.

Finally, I must acknowledge a place: the beautiful Waidner-Spahr library at Dickinson College, where I did much of my reading, writing, and thinking.

Writing the Past,
Writing the Future

Introduction

[T]he people of England well know, that the idea of inheritance
furnishes a sure principle of conservation, and a sure principle
of transmission, without at all excluding a principle of improvement. . . . By a constitutional policy, working after the pattern
of nature, we hold, we transmit our government and our privileges, in the same manner in which we enjoy and transmit our
property and our lives. The institutions of policy, the goods of
fortune, the gifts of providence, are handed down to us, and
from us, in the same course and order. Our political system is
placed in a just correspondence and symmetry with the order of
the world . . .
—Edmund Burke, *Reflections on the Revolution in France*

[T]here does exist a partial overlapping between memory and
the historical past that contributes to the constitution of an
anonymous time, halfway between private time and public time.
The canonical example in this regard is that of a narrative received from the mouth of one of our ancestors . . . a bridge is
constructed between the historical past and memory by the ancestral narrative that serves as a relay station for memory directed to the historical past . . .

    If we proceed along this chain of memories, history tends to
become a we-relationship, extending in continuous fashion
from the first days of humanity to the present.
—Paul Ricoeur, *Time and Narrative*

The word "aporia" appears in person in Aristotle's famous text,
Physics IV (217b), which reconstitutes the aporia of time *dia
ton exoterikon logon* . . . (*Diaporeo* is Aristotle's term here; it
means "I'm stuck . . . I cannot get out, I'm helpless.") Therefore, for example—and it is more than just one example among
others—it is impossible to determine time both as entity and as
nonentity.
—Jacques Derrida, *Aporias*

TIME. ITS NATURE HAS PERPLEXED PHILOSOPHERS FOR THOUSANDS OF
years. Aristotle began his analysis of time by noting its paradoxical
character: "Some of it has happened and does not exist, and some
of it is in the future and does not yet exist; these constitute both

13

the infinite stretch of all time and the time that is with us at any moment; but it would appear to be impossible for anything which consists of things that do not exist to exist itself." Aristotle later wondered at the fact that "time is not change, but at the same time . . . it does not exist without change."[1] Augustine's mind "burn[ed] to solve this intricate puzzle" of time and eternity, going so far as to ponder the question of what God was doing before he created time.[2]

This old question about the nature of time assumes new importance in eighteenth- and nineteenth-century Britain, becoming a matter not just for philosophers and theologians, but for an increasing segment of the population, in response to a number of scientific developments, the emergence of new ideas about history, and the cataclysm of the French Revolution. The period from the late eighteenth through the mid-nineteenth centuries reveals a tremendous interest in situating the contemporary era in relation to the past, a collective desire for the kind of "bridge," in Ricoeur's terminology, "between the historical past and memory." Edmund Burke's *Reflections on the Revolution in France* provides a national version of this "ancestral narrative" by characterizing English history as a continuous chronicle of generations and values, a steady and uninterrupted movement from the past toward the future, like Ricoeur's "chain of memories." Burke repeatedly emphasizes order, symmetry, and progression, which he contrasts to the chaotic events taking place in France. In effect, he views English history, both its political history and the history of its peoples, as an unbroken and orderly narrative "to the end of time." He frequently employs literary analogies: he uses Horace's *Ars Poetica* to draw a parallel between the construction of poems and states, he characterizes the events across the English Channel as a tragic drama, and he makes allusions to Aristotle's theories of drama and to the contemporary actors David Garrick and Sarah Siddons. If English history is a narrative, then the French Revolution is to be feared for its narrative discontinuities as well as for the political upheavals it has caused, in a century already possessed, as Robert Miles puts it, of an "anxious conception of its place in history."[3]

Nor was Burke alone in drawing analogies between literature and history. In fact, history and fiction inform each other in the second half of the eighteenth century. Representations of history become increasingly "literary" during this period. For example, Gibbon's *The Decline and Fall of the Roman Empire* (1776–88), is strongly marked by a narratorial presence. The desire to create stories out of chronicles of events, "to make a plausible story out of a congeries of 'facts,' which, in their unprocessed form, make no sense at all" is reflected in the process that Hayden White calls "emplotment."[4] We see this process at work in the popular fiction of the period as well, and one genre that illustrates this phenomenon is the Gothic romance. Gothic novels first create and then resolve chaos and confusion by means of increasingly complex plots, a characteristic satirized most famously in Jane Austen's *Northanger Abbey*.[5] Moreover, if the English national identity is represented in narratological terms by Burke, and there is a "just correspondence and symmetry" between the world of nature and all that constitutes England for Burke—its property, lives and political system—then it is not surprising that central to many of the immensely popular Gothic novels during the 1790s is the issue of identity, where that identity is figured in terms of one's relation to past generations. The typical heroine of an Ann Radcliffe novel must uncover her identity, which usually involves solving the mystery of a maze of relationships that are seldom as they initially seem. For example, *The Mysteries of Udolpho*'s Emily St. Aubert must figure out who she is, in part by discovering the identity of the mystery woman at whose likeness her father longingly gazed—a likeness referred to twice on the same page as "a lady, not her mother."[6] In solving this mystery, Emily must construct a narrative of the past that will, among other things, determine her legitimacy (hence the coherence of her generational narrative), because the text encourages us to believe that the mystery woman, who so closely resembles Emily, is indeed her mother, when in fact we eventually learn that she is Emily's aunt.

At the other end of the political spectrum from Burke, William Godwin and other radicals believed strongly in human "perfectibility," the notion of continuous progress toward a perfection never ultimately to be achieved:

> [M]an is perfectible. This proposition needs some explanation.
>
> By perfectible, it is not meant that he is capable of being brought to perfection. But the word seems sufficiently adapted to express the faculty of being continually made better and receiving perpetual improvement; and in this sense it is here to be understood. The term perfectible, thus explained, not only does not imply the capacity of being brought to perfection, but stands in express opposition to it. If we could arrive at perfection, there would be an end to our improvement.[7]

Note that perfectibility does not suggest the *achievement* of perfection, but "stands in express opposition to it," for achieving perfection would put an end to progress. It is the movement that is all-important. Despite vast differences in political philosophies, Burke and Godwin both emphasize the principle of movement, from past to present, and from present to future. Both view time as a narrative of human (and, in Burke's case, particularly British) development. This regarding of time as a progressive flow, with narratological properties, is a characteristically eighteenth century concept of temporality, and such a view informs the popular fiction of the period. The Gothic novel illustrates the eighteenth century's preoccupation with time by its emphasis on the relationship between past and present. Following the pattern established by Horace Walpole's *The Castle of Otranto* in 1764, most Gothic romances are set in the past and are concerned with buried secrets that threaten order and stability in the novel's present. These secrets often involve the usurpation of property or titles, placing inheritance (the instrument of Burke's "sure principle of transmission") at risk.

Since the blossoming of interest in the Gothic that began in the 1970s, the majority of critics have been fascinated by the genre's exploration of the psychology of the self or its treatment of matters of gender and patriarchal power, in part because Gothic narratives often feature the confinement of young female protagonists. Indeed, the term "Female Gothic," which entered the lexicon via Ellen Moers's *Literary Women* in 1976,[8] has for a time become nearly synonymous with "Gothic." The work of feminist and psychoanalytic critics has helped to focus attention on a genre that traditional historiographers of the novel dismissed as having "little intrinsic merit" and being at "the level of mediocrity and worse."[9] This revival of interest in the Gothic has helped us view texts such as *Otranto,* Clara Reeve's *The Old English Baron,* and Ann Radcliffe's romances in exciting new ways. Yet while these readings have revived interest in the genre, and have occasionally addressed issues such as inheritance, their emphasis has been on the extent to which history and law have been symbols of patriarchal power.

Jacqueline Howard takes a different approach. Viewing Gothic romances dialogically, as texts that encode a range of discourses, Howard uses M. M. Bakhtin's theories of dialogism to explore the intertextual relations of Gothic novels at the time of their writing, identifying a series of contemporary discourses in the text of Radcliffe's *The Mysteries of Udolpho.*[10] These range from discourses on sensibility and taste, politics, and even late eighteenth-century debates on the aesthetics of landscaping, when Quesnel and St. Aubert argue over Quesnel's proposed "improvements" to his estate in Gascony, including whether to cut down the stately old chestnut that St. Aubert refers to as "the glory of the estate."[11]

There are some obvious advantages to a critical methodology that does not depend on gender, as a number of critics have resorted to splitting the Gothic genre into subgenres to accommodate novels that do not fit easily into a gender-based taxonomy. For example, Matthew Lewis's *The Monk* has sometimes been placed into an aberrant category of masculine horror-Gothic, in contrast to the more typical female terror-Gothic (e.g., Radcliffe et al.). But even this approach is doomed to be problematical. For example, where does one place Charlotte Dacre's *Zofloya*? When mentioned at all by critics, *Zofloya* is usually seen as a female version of *The Monk*, with a female author and protagonist, so it becomes, if our model depends on gender, an aberration of an aberration, or simply what Diane Long Hoeveler called "the most eccentric female Gothic ever penned."[12] Viewing Gothic fiction dialogically, rather than monologically, however, tends to open these novels to a variety of readings. *The Monk*, for example, can be seen not as an exception to the model, but as encoding its own particular set of discourses, in this case, discourses on French sensationalism, the *Sturm und Drang* movement, and Germanic folk and fairy tales. I want to employ a similar approach to examine the discourses of temporality that are encoded in several popular novels of the eighteenth and nineteenth centuries, discourses that often reveal anxieties about the changing perceptions of time.

Consider, for example, the discourses on the past that are a common feature of Gothic romances. Indeed, a setting in the distant past is regarded as one of the standard Gothic conventions, yet it is seldom given serious attention, beyond noting, as David Punter does, that Gothic novels are much less concerned with historical accuracy than "conjuring a sense of 'past-ness.'"[13] In fact, I maintain that there is more to the Gothic romance's temporal setting than mere atmosphere. The past setting enables the Gothic romance to narrate anxieties about genealogical coherence from a safe distance, which explains the emphasis in these novels on themes of usurpation and inheritance.

The Gothic novel's concerns about genealogy—figuring one's identity in terms of one's relation to past generations—are echoed in the sensation novel of the 1860s, which many critics from Punter onward have associated with the Gothic. My choice of Gothic and sensation fiction as two of the subjects of my study is not dictated by a desire to undertake an historiographic approach—to write the history, or rise, or development of the novel—or even to make a claim that one genre necessarily led to the other. The two genres have elements in common, but such

Gothic elements inform much popular fiction, not just the genre of the sensational. (Consider Dickens, who employed devices such as Gothic atmospherics, suspense, and mysteries of genealogy and identity in novels such as *Oliver Twist, Bleak House,* and *Our Mutual Friend.*) I do not intend to show how (or if) Gothic *became* sensation fiction, but wish only to focus on several "moments" in eighteenth- and nineteenth-century popular fiction. I regard the movement from the Gothic romance to the sensation novel as less a "movement"—implying a state of evolution—than as an example of the type of dialectic that informed Wordsworth and Coleridge's plan for the *Lyrical Ballads.* Coleridge, writing of this decision nearly two decades later, referred to his frequent discussions with his friend on:

> the two cardinal points of poetry, the power of exciting the sympathy of the reader by a faithful adherence to the truth of nature, and the power of giving the interest of novelty by the modifying colours of the imagination. . . . The thought suggested itself . . . that a series of poems might be composed of two sorts. In the one, the incidents and agents were to be, in part at least, supernatural; and the excellence aimed at was to consist in the interesting of the affections by the dramatic truth of such emotions, as would naturally accompany such situations, supposing them real. . . . For the second class, subjects were to be chosen from ordinary life; the characters and incidents were to be such, as will be found in every village and its vicinity, where there is a meditative and feeling mind, to seek after them, or to notice them, when they present themselves.[14]

The Gothic romance, despite Ann Radcliffe's use of what has often been called the "explained supernatural" still falls into Coleridge's first "sort."[15] As Tzvetan Todorov classified it, "we generally distinguish, within the literary Gothic, two tendencies: that of the supernatural explained (the 'uncanny'), as it appears in the novels of Clara Reeves and Ann Radcliffe; and that of the supernatural accepted (the 'marvelous'), which is characteristic of the works of Horace Walpole, M. G. Lewis and Maturin." Even though the situations in Radcliffe's novels, by Todorov's definition, ultimately are classified as uncanny, "the effect of the fantastic is certainly produced . . . in Ann Radcliffe, up to the moment when we are sure that everything which has happened is susceptible of a rational explanation."[16] Indeed, such explanations are sometimes deferred for hundreds of pages.

Sensation fiction falls into Coleridge's "second class" of subjects; in Wordsworth's own terminology, his intention was "to choose incidents and situations from common life, and to relate or describe them, throughout, as far as was possible, in a selection of language really used by men; and at the same time, to throw over them a certain colouring of imagination, whereby ordinary things should be presented to the mind in an unusual way . . ."[17] One could argue, of course, that the incidents often depicted in sensation fiction—adultery, bigamy, madness, and murder—are anything but ordinary. In fact, the possibility that they *are* ordinary was precisely the cause of all the contemporary anxiety about the genre. As H. L. Mansel put it in his 1863 review of two dozen sensation novels, "The man who shook our hand with a hearty English grasp half an hour ago—the woman whose beauty and grace were the charm of last night, and whose gentle words sent us home better pleased with the world and with ourselves—how exciting to think that under these pleasing outsides may be concealed some demon in human shape, a Count Fosco or a Lady Audley!" In Henry James's words, these novels depict "those mysterious of mysteries, the mysteries which are at our own doors."[18] And they not only *depict* such mysteries, they might, according to the fears of the critics, *contribute* to such transgressions. Here is Mansel again, expressing the view of many critics:

> Excitement, and excitement alone, seems to be the great end at which they [the writers] aim. . . . And as excitement, even when harmless in kind, cannot be continually produced without becoming morbid in degree, works of this class manifest themselves as belonging, some more, some less, but all to some extent, to the morbid phenomena of literature—indications of a wide-spread corruption, of which they are in part both the effect and the cause; called into existence to supply the cravings of a diseased appetite, and contributing themselves to foster the disease, and to stimulate the want which they supply.[19]

Another reviewer in 1863 expressed fears "about women's mental impressionability" and complained that sensation novels "drugged thought and reason" and adversely affected women's nerves and their intuition. Of even more concern, such fiction could "open out a picture of life free from all the perhaps irksome checks that confine their own existence."[20] Thus, the Wordsworthian goal of making the ordinary—or what might lie behind the ordinary—interesting, could be dangerously interesting.

In any case, in the sensation novel, the construction of the past narrative (again, often involving questions of identity) is usually accomplished by an amateur detective, or perhaps by means of a series of narrators, as in Wilkie Collins's *The Woman in White* or *The*

Moonstone, in which the reader plays the role of the detective assembling evidence. In fact, Hayden White draws a parallel between the role of the historian and the role of the "competent detective" in his discussion of what R. G. Collingwood called "the constructive imagination." Both the historian and the detective must fashion a coherent narrative from the accounts of multiple (and at times, conflicting) viewpoints and from fragmentary evidence: "The events are *made* into a story by the suppression or subordination of certain of them and the highlighting of others, by characterization, motific repetition, variation of tone and point of view, alternative descriptive strategies, and the like."[21]

The narratives of past events in Gothic and sensation fiction almost always reveal discontinuities of some kind, such as the Gothic's preoccupation with usurpations of property or titles, either by someone of another social class (Horace Walpole's *The Castle of Otranto*) or more often by a second son (Schedoni in Radcliffe's *The Italian,* Heathcliff in *Wuthering Heights*), causing a disruption of primogeniture. This usurpation presents a mystery that must be decoded, and the mystery is often as convoluted as the passages of the crumbling castle in which the protagonist has been confined. Consistent with the Victorian anxieties about the integrity of the domestic sphere, in sensation fiction, the discontinuity or figurative usurpation may stem from a domestic transgression, such as a secret prior marriage (Mary Elizabeth Braddon's *Lady Audley's Secret* or *Aurora Floyd*) or the birth of a child (Collins's *The Dead Secret* or *The Woman in White*). All these issues involve complications that affect the orderly transmission of property. We might view primogeniture as a desire for a coherent, ordered, Burkean narrative from the past to the future, a narrative written with property, and one that has often been complicated by the problem of younger sons. (Note that Burke explicitly links government, privileges, property, and lives, in his "sure principle of transmission.")[22] Both the Gothic and the sensation novel reveal anxieties about this "primogeniture narrative."

We have seen this anxiety about succession as early as *The Castle of Otranto* in 1764 and *The Old English Baron* in 1777. And while the French Revolution certainly influenced Burke and could well have influenced Ann Radcliffe's novels of the 1790s, it is rather difficult to account for how it might have contributed to Walpole's novel a quarter-century earlier. A more compelling explanation is that these precursor texts (Walpole and Reeve) emerged in response to the century's growing concerns about the aporetic nature of time. An *aporia* is a rhetorical figure marking hesitation. The word literally means "without passage" in the Greek—Derrida translates the term as "I'm stuck." It was used most famously by Aristotle in the *Physics,* in his discussion (particularly germane to our purposes) of the being and non-being of time. Therefore, the term conveys the added sense of "inarticulable contradiction." Throughout this project, I will be using *aporia* in both connotations—that of hesitation or "stuckness," as well as a paradox or contradiction that resists articulation.

In *Time and Narrative,* Paul Ricoeur analyzes the temporal perspectives of Aristotle, Augustine, and Heidegger, all of whom posed penetrating questions on the nature of time. One of the central aporias that Ricoeur investigates concerns our attempt to reconcile phenomenological time and cosmological time, to situate ourselves and our own experience of time in the context of the time of the universe. Ricoeur maintains that we bridge this gap in three ways: first, calendars and related mechanisms are connectors because they "make historical time conceivable and manipulable." The calendar belongs to both human and astronomical universes, using the measurement of the motions of heavenly bodies, to keep track of human events. The second connector is the succession of generations, because we can use them to travel back in time through a chain of ancestral memories, and thus "situate our own temporality in the series of generations, with the more or less necessary help of calendar time." The third connector is narrative, which performs a "mediating role" by refiguring the historical past, reinscribing lived time on the time of the world. Time and narrative, Ricoeur asserts at the outset of his study, exist in a dialectical relationship. "Time becomes human time to the extent that it is organized after the manner of a narrative; narrative, in turn, is meaningful to the extent that it portrays the features of temporal existence." The Burkean "narrative of generations," then, unites two of these mechanisms of temporal reconciliation in a powerful metaphor that informs some of the most popular fiction of the Romantic and Victorian periods.[23]

This process of temporal reconciliation is not limited to narratives of past generations. The eighteenth- and nineteenth-century fascination with time often took the form of extrapolation into the future. The third type of novel that I will examine in this book is the apocalyptic "end of the world" romance that enjoyed a brief popularity in the first few decades of the nineteenth century. If Radcliffean Gothic novels situate one's identity in terms of one's relation to past generations, then the apocalyptic novel, which often employs the Gothic affect of terror and horror, projects the series of generations forward to some ultimate end. They satisfy "our deep need for intelligible Ends. We project ourselves—a small, humble elect, perhaps—past the End, so as to see the structure [of our lives] whole, a thing we cannot do from our spot of time in the middle."[24]

Originating in eighteenth-century "last of the race" myths of noble Celtic bards that were the product of nostalgia for a lost past,[25] many of these futuristic romances depict "comets, burning forests, [cities] in ruins, a dimmed sun, darkness and death."[26] Byron's 1816 poem "Darkness" adapts this model to portray his vision of the end of the world as synonymous with the end of all energy and motion.[27] Like Aristotle and Augustine, Byron seemed to associate time with motion—in the absence of the latter, the former ceases. These end-of-the-world romances appeared to be a product of contemporary fears of degeneration and decay in the cosmic order—such as planetary systems winding down.[28] Therefore, Burke's narrative of generational succession could either be seen as preservative of English law, property, and civilization (or in Godwin's hands, shaped into a progressive model), or it could just as easily be inverted to a degenerative model suggesting a clockwork mechanism winding down toward chaos, transmitting, not order, but disorder (entropy). Mary Shelley's *The Last Man* cleverly associates this pattern of decay with the natural world, using a worldwide plague as its agent. Ironically, in Burkean terms, the plague "work[s] after the pattern of nature." Appearing out of the east and moving westward just as the sun does, it is transmitted from one person to another.

The resonance and mythic power of Burke's metaphor may be explained by two particularly dramatic shifts in thinking about temporality that emerged during the second half of the eighteenth century and continued well into the nineteenth: changes in notions of the age of the universe, and the attitude toward history and the past. The temporal attributes of Gothic fiction that are often regarded simply as stock conventions emerged at a particular moment in response to the interplay of these two changes in the perception of temporality.

The entire scope of cosmological time underwent a dramatic shift during the century before Charles Darwin. The universe became dramatically older, from the previously accepted Biblical six-thousand-year universe to one literally thousands of times older. This model of the universe, influenced by the Protestant Reformation and certain eschatological views, had become solidified with the publication of Archbishop James Ussher's *The Annals of the*

World Deduced from the Origin of Time in 1658, giving creation a specific chronology at about the time that Cartesian thinking seemed to demand such an enumeration.[29]

But the literal Biblical chronology began to show signs of strain in the late eighteenth century as inconsistencies emerged from a number of fields of scientific endeavor. The resolution of these observed inconsistencies required the construction of a new "bridge" to the past, a revised narrative that would explain the universe's origins. Appearing in 1755, Immanuel Kant's first book, the *Universal Natural History and Theory of the Heavens,* interpreted the "small luminous patches" in the night sky seen through telescopes, as reported by Maupertuis in 1742, to be galaxies of individual stars seen from incredibly far away and proposed that Nature may have evolved from chaos to order over a period of "millions of years and centuries."[30] Kant thus greatly expanded both the size and age of the universe. Although Kant's *Universal Natural History* was not widely read, because its publisher went bankrupt as it was being printed and copies were impounded, his ideas were known in at least some circles.[31] A book that *was* widely read, however, was Georges Louis Leclerc, Comte de Buffon's 1778 *Epochs of Nature,* which calculated how long it would take each planet to cool to a temperature that could sustain life. Buffon arrived at a figure of nearly seventy-five thousand years for the age of the earth, not too far off from an earlier estimate by Sir Isaac Newton of about fifty thousand years, but which Newton had declined to publish due to conflicts with his own religious views.[32]

By the late eighteenth century, the aporetics of temporality therefore became more marked. If generations and calendar time make it "possible for every one of us to situate our own temporality in the series of generations"[33]—continuing the process begun and then extended through the genealogies in the biblical books of Genesis and Matthew—then the scope of this process changes dramatically. Instead of a cosmos thousands of years old, perhaps two hundred or so generations, one lifetime now had to be situated in relation to a universe several thousand lifetimes old (Buffon's figures), or hundreds of thousands, perhaps millions, of lifetimes in duration (Kant's). The "chain of memories" back to Adam was now too long to comprehend, and the length of one human life was therefore dwarfed almost into insignificance. Fiona J. Stafford notes that, while evolutionary theory is thought to be primarily a nineteenth-century phenomenon, "the insistent questions about the fixity of species and the Mosaic timescale of six thousand years were beginning to have significant psychological effects"[34] in the second half of the eighteenth century.

It seems only "natural" that popular fiction would be informed by this changing conception of cosmic time, because both generational succession and narrative are mediators between "the time of the soul and the time of the world"[35] and exist in a dialectical relationship with temporality. Hence the Gothic's emphasis on the "proper" succession of titles and property—think of Burke's "sure principle of transmission"—because if there is not a coherent narrative of generations, then all that one values becomes increasingly meaningless in the increasingly vast scale of time. The themes of usurpation and identity that pervade much popular British fiction from the 1760s through the 1860s reflect anxieties about the orderly transmission of property and cultural values across generations, anxieties that may have been exacerbated by the French Revolution. England's cultural identity during this period seems to depend on just such ideals of order and coherence. Much popular fiction, including the Gothic and the sensational, attempts to effect this coherence through narrative. In the past, whether it is the distant past of the Gothic novel or a character's personal past in the sensation novel, there is a secret transgression that poses a threat to this orderly and coherent transmission or property and identity, a shadow of the past that looms across the present. After a number of plot turns, the secret past is successfully narrated and the discontinuities usually resolved, so that coherence is achieved in the present and can in turn be transmitted to the next generation. This explains the emphasis on resolution through marriage that characterizes both types of novels, a resolution that often perplexes feminist critics who view such novels as primarily subversive of a patriarchal domestic ideology, and see the dominant social order ultimately reasserted, the subversion itself subverted.[36] But I will argue that these novels are not subversive as much as they are a means of negotiating discursive tensions. These tensions extend deeper than domestic ideologies and are bound up with the aporias of time itself, hence the preoccupation with situating the past in relation to the present and the desire to resolve these aporias through a variety of narrative strategies.

Besides the "aging" of the cosmos, the other shift in thinking about time that took place during the eighteenth century concerns attitudes toward history. Reinhart Koselleck identifies a "statistically measurable" German linguistic shift that occurred about 1750, from the "naturalized foreign word *Historie* . . . toward *Geschichte*," the former word referring to a report, or account, and the latter word, which means both "history" and "stories," combining the concepts of past events themselves as well as their representations. This linguistic shift corresponded to a recognition of time as a dynamic force that acted upon history and imparted a relativism to it: "History was temporalized in the sense that, thanks to the passing of time, it altered according to the given present, and with growing distance the nature of the past also altered." Koselleck quotes Goethe as having said "There remains no doubt these days that world history from time to time has to be rewritten . . . because new views emerge." Yet at the very same moment that history becomes increasingly relative, opening the way to multiple views of history, the word *geschichte* "condensed" from a plural form to a collective singular—*one* history—and the phrase "history itself" came into being.[37]

The paradox of one history that nevertheless contains multiple views over time, history becoming, in effect, a moving target, is of a piece with the aporias of time and motion addressed by both Aristotle and Augustine. Aristotle's conundrum that time is not movement and yet is not independent of movement (for we do not perceive any passage of time if we do not perceive change) is echoed by Augustine's claim that time is never still, and derives its length from movement.[38] A similar linguistic phenomenon occurs with the German word for *progress,* which emerges toward the end of the eighteenth century and is also, like the word for *history,* a collective singular. This is an intriguing development for a number of reasons. Koselleck points out that "the divide between previous experience and coming expectation opened up, and the difference between past and present increased, so that lived time was experienced as a rupture, as a period of transition in which the new and the unexpected continually happened."[39]

Progress, then, was associated with movement and transition. It was a carrier of the "new and the unexpected." M. M. Bakhtin's theories of heteroglossia are helpful here, for not only do novels incorporate multivoicedness because they contain multiple discourses, but Bakhtin refers to "the internal dialogism of the word . . . the dialogism that penetrates its entire structure." This "internal dialogism of the word finds expression in a series of peculiar features in semantics, syntax and stylistics."[40] *Geschichte* embodies this dialogism semantically in the way that it means both "history" and "stories"—what happened, as well as the way the events are described, their representation. Furthermore, both the words for *history* and *progress* are syntactically dialogic in that they are collective singulars. They transcend the binary structure of singular *or* plural by being both singular *and* plural, singular in form, and plural in meaning. There is a play of differences at work here, a discursive tension, that informs, "penetrates," the way that time and history were being thought of at the end of the eighteenth century.

Robert Miles has observed that the decade of the 1780s was "haunted by a sense of social and metaphysical dislocation," and the Middle Ages were now seen as "a period uncursed with the modern 'dissociation of sensibility.'"[41] This sense of separation from the continuity of the past, the experience of lived time as a "rupture" was intensified by "the swift change of experience embodied in the French Revolution. The break in continuity appeared to uncouple a past whose growing foreignness could only be illuminated and recovered by means of historical investigation."[42] Benedict Anderson has pointed out that this disruption of history led, first, to the proclamation of a new calendar by France's Convention *Nationale,* to begin on 22 September 1792, and, second, to the establishment, within twenty years of the Proclamation of the Year One, of history as a discipline, with its own journals and academic chairs.[43]

Nor was this sense of disruption, of a break with the past, peculiar to the 1790s. As the nineteenth century unfolded, it revealed a steady stream of developments in geology, biology, and history, all emphasizing that the present was not like the past. "When [the Victorians] thought of themselves as an Age, and they soon came to do so—the adjective 'Victorian' was coined as early as 1851—they were deeply impressed by their uniqueness."[44] The gathering pace of industrialization and the advent of the railway standardized time across Britain and made people highly conscious of time. Consequently, a whole new set of temporal anxieties emerged. These ranged from fears of missing trains to, at the other extreme, difficulty in passing the time until one's train was due to leave—young Robert Audley in Braddon's *Lady Audley's Secret* experiences both of these complaints.

Despite a multitude of developments in science and technology, the claim for the most powerful effect on the popular imagination must belong to evolutionary theory. Evolution certainly did not begin with Charles Darwin; the work of scientists such as Kant, Buffon, Erasmus Darwin, Sir Charles Lyell, Robert Chambers, and a host of other figures evolved (so to speak) toward *The Origin of Species:* "Far from introducing the idea of evolution *per se* to a totally unprepared public or initiating the religious doubts which were to trouble so many minds in the years to come, *The Origin of*

Species was largely a brilliant synthesis of many scientific ideas already current, with one or two crucial additions."[45]

Still, evolutionary theory is most often associated with Darwin and there is little doubt that Darwin's publication of the *Origin* in 1859, followed in 1871 by *The Descent of Man,* encapsulated popular anxieties about the implications of deep time. While the *Origin* ends with a vision of "endless forms most beautiful and wonderful [that] have been and are being evolved,"[46] a vision that Richard Altick observes "might have been interpreted as substantiating the Victorian faith in progress as a built-in attribute of the universe," nevertheless, "a close, candid reading of Darwin's account made it obvious that evolution did not necessarily imply progress."[47] If Burke's *Reflections* provides convenient shorthand for a narrative model of human inheritance, preserving property and values across the generations, then Darwin's work offers a competing narrative of generations that is not limited to humanity. It is these two competing narratives—Burke's and Darwin's—that form the poles of our discussion of temporal discourses in popular fiction. Burke and Darwin provide ideologies of transmission, the former largely conservative, the latter entirely dependent upon change—one species not remaining constant to the end of time, but evolving into other forms. These two narratives form a dialectic of movement and nonmovement reminiscent of Aristotle's analysis of the nature of time. They also provide ideological tools by which the late eighteenth and early nineteenth centuries explored the issues of time amid the discursive tensions engendered by a complex array of forces.[48] These forces include changing conceptions of the size and age of the universe, changing notions of the historical past and its relation to the present, the political and social cataclysm of the French Revolution, evolutionary theory, and sweeping technological change.

This book will examine the way six novels by six different authors over a seventy-year period—approximately the span of a human life—articulate these temporal discourses.

The *chronotope* (Bakhtin's word for "time space"[49]) of Ann Radcliffe's *The Mysteries of Udolpho,* for example, set in an imagined past before the eighteenth century's rupture, uses embedded genres such as poetry and travel writing, the prolonged suspension between memory and expectation, the superimposition of the past upon the present, and the repetition of incidents and characters to create a dreamy temporality reminiscent of Augustine's three-fold present, where time as we understand it seems not to exist. In chapter 1, "No Time Like the Present," I argue that *Udolpho*'s construction of an alternative temporality was a response to the fears of the French Revolution and the gathering perception of a present detached from the past. The novel creates its own peculiar temporality, a "radically unformed temporal experience,"[50] in which movement and nonmovement, concord and discord, the feudal past and modern present, can coexist coherently.

Charles Robert Maturin's *Melmoth the Wanderer* is a novel obsessed with time and narrative. In chapter 2, "The Clock is Ticking," I argue that this novel represents a sustained quest for coherence in the face of a series of aporias. This quest ultimately takes the form of a dialectic of coherence and incoherence, a "humanizing" of what Frank Kermode calls the "disorganized time" represented by "the interval between *tick* and *tock*."[51] The clock had begun to assume more and more power over the regulation of people's lives because the factory, the mail coach system and more accurate timepieces all made large segments of the population increasingly subject to schedules. In *Melmoth,* Maturin dramatizes his concerns about the dehumanizing effects of this rigidly structured temporality by depicting the institutional transformation of people into clock-watching mechanisms. The need to *humanize* the clock and its intervals is greater than ever in consequence of industrialization and horological developments. The solution to time's aporetic aspect is not to divide the expanse of time into smaller and smaller temporal increments, but to organize it "after the manner of a narrative,"[52] which refigures the infinite in human terms. We see this storytelling alternative dramatized in the novel's peculiar structure of embedded tales with images of acts of narration and transmission, both oral and written. In these narratives, time's subjectivity—the way it can seem to expand or contract under certain conditions—is emphasized. Maturin's narrative therefore proposes alternative forms of temporality to the incessant clock-watching that is becoming increasingly prevalent in the modern, industrialized world.

In chapter 3, "Transcending Time," Mary Shelley's apocalyptic narrative, *The Last Man,* weaves together memory and Sybilline prophecy to test the power of narrative to attain a perspective that encompasses all of human history, transcending, and even reversing, linear time. In a world of only one human being, there is no society and therefore no time. As a result, Ricoeur's "circle of narrativity," in which "[t]ime becomes human time to the extent that it is organized after the manner of a narrative; [and] narrative, in turn, is meaningful to the extent that it portrays the features of temporal existence,"[53] is broken. Time is shaped and given meaning by human relationships—the intimate, as well as the relationships with the wider world of society. One is part of one's cultural moment, and, absent a network of human relationships, not only do Shelley's characters and the narratives they inhabit become aporias, but time itself can become inarticulable. At the end of *The Last Man,* neither narrative nor human time applies, so the Burkean model has been demolished. There is only an inarticulable and aporetic no-time.

Finally, in chapter 4, "Aporia in the House," I consider three novels from the early 1860s that are usually regarded as the foundations of the sensation fiction genre: Wilkie Collins's *The Woman in White,* Mary Elizabeth Braddon's *Lady Audley's Secret,* and Mrs. Henry Wood's *East Lynne.* All three novels abound with references to the contemporary world of railways, time consciousness, and assumed identities. All three emphasize a comprehensive investigation of the past and the construction of a narrative that seeks to make sense of that past, and therefore the present. This process mirrors the effort of Victorian science to construct a plausible narrative of the earth's (and the human race's) past. But such an effort produces as many anomalies as it attempts to resolve. Indeed, all three novels reach a state of narrative failure, suggesting that time's chaotic and aporetic nature may be beyond our ability to "humanize" it through narrative, exposing the Burkean model for the construct that it is.

As revolution and evolution have left their marks upon public perceptions of temporality, and new anxieties have accompanied developments in applied technology, in law, and in the theories of science and history, public time assumes greater importance. During the period from the 1790s through the 1860s, popular conceptions of time have been transformed. The "deep time" of the astronomers, geologists and biologists has resulted in so much more time for which to account. Yet, paradoxically (as paradox is often associated with temporality), time has become foreshortened in the public awareness because railway travel and the telegraph have sharply reduced the elapsed time in travel and communications, resulting in a heightened consciousness of the present moment. It is not a rich, thick three-fold present as Augustine theorized, but a more anxious, "now-saying" moment.

Another way of stating that public time has assumed greater importance, is to say that there is an increase in the extent to which time has become socially constructed during this period, a temporal phenomenon that these selected novels have certainly demonstrated. Largely absent from *The Mysteries of Udolpho,* socially constructed time has begun to emerge by the time *Melmoth the*

Wanderer appeared in 1820. We see this in the novel's preoccupation with clocks and bells, and more dramatically with its anxieties about humans being transformed into mechanisms. Some of Mary Shelley's short fiction and in particular her novel *The Last Man,* expresses an apparent desire to escape from linear time altogether—to view it from a vantage point that encompasses all of history, to fictively reverse its direction, and even to render it "null" (as Shelley referred to it in her journals[54]) in the absence of human society. Finally, in *The Woman in White, Lady Audley's Secret,* and *East Lynne* we will see society further standardizing time through the railway timetable and demanding that its members be conversant with this new definition of time. But social changes such as divorce, a growing middle class, and more permeable class boundaries also alter notions of identity. This takes place even as scientific developments such as evolutionary theory and the laws of thermodynamics spark widespread fears of degeneration. Evolution provides a narrative of generations that contests the Burkean model of preservation through inheritance. But despite the emergence of this competing narrative, and despite growing evidence that the ability to construct a coherent account of "origins and ends" is beyond the power of narrative, I hope that my analysis will demonstrate that the *desire* for "emplotment" shows no sign of diminishing. If anything, the advent of the sensation novel, and the detective novel that will follow, reflect an increased desire to fashion narratives that explain the pattern of the evidence at hand, "to make a plausible story out of a congeries of 'facts,' which, in their unprocessed form, make no sense at all."[55] The more the world seems to "make no sense at all," the stronger the need to render intelligible what Walter Hartright calls "the ways of our unintelligible world."[56]

1

No Time Like the Present:
The Mysteries of Udolpho

Suppose that I am going to recite a psalm that I know. Before I
begin, my faculty of expectation is engaged by the whole of it.
But once I have begun, as much of the psalm as I have removed
from the province of expectations and relegated to the past now
engages my memory, and the scope of the action which I am
performing is divided between the two faculties of memory and
expectation, the one looking back to the part which I have already recited, the other looking forward to the part which I have
still to recite. But my faculty of attention is present all the while,
and through it passes what was the future in the process of becoming the past.

—Augustine, *Confessions*

While Dorothée spoke, Emily was still looking at the lute, which
was a Spanish one, and remarkably large; and then, with a hesi-
tating hand, she took it up and passed her fingers over the
chords. They were out of tune, but uttered a deep and full
sound. Dorothée started at the well-known tones . . .

—Ann Radcliffe, *The Mysteries of Udolpho*

[L]iterature is the irreplaceable instrument for the exploration
of the discordant concordance that constitutes the cohesiveness
of a life.

—Paul Ricoeur, *Time and Narrative*

As WE HAVE SEEN IN THE PREVIOUS CHAPTER, ATTITUDES TOWARD TIME
and history began to change as the eighteenth century drew to a
close. If the century suffered anxieties about its place in history and
the period was characterized by a "dissociation of sensibility,"[1]
then the French Revolution further shattered the already unsettled
notions about lived experience. "[L]ived time," as Reinhart Koselleck points out, "was experienced as a rupture" between past and
future. Nor can we discount the effect of the proximity of the end
of the century. "Our sense of epoch," Frank Kermode has written,

"is gratified above all by the ends of centuries."[2] The close of the eighteenth century, particularly in the turbulent atmosphere of the French Revolution, almost certainly contributed to a sense of gathering apocalypse that made the past seem a welcome refuge.

In the decade of revolution that was the 1790s, Ann Radcliffe became a publishing phenomenon, emerging from anonymity to become one of the most successful novelists of her time. Although Horace Walpole's *The Castle of Otranto* is widely regarded as having begun the Gothic genre in 1764, it was Radcliffe who really seemed to codify many of the characteristics that define the Gothic, and the term "Radcliffean Gothic" is almost a tautology.[3] Four of the five romances Radcliffe published between 1789 and 1797 feature exotic settings in the historical past, from the feudal Scotland of *The Castles of Athlin and Dunbayne* to the seventeenth-century France of *The Romance of the Forest*. (*The Italian* is the lone exception, set in Italy between 1742 and 1758.) Yet her most famous novel, *The Mysteries of Udolpho,* is most thoroughly imbued with discourses on temporality, four aspects of which I will address in this chapter: the novel's explicit references to time, for example, its past setting, or conversely, its noticeable *absence* of definitive temporal markers such as seasonal descriptors; the castle as a trope of time; the role of repetition as a temporal motif; and the protagonist's prolonged suspension between memory and expectation in an extended, "unruptured" present. I will argue that the novel's embedded discourses on temporality were a response to the unprecedented forces that were reshaping the concept of time in England, and that the novel's construction of an alternative temporality contributed to the novel's popular reception. In response to the gathering perception of a present growing increasingly detached from the past, *The Mysteries of Udolpho* offered an imaginatively compensatory version of this new temporal reality. I want to suggest that Radcliffe's novel served as an antidote to revolutionary fears and also to the whole idea of progress and its temporally dissociative effects, these antidotal properties contributing to its success during this decade. The way that the novel accomplished this feat, through a complicated series of temporal discourses, is the subject of this chapter.

REFERENCES TO TIME

In a nod to Cartesian specificity, *Udolpho* is nominally set in 1584, 210 years prior to its publication, but, as is common in Gothic fiction, the use of the past is more atmospheric than historical.[4] Despite the reference to the year, which occurs twice in the novel—including its opening sentence—we cannot really locate the novel in a particular era, and Radcliffe ignores references to particular historical events of the period. In fact, the discourses contained in the novel involve, not late sixteenth-century, but late eighteenth-century issues, such as sublimity, sensibility, and taste, and the characters drink coffee and use dinner forks nearly a century before either practice was introduced to western Europe.[5] And when the Count De Villefort, on a journey through the Pyrenees late in the novel, speaks of:

> the mineral and fossile substances, found in the depths of these mountains,—the veins of marble and granite, with which they abounded, the strata of shells, discovered near their summits, many thousand fathoms above the level of the sea, and at a vast distance from its present shore;—of the tremendous chasms and caverns of the rocks, the grotesque form of the mountains, and the various phænomena, that seem to stamp upon the world the history of the deluge (602),

he echoes the prevailing eighteenth-century catastrophist view of geology, as articulated in Thomas Burnet's *The Sacred History of the Earth* (1681–89).[6] Radcliffe has established a discursive tension in the temporal realm, a state of dissonance between the supposed specificity and the vague historicity of her setting.

Robert Miles argues that Radcliffe sets the novel in a period that Miles calls "the Gothic cusp," a "moment of passage from a feudal to a modern world," so that she can dramatize the tensions between the two periods and their respective world-views.[7] Seen in this context, the apparent conflict between Radcliffe's choice of temporal settings with a particular purpose in mind (Miles's argument) and her disregard for historical accuracy, exemplify discursively the very tension that her settings explore, the conflict between the feudal and the modern. This is just one of a whole network of dialectical relationships that *Udolpho* imaginatively resolves, dialectics of sense and sensibility, reality and fantasy, movement and stasis, difference and repetition, past and present, memory and expectation. Synthesizing these dialectics is the work of Radcliffe's narrative, and as we shall see, Augustine's recitation of the psalm becomes the figure for this great synthetic project. Augustine's example is particularly applicable to my analysis of *Udolpho* because the psalm's recitation emphasizes that the resolution of apparent paradoxes (in Augustine's case, that between time and

eternity) takes place in the mind, is bound up with issues of temporality, and is accomplished narratively. Augustine's recitation is a
narrating instance that is in turn described through an act of narration. This act fashions coherence by uniting past, present and future, memory and expectation, in an extended present. It is just
such a model that *Udolpho* employs to accomplish its own peculiar
coherence by its synthesis of temporalities.

The conflict between feudal and modern that Miles addresses
was a particularly late eighteenth-century concern, especially in
the decade of the French Revolution, which played such a prominent role in disrupting history. Such a disruption prompted Burke
to write his *Reflections on the Revolution in France,* which invokes
the British national past and emphasizes, in contrast to France, its
lineal relationship to the present, from the "hereditary succession"
of the crown to the "sure principle of transmission" of government,
property, and life itself.[8] Radcliffe's temporal setting accomplishes
a connection to the past in a more complicated way. The past in-
voked by *Udolpho* is reminiscent of M. M. Bakhtin's epic past in
several ways. First, it is set in "the national heroic past . . . a world
of 'beginnings' and 'peak times' in the national history, a world of
fathers and founders of families, a world of 'firsts' and 'bests.'"[9]
This national heroic past is a "Gothic" past, because, in the eighteenth century, "Gothic," as applied to literature, art and architecture, becomes an especially desirable attribute. With specific
application to Britain, what had been regarded as wild and barbaric
begins to be valued. Describing this shift in cultural attitudes,
David Punter states that "the fruits of primitivism and barbarism
possessed a fire, a vigour, a sense of grandeur which was sorely
needed in English culture . . . and . . . the way to breathe life into
the culture was by re-establishing relations with this forgotten,
'Gothic' past."[10]

And yet, in Bakhtin's schema, the epic past is sealed off from the
present: "The epic world is constructed in the zone of an absolutely
distanced image, beyond the sphere of possible contact with the developing, incomplete and therefore re-thinking and re-evaluating
present." We can see this absolute distance in the way that there is
no apparent line of descent from Emily St. Aubert to Ann Radcliffe's present. The St. Auberts are a mythic family rather than a
real one, yet Bakhtin notes that the authorial perspective of the
epic is that of "the reverent point of view of a descendent." The St.
Auberts become ancestors of us all. If not their literal descendents,
we are at least their spiritual and moral offspring through a
Burkean kind of national descent. (Of course, the St. Auberts are

not British, but neither does such a detail prevent the British appropriation of the Goths as paragons of Britishness.) Bakhtin's construction of the epic past as simultaneously "walled off absolutely from all subsequent times," and as an age of heroes from whom "we" nevertheless descend, embodies exactly the kind of discursive tension between past and present that we have been considering.[11] It is 1584 and it is not, because the characters drink coffee and talk about sensibility and taste. In the postmodern era, we perceive such details as anachronistic because we think of different periods of the past as separate and distinct objects. But Radcliffe was invoking a past in which time was imagined as being continuous rather than dissociated into discrete segments, a fitting antidote to the "dissociation of sensibility"[12] that characterized the late eighteenth century.

This representation of time as continuous and unsegmented may explain the novel's nearly total absence of references to days of the week, months, or seasons, and helps to reinforce the dreamlike quality of the novel.[13] (There are, as we shall see, constant references to mornings, evenings, and nights.) If we attempt to trace the seasons that pass in the course of the novel, we discover that they do not "add up"—they do not arrange themselves into a quantitative linearity. The novel's opening chapters are suggestive of summer, or at least spring ("flowery turf," "balmy air" [8]; "midsummer's eve" in the poem "The Glow-Worm" [16]). After the death of Emily's mother, on her journey through the Pyrenees with her father, they encounter peasants dancing to "the joyous music of the vintage" (65), yet a few pages later, Emily's poem, "The First Hour of Morning," alludes to "the breath of May" (74), although here the reference may be more figurative than literal. In any case, subsequent to St. Aubert's death and some period of mourning, Valancourt's courtship of Emily (and Montoni's of Madame Cheron) occupy "the winter months" (140). In the next chapter, the time of Emily's initially planned marriage to Valancourt—usurped by her aunt and Montoni[14]—it is spring (141). It is still spring when they travel through Italy, and the Carnival at Venice, Terry Castle notes, takes place in the week before Lent.[15] Some days or weeks pass by in Venice, but the narrative does not enumerate them. After spending an unspecified period of time in Castle Udolpho, Emily is temporarily removed from the castle for reasons of safety. During her sojourn in the countryside, there is a reference to "the sun's rays, streaming through an autumnal cloud" (401). Not long after this, when she escapes from the castle, the narrator makes several remarks about the "intense heat," "sultry hours" and "profusion of fragrant flowers" in the valley of Arno (455–57). Although these descriptions of flowers and heat could still refer to autumn in Italy, the reader experiences a sense of having looped backward in time to the summer months, like the retrograde motion of an outer planet among the stars, assuming that the reader has noticed the earlier autumnal references at all, amid the lush, even cinematic, descriptions of sublime landscapes.[16]

Udolpho constantly works to frustrate the linearity of time. Its time is more akin to the "miraculous" time of the chivalric romance, exhibiting "a *subjective playing with time,* an emotional and lyrical stretching and compressing of it."[17] After Emily's return to France, there are more references to autumn ("autumnal lights upon the mountains" [592]) and later "a grey autumnal evening toward the close of the season" is described (619). On this evening, Emily reflects upon having been "tossed upon the stormy sea of misfortune for the last year," so clearly the novel's events are meant to comprise approximately a year. However, there is no way for the reader to determine this in the absence of any specific durational cues, and, as we have seen, what seasonal references there are suggest that more than a year has passed. (At the time of her reflection, we've seen two summers, and this must be the second autumn, although such an analysis is no more productive than counting the number of Christmases in Tennyson's *In Memoriam.*) The lack of precise dateability, which we associate with public, or calendar, time, signals that *Udolpho*'s time is not what Paul Ricoeur terms "the time of the world." We use the calendar to bridge the human and astronomical universes, "mak[ing] historical time conceivable and manipulable,"[18] but *Udolpho*'s rhythms are not those of the heavenly bodies, whose movements order the passage of time (as Aristotle noted when he observed that, while time is not motion, time is still a *measure* of motion and cannot exist without it.[19] Nor can we say that the novel's rhythms are those of Emily's various journeys, because, as we shall see, the descriptions of those journeys resemble each other so much that they seem more like a single journey, endlessly repeated.

The "pieces of poetry" that are "interspersed" throughout the text (the very use of the term "interspersed" on the title page of the novel connoting that the poetry will appear at irregular intervals, disrupting the linear sequence at more or less random moments) also influence our perception of time in the novel. Besides Radcliffe's chapter mottoes, which primarily originate from poets such as Shakespeare, James Thomson, Milton (the lyrics), William Collins, and James Beattie, there are twenty-one original poems.[20]

Nearly all of these depict the beauties of nature or pastoral scenes[21] and just over half (twelve) were composed on Emily's various travels in the Alps, Pyrenees, and Venice. The longest gap without an interspersed poem—some 207 pages—corresponds to the period of Emily's incarceration in Castle Udolpho, when she had little contact with nature, except for what she could observe from the castle. Only six of the twenty-one poems in *Udolpho* contain any seasonal references, one each to summer and autumn, and four to spring.[22] But all except four have specific time-of-day references, three to the morning, twelve to evening and/or night (three contain both), and two, the longest poems in the novel ("The Sea-Nymph" [179–81] and "Stanzas" [206–8]) span an entire day, both beginning *and* ending at sunset. *None* of the poems spans longer than a day, and, while three times as many poems mention time of day as time of year (i.e., season), a spring or summer day is almost always implied, and the period of sunset and evening twilight is a recurrent setting. In fact, the prose of the novel abounds with references to this time of day as well. It is the time most often associated with both sublimity (such as the first sight of both Castle Udolpho [226–27], and the Chateau-le-Blanc [467]), and tranquil reflection (e.g., 90, 175, 206). Sunset is also a time of transition, that looks backward to the day and forward to the night. The parted lovers promise to "constantly watch the sun-set" so that they may "meet . . . in thought," happy that their "minds are conversing" (163). At times, the novel seems one long succession of sunsets, like a slide-show by an uncle who rarely photographs anything else. Or perhaps it is just one long sunset, and we are constantly poised upon the cusp between day and night, holding it in the mind like St. Augustine's psalm.

These interspersed pieces of poetry are an excellent example of what Bakhtin calls an "incorporated genre." In "Discourse in the Novel" he notes that:

> [t]he novel permits the incorporation of various genres, both artistic (inserted short stories, lyrical songs, poems, dramatic scenes, etc.) and extra-artistic (everyday, rhetorical, scholarly, religious genres and others) . . .
>
> Each of these genres possesses its own verbal and semantic forms for assimilating various aspects of reality. The novel, indeed, utilizes these genres precisely because of their capacity, as well-worked-out forms, to assimilate reality in words.[23]

The poetry transforms the temporality of the novel by transmitting the temporal reality of the lyric. One way we see this is in the way

the linear movement of the narrative (and often the physical progress of the traveling party across the landscape as well) is stalled
while we experience these pastoral, descriptive passages, during
which nothing much is happening except the movement of the observer's eyes, like the motion of the camera in the cinema. The only
action is the act of observation, and the reader's eyes on the page
are analogous to the observer's eyes as she "reads" the landscape.
The act of reading in these passages is mimetic of the act of observing, and the reader seems to enter the textual world, a world characterized by a pace that allows time to contemplate the scenery.
The recurring pattern by which the embedded lyrics slow down the
reader's progress suggests a desire to retard the "progress" of late
eighteenth-century Europe.

Another way the poetry transforms the novel's temporal reality is
in the idealization of the day, as the longest unit with which the
novel is concerned. The two long poems in particular ("The Sea-
Nymph," 179–81, and "Stanzas," 206–8), both emphasize the day,
starting and ending at sunset, resulting in the establishment of a
diurnal rhythm that is periodically reaffirmed each time we encounter another "interspersed" poem.

The exceptions to this emphasis on the day unit are sufficiently
few as to be noticeable: the reference to the year 1584, Emily's
reflection of her misfortunes over the course of a year, and a few
scattered seasonal references, all previously mentioned; some references to events that take place over a period of a few days, such
as Emily's vigil "during two days and two nights, with little inter-
mission, by the corpse of her late aunt" (375–76); and a few references to weeks, which, curiously, are often associated with
emotional ordeals, or the period of recovery from such ordeals.
Here is the description of the period of sharpest grief after the
death of Emily's mother: "What reason and effort may fail to do,
time effects. Week after week passed away, and each, as it passed,
stole something from the harshness of her affliction, till it was mellowed to that tenderness which the feeling heart cherishes as sacred. St. Aubert, on the contrary, visibly declined in health"
(24–25). This pattern is repeated after the death of her father,
when "[s]everal weeks passed away in quiet retirement, and Emily's affliction began to soften into melancholy" (99). Another example of the power of weeks to soften sorrow occurs when, stricken
with his separation from Emily, "[t]o forget himself and the grief
and anxiety, which the idea of her recalled, . . . [Valancourt] would
quit his solitude, and again mingle in the crowd. . . . Thus passed
weeks after weeks, time gradually softening his sorrow . . . " (293).

Days or weeks also suggest intervals of suspense or fear: When Emily remains in her room in Castle Udolpho, anxiously waiting for confirmation of the identity of a fellow prisoner whom she suspects to be Valancourt, "[s]everal of her succeeding days passed in suspense" (442), and soon after, "[a] week elapsed, before Ludovico again visited the prison" (444); and later, afraid of meeting Valancourt, who had seemingly fallen into wicked ways, Emily forbore "to visit the gardens, for several days. When, after near a week, she again ventured hither, she made Annette her companion . . ." (587). But such longer intervals of time are rare in the novel. Only grief, or a period of suspense while awaiting a desired outcome, makes Emily conscious of the passage of time to the extent that it is noted. Otherwise she lives from day to day.

While the novel seems to emphasize and idealize the diurnal rhythm, in a strange way, *Udolpho* also seems to have no noticeable rhythms at all, perhaps because its rhythms are associated more with contemporary aesthetic theory than with action. Miles, pointing out that Radcliffe's "narrative art" works on the reader's nerves, proposes an aesthetic rhythm that alternates between the suspenseful and the comic, the sublime and the picturesque.[24] The "cinematic word-paintings" that Rhoda L. Flaxman describes, as well as the interspersed poetry and Miles's aesthetic rhythms, all combine to produce for the reader a "metaphorical journey through a landscape [that] represents a kinesis within stasis"[25]— another kind of discursive tension. Flaxman's "kinesis within stasis" represents a dialectic that stands as a figure for the temporal paradoxes that fascinated Augustine and Aristotle. It is easy to see why the novel has so often been read as a story of an inner journey—or perhaps not a journey at all, for "journey" implies "progress" and whether any occurs in *Udolpho* is debatable—but read at least as a narrative of inner space. D. L. Macdonald states that "since Emily learns nothing she does not already know from her experiences, there is no reason for them not to repeat themselves over and over. . . . Since nothing is happening in the novel, there is no reason for it ever to stop."[26] This pattern of repetition is reminiscent of Bakhtin's characterization of the setting of the provincial town in many nineteenth century novels: "Here there are no events, only "doings" that constantly repeat themselves. Time here has no advancing historical movement; it moves rather in narrow circles: the circle of the day, of the week, of the month, of a person's entire life. . . . Time here is without event, and therefore almost seems to stand still."[27] Emily's time seems to "move" in similar, narrow circles, the "circle of the day."

Aristotle's paradox that time is not motion even while it is still a measure of motion is dependent on his assertion that "time cannot exist without change," for we cannot perceive any passage of time if nothing has changed. Augustine similarly claims that time is never still and derives its length from movement.[28] If there is no change, then time, as we know it, seems not to exist, as Macdonald implies when he states that "nothing is happening," another way that that novel subverts the idea of progress. Certainly, the situation at the end of the novel is remarkably similar to the one at the beginning, suggesting that nothing really did happen. Ian P. Watt's discussion of Walpole's *The Castle of Otranto* is just as applicable to *Udolpho*'s often dreamy quality: "In dreams, time is intensely real in the sense that we are immersed in a series of scenes which follow each other with hallucinatory vividness: it is very much a question of now, and now, and now."[29] Thus, the events in *Udolpho* seem vivid enough, but they cannot be situated according to an external, or public, time scale. As a result, they are perceived as being without beginning or end, and therefore seem random and chaotic. This is a manifestation in the temporal dimension of what Linda Bayer-Berenbaum, in her discussion of the Gothic fascination with ruins, calls a desire "for the random, the wild, and the unbounded."[30]

We see this desire for the unbounded in the physical dimension throughout the novel, as Emily apprehends nature as both awe-inspiring for its sublimity as well as soothing for its picturesque qualities, no matter how dreadful her circumstances. She is always inspired or soothed by nature. Those who do not possess such sensibility, such as Mademe Quesnel and the Countess de Villefort, both of whom despise rural life in favor of the charms of the city, are clearly disparaged. Madame Quesnel and her husband, who shares her tastes, prefer a world of politics and magnificent balls, Quesnel himself admitting he has "so many affairs of moment" on his hands that he can rarely "steal away even for a month or two" (12). Quesnel's choice of words here is revealing, for "moment," in this context, superimposes the important upon the ephemeral. The word refers to "weight" or "importance," but also carries the more common temporal meaning of "an instant," particularly the present moment. And indeed, the progressive Quesnels wish to bring the ancient estate up to date. Their proposed "improvements" are described in terms of cost ("thirty or forty thousand livres," 12), and they plan to cut down a number of the estate's trees, including a centuries-old chestnut (severing, like progress itself, the continuity of the past and coincidentally the metaphor used to describe genealogy), to plant Lombardy poplars like those found at the Venetian estates of Madame Quesnel's uncle. The poplars' forms might "adorn[] the scene" in Venice, St. Aubert remonstrates, but they are out of place "among the giants of the forest, and near a heavy, gothic mansion" (14), and thus represent an assault upon good taste.[31]

The Countess de Villefort and her husband differ rather strongly in their landscape preferences and this contrast is painted in rather sharp terms. She calls the Chateau-le-Blanc "dismal," "barbarous" and "savage" (469), prompting two rejoinders from her husband, who finally tells her in exasperation that her conversation "discovers neither good taste, or good manners" (471). Thus, good manners are associated with good taste, which is defined as an appreciation for the charms of the wild, romantic, anti-progressive countryside. The desire for the unbounded is privileged in the novel. In the temporal dimension, this desire can be seen in an endless succession of sublime or picturesque sunsets that paint oceans and mountains and crumbling Gothic castles.

THE CASTLE

The fascination with ruins fuses the desires for randomness in both the spatial and the temporal realms because ruins are physical examples of time's passage, breaking down organized forms into more disordered ones, time acting on space. The castle itself constitutes a second key element of temporality in *Udolpho*. The castle becomes what Bakhtin terms a *chronotope,* "literally 'time space,' . . . the intrinsic connectedness of temporal and spacial relationships that are artistically expressed in literature." In the chronotope, Bakhtin goes on to say, "[t]ime, as it were, thickens, takes on flesh, becomes artistically visible; likewise, space becomes charged and responsive to the movements of time, plot and history."[32] We can almost see time taking on flesh in the figure of the castle. The castle has received a great deal of attention by modern critics as a representation of the body or as an oppressive, enclosing, patriarchal space and yet relatively little attention has been paid to it as a trope of time.[33] Such feminist and psychoanalytic readings are oriented spatially rather than temporally, and while illuminating, they obscure the fact that Radcliffe's contemporaries would have seen the crumbling old castle primarily as a figure of antiquity and sublimity. They would have seen it in temporal, as well as spatial, terms. Archibald Alison's 1790 *Essay on the Nature and Principles of Taste* notes that "The Gothic castle is still more sublime than all [other forms of architecture], because, besides the desolation of time, it seems also to have withstood the assaults of war."[34] The castle is the material and therefore spatial inscription of time. Ian P. Watt discusses the late eighteenth century's fascination with the tension between past and present, as evidenced in its preoccupation with ruins in art, architecture, and landscape, and observes that "in the Gothic novel, the castle becomes connected with the family because it is essentially the material survivor of a powerful lineage, a symbol of the continuing life of its founder."[35] Watt thus associates the figure of the castle with generational succession. Generational succession is one means of reconciling the aporias— the inarticulable contradictions—of time by providing a connection between historical time and the time of one's own experience, a way we can travel back along the path of our ancestors' memories.[36]

Bakhtin's description of the castle seems to invoke Edmund Burke in its representation of the transfer of power and property rights in an unbroken line: "The castle is the place where the lords of the feudal era lived (and consequently also the place of historical figures of the past); the traces of centuries and generations are arranged in it in visible form as various parts of its architecture, in furnishings, weapons, the ancestral portrait gallery, the family archives and in the particular human relationships involving dynastic primacy and the transfer of hereditary rights."[37] The "material survivors," in Watt's terminology, the castles in Gothic novels, are always in terrible states of disrepair, crumbling on the outside, dusty, rotting, and damp on the inside, bearing, in other words, all the scars of their survival. For a century so concerned with matters of taste, one wonders about their standards of housekeeping, given all the damp furniture and rotting wall-coverings (and even walls, for that matter). Most Gothic castles have a neglected wing or two, and even responsible homeowners miss some details: The Count De Villefort does a fine job of restoring the Chateau-le-Blanc to its former glory, but manages to overlook the north apartments, shut up for twenty years (546), while less capable castle owners, such as Montoni, effect only those repairs needed to withstand a siege. And even a heroine with the most refined sensibilities hardly hesitates a moment before sleeping in a bed whose appearance must be extremely doubtful (not to mention its likely tiny inhabitants.)[38] A reader with twenty-first-century sensibilities thinks about hygiene, but our century is more focused on the body, and psychoanalytic and feminist Gothic readings tend to refract such concerns. To an eighteenth-century reader, however, these crumbling old castles and their dusty apartments do not encode discourses on hygiene, but on temporality and sublimity.

This eighteenth-century sensibility is vividly demonstrated by a famous passage in the novel. Shortly after Emily apprehends the castle of Udolpho for the first time, Radcliffe's narrator's description contains numerous references to both the sublimity of the castle's appearance and its antiquity. It is described as "vast, ancient and dreary"; its crumbling aspect, beheld (naturally) in the fading light of the dying day, seems to invoke the past, as well as the disorder caused by entropy. Emily perceives "two round towers, crowned by overhanging turrets, embattled, where, instead of banners, now waved long grass and wild plants, that had taken root among the mouldering stones, and which seemed to sigh, as the breeze rolled past, over the desolation around them" (227). In Radcliffe's description, the very plant life is a metaphor for antiquity, since it is taking root among the stones, the natural world battling the artificial, working, slowly but inexorably, to undo human accomplishments, much as Percy Shelley would later represent nature's erosion of human works in "Ozymandias." The human life that is associated with the castle is also old: As Emily "gazed with awe upon the scene . . . an ancient servant of the castle appeared." Even opening the door is a process characterized as a slow transformation, akin to the grass's slow progress over the stone. The bolts of the door must be withdrawn, the "huge folds of the portal" must be "force[d] back," the "carriage wheels roll[] heavily under the portcullis" (227).[39]

These prolonged descriptions of representations of the past require time to narrate and time to read, further slowing the pace of the narrative, and therefore bringing the reader's temporal experience closer to Emily's, as was the case with the landscape descriptions. Gérard Genette observes that "written narrative exists in space as space, and the time needed for 'consuming' it is the time needed for *crossing* or *traversing* it, like a road or a field. The narrative text, like any other text, has no other temporality than what it borrows, metonymically, from its own reading."[40] Our time to "cross" this ponderous narrative passage corresponds to Emily's temporal experience of the carriage crossing under the portcullis, juxtaposing our temporal reality with hers.

REPETITION

This description of the castle also illustrates a frequent pattern in the novel, whereby the narrator makes a point of explicitly juxtaposing past and present. The characters do this as well, especially in the way they invest the castle with the spiritual presence of departed inhabitants. After hearing the story of the Marchioness de Villeroi from Dorothée, the housekeeper of the Chateau-le-Blanc, Emily "felt a thrilling curiosity to see the chamber, in which the Marchioness had died, and which Dorothée had said remained, with the bed and furniture, just as when the corpse was removed for interment" (529). Emily's "thrilling curiosity" is to behold this chamber, frozen in a moment of time twenty years past. It is undoubtedly the prospect of an uncanny experience that produces the thrill and the fact that the subsequent entry is clandestine adds to this quality.[41] The two women steal into the neglected north apartments without the knowledge of the Count, so as not to "displease" him. As the two explore the chambers, the narrative incessantly refers to the rooms having been left exactly as they were twenty years before. Dorothée observes that "the last time I passed through this door—I followed my poor lady's corpse!", noting that "all the time between then and now seems as nothing" (531–32). The past becomes a doppelgänger that haunts the present, from which the uncanniness of this episode derives.[42] The past is so vividly imposed on the present that the dead seem to come to life again, another form of retrograde motion. Emily, approaching the bed, observes "the high canopied tester of dark green damask, with the curtains descending to the floor in the fashion of a tent, half drawn, and remaining apparently, as they had been left twenty years before." At least for the excitable Dorothée, the illusion is so effective that the housekeeper almost convinces herself that her former mistress is still present: "Holy Virgin! Methinks I see my lady stretched upon that pall—as when I last saw her!" (532–33). Both frightened and fascinated, she then makes the apparition real, by having Emily stand beside the Marchioness's portrait, so that she can "exclaim[] again at the resemblance" (533). And, when Emily looks at the Marchioness's clothing, "scattered upon the chairs, as if they had just been thrown off," the very disorder, a tableau of frozen haste— "kinesis within stasis"—joins the scene to Emily's own time. But the tableau cannot be left alone. The past must be reanimated again in the present, as Dorothée does when Emily picks up a black veil, "dropping to pieces with age":

> "Ah!" said Dorothée, observing the veil, "my lady's hand laid it there; it has never been moved since!"
> Emily, shuddering, immediately laid it down again. "I well remember seeing her take it off," continued Dorothée. . . .

Dorothée wept again, and then, taking up the veil, threw it suddenly over Emily, who shuddered to find it wrapped round her, descending to her feet, and, as she endeavoured to throw it off, Dorothée intreated that she would keep it on for one moment. "I thought," added she, "how like you would look to my dear mistress in that veil;—and may your life, ma'amselle, be a happier one than hers!" (533–34)

Dorothée tries to prolong the moment beyond Emily's desire, and the resemblance is indeed uncanny—so much so that Emily will later drive Agnes/Laurentini to distraction: "It is her very self! Oh! There is all that fascination in her look, which proved my destruction!" (644).[43] Not only Emily, but "every object" in the room—an open prayer book, a crucifix—"seemed to speak of the Marchioness." Radcliffe permits the lady's lute to have gone out of tune in the intervening twenty years, but the strings still "utter[] a deep and full sound" (534). We associate an untuned instrument with dissonance and discord, but Radcliffe's language qualifies that. The dissonance is not emphasized, but rather the depth and fullness of the sound, and the "well-known tunes" of the lute trigger a fond memory in Dorothée of the last time she heard her mistress play it, a song that, although mournful, is characterized as "sweet," as she sang "a vesper hymn, so soft and so solemn." The lute becomes a lyrical voice, and its dissonance is productive, a musical figure for the discursive tension that we see so often in the novel. Its discordance is strangely concordant, a paradox to which we shall return later.

In the scene in the Marchioness's chamber, there is a multiplying of temporalities at work, much as Wordsworth will contemplate the landscape near Tintern Abbey in 1798 and see his second visit as both a repetition of the one five years earlier ("The picture of the mind revives again") and a realization that the second visit is not exactly the same ("I cannot paint / What then I was").[44] Ricoeur's analysis of Heidegger notes that:

The cardinal function of the concept of repetition is to reestablish the balance that the idea of a handed-down heritage tipped to the side of having-been, to recover the primacy of anticipatory resoluteness at the very heart of what is abolished, over and done with, what is no longer. Repetition thus opens potentialities that went unnoticed, were aborted, or were repressed in the past. It opens up the past again in the direction of coming-towards. By sealing the tie between handing-down and resoluteness, the concept of repetition succeeds at once in preserving the primacy of the future and in making the shift toward having-been.[45]

In other words, the apparent closure of the past is reopened and infused with new potential. Repetition is a unifying act involving all the temporal dimensions because "repetition is the name given to the process by which . . . the anticipation of the future, the recovery of fallenness, and the moment of vision (*augenblicklich*) in tune with 'its time' reconstitute their unity." On the banks of the Wye, Wordsworth experiences a doubled awareness—how he feels *now*, and (in memory) how he felt *then*, a process Ricoeur terms "[t]he double intentionality of recollection." In Ricoeur's system, "expectation [is introduced] into memory itself, as the future of what is remembered," and "retroactively . . . color[s] the reproduction of the memory."[46]

This is exactly the kind of doubled awareness that Gilles Deleuze had in mind when he said, "the active synthesis of memory may be regarded as the principle of representation under this double aspect: reproduction of the former present *and* reflection of the present present,"[47] a kind of dialogue between past and present in which the temporalities interpenetrate each other. Details such as the scene in the Marchioness's chamber are part of *Udolpho*'s preoccupation with repetition and difference. The novel abounds with repetitions, or almost-repetitions, of characters and events. Terry Castle observes that "characters in *Udolpho* mirror or blur into one another." Both the friar who comforts Emily after her father's death and the Count de Villefort remind her of St. Aubert; Du Pont is taken for Valancourt; Emily even sees herself reflected in Valancourt.[48] Robert Miles refers to these dualities as antitheses of each other (Emily and Laurentini, St. Aubert and Montoni, and even, in an apparent reference to Valancourt's gaming, the two Valancourts ["the same . . . not the same," as Valancourt himself cries, 513]).[49] These character doublings correspond in the temporal dimension to repetitions of narrated events. There are four excursions over the mountains in carriages: the Pyrenees with Emily's father, the Alps and later Apennines, with Montoni, and the Pyrenees again with the Count De Villefort. There are two shootings of Valancourt, two attempts to kidnap Emily and two trips to the castle (along with corresponding departures). All of these repeated incidents "mirror or blur into one another," just as the characters do. We perceive them as both similar—as repetitions—and as different. The tension between similarity and difference is sufficient to produce the uncanny effect, to render the incidents doppelgängers.

In fact, the whole episode of entry into the Marchioness's chamber becomes a striking example of a multilayered repetition, akin to the repetition in Gothic art that Bayer-Berenbaum associates with infinity, "an organizing principle . . . that replaces symmetry."[50] This incident is a narrative tour de force that has received almost no critical attention, perhaps because it lies outside the Castle Udolpho portion of the novel that so fascinates critics. David Punter's claim that "[t]he incidents at Le Blanc are pallid beside the richly coloured and terrifying Udolpho scenes" is a typical response.[51] In this episode, Radcliffe embeds romance within romance and temporality within temporality, blurs the barriers between fiction and "reality," and parodies the "magnificent machinery" of her own novel. Two chapters subsequent to the secret visit by Emily and Dorothée, they enter the chamber again with the Count and Ludovico, preparatory to the latter's spending the night there, in order to quell the rumors of ghosts that have frightened the servants. Entering the room, the Count recalls it as it was in its former splendor (547), in a scene that Terry Castle notes is reminiscent of Burke's description of Marie Antoinette in his *Reflections*.[52] The well-read, contemporary reader thus experiences a multiplied set of remembrances: the previous visit of Emily and Dorothée (of which the narrator reminds us by observing, as they enter, that Emily and Dorothée had rested there), a secret the reader shares with them, and Burke's description of the French queen, a secret known only to that reader. (And of course, there is the Count's own recollection of his past visits, to which the reader is not privy at this moment.) The embedded temporalities in this episode grow in complexity. Left alone, Ludovico first notices the portrait of the deceased Marchioness "with great attention and some surprise," presumably because of the resemblance to Emily, although this is never explicitly stated—another secret shared with the reader (549). Ludovico passes the evening in the chamber by amusing himself with a volume of Provençal tales. The narrator comments on this literary genre, noting that:

> [t]he fictions of the Provençal writers, whether drawn from the Arabian legends, brought by the Saracens into Spain, or recounting the chivalric exploits performed by the crusaders, whom the Troubadours accompanied to the east, were generally splendid and always marvelous, both in scenery and incident; and it is not wonderful, that Dorothée and Ludovico should be fascinated by inventions, which had captivated the careless imagination in every rank of society, in a former age. Some of the tales, however, in the book now before Ludovico, were of simple structure, and exhibited nothing of the magnificent machinery and heroic manners, which usually characterized the fables of the twelfth century. . . . (551)

Radcliffe might be referring to her own romance; besides the self-parody evident in the allusion to "magnificent machinery" and tales set in the remote past, the invocation of the "Arabian legends" reminds us of one of the most famous works of framed tales. And in fact, an embedded tale does follow, one whose telling is interrupted three times. These interruptions contribute to a particularly uncanny affect, because they seem to juxtapose a narrated past and the novel's "present," just as we saw when Emily and Dorothée visited the Marchioness's chamber. Ludovico's reading a romance set in a mythical past is strikingly akin to our reading of *Udolpho,* a narrative strategy similar to the one employed by Chaucer, when his Criseyde, in a city besieged, reads a romance of the siege of Thebes, a romance that tells of the ancestry of her future lover, as if Criseyde is, as Carolyn Dinshaw has noted, reading her own narrative.[53] The episode in the Marchioness' chamber has a similarly self-reflexive quality; Ludovico could be reading *this* tale, as it contains so many elements of the Gothic romance. Not only do the characters mirror one another, but the text seems to mirror itself.

In the Provençal tale, a Baron, alone in his chamber, sees an apparition of a stranger who promises to reveal a terrible secret, of "consequence to you and your house," a situation hauntingly similar to the terrible secret hidden in the papers of Emily's father. The Baron's secret is so important that the Knight tells the Baron that "[I]n future years, you will look back on this night with satisfaction or repentance, accordingly as you now determine" (553). The Baron is led through a number of secret passages in his castle to a forest site where lie the bones of an old knight who had been murdered—the very bones, we realize, of the Baron's ghostly midnight guide. This episode invokes associations with Gothic archetypes. The secret passages and buried bones recall Clara Reeve's *The Old English Baron,* and the concern for future generations recalls both Reeve's novel and Walpole's *The Castle of Otranto.* The fact that Ludovico, alone in a chamber late at night, reads a tale in which a Baron sees an apparition while alone in his chamber, a tale of usurpation and labyrinthine passages, blurs the lines between the fictive "realities" of the embedded tale and *Udolpho* itself. As is the case with the interspersed lyrics, this interpolated tale represents one of Bakhtin's "incorporated genres," which genres, we recall, cause the novel to "assimilate [their] reality."

Moreover, Ludovico's reading experience seems to mirror our own, particularly in the way Radcliffe handles the interruptions. The first of these occurs about one third of the way through the tale, when Ludovico imagines he hears a noise in his chamber—

exactly the sort of occurrence that is common to Radcliffe's characters in such stressful situations.[54] The experience of reading a tale, or a tattered manuscript, stretches the characters' nerves to such an extent that they imagine various noises, as if the prolonged suspension in the realm of the fantastic—between the uncanny and the marvelous, as Todorov defines the term[55]—can affect their own "reality." We more or less accept the embedded narrative, whether spoken or read from a crumbling manuscript, as one of the stock devices of Radcliffean Gothic, and may smile at the characters' excess of sensibility. But in this case, subsequent interruptions suggest that the embedded tale will not remain embedded, and the world of the metanarrative increasingly informs the world of the narrative. Elizabeth MacAndrew observes that when characters hear a narrator describe "people and events they know nothing of, this narrative method places the reader in the same relation described as the listeners to the tale."[56] In the Provençal tale, the Baron, shivering in the windy blasts, feels the contrast between his "present situation" and the cozy fire in the bedchamber he left behind, and at this point Ludovico looks at his own fire and gives it a stir (555). The embedded reality has penetrated Ludovico's own. In the third interruption, just as the Baron hears a voice that identifies the remains of Sir Bevys of Lancaster, Ludovico looks up, imagining he has heard a voice in his own chamber (556). The frequency of these metalepses, to use Gérard Genette's term, seems to blur the boundaries between the fictive levels.[57] As if to emphasize this phenomenon, Ludovico goes to sleep after he finishes the tale and his dream conflates the two realities: "In his dream, he still beheld the chamber where he really was, and, once or twice, started from imperfect slumbers, imagining he saw a man's face, looking over the high back of his armchair. This idea had so strongly impressed him, that, when he raised his eyes, he almost expected to meet other eyes, fixed upon his own, and he quitted his seat and looked behind the chair, before he felt perfectly convinced, that no person was there" (557). The interpenetration of one fictive reality by another through a combination of embedded narrative and dream may make the barrier between our own reality and the world of the novel seem less impenetrable as well, a factor that may have contributed to the novel's popularity in the revolutionary decade. Reading this incident, particularly while alone, may produce a brush with the uncanny not unlike Ludovico's own experience. We identify with Ludovico's act of reading; when he hears a noise and looks up, we seem to experience a frisson of fear. Do we, in turn, look up? Or, is it the sounds from our world that have penetrated the text, and Ludovico is looking up at us?

In fact, fantasy and reality form one of the most pervasive of the novel's numerous dialectics, one that is bound up with the debate over Radcliffe's famously controversial narrative device, the "explained supernatural." An early review of the novel in the *British Critic* notes that "[t]he endeavour to explain supernatural appearances and incidents, by plain and simple facts, is not always happy."[58] Sixteen years later, Anna Letitia Barbauld would point out that the device is not entirely unsuccessful, observing that, while "all the strange and alarming circumstances brought forward in the narrative are explained in the winding up of the story by natural causes . . . in the mean time the reader has felt their full impression."[59]

A certain degree of sensibility seems to be called for. Emily St. Aubert must constantly negotiate a passage between sense and sensibility. She must heed her father's warnings against excess ("all excess is vicious," he advises her after her mother's death [20]) and his admonishments to obey "the duty of self-command." Yet clearly, without sensibility, she would not be able to apprehend the sublime and the beautiful, and would be like the Quesnels, who lack good taste. Moreover, despite his warnings about excess, Emily's father is a dreamer: "I remember that in my youth this gloom used to call forth to my fancy a thousand fairy visions, and romantic images; and, I own, I am not yet wholly insensible of that high enthusiasm which wakes the poet's dream" (15), so he too negotiates this "sense and sensibility" passage. Emily constantly worries about her fears, which she associates with superstition, and the long-delayed rational explanation of the mysteries. Yet when Emily decides to resist Montoni's demands to yield title to her estates to him, he complains "contemptuously" that she "speak[s] like a heroine" (381). E. J. Clery calls this encounter "a rite of passage" for Emily. Her resistance, though the stuff of romantic fiction, strengthens her resolve, makes her a "real" resisting heroine, and signals her ultimate triumph over him. Clery points out that "Montoni echoes the hackneyed complaints of critics of the novel and its female audience . . . [and] associates the main female character with romance-reading, accusing her of entertaining paranoid fantasies and of self-dramatisation. . . . When the heroine is vindicated, so too is the exemplary 'truth' of fiction."[60]

Thus, the fictive values are affirmed in "reality" (although this reality is of course still that of a romance). And not only heroic values but other elements of romance are affirmed. As Dorothée seems to see her dead mistress when she and Emily re-enter the Marchioness's chamber, so do characters in the novel constantly seem surrounded by spectral images of absent loved ones who are separated by time or space: "The supernatural is not so much explained in *Udolpho* as it is displaced. It is diverted—rerouted, so to speak, into the realm of the everyday. Even as the old-time spirit world is demystified, the supposedly ordinary secular world is metaphorically suffused with a new spiritual aura."[61] This dialectic of fiction and reality is labyrinthine. The novel always seems to raise the specter of romance and the supernatural and then to deny it. The repetition of the device of the explained supernatural is a case of the narrative visibly asserting itself. Such a device affirms the values of the rational and everyday world,[62] but it can become a cliché, an obvious artifice, and it is this aspect that seems to have offended some critics, most famously Sir Walter Scott, who attacked the device *qua* device in a review of a novel by Dennis Jasper Murphy (actually Charles Maturin): "[W]e disapprove of the mode introduced by Mrs. Radcliffe and followed by Mr. Murphy and her other imitators, of winding up their story with a solution by which all the incidents appearing to partake of the mystic and the marvellous are resolved by very simple and natural causes . . . it is as if the machinist, when the pantomine was over, should turn his scenes, 'seamy side out', and expose the mechanical aids by which the delusions were accomplished."[63] In its artificiality, its "seamy-side-out-ness," then, the explained supernatural becomes its own inverse deus ex machina, a too visible intrusion of the narrative act into the narrative it produces, dissolving the blood-brain barrier between mimesis and praxis, *sjužet* and *fabula*.

Such a dissolution of the boundaries between realities also blurs the boundaries between multiple temporalities. Ludovico reads an old tale of an older crime and older bones, a tale of actions taken for the sake of the "house," the spatial metonym for future generations. Although the apparent age of the tale (twelfth century) suggests that these future generations are in the past, from the perspective of the novel's (ostensibly sixteenth century) present, we cannot be sure, because we tend to look for connections to Emily's circumstances, to see the tale as part of a pattern. We begin to engage in what Hayden White calls "emplotment," the process by which we "make a plausible story out of a congeries of 'facts,' which, in their unprocessed form, make no sense at all."[64] But in this case the pattern is misleading, for ultimately, there are no hidden bones in *Udolpho;* the horror behind the veil in the picture gallery is made of wax; and Laurentini was not murdered. But, at this point, the reader does not know that. We are constantly uncertain whether the Provençal romance is a repetition of Emily's situation or not, just as we wonder at the identity of other apparent repetitions: Was it Valancourt whom we heard, as we (and Emily) believe? Or was it Du Pont?

Such repetitions are not always imposed upon the characters by the narrative; sometimes repetition is desired, and actively sought, by them. Despite an open invitation to stay at the Chateau-le-Blanc, Emily wants to go to the nearby convent so she can "sigh, *once more,* over her father's grave" (492, emphasis added). Perhaps most peculiar of all is Valancourt's behavior after Emily's departure, behavior that to our modern sensibilities seems obsessive and even somewhat perverse. Terry Castle describes the novel's fascination with investing objects with the spirits of those who are absent (either dead, or just separated in space). Theresa, the old servant of Emily's father, informs her that, after Emily had left La Vallée, Valancourt would wander through the rooms of Emily's house, particularly in the south parlor that had been hers, looking at her pictures, playing her lute, and reading the books she'd read (but, as Theresa pointed out, not really reading, just holding them and talking to himself about Emily [593–94]). We might call this behavior evidence of a fetish (in her brief mention of the incident, Terry Castle refers to Valancourt's behavior as "obsessive")[65] yet the very placement of this description in the novel clearly undermines such an interpretation. Rather than suggesting the need for a restraining order, Valancourt's behavior is related in the context of his rehabilitation, and used to emphasize his constancy and sensibility, although Theresa does briefly worry that Valancourt is "out of his reckoning" (594). While Valancourt laments the loss of Emily at this point and has no hope for a future with her, these fantasies of her presence as he handles objects associated with her seem to console him. He still talks to her as if she were present, and in a way she is. "A scar is the sign not of a past wound but of 'the present fact of having been wounded,'" Deleuze observes, and goes on to state that "the contemplation of the wound . . . contracts all the instants which separate us from it into a living present."[66]

Further, the description of this behavior is what Genette would categorize as "iterative" or repetitive (i.e., "he *would* go . . ."). In other words, it is "narrating one time, what happened *n* times."[67] For Valancourt, wandering through her rooms and talking to Emily represent a poignant realization of the present, a totalization of his memories and hopes in an extended present that embraces all the temporal axes, just as Martin Heidegger characterizes repetition as unifying the *ecstasies* of time ("the phenomena of future, having been, and present").[68] It is interesting that the German word *Wiederholung* that Heidegger uses to discuss repetition can also be translated "recapitulation," with a musical connotation. As Heidegger's translator, Joan Stambaugh, notes, "[I]n music (specifically in the sonata form) recapitulation refers to the return of the initial theme after the whole development section. Because of its new place in the piece, that same theme is now heard differently"[69]—just as, to invoke another musical analogy, Wordsworth now perceives "the still, sad music of humanity," even while he's aware he's lost the "aching joys" and "dizzy raptures" of the past five years before.[70] Those five years have been the development section of the sonata. Given the recurring role of music in *Udolpho*, this connotation of repetition as recapitulation is particularly apt. Valancourt's strange behavior contracts time into an ecstatic unity that resonates in the musical spectrum of the novel, another Bakhtinian "incorporated genre." It suggests Augustine's experience in reciting a psalm he has memorized. He is "engaged by the whole of it" even as the act of recitation causes parts of the psalm to pass from expectation into memory. In the grasping of the whole of it, there is a kind of unity of past, present, and future that Heidegger terms *ecstatic*.[71] This grasping of the whole provides coherence, so the repetition motif becomes productive. According to Ricoeur, "Heideggerian repetition . . . holds together, in the most improbable manner, mortal time, public time, and world time." It provides one type of resolution to the aporia that is represented by "the oscillations of an existence torn between the sense of its mortality and the silent presence of the immensity of time enveloping all things."[72]

MEMORY AND EXPECTATION

Heidegger's ecstatic unity is akin to sublimity in the temporal realm. Edmund Burke identified terror as an important source of the sublime in his *Philosophical Enquiry,* and *Udolpho* makes many explicit references to the sublimity of terror.[73] Radcliffe herself, in her 1826 essay, "On the Supernatural in Poetry," drew a distinction between Terror and Horror, noting in fact that the former "expands the soul and awakens the faculties to a high degree of life"—just what the sublime does—while the latter "contracts, freezes and nearly annihilates them."[74] Robert Hume's 1969

"Gothic versus Romantic" essay builds upon this distinction and uses it as the means to separate Terror-Gothic, which Hume associates with Horace Walpole and Radcliffe, and Horror-Gothic, which he associates with Matthew Lewis, William Beckford, Mary Shelley, and Charles Maturin.[75] I want to argue that there is a temporal component to this distinction that is consistent with Radcliffe's assertion that terror expands while horror contracts. For example, having just entered the castle of Udolpho for the first time, and still very much under its spell, Emily experiences a curiously dilated sense of time as Montoni paces thoughtfully in front of Emily and her aunt, awaiting the return of the servant who is bringing wood to light a fire. All seems suspended: "From the contemplation of this scene, Emily's mind proceeded to the apprehension of what she might suffer in it, till the remembrance of Valancourt, far, far distant! came to her heart and softened it into sorrow" (229).

In a single sentence, Emily, immersed in the present gloom of the ancient castle, moves, first to anticipation of what she might suffer, then to a recollection of Valancourt, distant in both space and time. The castle's brooding presence haunts not just its ancient past, but looms over her future, as well. Her awareness in this passage is not confined to a point-like now (or even to a succession of nows, which Heidegger characterizes as the "vulgar understanding" of time[76]), nor does she experience time as fleeting. Emily's temporal awareness is more akin to the *distentio animi* ("extension of the mind") of Augustine's three-fold present:

> [I]t is abundantly clear that neither the future nor the past exist, and therefore it is not strictly correct to say that there are three times, past, present, and future. It might be correct to say that there are three times, a present of past things, a present of present things, and a present of future things. Some such different times do exist in the mind, but nowhere else that I can see. The present of past things is the memory; the present of present things is direct perception; and present of future things is expectation.[77]

Contrast this "extension of the mind" to one of the truly singular moments of horror in the novel, at the point when Emily obtains her first, brief, glimpse of what lies beneath the veil in the picture gallery. Emily falls senseless to the floor: "When she recovered her recollection, the remembrance of what she had seen had nearly deprived her of it a second time. She had scarcely strength to remove from the room, and regain her own; and, when arrived there, wanted courage to remain alone. Horror occupied her mind, and *excluded, for a time, all sense of past, and dread of future misfor-*

tune" (249, emphasis added). Clearly horror "contracts" Emily's temporal faculties, obliterating memory and expectation alike, stripping the present moment of its richness and freezing her in a narrow now.

But this passage is an exception. For the most part, the novel is filled with examples of the Augustinian threefold present: During one of the many occasions in which Emily hears distant music, she recognizes one of the songs her father had sung to her as a child, and this invokes, first, memories of her childhood in her native country, then memories of having heard it (sung by someone else— actually Du Pont, although she does not know that at this point) in her father's fishing-house, and then a complicated dilation of the present to include the future and memories of multiple pasts:

> Assisted, perhaps, by the mystery, *which had then accompanied this strain,* it had made *so deep an impression on her memory* that she had never since entirely forgotten it; and the manner in which it was now sung convinced her, however unaccountable the circumstance appeared, that this *was the same voice she had then heard.* Surprise soon yielded to other emotions; *a thought darted, like lightning, upon her mind, which discovered a train of hopes, that revived all her spirits.* Yet these hopes were so new, so unexpected, so astonishing, that she did not dare to trust, though she could not resolve to discourage them. She sat down by the casement, breathless, and overcome with *alternate emotions of hope and fear;* then rose again, leaned from the window, that she might catch a nearer sound, listened, now doubting and then believing, softly exclaimed the name of Valancourt, and then sunk again into the chair. Yes, it was *possible, that Valancourt was near her,* and *she recollected circumstances,* which induced her to believe it was his voice she had just heard. She remembered he had more than once said that the fishing house, *where she had formerly listened to this voice and air,* and where she had seen pencilled sonnets, addressed to herself, had been his favorite haunt, *before he had been made known to her;* there, too, she had herself unexpectedly met him. (386–87, emphasis added)

She remembers the sound of this voice, back to an earlier time in her father's fishing house, before she knew Valancourt, to the implied time when she first knew him. There are many other instances of this multiplied present. As Emily is conducted back into the castle by Montoni's men after a brief sojourn outside its walls, the sight of the familiar gate fills her with terror: "The little remains of her fortitude now gave way to the united force of remembered and anticipated horrors, for the melancholy fate of Madame Montoni appeared to foretell her own" (427). Earlier, in a more sublimely tranquil moment, Emily gazes at the stars: "They brought a retrospect of all the strange and mournful events, which had occurred since she lived in peace with her parents. . . . She wept to think of what her parents would have suffered, could they have foreseen the events of her future life" (329).

As Reinhart Koselleck has noted in his discussion of the latter half of the eighteenth century, "experience is present past, whose events have been incorporated and can be remembered. . . . expectation also takes place in the today: it is the future made present; it directs itself to the not-yet, to the nonexperienced, to that which is to be revealed."[78] Although Emily's awareness, to cite Ian P. Watt again, is "very much a question of now, and now, and now," it is the kind of present that Paul Ricoeur, in his discussion of Augustine's analysis of time, calls a "thick" present (containing both protention, or future intention, and retention), not a point-like now. Time "thickens, takes on flesh," Bakhtin told us, using the same metaphor.[79] In contrast to the memory and anticipation that saturate Emily's awareness during most of the novel, her long-anticipated future seems "a dreary blank" when she feels she has lost Valancourt, who in Emily's mind is always connected to the future. "Valancourt seemed to be annihilated, and her soul sickened at the blank, that remained" (581). Without the richness of the threefold present, her existence seems thin and meaningless, because the experience of the threefold present may partake of some of the sublimity of God's experience in eternity, which, Augustine tells us, is of an eternal present, without past or future, and thus infinitely "thick": "It is in eternity, which is supreme over time because it is a never-ending present, that you are at once before all past time and after all future time. For what is now the future, once it comes, will become the past, whereas *you are unchanging, your years can never fail.* . . . Your years are completely present to you all at once, because they are at a permanent standstill. . . . Your today is eternity."[80] Even though we mortals are "in time," *Udolpho*'s frequent passages about sublimity suggest an association with "the Great Author" during these sublime moments. "Blanche's thoughts arose involuntarily to the Great Author of the sublime objects she contemplated" (475). Ascending the Alps, Emily "seemed to have arisen into another world, and to have left every trifling thought, every trifling sentiment, in that below." The world of trifling thoughts and trifling sentiments she leaves behind is the world of time, and "grandeur and sublimity now dilated her mind" (163).

Even in her less sublime moments, throughout *Udolpho,* and not just in the one-third of the novel that she spends imprisoned in the castle, Emily is constantly suspended between memory and expectation. Anticipation, as Carly Simon might have put it, is making Emily wait, and while she waits, she broods about the past. Such a contemplation of the past makes it seem to live in the present. One way this phenomenon is represented is through the novel's investiture of objects and places with the spirits of the departed, as explored by Terry Castle in her essay "The Spectralization of the Other in *The Mysteries of Udolpho*." Despite Castle's analysis of the implications of the dissolution of the barrier between life and death, it seems to me that there is a temporal component to this motif in the novel as well, because the dead who are ever-present are not just dead but are associated with her past, yet that association occurs in the present. ("They're here!") Emily is surrounded and enclosed by these spirits, but this is a happy, soothing, thickening kind of enclosure, not the material enclosure often described by critics of the Gothic, who see the castle only as an oppressive space. The womb is a better analogy here, because the womb is about both space and time. It is productive; it ripens the foetus that "takes on flesh," just as time does for Bakhtin.

As Emily is suspended temporally in her extended present, so too is the reader subjected to the same temporal suspension by the narrative, a strategy that Radcliffe employs to a greater extent in this novel than in her other Gothic romances. The result of this narrative strategy has at times perplexed critics. Donald Williams Bruce complains that, "[t]he plot of *The Mysteries of Udolpho,* although Emily is forever on the move, is static in effect, possibly because of the frequent descriptive passages."[81] And we have seen the role of Radcliffe's interspersed poems in slowing down action in order to describe scenes, to impose the temporality of the lyric on the narrative. We have also seen that the constant repetitions of incidents, which are interlaced with postponements, work to delay forward progress. For example, consider the private staircase in Emily's bedroom in the castle (which Annette refers to as the "double chamber," yet another doppelgänger [234]). On at least six occasions spanning more than 180 pages, Emily fears, recalls, or proposes to explore this staircase. Sometimes her intentions to explore it are foiled because the door is locked (272); on two occasions, it is unlocked and, fearing someone will enter her room, she tries to secure the doorway by blocking it with furniture (320, 438). Another example of this motif of repeated postponements is Dorothée's narration of the mysterious fate of the Marchioness, also delayed a number of times: at first she is too overcome with emotion to begin (492); later, she starts telling the story but is interrupted by the horn for dinner (498–99); on two different occasions, despite the build-up of suspense about this story, Emily herself is distracted by her circumstances and *forgets* her appointments with Dorothée (504, 518). The housekeeper finally begins the story, only to be briefly interrupted by "music of uncommon sweetness" (523) before she is able to resume. The story having been finally told, Emily wants to see the Marchioness's picture to examine the strange resemblance to herself, but this has to be postponed because "[t]he night was too far advanced" (529).

And poor Ludovico, whose reading of the Provençal tale was interrupted several times by noises in the chamber, disappears from the Marchioness's chamber, his fate unknown for some fifty-five pages before he reappears in the hideout of the banditti. But the explanation of this mystery is deferred for another fifteen pages and several interruptions. Thus our anticipation continues to build as these mysteries overlap. For example, shortly before her escape from the castle, the mysteries of Udolpho still unresolved include: the secret hidden in the papers of Emily's father; Laurentini's story; the murdered figure behind the veil; the ghostly figure seen walking on the castle terrace; the music that haunts Udolpho; the voice that convicts and questions Montoni during his councils with his fellow banditti; and the chest found in Emily's bedroom. These overlapping mysteries, most of which are not resolved until the final pages of the novel, leave the reader poised between the memory of their previous apparitions and the expectations about what they might signify. We also find ourselves suspended, along with Emily, in Todorov's fantastic, that realm that lies between the uncanny and the marvelous. Scott Mackenzie has characterized as "innovative" Radcliffe's strategy of "synchoniz[ing] her plotted lacunae, sometimes literal gaps in writing, sometimes figural gaps in knowledge, with the overall structure of the narrative and the self-realization of its heroine. Mysterious tunes, words, and figures, gaps in a manuscript, mistaken resemblances and so on, have equivalent spaces in the novel, spaces that will be filled in later, with direct consequences for its heroine, Emily St. Aubert." The blankness of Emily's imagined life without Valancourt and the mystery of what lies behind the veil in the picture gallery are lacunae that, Mackenzie claims, interrupt "the onward rush of narrative," examples of literal aporias, "rhetorical figure[s] marking hesitation."[82] Todorov uses the language of "hesitation" to characterize the duration of our experience of the fantastic: "The fantastic . . . lasts only as long as a certain hesitation: a hesitation common to reader and character, who must decide whether or not what they perceive derives from 'reality' as it exists in the common opinion."[83] We think of hesitation as occupying only a moment, but moments are richly and thickly prolonged in *Udolpho*. We remain suspended in the momentary realm between the uncanny and the marvelous as mysteries remain unresolved. The hesitations, in a curious way, "propel" the narrative, but not linearly. They instead make suspensions productive, in much the same way that Mackenzie states, "What I am calling lacunae should not be understood as spaces that are simply empty. They are spaces which signify doubly and more than doubly."[84]

THE GOTHIC LINE: DISCORDANT CONCORDANCE

In addition to being suspended between memory and expectation, Emily is also suspended generationally. She is at once the focus of the novel, and the focus of generations, all of which converge on her, as her multiple inheritances attest. At the end of the novel, she not only marries Valancourt, but she inherits property from her father, St. Aubert; from her aunt, Madame Montoni; and a third of the personal property of Sister Agnes, (who is really Laurentini and who had helped to murder her other aunt, the Marchioness). The text even implies that Emily inherits Udolpho itself from Laurentini. The castle was Laurentini's, because Montoni was to inherit it if Signora Laurentini died unmarried; at this point in the novel, both are dead. Such a conclusion would probably not be supported by careful scrutiny, but the text is decidedly ambiguous. Note the key paragraph: "The legacy, which had been bequeathed to Emily by Signora Laurentini, she begged Valancourt would allow her to resign to Mons. Bonnac; and Valancourt, when she made the request, felt all the value of the compliment it conveyed. The castle of Udolpho, *also,* descended to the wife of Mons. Bonnac, who was the nearest surviving relation of the house of that name. . . ." (672, emphasis added)

Does the *also* in this passage connect the things that the Bonnacs inherit, or the things that Emily resigns to them? The text can be read either way. A similar ambiguity surrounds the flying of the banners of the Villeroi line, "which had long slept in dust" (671), and which are now apparently rehabilitated: It is unclear whether they fly in honor of Emily or Blanche, since both are married on the same day, and both are related to that family, Blanche as the daughter of Villeroi's cousin (de Villefort) who inherited the title, and Emily as the niece of the Marchioness. (We had previously been told that St. Aubert himself was buried, at his own request, "near the ancient tomb of the Villerois." In fact, he "had pointed out the exact spot" most specifically [87].) It is a double wedding, and a wedding of doubles, as Emily and Blanche are almost the same person, which the text's ambiguities about the inheritance affirm. At least figuratively, Emily may represent the successor to the Villeroi line. If anything, this association with the Villerois reinforces Rictor Norton's contention that Emily may in fact be the offspring of an incestuous union:

> The reader believes Agnes, who says that Emily is the daughter of the Marchioness de Villeroi, and that her father St Aubert was the Marchioness's secret lover—despite being her brother. Clues have been deliberately planted to lead us to the discovery that the Marchioness gave birth to Emily just before she died . . . . St Aubert's obsession with prudence is seen to stem from a passionate affair with the Marchioness. It is wholly unbelievable that St Aubert totally suppressed all knowledge of the existence of the Marchioness because he wished to spare his daughter the pain of learning merely that an aunt had died in mysterious circumstances. Emily, far from resembling St Aubert's wife, is on the contrary identical to the portrait of the Marchioness. At the end of the novel the significance of these clues is simply dismissed.[85]

While incest themes in Radcliffe are rare, compared to Gothic romances by other authors,[86] Norton's argument is rather compelling. That Emily is a "copy" of the Marchioness is suggested, not just by Emily's uncanny resemblance to her, emphasized repeatedly by Dorothée, Laurentini, and others, but by other factors. Her father's anxiety about Emily's reading his papers remains as mysterious as do the contents of the papers themselves—including the lines Emily inadvertently saw (recalling which, she "shuddered at the meaning they seemed to impart, almost as much as at the horrible appearance, disclosed by the black veil" [491])—lines that are never revealed to the reader, as if they were somehow unnarratable, an aporia in the sense of the inarticulable.[87]

There is also the matter of the "matrilineal" inheritance (the preservation of inheritance in the female line) that Kate Ferguson Ellis has pointed out is a recurring theme in the novel.[88] Emily inherits estates from her other aunt, Madame Montoni, so the fact that she inherits from the Marchioness does not in itself prove that the Marchioness is her mother, but, if her mother were also her aunt, the resulting multiplication of relationships would be akin to the infinite repetition and "intertwining motifs" that Bayer-Berenbaum identified as an organizing principle in Gothic art. We saw this intertwining as a figure for the narrative layering in the Provençal tale scene, Ludovico in the chamber seeming to read his own tale, the tale *we* are reading, a kind of narratological act of incest, a convoluted set of relationships to reality. Of the earliest evidence of what Linda Bayer-Berenbaum calls "Northern [i.e., Gothic] ornament," in a chapter in which she analyzes "the Gothic line," Bayer-Berenbaum writes: "The shapes are knotted and twisted together in a frantic, springy, undulating pattern. They separate from one another, run parallel, and then cross again in a maze of latticed activity, producing 'a fantastic spaghetti-like interlace' 'whose puzzle asks to be unravelled, whose convolutions seem alternately to seek and to avoid each other.'"[89] Bayer-Berenbaum's analysis of "the Gothic line" could just as easily refer to a genealogical—and therefore temporal—line as a spatial one. The puzzle of Emily's parentage and the exact nature of the relationship between her father and his sister beg to be unravelled as well. But it is a Udolphian mystery that remains unresolved, frustrating final closure, even while all of these generational lines from the past, all of the discontinuities, converge on, and tend toward a linear, Burkean resolution—"working after the pattern of nature, we hold, we transmit our government and our privileges, in the same manner in which we enjoy and transmit our property and our lives"—in Emily. At the very moment that the novel seems to assert the coherence of genealogical succession, it complicates such a reading via the textual ambiguities of the legacy passage and the "maze of latticed activity" of Emily's heritage.[90]

Udolpho's multivalence on the issue of inheritance constitutes yet another of the novel's many dialectics. Even more important, this generational convergence takes place in the extended present of the novel. Radcliffe gives us no scene of Emily as a mother, surrounded by her children. They and the future they represent are certainly implied, for we must assume that the generations will flow outward from Emily, presumably neat, untangled, Burkean lines now, but we do not see them, and children are never mentioned. As a result, this omission underscores the separation of Emily's Bakhtinian, epic, past, from which we are cut off even while we are simultaneously the descendants of its heroes. The narrative stops at this point, with Emily embodying the future like a reservoir of potential energy, but the emphasis is on the here and now, the rich, thick, extended, spectralized, present. The narrator intrudes here, asserting that innocence will triumph over misfortune, and hoping she has "beguiled the mourner of one hour of sorrow" (672). The reference to "one hour of sorrow" is of course rhetorical, as if to say, "if the reading of this four-decker, a work of many hours, could ameliorate even one hour of sorrow," but it occupies that slippery textual space in which a secondary implication also obtains—that the novel only takes an hour to traverse, because public time has no meaning here. And indeed, at the end of it, Emily seems to have come full circle, back to her point of origin. She has Valancourt, just as if the original wedding had taken place. *Udolpho* thus perfectly typifies the "adventure time" of Greek romance that Bakhtin describes:

> The first meeting of hero and heroine and the sudden flareup of their passion for each other is the starting point for plot movement; the end point of plot movement is their successful union in marriage. All action in the novel unfolds between these two points. These points—the poles of plot movement—are themselves crucial events in the heroes' lives; in and of themselves they have a biographical significance. But it is not around these that the novel is structured; rather, it is around that which lies (that which takes place) *between* them. But *in essence* nothing need lie between them. . . . It is as if absolutely nothing had happened between these two moments, as if the marriage had been consummated on the day after their meeting.[91]

All that apparent kinesis is only stasis, a kind of Aristotelian paradox of movement and non-movement. As MacDonald stated, "nothing is happening in the novel."[92] The Villeroi banners, flying again, seem to return us to the time of Dorothée's youth, or at least they superimpose that time on Emily's present; with Dorothée, we, too, can almost see the Marchioness again. As Valancourt said of himself, Emily is both "the same . . . [and] not the same" (513). All the genealogical discontinuities *seem* to have been set aright. It is true that people have died since the beginning of the novel, but their being dead does not mean that they're gone—to the contrary, as Castle points out: "Absence is preferable to presence. (An absent loved one, after all, can be present in the mind. One is not distracted by his actual presence)."[93] They're never *as* present as when they're dead, for then they surround us, but do not get in the way, so this spectralized present is even better than the original.

I have said earlier that the novel lacks any real *progress*. As I noted in the introduction, progress is associated with movement and transition, a way of thinking that sees the present as dividing past from future—a rupture.[94] And coincident with the development of the notion of progress is a desire for the past, perhaps for the fantasy of wholeness it seems to offer. David Punter notes that much of the fiction written during this decade of revolution "rejected direct engagement with the activities of contemporary life in favor of geographically and historically remote actions and settings," and it is certainly tempting to consider *Udolpho* as a response to the French Revolution, for its publication in May of 1794 indicates that it must have been written during the worst period of the Terror.[95] But it is impossible to say for certain how Ann Radcliffe personally responded to developments across the Channel, since the only extant journals are travel writing, beginning with journeys taken *after* the publication of the novel and excerpted in Thomas Noon Talfourd's memoir.[96] Thus, we cannot be sure if the novel's past setting (like the settings of most of her other romances) stems from a nostalgic desire to reach back to a time before the chaotic events in France that so unsettled Edmund Burke, and, in fact, much of the country. Nor can we be certain that the massive disruption of history that led to France's proclamation of a new calendar as well as the establishment, within twenty years of the Proclamation of the Year One, of history as a discipline and the first academic chairs in history,[97] influenced any of her discourses on time. We just do not know anything about Radcliffe's private thoughts.

Rictor Norton, however, has documented the extraordinary *response* of the public to Radcliffe's romances, particularly to *The Romance of the Forest* and *The Mysteries of Udolpho*. These responses ranged from tremendous popular and critical success—as evidenced by the number of reprintings, the unprecedented amounts she received for the sale of copyrights to her last two novels (£500 for *Udolpho* and £800 for *The Italian*), and the fact that "many of her contemporaries joined in one breath the names of Shakespeare, Milton, Ariosto, Radcliffe"—to the extreme: Some millennialists regarded Radcliffe's Gothic novels as communications from God.[98] But all testify to the novel's resonance with the public. And while we have said that Robert Miles has described the temporal setting of many of Radcliffe's novels as being on "the Gothic cusp," looking backward to the feudal and forward to the modern era, *Udolpho* alone must have been written during the time that I will call the "cusp" of the French Revolution, at virtually the sunset moment when British public opinion toward the revolution began to change. (*The Romance of the Forest* was published in 1791, and *Udolpho* in May of 1794.) Robert Miles considers the year 1792 to be pivotal in this regard, noting that, at the time Burke's *Reflections* was published in 1790, it reflected a minority view, the tide of public opinion having been largely in favor of the revolution until the massacres of 1792–93, but "[b]y 1794 the reaction against French

Revolutionary atrocities had reached a fever pitch. The hopeful mood of 1791 had turned very sour indeed. Habeas corpus was suspended; in 1794 the radical intellectuals John Thelwall and Horne Tooke (plus sundry others) were tried for high treason."[99] Like Emily, the public in England must have been filled with alternating hopes and fears as events across the Channel unfolded.

The contemporary response to the novel, even while we cannot know Ann Radcliffe's authorial intentions, uniquely illustrates Bakhtin's concept of *refraction*. Novels, Bakhtin tells us, incorporate a system of images of languages and the author's intentions move through these images "as if along a curve," in which "the distances between discourse and intentions are always changing . . . the angle of refraction is always changing. . . . In an era when the dialogue of languages has experienced great change, the language of an image begins to sound in a different way, or is bathed in a different light, or is perceived against a different dialogizing background."[100]

But the novel genre does not simply exist separately from this "background animating dialogue." It contributes to it, influences it, and is in dialogue with it, constantly reshaping it.[101] During this revolutionary decade, this era of great change, Radcliffe's own romances, especially *The Mysteries of Udolpho,* are on the cusp of change and can be read both radically and conservatively in the domestic and the political spheres. For example, the novel ends with a marriage, but consistently asserts the property rights of women. Despotic figures such as Montoni and forced marriages, or the threat of them, can represent the excesses of foreign tyranny, but they could just as easily encode a critique of aristocratic privilege and patriarchal power in England. The feudal past is multivalent in England at this time. On the one hand, it can be associated with the excesses that brought on the French Revolution in the first place, giving St. Aubert's warning that "all excess is vicious" as "deep and full [a] sound" as the strings of the Marchioness's lute. On the other hand, it is an idealized time "uncursed with the modern 'dissociation of sensibility.'" The very word *sensibility* is itself an excellent example of the Bakhtinian phenomenon of refraction. Despite its universality of appeal in the second half of the eighteenth century, by 1800 *sensibility* had become almost as universally tainted (along with associationism) by perceived associations with Enlightenment rationalism and the French Revolution.[102] This shift in attitude is mirrored by the response to Radcliffe's novels, wildly popular for awhile, and then falling almost as quickly out of fashion due to a glut of mass-produced imitations and perhaps a whiff of Jacobinism.[103] In her imitators we can see evidence of Radcliffe's novels shaping the background animating dialogue.

The Mysteries of Udolpho's construction of an alternative temporal experience functioned as an antidote to a decade of revolutionary fears, providing an imaginative resolution to growing cultural anxieties. And even though many of the familiar trappings of Radcliffe's romances were both imitated and parodied to such an extent that both she and her imitators soon became passé, in a curious way her novels, particularly *Udolpho*, "came to symbolize remembered youth . . . a prelapsarian world of lost happiness."[104] While we cannot say with certainty that Radcliffe set her novels in the past from motives of nostalgia, many readers regarded them nostalgically, fondly remembering the experience of reading them. This personal, "prelapsarian world," as we have seen, is a peculiarly timeless one. Entering it by way of *Udolpho*, even re-entering that world, becoming lost in its postponements and repetitions, its picturesque ruins and sublime sunsets, poised, at least for awhile, in a present rich with vivid memories and alternating hopes and fears, is akin to communing again with the spirits of the departed. It allows readers to connect themselves to a time before the dissociation of sensibility, before the rupture of the present, before the notion of progress, when time seemed whole again. The temporality created in *Udolpho* is mythic and nonlinear, not arbitrarily marked out into discrete segments, but whole, unbroken, un-dissociated, where time flows in circles of repetition, where the dead live again and surround the living, who not only commune with their spectralized presences but also *become* them, taking their forms, allowing them to exist simultaneously in multiple temporalities. The idealized past is thus heroically and epically national, as well as lyrically personal. The novel's use of these epic and lyric forms invokes the attributes of their temporalities, admitting access to a past made present, richly, thickly present, through the act of reading. "The narrative work is an invitation to see our praxis as it is ordered by this or that plot articulated in our literature,"[105] as Ricoeur reminds us. In the case of *The Mysteries of Udolpho,* the peculiar temporal attributes of that imagined world inform and penetrate our own reality, especially given the novel's characteristic blurring of boundaries between the real and fictional worlds. Our own world's temporality is transformed. *Udolpho*'s aporias are hesitations, a hesitation from the world of the French Revolution into Todorov's fantastic, into a world with "no advancing historical movement," where time "moves rather in narrow circles," where time "is without event, and therefore almost seems to stand still."[106]

There is considerable evidence that many readers of *The Mysteries of Udolpho* did return to the world of the novel, sometimes repeatedly. These repeat readers, among whom are Henry Crabbe Robinson, William Hazlitt, and Charles Bucke, obviously derived a satisfaction that could not have stemmed from a desire for suspense in the conventional sense of not knowing the solution to the mystery.[107] Ricoeur suggests an explanation for this phenomenon that takes into account the novel's association with an idealized national past and also invokes the concept of recapitulation in a sense that is consistent with our use of the term in a musical context:

> As soon as a story is well known—and this is the case for most traditional or popular narratives, as well as for those national chronicles reporting the founding events of a given community—to follow the story is not so much to enclose its surprises or discoveries within our recognition of the meaning attached to the story, as to apprehend the episodes which are themselves well known as leading to this end. A new quality of time emerges from this understanding.
>
> ... the repetition of a story, governed as a while by its way of ending, constitutes an alternative to the representation of time as flowing from the past toward the future, following the well-known metaphor of "the arrow of time." it is as though recollection inverted the so-called "natural" order of time. In reading the ending in the beginning and the beginning in the ending, we also learn to read time itself backwards, as the recapitulation of the initial conditions of a course of action in its terminal consequences.
>
> In short, the act of narrating, reflected in the act of following a story, makes productive the paradoxes that disquieted Augustine to the point of reducing him to silence.[108]

Ricoeur's analysis supports my belief that *Udolpho*'s refraction of desire for the past is more complicated than simple nostalgia for a simpler time. The temporality that the novel evokes is also more complicated than our circular figure suggests, for "circular" implies a degree of order and regularity that is not really present, and time only *almost* seems to stand still. All is not restored *exactly* as it was ("the same . . . not the same" again). We must return again to the strings of the Marchioness's lute: "They were out of tune, but uttered a deep and full sound," a sound that evokes a powerful memory for Dorothée. Ricoeur's reading of Aristotle's *Poetics* states that "Aristotle discerns in the poetic act par excellence—the composing of the tragic poem—the triumph of concordance over discordance," that is, imposing a sense of order on the chaotic nature of the world, including time ("the narrative consonance imposed on temporal dissonance"). But Ricoeur goes on to say that "so long as we place the consonance on the side of the narrative and the dissonance on the side of temporality in a unilateral fashion, . . . we miss the properly dialectical character of their relationship."[109] For example, Greek tragedy emphasizes the role of plot reversals (*peripeteia*), that complicate the straightforward resolution of the narrative problem.

Ricoeur further argues that Augustine's threefold present by means of an extension of the mind, his solution to the paradox of time and eternity, represents a "plea for a radically unformed temporal experience." Ricoeur calls this plea "the product of a fascination for the unformed that is one of the features of modernity," and as we have seen, Miles maintains that Radcliffe has set *Udolpho* on the cusp of modernity. It seems no coincidence, then, that this "fascination for the unformed" is strikingly akin to Bayer-Berenbaum's claim that the eighteenth-century fascination with ruins represents a desire "for the random, the wild, and the unbounded."[110] *Udolpho*—the novel as well as the castle—is a ruin, bearing all the signs of the work of time, a scar that is evidence not of a past wound, but of "the present fact of having been wounded."[111] The strings of the Marchioness's lute give unmuted testimony to this phenomenon. They are not in tune, in the sense of being organized according to predefined pitches, as we would mark out the days and months using a calendar, but their sound possesses a wildness and randomness that are not the chaos of noise, but the work of time, uncannily superimposing the Marchioness's past upon the novel's present. A "new quality of time" has indeed emerged. Augustine's solution to his contemplation of the paradox of time and eternity was his synthesis of past, present, and future into an extended, threefold present. The "faculty of attention" that illuminates Augustine's recitation of the psalm transforms the present into "the actualization of the future of what is remembered,"[112] and unites all the temporal axes through his narrative act. From the level of narrative to the lowest textual level, *The Mysteries of Udolpho* creates its own peculiar temporality, a "radically unformed temporal experience" in which movement and nonmovement, concord and discord, the same and not the same, the feudal past and modern present, can coexist coherently.

A generation later, a different kind of revolution will produce anxieties about the transformation of temporal experience. Once again, narrative will provide alternative views of temporality, in a quest to refigure time in human terms. This quest is the subject of the next chapter.

2
The Clock is Ticking: *Melmoth the Wanderer*

Let us take a very simple example, the ticking of a clock. We ask
what it *says:* and we agree that it says *tick-tock*. By this fiction,
we humanize it, make it talk our language. Of course, it is we
who provide the fictional difference between the two sounds;
tick is our word for a physical beginning, *tock* our word for an
end. We say they differ. What enables them to be different is a
special kind of middle. . . . The fact that we call the second of
the two related sounds *tock* is evidence that we use fiction to
enable the end to confer organization and form on the temporal
structure. The interval between the two sounds, between *tick*
and *tock* is now charged with significant duration. The clock's
tick-tock I take to be a model of what we call a plot, an organization that humanizes time by giving it form; and the interval between *tock* and *tick* represents purely successive, disorganized
time of the sort that we need to humanize.
　　　　　　　　　　　　　—Frank Kermode, *The Sense of an Ending*

[F]or any living thing that has reached its normal development
and which is unmutilated, and whose mode of generation is not
spontaneous, the most natural act is the production of another
like itself, an animal producing an animal, a plant a plant, in
order that, as far as its nature allows, it may partake in the eternal and divine. This is the goal toward which all things strive,
that for the sake of which they do whatsoever their nature renders possible. . . . Since then no living thing is able to partake in
what is eternal and divine by uninterrupted continuance . . . , it
tries to achieve that end in the only way possible to it . . . ; so it
remains not indeed as the self-same individual but continues its
existence in something *like* itself.
　　　　　　　　　　　　　　　　　—Aristotle, *De Anima*

PUBLISHED A GENERATION AFTER *THE MYSTERIES OF UDOLPHO,* CHARLES
Robert Maturin's *Melmoth the Wanderer* (1820) is, in part, a novel
about hours and generations, and about transmission: of property,
titles, and identity across generations. Generational succession is
one of humanity's strategies for reconciling our own brief existence

68

with the time of the world, and is an important Burkean figure for order and coherence. *Melmoth the Wanderer* is also about the generation and transmission of stories. Often regarded as marking the end of the first great wave of Gothic novels,[1] it is an unusual novel, with its own peculiar use of familiar Gothic devices such as imprisonment and interpolated narratives. Its images of claustrophobic oppression, both figurative (the highly structured environment of the convent in which Monçada is imprisoned) and real (Monçada's entrapment in the narrow, lightless tunnels beneath the convent, with a parricide for company), both spatial and temporal, reach a pitch of intensity not surpassed before or since. Because of its unprecedented approach to embedded narratives, its structure has often been described using misleading metaphors such as Chinese boxes (which suggest a symmetry that is not present in the novel), or beads on a string (which suggests a sequential relationship among the narratives that does not exist), or a set of random fragments (which implies authorial carelessness).[2] None of these metaphors quite seems to fit, although the first two are evidence of a desire by critics to impose, through misreading, a degree of structural coherence that may not exist, just as Burke does with British history. (I will have more to say about critical misreadings below.) A more accurate description is Chris Baldick's claim that *Melmoth the Wanderer* is "preposterously convoluted."[3] Linda Bayer-Berenbaum sees the novel's many convolutions (she includes structure, plot developments, setting, and characterization in her insightful study) as a figure for the "twisted Gothic line" in Gothic art, the lines that intertwine to infinity.[4] We considered this intertwining figure in our discussion of *The Mysteries of Udolpho*, but in *Melmoth the Wanderer* it is even more dramatically realized.

Melmoth the Wanderer is preoccupied—one might even say obsessed—with time and narrative, Paul Ricoeur's "circle of narrativity and temporality," in which time is one of the defining characteristics of narrative, and narrative in turn gives shape and meaning to time.[5] I want to argue in this chapter, first, that the novel represents a sustained quest for coherence—a quest that involves a dialectical relationship between coherence and incoherence—in the face of a series of aporias. In rhetoric, the term *aporia* refers to a moment of hesitation, the speaker's inability to articulate in the face of an inexpressible contradiction. Derrida reminds us of Aristotle's use of the term in his attempt to come to grips with the contradictory nature of time. As it was first used, the term *aporia* has an explicitly temporal context. It is worth citing Derrida's example again, because it has particular application to *Melmoth the*

Wanderer: "The word 'aporia' appears in person in Aristotle's famous text, *Physics IV* (217b), which reconstitutes the aporia of time *dia ton exoterikon logon* . . . (*Diaporeo* is Aristotle's term here; it means 'I'm stuck . . . I cannot get out, I'm helpless.') Therefore, for example—and it is more than just one example among others—it is impossible to determine time both as entity and as nonentity."[6] In *Melmoth,* the quest for coherence in the face of inarticulable contradictions has both generational and narratological components. It is a quest that invites, and even depends on, a collaboration among Maturin himself, his publisher and the reader. This quest ultimately takes the form of a dialectic of coherence and incoherence, a humanizing of what Frank Kermode calls the disorganized interval between *tick* and *tock.*

Melmoth the Wanderer's discourses on temporality develop a complicated relationship among time, space, and narrative. The desire to "partake," as Aristotle put it, "in the eternal and divine," is the desire to resolve the temporal aporia of mortality and eternity, and in *Melmoth the Wanderer* the strategies by which we usually attempt to resolve these aporias are regulated by institutions such as church and family. Such institutions control access to eternity, both direct access (the church) and indirect access through generational succession (both the family and the church), and in the world of the novel, these institutions can become corrupted, with unfortunate consequences. The novel's complicated relationships among time, space, and narrative are often marked by a series of literal aporias, moments of hesitation or "stuck-ness," which may be represented in a number of domains, including space, language, and the legal system. Because of the novel's intricate intertwining of time, space, and narrative, those literal aporias exist as metonyms for the underlying aporias of temporality.

The second argument I wish to make is that, whether it was Charles Robert Maturin's intention or not, *Melmoth the Wanderer* emerges at a moment when industrialization is beginning to arouse concerns about the effects of institutions on people's lives. One of the consequences of this process of industrialization was to transform notions of time as workers became concentrated in urban centers, often in factory settings where they had little direct contact with nature and its own temporal rhythms, and large portions of their lives were governed by their employers' schedules. More and more segments of society began to be *scheduled.* In 1784, "a unified network of public transport based on strict timekeeping was introduced throughout the length and breadth of England, the mail coach system."[7] This "strict timekeeping" was made possible by significant developments in the accuracy of timepieces. While Christiaan Huygens's pendulum clock had greatly increased the precision of timekeeping as far back as 1656 and made possible the addition of the minute hand to clocks, the true revolution in horological accuracy occurred in the eighteenth century, particularly with the instruments John Harrison developed to solve the "longitude problem" and navigate safely and accurately at sea.[8] "In the last quarter of the eighteenth century," David S. Landes points out, "the British turned the marine chronometer into an object of industrial manufacture and commercial use."[9] Thus, by the time Maturin wrote *Melmoth the Wanderer,* the clock had begun to assume increasing power over the regulation of people's lives.

It may have seemed to those engaged in the development of more accurate clocks and watches that measuring the flow of time with ever-greater precision was a solution to all the old aporias of temporal experience, a way of giving our lives meaning by dividing the gulf of time into smaller and finer increments. Maturin, however, sees this "solution" as a false one, leading to dehumanization, transforming people into clock-watching mechanisms, and corrupting the institutions that safeguard generational succession (i.e., church and family), both of which—dehumanization and corruption—*Melmoth* dramatizes. For Maturin, dividing the infinite gulf of time into smaller intervals and paying increased attention to them is no answer. On the contrary, the need to *humanize* the clock and its intervals, as Frank Kermode expressed the matter, is greater than ever in consequence of industrialization and horological developments. Storytelling provides a means of refiguring the infinite in human terms ("Time becomes human time to the extent that it is organized after the manner of a narrative"), and although the second part of Ricoeur's "circle of narrativity" states that "narrative, in turn, is meaningful to the extent that it portrays the features of temporal existence,"[10] Maturin demonstrates that these temporal "features" are not limited to a mechanistic sequence of identical increments. Rather, what we know of time is that it can seem to expand or contract under certain conditions, a temporal subjectivity that Monçada experiences several times in the novel, so Maturin's narrative proposes alternative forms of temporality to the incessant clock-watching that is becoming increasingly prevalent in the modern, industrialized world. In *Udolpho,* the "emotional and lyrical stretching and compressing" of time that Bakhtin associates with the "miraculous" time of chivalric romance,[11] operates as an implied alternative to progress and revolutionary fears. In *Melmoth,* the transformation of temporal experience is contrasted more explicitly with its alternative (clock-watching), than *Udolpho*'s. The novel accomplishes this transformation subjectively—terror, pain, anticipation, and the deprivation of food, water, and external stimuli all dilate time—and objectively, in the figure of the Wanderer himself.

TEXTUAL AND GENEALOGICAL TRANSMISSION

Melmoth the Wanderer has been granted a lifespan of 150 years,[12] provided he can find someone to take his place during that period; failing that, he is damned. Critics have sometimes called him a composite of the Wandering Jew, Mephistophiles, Faustus, Job's Satan, and perhaps Lazarus.[13] The presence of this unusual figure is often regarded as providing the common thread for what would otherwise be disparate tales, tales that extend from the seventeenth to the early nineteenth centuries. I suggest that Maturin's primary model is William Godwin's 1799 novel, *St. Leon: A Tale of the Sixteenth Century*, a romance about a man who is given the secrets of the philosopher's stone (unlimited wealth) and the elixir of life (immortality). As we shall see, Maturin recycles a number of details from Godwin's novel, even while he departs from it in several important particulars.[14]

Much is made of the fact that Melmoth does not seem to age. The fact that "[h]e constantly allude[s] to events and personages beyond his *possible memory*" and "the extraordinary fact of the [Wanderer's] being seen in various and distant parts of the earth within a time in which no power merely human could be supposed to traverse them" (26, 228, 326) are both noted.[15] Melmoth seems, by virtue of his extended life span, to be outside the generations, wandering in time as well as in space. The Wanderer himself tells Stanton that he is "independent of time and place" (44). This capability invests him with powers that considerably exceed those of Godwin's St. Leon, yet unlike St. Leon, he is not truly immortal; Melmoth's lifespan, while significantly extended, is still subject to the constraints of time, a limitation that is emphasized quite dramatically at the novel's climax. This important adaptation of the St. Leon myth effectively demonstrates Maturin's concerns about the degree to which public time rules the lives of individuals.

One striking aspect of *Melmoth*'s particular approach to temporality is its dual emphasis on the hour, as represented by the clock, and the generation, as represented by its theme of property inheritance. The novel seems to express a conflicted attitude toward ge-

nealogical coherence as a means of reconciling the temporal
aporias that exist between the time of one's own experience and
the time of the world. It struggles to affirm generational succession
even while, ironically, there is no lineal inheritance in the novel.[16]
Simultaneously, evident in the remarkable number of references to
clocks in most of the tales, the novel consistently disdains artificial
methods of tracking time, principally the role of the clock in regu-
lating both religious and secular affairs. Because of Maturin's ecclesiastical background, one might expect to find the church
offering a means of reconciling temporal aporias by providing the
master narrative of eternal salvation—the "long view" by which
one human life is placed into the context of God's eternal plan (as
well as the promise of an afterlife for the soul). Yet religious institutions in the novel offer instead stultifyingly short-sighted perspectives. Followers of Catholicism and Puritanism alike live lives
obsessively regulated by routine and mired in petty, and often
deadly, disputes. Nor does the extension of the human life span by
supernatural means offer a viable alternative to the problem of
death, for Melmoth the Wanderer himself comes to a catastrophi-
cally bad end. We seem to be left with the (nonlineal) affirmation
of coherent, generational succession as an alternative, more or less
by default.

In *Melmoth the Wanderer,* generational succession is a curiously
wrought alternative to Aristotle's "uninterrupted continuance";
not only is inheritance non-lineal, but second sons, often seen as
villains in Gothic romances because of their threat to primogeniture, emerge as the heroes more often than not, a point that apparently contests the Burkean model of inheritance. The younger John
Melmoth, who is the protagonist for the frame tale of the novel, is
"the orphan son of a younger brother" who inherits the estate of
his uncle, old Melmoth, including the ancient manuscript that provides the first of the embedded narratives (7). Moreover, Melmoth
the Wanderer himself, despite his claim to young Melmoth that
"you behold your ancestor" (536), is apparently not literally so, if
we accept old Biddy Brannigan's account of the family history:
"The first of the Melmoths, . . . who settled in Ireland, was an offi-
cer in Cromwell's army, who obtained a grant of lands, the confiscated property of an Irish family attached to the royal cause. The
elder brother of this man was one who had travelled abroad . . .
[i.e., Melmoth the Wanderer]" (26). There is no mention of Melmoth the Wanderer having had issue prior to his "death" and subsequent resurrection to his extended life span (499–500), and the
only person with whom Melmoth the Wanderer becomes intimate,

according to the text, is Immalee, whose child—and his—dies in the prisons of the Inquisition while still an infant. Therefore young John Melmoth is the orphaned son of a second son who was himself descended from a second son who lived on property confiscated as a reward for service to a usurper, a very unique twist on primogeniture indeed. Yet, these second sons ensure the coherent succession of generations. An obvious exception to this coherence involves Alonzo di Monçada himself, who is the elder son supplanted by his younger brother, Juan. But Alonzo, while of the same parents as his brother, is apparently illegitimate because he was conceived out of wedlock. He has no familial identity in the eyes of church and state, so his status is closer to that of a second son than a first-born.

This unconventional genealogical coherence is mirrored by the peculiar narrative coherence of the embedded tales. Referring to the various tales surviving in an intact form, Chris Baldick asserts that the novel is "secretly as much about transmission as it is about transgression," calling it "[a] noticeable symptom [of this emphasis on transmission] . . . that the layers of narration which one might expect to be marked by distinct narrative voices are in fact tonally continuous," while Kathleen Fowler complains that "[t]he language of a long series of narrators is irritatingly consistent."[17] One might well argue that the consistency of the narrative voices is a shortcoming of the novel, although it would try the skills of the most adept novelist to be able to faithfully represent the layers of narratorial voices and still produce a comprehensible account, given the complexity of the interpolation; indeed, I suspect the result would be far more annoying and incoherent to the reader than the consistency that Maturin achieves.[18] Nor is this phenomenon really unique to Maturin's novel, for Bakhtin reminds us that speech style differences are blurred and ultimately become the author's style: "Another's speech—whether as storytelling, as mimicking, as the display of a thing in light of a particular point of view, as a speech . . .—is at none of these points clearly separated from authorial speech: the boundaries are deliberately flexible and ambiguous, often passing through a single syntactic whole, often through a simple sentence, and sometimes even dividing up the main parts of a sentence."[19]

In *Melmoth*, the transmission of the text becomes a figure for the transmission, in the Burkean (and institutional) sense, of property, values, and identity. This is consistent with Peter Brooks's assertion that "the nineteenth century's frequent use of the framed tale which, dramatizing the relations of tellers and listeners, narrators and narratees, regularly enacts the problematic of transmission, looking for the sign of recognition and the promise to carry on, revealing . . . a deep anxiety about the possibility of transmission."[20] To be sure, one might find evidence in support of Baldick's claim that Maturin occasionally forgets who is speaking; in at least one instance, an *oral* narrative by Monçada, a narrative consisting of hundreds of pages rendered in the most exacting detail, is interrupted by the ellipses that characterize fragmented manuscripts (165).[21] Still, despite the lacunae that occasionally appear in the tales, there is a narrative coherence that binds them together. The traditional explanation for this coherence is the figure of the Wanderer himself, and there is some validity to this claim. For example, Monçada startles his listener in the midst of the recitation of a tale embedded within his own tale by referring to the Wanderer's visit to the Englishman Stanton, a tale that has no structural relationship to Monçada's at all, although this "connection" is never explored further (298). But Melmoth's presence in some of the tales (such as "The Tale of Guzman's Family" and even the "Tale of the Spaniard") is so limited, so minor, that it is difficult to ascribe to him the burden of narrative coherence.

What the tales really have in common is less the fact that Melmoth appears in them, than the similarity of the problem confronted in each. These similarities, along with the consistency of narrative voices, seem to provide whatever degree of coherence exists. Behind a series of problems that beset the characters of the various tales lies a central one. The question that drives the quest of the Wanderer himself, and informs each of the tales, is one that all humankind faces: We die, yet the world goes on. How can we find someone to take our places after we're gone? This is the Aristotelian aporia concerning the desire for mortal creatures to "partake in the eternal and the divine," another form of Augustine's aporia involving the time of the soul and the time of the world. *Melmoth* takes up this problem from several perspectives, posing the institution of the family, the prolonging of one's existence through supernatural means, and ultimately, narrative itself, as possible solutions.

Melmoth the Wanderer's own solution to the temporal aporia (making a pact with the devil) seems a less than viable alternative because it ends with his being dragged off to Hell when he cannot find anyone willing to change places with him. (This failure was singled out by Balzac in his 1835 parody *Melmoth Reconcilié*, Balzac noting that Maturin should have sent the Wanderer to Paris "where he would have found a thousand persons to one who would have accepted his power." A reviewer for the *Monthly Review*, however, found the Wanderer's failure "the only novelty . . . in the plan of the book," to which novelty the reviewer accorded "considerable praise.")[22] The Wanderer thus provides a false solution; after all, prolonging his existence does not resolve the problem, but only postpones it.

The institution of the family as a means of coherently transmitting values, property, and descendants to the future, as Burke might have put it, is another possible solution. Maturin emphasizes the family in all the tales: in each, a problem that has genealogical implications is the narrative discontinuity that propels the tale forward, but in each tale, some dysfunction undermines the family's ability to resolve that discontinuity, so that the genealogical solution is problematical, at best. Indeed, Kramer sees the "common thematic concern" of the novel to be the "perversion of love by institutions."[23] This dysfunction is a characteristic of each of the tales. In the frame tale, young John Melmoth is an orphan who must depend on the goodwill of a miserly uncle to pay his college expenses and secure a start in life. (His uncle is so miserly that he raps on the floor when summoning servants rather than pulling the bells, because he is afraid that he will wear out the bell ropes [13].) The story of the Englishman Stanton, recorded in the tattered manuscript found in the closet in Old Melmoth's house, is a cautionary tale about a man with no family. Stanton's genealogical problem is his lack of genealogy—his closest relative is a younger "cousin," a term used broadly in the nineteenth century.[24] Like the figure he eventually pursues, Stanton himself is a wanderer, his story opening with his travels in Spain, where he is "obtaining board and lodging [in convents] on the condition of holding a debate in Latin, on some point theological or metaphysical, with any monk who would become the champion of the strife" (28), a kind of "devil's advocate."[25] When Stanton becomes obsessed with Melmoth the Wanderer, his cousin tricks him into entering a madhouse (45–47), where he spends a year or two,[26] and where he is visited by the object of his pursuit. Attaining his release, Stanton continues to pursue the Wanderer for several years; in fact, his manuscript ends with his statement that "[t]he desire of meeting him once more, is become as a burning fire within me,—it is the necessary condition of my existence" (59). Stanton's lack of family ties and obligations may well render him more susceptible to this obsession.

As I have already mentioned, Alonzo di Monçada in the "Tale of the Spaniard" is a first son, but he is illegitimate. (For sake of clarity and simplicity, I shall refer to this tale hereafter as "Monçada's tale," since there are several tales set in Spain.[27]) Monçada's family's ecclesiastical "Director" refers to Monçada's status aporetically, when he "remotely hinted at something insurmountable and inexplicable" (80), and Monçada is sentenced to become a monk as penance for his parents' sin. In the hierarchical and patriarchal society that is Catholic Spain, his mother, who, besides the social disadvantages of being born female, is also from a lower social class, bears all the guilt and has promised her son to the church as expiation for her sin. She tells Monçada that his father "loved me, and forg[ave] my weakness as a proof of my devotion to him" (90). Because Monçada is a living discontinuity with regard to the church's definition of generational coherence, his becoming a monk is the "only means to restore peace to the family" (121), to ensure "the honour of one of the first houses in Spain" (83). Otherwise, he is more or less "stuck," without the ability to move forward in life, as he will later be literally stuck in the tunnel beneath the convent.[28] Monçada's is to be a life without property, cut off from society and from the consolation of reproduction, doomed to renounce any hope of a child of his body to carry on after him (who would thus transmit his aporetic status to another generation). Monçada's family is controlled by the Catholic church, which not only determines that his younger brother is the legitimate heir, but drives his mother mad with guilt over her elder son's conception out of wedlock. Thus the church, by sanctifying marriage and defining legitimacy, disciplines the family and regulates its role in transmission. It imposes its own means of determining what constitutes generational coherence, at the same time that it creates monastic environments that limit or frustrate the species' natural means of reproducing.

During his attempted underground escape from the convent, we learn that Monçada's guide has his own set of distorted "family values": he murdered his father by slashing his throat in order to steal his money to pay debts; later, he betrays a pair of secret lovers (the woman disguised as a male novice) by sealing them up in a cave and starving them to death, only to learn afterward that the woman was his sister. Monçada's guide not only murders the one who was responsible for giving him life, but the death of his only sister and her husband eliminates any possibility of further generations of this family.

Immalee's family, the di Aliagas, in the "Tale of the Indians," (which I will refer to as "Immalee's tale") has wealth but lacks the *right* genealogy, a growing problem for the bourgeois class in eighteenth- and nineteenth-century Britain. They are of "formerly high descent" (330), now "in trade" and willing to force their daughter into an unwelcome marriage to satisfy their dynastic ambitions, to obtain the legitimacy their mercantilism (and the elder Monçada's social gaffe of having married beneath his station) has clouded. They require an alliance with a noble family in order to strengthen the stature of the family tree—an apt image, as Don Fernan, Immalee's brother, refers to his plan to marry off his sister to one of the first families of Spain as a "graft on the stock" (337).

It is in Immalee's tale that Maturin intensifies his analysis of religion, examining Hinduism, Islam, Judaism, and most prominently Christianity, with its Catholic form found to be especially wanting as a solution to the temporal dilemma. (While anti-Catholic discourses are a common feature of Gothic novels, we shall see that, despite Charles Maturin's Anglican clerical background, certain Protestant beliefs do not fare much better than Catholicism at his hands.) Immalee's "natural religion" during her childhood alone on the island in the Indian Ocean is more valorized, as her experience is summarized by Melmoth the Wanderer in a story later told to Immalee's father: "[A]nd the child survived, and grew up a wild and beautiful daughter of nature, feeding on fruits,—and sleeping amid roses,—and drinking of the pure element,—and inhaling the harmonies of heaven,—and repeating to herself the few Christian words her nurse had taught her, in answer to the melody of the birds that sung to her, and of the stream whose waves murmured in accordance to the pure and holy music of her unearthly heart" (503).[29] In fact, Immalee's timeless, idyllic, Rousseauvian existence is placed at the exact center of the novel, not, as Null claims, her choice to become a Christian.[30] This Romantic theology has even been anticipated by Monçada's contemplation, one evening, of the convent's garden, "with its calm moon-light beauty, its innocence of heaven, its theology of the stars" (117). In contrast to her idealized existence on the island, even after Immalee decides that she will become a Christian because of the appeal of its doctrine of universal love, which seemed "so beautiful and pure," she later complains to Melmoth, "when they brought me to a Christian land, I thought I should have found them all Christians," but is disappointed to find "[o]nly Catholics" (344).

The Walbergs, the family of Guzman in "The Tale of Guzman's Family," (referred to hereafter as "The Walbergs' tale," since Guzman is offstage dying, or dead, throughout most of it) have their own set of complications, again intensified by the Catholic Church. As Guzman is childless, his sister, Ines Walberg stands to inherit his fortune, but heresy (from the Catholic point of view) is the problem: the Walbergs are Protestants, so their problem is similar to Monçada's in that their Protestantism renders them theologically illegitimate. They initially lose their challenge to the church's claims on Guzman's fortune in the secular courts, in an apparent repetition of Monçada's own failed appeal to the secular authorities, who fear the consequences of interfering with ecclesiastical authority as "too dangerous" (173), although the Walbergs eventually obtain justice when a good priest finds a later-dated will in which Guzman leaves all his property to his family (432). This outcome undercuts the reliability of systems of dating and the role of narratives in the transmission of property; they are seen as arbitrary and subject to corruption. But during the period in which it appears that the church will succeed in cheating the Walbergs out of their rightful inheritance, Walberg, himself tempted by the offers of Melmoth the Wanderer, and unable to bear seeing his family slowly starve, nearly murders his wife and youngest children, while his oldest son sells his blood to a surgeon and his oldest daughter narrowly avoids prostitution (424–30).

In "The Lovers' Tale" (I'll refer to it as "The Mortimers' tale," for there are several tales involving lovers), Sir Roger Mortimer's coherent line of succession is fractured by political and religious strife. The provisions of his will attempt to provide a solution by uniting the sundered branches of his family but knowledge of this provision, and the attempt to manipulate genealogy to fulfill it, leads ultimately to disaster. The lovers' happiness is ruined when John Sandal's mother informs him, on his wedding day, that he and his promised bride, his cousin Elinor, have the same mother. Motivated by her desire for the inheritance he will possess if he marries another cousin, Margaret, she invents a false genealogy (providing a discontinuity where none in fact exists) that prevents his wedding, and ultimately leads to his madness when he finally discovers the truth.

The Wanderer's own variation on the old human dilemma of finding one to carry on after him is that his replacement is not to be produced biologically but through an act of conscious choice. He comes closest to success with Immalee, but his love for her prevents him from letting her make such a fatal choice. On one occasion, he leaves her on her island and does not return, lest he tempt her (324). On a second occasion, he renounces their engagement and disappears from her sight (367). The Mortimers' tale is told by Melmoth to Immalee/Isidora's father, Don Aliaga, as a cautionary tale that contains the account of his own death and apparent resurrection, an account not at all favorable to his nature, in a passage that stretches the limits of narrative viewpoint in an embedded tale. In this tale, Melmoth achieves a remarkable feat in a further interpolation, adeptly characterizing himself from the perspective of an English clergyman who has become his enemy, one who knew him as one who "has traversed the earth in search of victims, 'Seeking whom he might devour'" (501). This narrative adroitness is comparable to Melmoth's (an agent of Satan's) defense of Protestantism against Catholicism related in a text written by a Jew and narrated by a Catholic.[31]

Even more important than debating whether Maturin lost track of the layers of his narrative (as Chris Baldick has claimed[32]) and the improbably consistent narrative voices is the fact that the reader's suspension of disbelief comes relatively easily, despite what sounds like a dizzying array of narrative levels. The wild improbability of the details of this layering are quite easily forgotten, only arrived at by careful, conscious thought and reconstruction of the text *as a narrative,* including the degree of its adherence to narrative conventions. We don't just suspend disbelief; we "want to believe," as Mulder's poster in his FBI office in *The X-Files* proclaims. To put the matter simply, we get carried away by the tales and supply the missing coherence by eliding the disjunctions.

Melmoth's account to Don Aliaga even provides a prophecy of his own downfall: "[h]e is yet to be subdued by a foe that he deemed of all others the least invincible—the withered energies of a broken heart" (501). Yet Don Aliaga, "whose faculties were somewhat obtuse," (502), doesn't see the tale's "application" to him, so Melmoth gives a more explicit warning, telling the true story of Immalee's parentage and childhood on the island (Don Aliaga eventually beginning to comprehend the strange similarity to his own family circumstances), until Melmoth finally exclaims, "There is an arm extended to seize her, in whose grasp humanity withers!—That arm even now relaxes for a moment,—its fibres thrill with pity and horror,—it releases the victim for a moment,—it even beckons her father to her aid!—Don Francisco, do you understand me now?—Has this tale interest or application for you? . . . If it has . . . lose not a moment to save your daughter!" (503) Don Aliaga's obtuseness derives from his limited imagination. His is the stereotypically literal, mercantile, mind. He is unable to connect any aspects of the story the Wanderer narrates to his own situation and family. His inability to imaginatively make connections, to connect the dots, renders him "coherence-challenged," so the Wanderer's story is incoherent to him. Thus this tale is especially rich in discourses exploring the power of narrative. It seems to invite us to supply narrative coherence where a too literal consideration of details of the narrating event (the improbability of Melmoth the Wanderer's being able to achieve such a multilayered reversal of perspective, rendered accurately in a multiply-embedded tale) would undermine such coherence. In effect, it invites a noncritical misreading while providing an example of a character who is himself unable to render a tale coherent.

TIMEKEEPING MECHANISMS

In marked contrast to *Udolpho,* where the time of clock or calendar is rarely mentioned, *Melmoth* is filled with references to timekeeping. The year is often mentioned with regard to events of the frame narrative and embedded tales, such as the date of the novel's opening ("autumn of 1816" [7]), the date of the famous portrait of the Wanderer (1646 [18]), the date of Stanton's travels in Spain (1676 [28]) and London (1677 [39]), various dates relative to Immalee (we are told she is seventeen years old in 1680, for example [281], and she is seen in Madrid in 1683 [327]), and the year the Spanish travellers encounter Melmoth the Wanderer (1683 [327]).

Martin Heidegger's analytic of temporality distinguishes between an "authentic," existentially realized temporality, in which time is a unity of the three temporal "ecstasies," and what he terms the "vulgar understanding" of time, characterized by the perception of time as a "pure succession of nows, without beginning and without end, in which the ecstatic, self-transcending character of primordial time is levelled down," or diminished. Clock time is an aspect of this leveling down, as it reflects the three characteristics associated with ordinary, or vulgar, time: the clock is a phenomenon of *datability,* it can be used to measure or identify *duration* of time, and it is *public.* The clock artificially subdivides the "'most natural' measure of time, the day," and looking at the clock and "orienting oneself *toward time*" is a phenomenon that Heidegger disparagingly calls "*now-saying.*"[33] Maturin's novel is preoccupied with this now-saying in the image of the clock. Old Melmoth, the miserly uncle of the protagonist of the novel's frame tale, has "a timekeeper dumb for want of repair" alongside "a tattered almanack from 1750" (25), implying he once paid heed to time but does so no longer. His case, however, is the exception. From the moment that "the sound of the clock striking twelve made him [John Melmoth] start" and prompted him to open the Stanton manuscript (27), the novel is obsessed with time, frequently represented in characters who are dominated by it, often to the extent that it undermines their grasp of reality. One of Stanton's neighbors in the asylum, a "puritanical weaver," is possessed of a madness of a uniquely temporal character. This weaver, "who had been driven mad by a single sermon from the celebrated Hugh Peters . . . regularly repeated over the *five points* while day-light lasted, and imagined himself preaching in a conventicle with distinguished success; towards twilight his visions were more gloomy, and at midnight his blasphemies became horrible" (49).

Maturin's depiction of the mad weaver is strikingly similar to Burke's description of infinity as a source of the sublime, and his association of infinite repetition with madness. After describing the way our senses respond to repetitive stimuli even after they are no longer present (we continue to feel dizzy even after we have stopped whirling around), Burke states that this inability of the senses to "change their tenor" is "the reason of an appearance very frequent in madmen; that they remain whole days and nights, sometimes whole years, in the constant repetition of some remark, some complaint, or song; which having struck powerfully on their disordered imagination, in the beginning of their phrensy, every repetition reinforces it with new strength."[34] In this case, it is interesting that the madman is a weaver, an occupation that involves convolutions and intertwinings, the quest for infinity of the Gothic line to which Bayer-Berenbaum referred. But the repetitive behavior of Stanton's neighbor is echoed by other, more "rational" characters in the novel, and is related to the novel's link between the clock and the tedium of monotonous regularity. One of the first, and most vivid, images of this occurs in the statement by the old monk Fra Paolo in the "Tale of the Spaniard," when he tells Monçada, "I am a clock that has struck the same minutes and hours for sixty years. Is it not time for the machine to long for its winding up? The monotony of my existence would make a transition, even to pain, desirable. I am weary. . . . I hated the monastic life. . . . For sixty years I have cursed my existence. I never woke to hope, for I had nothing to do or to expect" (110–11). The obsessive regulation of the hours in the monastic life is characterized as unnatural and mechanistic as the old monk continues his complaint: "I never ate with appetite, because I knew, that with or without it, I must go to the refectory when the bell rung. I never lay down to rest in peace, because I knew the bell was to summon me in defiance of nature, whether it was disposed to prolong or shorten my repose." When one of the other monks praises him for the punctuality of his devotions, Fra Paolo responds, "That was mechanism" (111).

Fra Paolo's description is reminiscent of a phenomenon that Burke describes when he refers to the way that "the mind by a sort of mechanism" allows us to experience repetition where it no longer continues. The bell, closely associated with the clock in the way that it regulates all activities in the monastery, even deprives the brothers of human society, as Monçada learns when he is punished for his defiance of monastic authority: "the bell was rung,— that terrible bell, that requires every member of a convent to plunge into his cell, as something extraordinary is going on in the house. At the first toll I lost all hope. I felt as if not a living being was in existence but those who surrounded me, and who appeared, in the livid light of one taper burning faintly in that dismal passage, like spectres hurrying a condemned soul to his doom" (143–44). Like the clock, the bell is unnatural and transformative. In this case it changes human beings, not into mechanisms, but into spectres, depriving them of the quality of transcendence, of an ecstatic unity of the temporal axes that is characteristic of a primordial temporality. Later, in the Inquisition, Isidora is summoned to "the hour of her trial" by a bell (528).

So dependent is even the defiant Monçada on temporal markers, that, without them, he nearly goes mad. Confined alone in a lightless, reptile-ridden stone chamber as punishment, he misses, first, the light of day, and next, the means "to watch those divisions of time, which, by measuring our portions of suffering, appear to diminish them. When the clock strikes, we know an hour of wretchedness is past, never to return. My only time-keeper was the approach of the monk, who every day renewed my allowance of bread and water. . . . Those æras by which we compute the hours of darkness and inanity are inconceivable to any but those who are situated as I was" (144–45). There is a bitter consolation in being able to measure one's "hour[s] of wretchedness." Monçada's plight is a perfect realization of, in Heidegger's terms, the levelling down of *Care* (an aspect of *Da-sein*, or "being-in-the-world" that involves self-awareness, an awareness that looks toward one's future potential) to mere *preoccupation* (one's loss of perspective by becoming tangled in the minutiae of daily existence.)[35] It is worth nothing that Immalee/Isidora laments that her former life on her island was "all anticipation" while her present life in Spain is "all retrospection. *The life of the happy is all hopes,—that of the unfortunate all memory*" (344). Deprived of any other stimuli, the minutes become the minutiae; deprived of any means of apprehending the passage of time, Monçada embodies old Fra Paolo's complaint even more literally, by turning himself into a timekeeping mechanism:

> I had calculated with myself, that sixty minutes made an hour, and sixty seconds a minute. I began to think I could keep time as accurately as any clock in a convent, and measure the hours of my confinement or—my release. So I sat and counted sixty; a doubt always occurred to me, that I *was counting them faster than the clock.* Then I wished to be the clock, that I might have no feeling, no *motive for hurrying on the approach of time.* Then I reckoned slower. . . . Thus I oscillated, reckoned, and measured time on my mat, while time withheld its delicious diary of rising and setting suns,—of the dews of dawn and of twilight,—of the glow of morning and the shades of the evening. When my reckoning was broken by my sleep, (and I knew not whether I slept by day or by night), I tried to eke it out by my incessant repetition of minutes and seconds, and I succeeded; for I always consoled myself, that whatever hour it was, sixty minutes must go to an hour. Had I led this life much longer, I might have been converted into the idiot, who, as I have read, from the habit of watching a clock, imitated its mechanism so well, that when it was down, he sounded the hour as faithfully as ear could desire. (146–47, emphasis original)

What Monçada misses are the earth's natural rhythms, the "delicious diary of rising and setting suns," for which the clock is a poor, unfeeling substitute, a mechanical repetition of equidistant marks—Burke's concept of madness as a source of the sublime. This theme of humans *as* clocks is a persistent one in the novel. After he reads the letter from his brother promising his help in escaping the convent, Monçada feels "like a clock whose hands are pushed forward, and I struck the hours I was impelled to strike" (181). His sense of being "pushed forward" suggests once again concerns about the pace of time's movement which does indeed vary in the novel. In the previous passage in which Monçada obsessively counts the minutes, it is interesting that he worries about his ability to record the passage of time accurately as well as the danger of becoming *so* accurate in his imitation of the clock's mechanism that he will become an idiot.[36] He takes consolation in the mere fact that, however fast or slow, the hour is comprised of sixty minutes, as if the raw process of counting from one to sixty is sufficient. (Curiously, old Fra Paolo has "struck the same minutes and hours for sixty years," repeating the emphasis on the number sixty.)[37]

Maturin's motif of mechanism may provide a commentary on the growing pace of industrialization. Concerns about the factory system and child labor are evident in Britain at least as far back as

Blake's *Songs of Innocence* in 1789, but vandalism against factory machines such as power looms, beginning in the midlands and the north of England around 1792, intensified with the Luddite Riots of 1811–12.[38] This was still the comparatively recent past during the time Maturin was writing *Melmoth*. The relative dearth of biographical information on Charles Robert Maturin makes it difficult to determine how he felt about such events, although his views on some subjects, such as his Irish patriotism and anti-Catholic sentiments, are fairly well established.[39] But the novel's persistent anxieties about the mechanization of human existence are in accord with some contemporary concerns. Maturin translates this mechanism anxiety from the realm of the factory into the spiritual realm by fusing it with the monastic system of canonical hours. The tradition-bound Catholic church may seem an unlikely metaphor for the effects of industrial technology on human lives; nevertheless, the degree of control that the church as an institution exercised over one's temporal experience, particularly in the environment of the monastery or convent, is strikingly similar to that exercised by the factory owner. In both cases, the result is a heightened time-consciousness.

Monçada's anxiety about whether one's own accounting of time is in accord with *public* (i.e., "official," ecclesiastical) time is also seen in Donna Clara's household in Immalee's tale. The mother of Immalee, who "fretted about every thing," would "fret about the family clock not chiming synchronically with the bells of the neighbouring church where she performed her devotions" so that she can order her prayer rituals (368).

Donna Clara's fretting is in striking contrast to Immalee herself, who, as we have seen, spent her childhood alone on an island off the coast of India after a shipwreck, and who "took 'no note of time.'"[40] For Immalee, there can be no ritualistic, fretting, behavior, for "the tale of yesterday, or the record of past centuries, were synchronized in a mind to which facts and dates were alike unknown" (297). Maturin's choice of the word *synchronized* draws an especially effective distinction between Immalee and her mother's perspective, in the way that the two make temporal comparisons. They both synchronize, Donna Clara bells to bells, Immalee yesterday to the distant past. While on her island, Immalee does have an awareness of the relational structure of time; she knows that she is older than the roses, because she has seen them decay and be replaced by others, and that she is "much older than the moon, for she had seen it waste away till it was dimmer than the light of a firefly" (283–84). She regards time as part of the natural, or primordial world of temporality, based on the natural cycles of the day and the lunar month, not yet "levelled down" or corrupted by clock-time. She has seen multiple generations of roses and the moon, while she has remained. Unlike her mother's absolute sense of time, Immalee's is relative—she measures time in relation to the life around her.[41] She is not now-focused, for she can both remember and anticipate. Her memory (retention, in Heidegger's schema) includes words from childhood and the knowledge that earlier generations of roses were "a great deal larger and brighter—that, in fact, everything had grown small latterly" (283), for she can now reach fruit that she could not reach before. She is not unaware of longer rhythms of change, or that she herself has changed—grown taller—although she is "unacquainted" with "the linked progress of events" (297). Immalee also possesses anticipation. She knows the moon will decline (284), and that "flowers wither and die their beautiful death of nature" (286). Like the Wanderer himself, she has a multi-generational view of life, even if her points of comparison seem somewhat ephemeral.

How different is her temporal perspective from her mother's, whose orientation, despite the fact that it is couched in piety and we might therefore expect it to be oriented toward eternity, is instead particularly short-termed, filled with anxieties about synchronizing her clock-driven devotions with the bells of the nearby church. Donna Clara's devotions are regulated like those of the monks in the convent, whose argument about the proper hour for matins, a debate over a difference of "*[f]ull five minutes*" (102, emphasis original), is so sharp it threatens to split the community.

We also see this mechanistic approach to time in the monastic life used to ironic effect: As the convent's Superior plots with some other monks to drug Monçada so that he cannot meet with the visiting Bishop, and responds to the fears one monk expresses about taking so drastic a step by asking "But who can know it?," an "old ascetic monk . . . who had accustomed himself to the exclamation, 'God knoweth all things,' whenever the clock struck" makes his proclamation.[42]

And yet time in *Melmoth* has a dual nature. On the one hand it is artificial and unnatural, but, once regulated by it (as Immalee had not been, while on her island), one can go mad without it. Time is dialogic in that it has multiple voices, both figuratively and literally. This dialogism is expressed in the very *sound* of the clock's ticking, which for Monçada seems to strike "every minute the alternate sounds, '*There is hope,—there is no hope*'" (174). Time expresses a dialectic of both hope and fear. As Kermode observed, we "provide the fictional difference" between the clock's sounds *tick* and *tock*.

Clock-striking reaches a feverish pitch in the often-discussed chapter that details Monçada's escape from the convent with a parricide for a guide (volume 2, chapter 8). In this chapter, Maturin seems to provide alternative conceptions of time, for it does not always unfold as a sequence of identical segments. Clock images abound; in fact, the intensity of time-consciousness in the chapter refigures in the temporal dimension the intensity of its spatial claustrophobia. The chapter begins on the eve of Pentecost, at two a.m., when Monçada enters the chapel for his allotted hour of prayer. He meets his co-conspirator, who describes to him the plan for their escape on the following night. The parricide advises him, "we have no time to lose. You have but an hour to remain in the church, and I have much to tell you in that hour" (183). This early establishes a tone of temporal constraint (to which even Melmoth the Wanderer himself is ultimately subject): there is only an hour, and much to do in that hour, before the bell will ring and other monks will appear for their allotted time of devotions. Just as the parricide finishes his explanations of the escape plan and they part, "[t]he clock struck three, its sound reminded me that my hour had expired" (187). The day that follows, as he anticipates his escape, is an aporia both in the sense of an inability to articulate and in the sense of a hesitation, a suspended moment. Monçada says he has "no more power of describing" that day, likening his ordeal to a sultan's in an unidentified "eastern tale" who imagines an extraordinary series of adventures in the moments in which his head is plunged into a basin of water. Again, the dialectical nature of time is emphasized, and again it is associated with sound imagery, the multivoicedness of the bell, Monçada "oscillating between hope and despair. I seemed to myself that day to be pulling the rope of a bell, whose alternate knell was *heaven—hell,* and this rung in my ears with all the dreary and ceaseless monotony of the bell of the convent" (188). He enters the church at night, only to be delayed by an old monk praying for relief from a toothache so severe that the pain has spread *"from the lower jaw to the upper"* (189; emphasis original). The image of the toothache is a profound one, for who has not felt the passage of time more slowly and keenly than in such moments? Maturin's peculiar way of emphasizing (italicizing) such phrases as the spread of pain reinforces the impression of mounting anxiety, almost to the point of hysteria. In the midst of this delay of Monçada's plans, the clock strikes two once more, seeming to annihilate the difference from one day to the next, as if

time has moved backward to two a.m. the previous morning, an effect heightened by the fact that this occurs only one paragraph later
than the events of the previous night.

Textually, Maturin has blurred the distinctions between days,
trapping the reader in that feverish hour between two and three
o'clock, like a dream of prolonged terror that one, along with
Monçada, is incapable "of analysing . . . to its component parts of
sanity, delirium, defeated memory, and triumphant imagination"
(187). The motif of the conspirators only having an hour to accomplish their purpose is repeated on this, the second night, and their
efforts are frustrated by a recalcitrant lock on the door to their escape passage. With the sound of the clock ringing in Monçada's
ears "like the trumpet of the day of doom" (190)—and thus, presumably, alternatively heaven and hell, as he observed before—
they at last open the door and descend into the tunnels beneath
the convent.

In the subterranean passage, where their "wanderings . . .
seemed to be endless," they lose track of time ("for minutes are
hours in the *noctuary* of terror,—terror has no *diary*" [192]), and
Monçada becomes stuck in a constricted passage. He remembers a
tale of a traveler in the vaults of the Egyptian pyramids who, finding
himself in a similar plight, heard his companions proposing to dismember him so that those behind him could escape. Time for
Monçada seems to have dilated (consistent with Radcliffe's assertion that Terror "expands the soul"[43]), even as the unhappy traveller in the pyramids swelled in size due to his terror. He finally
manages to extricate himself as their lamp expires ("I had watched
it like the last beatings of an expiring heart," Monçada relates), but,
before they have found their way to freedom, at that very moment
they hear "the chaunt of matins . . . which was now begun in the
chapel now far above us" (194). Suspended below the earth, in a
lightless, timeless void, the pair hear the chant from the world of
time far above them. Once again, as was the case of Monçada's solitary confinement, even the over-regulated monastic life he was trying to escape seems preferable to an infinity of darkness and
timelessness, in which both space and time are unmarked and un-
humanized. Monçada exemplifies Ricoeur's "oscillations of an existence torn between the sense of its mortality and the silent
presence of the immensity of time enveloping all things."[44]

Finding themselves, at daybreak, within reach of the tunnel's
exit into the convent garden, the two must prolong their stay another whole day, because workers have already entered the garden,
another constraint imposed by public time. This chapter (volume

2, chapter 9) is filled with references to the length of time to be spent without food or water, Monçada trying to console himself that the hours they must wait are nothing, compared "to the eternity of hours that must otherwise be wasted in a convent" (196). But those hours so near to escape are indeed a severe trial, as Monçada must listen to the parricide's dream-inspired recounting of the details of his father's murder. Soon, Monçada can think of nothing else but "the prospect of seclusion here for a whole day amid famine, damps, and darkness, listening to the ravings" of his companion (201). Because Monçada cannot stand to let his companion go to sleep and audibly relive the horrors of his crime, Monçada asks him to sing to keep awake, but the parricide sings "songs that would have made a harlot blush" (202–3). Ultimately narrative provides a solution—however perverse, in this case—to the problem of passing the time. Because "time becomes human time to the extent that it is organized after the manner of a narrative,"[45] it humanizes an otherwise intolerable interval; noticing that the vaults beneath the convent seem familiar, the parricide proceeds to narrate the story of a pair of secret lovers whom he had helped to escape through those very tunnels, but whom he ultimately betrays, trapping them and starving them to death. (It is only after their deaths that the parricide realizes that the woman is in fact his sister.) The parallels to Monçada's own situation are soon obvious even to him, and he confronts his guide with the fact that he is "tracing my course this night step by step" (208). His companion makes no effort to deny this, asserting that Monçada is in his power and he could summon half the convent in a moment.

After the acute emphasis on the passage of time during the two traumatic chapters of escape, Monçada collapses into insensibility—an aporetic hesitation in his awareness—while "[m]any a month of gloomy unconsciousness rolled over me, without date or notice"—four months in fact, in the prisons of the Inquisition to which his treacherous companion has betrayed him (216). When he recalls the circumstances of his escape, and his brother's murder at the moment of it, "the recollection of all the past" strikes him "like a thunder-bolt" (217). This pattern of acute awareness of time followed by insensibility is repeated when Monçada escapes from the Inquisition when much of it is destroyed in a catastrophic fire, during which he sees the steeple of a nearby church against the flames:

The night was intensely dark, but so strong was the light of this conflagration, that I could see the spire blazing, from the reflected lustre, like a meteor. The hands of the clock were as visible as if a torch was held before them; and this calm and silent progress of time, amid the tumultuous confusion of midnight horrors,—this scene of the physical and mental world in an agony of fruitless and incessant motion, might have suggested a profound and singular image, had not my whole attention been rivetted to a human figure placed on a pinnacle of the spire, and surveying the scene in perfect tranquillity. . . . The hopes of my justification made me forget every thing. (242)

Melmoth's apparition on the pinnacle of the spire, where he is *above* time, is a demonic inversion of Augustine's image of God, "outside time in eternity," an eternity "for ever still" (just as the Wanderer is in perfect tranquillity) while time "is never still," like the tumultuous scene before Monçada, with its "incessant motion."[46] The figure on the spire is of course that of Melmoth the Wanderer.

Following this vision and his escape in the confusion, Monçada collapses in the home of the Jew, "Don Fernan di Nunez" (his Christian name), where "[m]any days elapse[]" before he comes to his senses again (250). When "Don Fernan" is taken by the Inquisition, "under the suspected character of a relapsed Jew" (261), Monçada escapes through an underground passage that connects that home to the home of a second Jew, Adonijah. This is one of an array of almost-repetitions that occur in this section of the book, doublings that are the same, but not the same, as we saw in the case of *Udolpho*'s Valancourt. More apropos of *Melmoth the Wanderer*, these doublings resemble the clock's *tick* and *tock*, which are the same, but are apprehended differently. Such doublings and almost-doublings once again suggest the repetition of the Gothic line as a figure for the infinite, because they constantly multiply themselves. This system of tunnels is a kind of Jewish version of the tunnels under the convent; two sets of tunnels, and two Jews, one of whom pretends to be a Christian, maintaining two sets of names for himself and his family, and one who apparently does not. Adonijah himself is a kind of anti-Melmoth, both like and unlike the Wanderer. At 107 years old, his life has been "prolonged beyond the bounds allotted to mortality" (267; a statement that is repeated on p. 269), presumably until his tales can be collected and transcribed, a testament to the temporally transcendent power of narrative. Adonijah, having himself spent sixty years in the transcription of his tales, seems to intend Monçada to be his successor in this endeavor; like the Wanderer, he also seeks one to take his place, recalling Aristotle's organism's striving to continue its existence "in something *like* itself." Adonijah is perhaps closer to the true figure of the Wandering Jew as represented by Godwin's *St. Leon* than Melmoth the Wanderer, because Maturin's character has none of the Mephistophilean traits of Godwin's. Adonijah is also both like and unlike Fra Paolo. The sixty years of his labors (also mentioned twice [265, 267]) recall the old monk's sixty years of "mechanism."

We saw the way that Maturin seemed to blur the interval between days in the chapter detailing Monçada's escape, when the events of two succeeding nights were both taking place between two and three o'clock. A similar strategy is employed, to more pronounced effect, in Immalee's tale, one of the tales that Monçada translates from Adonijah's scrolls, when he seems to dissolve the interval between the writing of the letter from Don Francisco to his wife, Donna Clara. Here, however, it is not just an hour, but an exact moment, marked out by the striking of the clock. Don Francisco writes to his wife of his encounter with the stranger whom we know to be Melmoth the Wanderer:

> "overcome with horror at this second visitation, I fell back on my pillow almost bereft of the use of my faculties, I remember the clock struck three."
>
> As Donna Clara and the priest (on their tenth perusal of the letter) arrived at these words, the clock in the hall below struck three. "That is a singular coincidence," said Fra Jose. "Do you think it nothing more, Father?" said Donna Clara, turning very pale. (383)

As Linda Bayer-Berenbaum points out, "[s]trange twists in the time sequence of the novel cause different episodes to buckle over upon themselves in order to occur simultaneously." She notes that, in this case, "Maturin makes much of this coincidence, leading the reader to think that somehow time has stood still, that the writing of the letter and its later reading are happening at the same time," lending an immediacy to the narrative.[47] What causes the illusion of simultaneity in this scene, the "singular coincidence" (if not something more), is the striking of the clock in both Don Francisco's letter and Donna Clara's house. Without these clock strikes, there would be no reason for Donna Clara to turn pale at all—and in fact, the coincidence only takes place "on their tenth perusal of the letter," as the tale's narrator (presumably Adonijah, as told by Monçada to the young Melmoth, but Adonijah's source is not made clear) parenthetically notes.

The coincidence then, is a forced one, caused by Donna Clara's obsessively repetitive behavior. She has spent the entire preceding

day "reading over and correcting her answer to her husband's letter" (377), in a wonderfully comic passage in which Maturin relates all her repeated corrections and alterations of the letter to her
current needlework project, in which she is "*overcasting* a piece of
tapestry wrought by her grandmother. . . . The new work, instead
of repairing, made fearful havock among the old" (377). That letter
having been finally dispatched, she and Fra Jose read "over and
over" Don Francisco's "extraordinary letter" (381). Donna Clara
seems unable to finish anything, or to make any progress at all. Re-
sembling Burke's madman and his infinite repetitions, exhibiting
what we would today call obsessive-compulsive behavior, she can
only go back over previous territory, or at best be a slave to the moment, her perspective warped by compulsive attention to details,
whether it is needlework, letter-writing or synchronizing her devotions to the nearby church bell. The reply to Don Francisco's first
letter was able to be completed only through Fra Jose's dictation,
and was sent at all only because the priest himself folded and sealed
it, swearing "by the habit he wore, he had rather study twenty pages
of the Polyglot fasting, than read it over once more" (380).

Indeed, so warped is Donna Clara's judgment that, on an outing
in Madrid with her daughter, Isidora (as Immalee is now called)
instinctively knows that a mendicant woman's naked child is not
her own, because the woman is clothed while the infant is not (presumably no real mother would permit such an imbalance), although Donna Clara had been deceived by the woman's subterfuge.
In other words, Isidora can read the tale of generations; she knows
more of being a mother than her own mother does.

And yet Maturin's clock-striking device is successful, for despite
the fact that Donna Clara is perusing the letter for the tenth time,
the chiming of the clock does produce a singular effect in the
reader, who links it to the significance of three a.m. in Monçada's
tale, where it had struck on two successive nights, "ringing like the
trumpet of the day of doom." Furthermore, we know that Melmoth
and Isidora/Immalee are to be married that very night. In fact, she
and her lover left the house two hours before, their departure
marked by a noise that Fra Jose had briefly noted, a noise that
Donna Clara imagines she has heard only now. It is the clock striking three that breaks the cycle of repeated perusals of the letter that
in turn causes Fra Jose and Donna Clara to notice the open case-
ments and eventually the empty bed in Isidora's apartment. The
tale's narrator makes a point of telling us that the priest's "It is too
late" echoes "the ominous words quoted in the letter of Don Fran-

cisco" (384), which adds to the sense of simultaneity, of temporal and spatial moments collapsed into one another.[48]

Donna Clara's obsession with time, as we have seen, is consistent with Maturin's complaints about Catholicism as practiced in Spain. Two of the novel's embedded tales depict Protestant families, and it is interesting to see how they are characterized with regard to time's influence over them. Both the Walberg family in the "Tale of Guzman's Family" and Elinor's family in the "Lovers' Tale" are Protestant, but the two tales' outcomes could not be more different. In the former, the Walbergs, who are German Protestants, are visiting Spain as old Guzman, long-estranged brother to Ines, lies dying. Guzman, we are told, was "inflexible," and "a man of fixed habits," but he was able to transcend his habitual nature, defy the conniving priests, and invite his sister to Seville for a reconciliation.

The Walbergs lack the obsessive fixation on time that seems to characterize much of the Catholic world in the novel. Only their immersion in the environment of Catholic Spain awakens in them a heightened awareness of time, as when, during their long ordeal prior to Guzman's death, they "sat in profound silence, interrupted only by the ticking of the clock, which was distinctly and solely heard, and which seemed too loud to their quickened ears, amid that deep stillness on which it broke incessantly" (409). The mechanical ticking is an intrusion on their "profound silence." Yet the family is not without certain time-based habits and rituals. In their Spanish lodgings, Walberg hears "the clock strike the hour at which he had been always accustomed, in prosperity or adversity, to summon his family to prayer" (406). But somehow this regularity does not reach the level of monotony that we see in Monçada's convent or Donna Clara's house. Indeed this family is treated with particular care by the narrative. They are usually depicted through explicitly painterly images that stress their domesticity: "[A] painter, who wished to embody the image of domestic felicity in a group of living figures, need have gone no further than the mansion of Walberg" (404). The narrator dwells on the pleasing contrast among the generations, from Walberg's children to his parents, figured in seasonal terms, spring to winter. They are the idealized "beautiful family"— the only family in the novel whose members all seem to care for each other.[49] The painterly language seems to fix them in time, in a tableau of aging that is itself ageless, the work of time painted in sympathetic colors. And indeed, their prayer, in their time of family devotions, is "to pass through things temporal, that they might not finally lose the things eternal" (406)—a sentiment completely opposite those of Monçada's family's "Director," who subordinates the future to the needs and machinations of the present, as he attempts to force Monçada to become a monk: "How well religious persons understand the secret of making every event of the present world operate on the future, while they pretend to make the future predominate over the present" (89). In Heidegger's terms, the Walbergs are more existentially authentic, because their temporality is future-directed, focused on their potential for eternity, the realm of God's unchanging Being outside time. The Director and his cronies, on the other hand, are "levelled down," representing the diminishing of Care to Preoccupation—preoccupation with the petty disputes of this world, embodying a loss of both retention (memory) and awaiting (expectation).[50] The Walbergs' temporality is idealized, and Guzman's sister Ines's especially so. Soon after their arrival in Spain, while Guzman is still alive, but resolved not to see them even while he supports them financially, the family lives "in luxury," and only Ines has any anxiety that their situation may be only temporary:

> The wife of Walberg, during this interval, which seemed one of undisturbed felicity to all but her, sometimes suggested a gentle caution,—a doubtful hint,—a possibility of future disappointment. . . . At times . . . she led [her children] anxiously in the direction of their uncle's house. She walked up and down the street before his door with her children, and sometimes lifted up her veil, as if to try whether her eye could pierce through walls as hard as the miser's heart, or windows barred like his coffers,—then glancing on her children's costly dress, while her eye darted far into futurity, she sighed and returned slowly home. (408–9)

Under the circumstances, Ines's concerns do not seem obsessive, but what we would probably call realistic. Note the number of terms that refer to moderation, such as "gentle caution" and "possibility of future disappointment." Ines is more future-directed than her family, but in a novel populated with characters whose attitudes toward time are often bizarre and extreme, her attitude is refreshingly reasonable.

The Walbergs' "good rituals" are further valorized by their interruption: one of the signs that matters are amiss is that they actually break their prayer ritual. This occurs on two occasions, first when they are too excited by hope that they will win their share of the inheritance due them, and later when they are too distressed by the prospect of losing their appeal to the civil authorities. Old Walberg, "lifting up his withered hands, and speaking with an energy he had not showed for years,—[said] 'thus, O my God! prosperity and adversity alike furnish us with excuses for neglecting thee!'" (413). Rituals are not always bad, it seems.

But the other Protestant family, in the "Lovers' Tale," has the kind of overdetermined routine that Maturin has associated with the oppressive environment of the convent. The Mortimer family, descended from the age of the Norman Conquest, unbroken by the Wars of the Roses, is split along both political and theological lines by the English Revolution. Elinor is the granddaughter of Sir Roger Mortimer by his second son, who had "embraced the Puritanic cause, and, lapsing from error to error, married the daughter of an Independent, whose creed he had adopted" (447). She laments, just after she has met her cousin John Sandal, who had immediately captured her heart, that she must return to her grandfather's castle, for its hours are "scrupulously observed" (466). Here the regular routine interrupts what seems a more "natural" process of falling in love. And the chaplain's reading the evening prayers is referred to as "a form so strictly adhered to at the Castle, that not even the arrival of a stranger was permitted to interfere with its observance" (468). Later, after John Sandal's mother's success in foiling her son's union with Elinor by convincing him that Elinor was in fact his own half-sister, Elinor, in a state of despair, goes to live with her Puritanical aunt. In this rigidly Calvinist household, Elinor's life is hauntingly similar to that of the old monk, Fra Paolo; in fact the language used to describe it is nearly identical; note the repetition of the old monk's use of terms like "mechanism" and "winding up": "[S]he prayed without unction, and fed without appetite, and retired to rest without the least inclination to sleep. Her life was mere mechanism, but the machine was so well wound up, that it appeared to have some quiet consciousness and sullen satisfaction in its movements" (475). Making the analogy even more explicit, her life is characterized as one of "monastic rigour" (481).

The novel's persistent images of clocks even involve Melmoth himself. Prior to assuming his extended life span, he apparently dies, and he and a companion fix their eyes "intently on the slow motion of the clock," Melmoth expiring precisely at twelve (500). But the most intense use of clock imagery takes place in the final embedded tale, "The Wanderer's Dream," combining clocks and bells in one horrifying spectacle of damnation. Though his clock measures years rather than hours, it is no less inexorable and is accompanied by the tolling of a bell. Held by "a gigantic outstretched arm" over a precipice above an ocean of fire, his attention is directed upward to a dial-plate fixed on the top of that precipice, and which the flashes of that ocean of fire made fearfully conspicuous. He saw the mysterious single hand revolve—he saw it reach the appointed period of 150 years—(for in this mystic plate centuries were marked, not hours)—he shrieked in his dream. . . .

His last despairing reverted glance [as he fell] was fixed on the clock of eternity—the upraised black arm seemed to push forward the hand—it arrived at its period—he fell—he sunk—he blazed—he shrieked! The burning waves boomed over his sinking head, and the clock of eternity rung out its awful chime—"Room for the soul of the Wanderer!" (539)

This is the culmination of all the clock-watching that occurs throughout the novel, from Donna Clara's synchronizing of the bells to Monçada's own hyperattentiveness to the hours in the chapel or his counting to sixty, and is a disturbing reminder of the fact that even the Wanderer's extended existence is subject to a cosmic temporality that is inexorable. This scene marks a significant departure from Godwin's *St. Leon,* who is subject to no such temporal limitation. This disturbing scene further taints— retroactively—all the mechanistic imagery that has gone before, with the result that we are "reading the ending in the beginning and the beginning in the ending."[51] It is as if all of the characters who are preoccupied with time are headed for a similarly nightmarish fate.

Moreover, the characters in the various tales seem to represent a continuum of degrees of temporal awareness, from Monçada's four-month period of insensibility (216), through Immalee's idealized primordial time-sense, through a range of "now-saying": Fra Paolo, whose life is highly regulated by external authorities; Donna Clara and the Calvinistic aunt in the Lovers' Tale, both of whom have internalized fixed routines, repetitive and ritualistic; to anxiety: Monçada in the chapel at two a.m.; and finally to hysteria and madness: Monçada obsessively and repetitively counting to sixty in his cell, and Stanton's mad companions. At one end of this continuum is inertness; at the other is madness. The novel also depicts a continuum of awareness of temporal *intervals.* Melmoth the Wanderer thinks in terms of centuries (although, in the final analysis, he is as much governed by the clock as Donna Clara or Fra Paolo), while Donna Clara thinks only of the present moment; Ines Walberg's "eye dart[s]far into futurity" while the monks seem able to comprehend no time more far-reaching than the daily canonical hours, and dispute differences of five minutes. In between lies Immalee's primordial sense of time; her awareness of intervals is determined by the rhythms of nature—the "periodical regularity" of "the alternation of night and day," the waxing and waning of the moon, and the fading of the rose "every six moons" (280, 284, 282). Immalee's temporal awareness is more truly Burkean, in the way that it "work[s] after the pattern of nature."[52]

The Limits of Narratibility

Melmoth the Wanderer emphasizes the act of narration as persistently as it emphasizes clock time. Narrative seems to provide a degree of coherence and simultaneously frustrate it, just as we saw the novel affirming the transmission of property even while this transmission is complicated by a series of nonlineal inheritances. We have already considered the peculiar—and for some readers, annoying—consistency among the narrative voices of the novel. But if the narratorial voices are strangely consistent, the novel's unusual structure would seem to suggest anything but coherence and consistency, although I want to argue that a closer examination yields a different result. The relationship between the narrative and generational coherence of the tales is most revealing. Of the five major tales (Stanton's, Monçada's, Immalee's, Guzman's family's, and the Mortimers'), two (Stanton's and Monçada's) do not reach closure, and two come to unhappy endings (death and/or madness, in Immalee's and the Mortimers' tales). Stanton's crumbling manuscript trails off in midsentence, his fate very much in doubt, and he is never heard from again, except for the brief mention of him in Monçada's tale. This second reference to Stanton actually frustrates closure, as John Melmoth's interruption of Monçada's tale to express his astonishment is dismissed with an appeal to patience, although his (and our) patience goes unrewarded, as this anomalous connection is never explored further (298). Stanton, like the manuscript that recorded his tale, subsides into illegibility. With no apparent descendants, his *line* comes to an end even as do the *lines* in his manuscript. Monçada's tale becomes a vehicle for the transmission of other texts, of which we only see Immalee's (both Immalee's tale, and Monçada's that encloses it, conclude at the same time), and that weirdly hybridized: transcribed from parchments written by a Jew using Greek characters in the Spanish language, narrated orally to John Melmoth, and edited and annotated by Charles Robert Maturin.

There are other tales, but we don't see them. We do see the subjects of legends coming to life through the act of narration.

Monçada's narrative is embedded within John Melmoth's story, and having told it, Monçada "rises" to become part of the frame tale. John Melmoth prepares to hear the sequel to Monçada's tale, only to be interrupted by the appearance of Melmoth himself. In both cases, the characters in the tales emerge to take control of the author's world, similar to the phenomenon that Gérard Genette refers to as an "intrusion by the extradiegetic narrator or narratee into the diegetic universe," and similar to what Ludovico thought he experienced in the Provençal tale scene in *The Mysteries of Udolpho*.[53] Immalee's tale terminates the di Aliaga line, as she, her infant child, and her brother all perish. Her family's dynastic ambitions are not only frustrated but their family will come to an end, once Immalee's father condemns her and his granddaughter to the Inquisition, in a kind of reversal of Monçada's parricide, completing the ironic inversion of both parts of Melmoth's statement to Immalee on her island, that Christianity requires its followers "to honour their parents and to cherish their children" (296). Instead of future generations for the transmission of values, Immalee's parents are left with only their mercantilism and mechanism.

"The Lovers' Tale" achieves closure, but it ends unhappily; the Mortimer line comes to an end when Margaret, Sir Roger's granddaughter and heir to the estate, dies in childbirth after delivering stillborn twins, a birth rendered the more tragic for being doubled. John Sandal succumbs to madness when he learns of his mother's deception, and Sandal is cared for until his death by Elinor, who herself dies soon after, leaving "the estates and title [to go] to the distant relative named in [Sir Roger's] will" (494). In fact, as Jack Null points out, the first tale which comes to a definite conclusion is "The Tale of Guzman's Family,"[54] which ends 434 pages (or approximately eighty percent of the way) through the novel, the fourth major tale we've encountered to that point. This tale ends with its idealized portrait of Walberg generations and with an unusual use of the present tense; Walberg's father dies in peace and is buried in consecrated ground, and the Walbergs "*reside* in prosperous felicity" (434, emphasis added), as if they can still be seen, living portraits in a gallery. The only shadow cast on this felicity, however, is the realization that the teller of this happy and coherent tale, who is "only a writer . . . a man of no importance in public or private life" (and who also has other tales to tell), is found dead in his bed at the inn, an apparent victim of Melmoth the Wanderer. A second stranger (actually Melmoth himself), informs Don Francisco that the writer died because, in seeking "the possession of a desperate secret," his "presumption exceed[ed] [his] power" (439).

So much for a writer's rewards; this one evidently perished of *hubris*. The dead writer is both like and unlike Adonijah; both are collectors of tales about Melmoth the Wanderer, but whereas the writer's life is cut short by his presumption, Adonijah's is in fact prolonged by his need to complete his narratives, his solemn vow to God.

Kathleen Fowler suggests that *Melmoth the Wanderer*'s various tales "are not only left without closure; they are internally incomplete as well," which she acknowledges may be "partly the result of the perishability of the documents in which they are preserved."[55] But I would argue that most of the narratives are extremely well preserved indeed. Stanton's is the stereotypical fragmented, crumbling Gothic manuscript, its lacunae sometimes occurring in midsentence. There are also stereotypically Gothic ellipses in Monçada's brother's correspondence to him, lines "unintelligible . . . apparently from the agitation under which they were written" (122), but these "defaced page[s]," like Stanton's, are closely associated with narratives of conventionally Gothic oppression and imprisonment. Adonijah's scrolls—which account for a large portion of the novel—are seldom interrupted: once by an explicit reference to "several pages [having been] destroyed and the contents of many following, wholly obliterated" (356), this occurring some eighty-four pages into Immalee's tale. There are a few instances where asterisks mark material edited from Donna Clara's and Don Aliaga's letters (the narrator making a point of indicating that these letters are extracts from a more voluminous correspondence [378, 381]), and part way through the Walbergs' tale, asterisks begin to appear (411), but they seem to represent not textual lacunae but the passage of time, as there are no obvious breaks in the narrative—certainly not the kinds of breaks we associate with crumbling manuscripts. These continue through to the end of Immalee's tale and reflect editorial decisions by the narrators. When the Spaniard begins his tale, the frame tale's narrator, out of "mercy to the reader," advises that he "shall give [Monçada's narrative] without the endless interruptions and queries, and anticipations of curiosity, and starts of terror, with which it was broken by Melmoth" (73). In that portion of the novel, there are two places where Monçada pauses due to fatigue or excess emotion (130, 173), but these again seem to be a nod to narrative convention. And of course, there is the inexplicable ellipsis in the oral narrative mentioned earlier (165). But for the most part, the tales are orally relayed from their written sources without fault (*so* reliably that, as we have seen, it strains credulity) by Monçada to young John Melmoth.

One theory that accounts for Maturin's not bringing all the tales to closure is his possible desire to reserve room for a sequel.[56] Virtually everyone has more tales to tell, presumably to be narrated in forthcoming volumes. Besides the stranger who told the tale of the Walbergs to Don Francisco, Monçada intends to relate other tales that he has translated, as well as continue his own tale by describing his escape from Adonijah. At the end of the novel, Melmoth himself is apparently gone from the scene (although he has already been resurrected once, following his first "death"), but we might still speculate about other tales of his interactions with mankind, including those that comprise the rest of Adonijah's manuscripts. The tales, in other words, seem to go on, although we do not have them all.

The novel's lack of closure would seem to work at cross-purposes with the concept of coherence, since we want to associate coherence with closure. Kathleen Fowler complains that the reader is led "into the interior of a labyrinth" and "abandoned somewhere within the maze seemingly without a map, or even a thread," lacking the reader's "expected closure." But when we recall Chris Baldick's assertion that the novel is "secretly . . . about transmission," then the prospect of the transmission of further tales seems to make sense; there will be another "generation" of tales to read. What becomes more important than closure is continuity, transmission transcending completion, just as in Aristotle's example of a living creature's life being extended, not by the "uninterrupted continuance" of its existence, but "in the only way possible to it," by "continu[ing] its existence in something *like* itself."[57] The novel is nearly as preoccupied with accounts of tales and their narration as it is with images of clocks. All of the interpolated tales contain descriptions of the writing or telling of tales, letters, confessions, or appeals, down to the level of sub-atomic invisibility. These tales are told by numerous narrators to a variety of audiences, for many ostensible purposes. The five primary embedded tales alone are told by five different narrators in as many situations and for as many purposes. (See Table 1, "Narrators, Purpose, and Disposition of Tales.") Some narratives are read or listened to while traveling: Don Francisco is a captive audience to two tales, the tale of the Walbergs (by the writer/stranger) and that of Elinor Mortimer (by the Wanderer himself). Some are clearly meant as warnings, such as Melmoth's narration of Elinor Mortimer's tale to Don Francisco. Some tales are even told to prove the veracity of other tales: Monçada tells John Melmoth the story of Immalee in the first place "to substantiate his own extraordinary story" (299), although this

TABLE 1

Melmoth the Wanderer: Narrators, Purpose, and Disposition of Tales

(Page numbers refer to the Oxford edition but proportions are comparable in other editions)

Narrative/ Pages	Level	Teller	Auditor	O/W*	Purpose	Disposition of text	Outcome	%-age of novel
Frame (7–27; 59–73; 534–42)	1	Maturin's narrator	Novel reader	W	Earn a living		Monçada & John Melmoth return home	7.75%
Stanton (28–59	2	Stanton	John Melmoth	W	Personal	Unknown	Incomplete; fragmented	5.72%
Spanish Woman's tale	3	Spanish woman	Stanton	O	Pass time?	Incomplete/ Unknown	Death	1.29%**
Inquisition Report	4	Spanish woman?	Stanton	W/O	Official report	Unknown	Death?	
Prisoner's Confession	5	"Contumacious monk" (37)	Inquisitors	W/O	Response to torture	Obliterated	Unknown	
Spaniard (73–534)	2	Monçada	John Melmoth	O	Explanation	Incomplete	Open?	36.72%
Letters from Juan	3	Juan Monçada	Alonzo Monçada	W	Plan escape	Swallowed (by Alonzo)	Escape	
Alonzo's appeal ("confession")	3	Alonzo Monçada	Secular official	W	Effect release from convent	Sent to "advocate"	Appeal rejected	

TABLE 1 (Continued)

Narrative/ Pages	Level	Teller	Auditor	O/W*	Purpose	Disposition of text	Outcome	%-age of novel
Parricide's Tale	3	Parricide	Alonzo Monçada	O	Recognizes vault		Death, madness	
Indians (272–534)	3	Adonijah?	Monçada	W/O	Adonijah's "requirement"	Written MS: unknown	Death	31.37%
Guzman (399–434)	4	Stranger (writer)	Don Francisco	O	Pass time during storm	Related orally	Happy	6.46%
Lovers' (444–501)	4	Melmoth	Don Francisco	O	Warning	Ignored	Death, madness	10.52%
Clergyman's Tale (498–501)	5	Clergyman	Elinor	O	Resistance		Info about Melmoth heeded	
Other tales . . .	2, 3	Adonijah/ Monçada	John Melmoth	W/O		Not told		
Wanderer's Dream (538–39)	2	Maturin's narrator	Reader	W	Foretells fate		Damnation	0.37%

Primary tales are in italics

* Oral/Written

** Includes embedded tales

is a curious kind of justification. How is this substantiation accomplished? Could not Monçada, whom we know to be imaginative, and to have suffered extreme psychological privations and ordeals, have made up the story of Immalee? Could this tale represent a more rational form of the same hysterical ravings of those who inhabit the cells adjacent to Stanton in the madhouse?

David Punter points out that, in *Melmoth*, "a narrative is begun, which appears to be highly improbable. Before it ends, another narrative begins which offers 'separate' corroboration of the first," and goes on to say that "No single character in *Melmoth* claims to be in absolute possession of the truth; no single sub-text claims authority independently of the others. Maturin simply piles on the evidence, selecting his fields as widely as possible, so that the audience is brought gradually nearer and nearer to a kind of circumscribed credence necessary for continued interest."[58] Presumably, the skeletons in Adonijah's closet would offer a form of tangible proof of at least part of Monçada's tale, but, again, no one else has seen them. To the reader, they constitute just another textual description. Monçada apparently has no written extracts of the strange Greek-Spanish manuscript he translated while in Adonijah's underground tunnel, but recounts it entirely from memory, a fact that challenges the credulity of some critics.[59] We must take Monçada's word for it that such a manuscript even exists.

Unlike the outward transmission of corroborating evidence that the love letters of Felix and Safie represent in *Frankenstein* (where the creature provides copies of this correspondence to "prove the truth of my tale"), in *Melmoth,* there is an inward movement until the layers of concentric narration collapse, like the final moments in the life of a star that has exhausted all its thermonuclear fuel, the outward pressure of radiation no longer able to overcome the inward pressure of gravity.[60] In Maturin's novel, there are two kinds of narrative limits: structural limits to how many levels of interpolation the narrative can support, and semantic limits—limits to what can be represented. Leigh A. Ehlers terms this second kind of limit the "sense of the inability of reason to narrate certain tales, the recognition that some experiences, particularly the horror of human depravity, are beyond man's ability to explain, organize, and narrate complacently and safely," a kind of aporetics of horror.[61] Although *Melmoth the Wanderer* is a romance, and Maturin imposes continued demands on the reader's willing suspension of belief, there are limits to what can be demanded, boundaries of representation beyond which an early nineteenth century novel cannot penetrate.

EMPLOTMENT

Let us consider further the functions of the novel's various texts as vehicles of transmission, as well as their relationship to the narrating instances that transmit them. One of the first texts we encounter—although only diegetically—is old Uncle Melmoth's will. This document is read "before proper witnesses" and transmits all his property to his nephew, John. It is a Burkean narrative, an instrument of coherent transmission to the next generation. Uncle Melmoth has also provided a handwritten codicil that refers to the portrait of the Wanderer and to the manuscript we subsequently learn to be Stanton's. This manuscript is "among some papers of no value, such as manuscript sermons, and pamphlets on the improvement of Ireland, and such stuff," and may be "distinguish[ed] . . . by its being tied around with a black tape, and the paper being very mouldy and discolored." Melmoth suggests that his nephew "may read it if he will;—I think he had better not" and further advises that he should burn it (21). The codicil is referential—a hypertextual link to another text, which is described in doubtful terms due to its proximity to "papers of no value," guilty by association. Thus, a coherent, valorized text (the will), effectively ending young John's poverty as well as the absurdity of his uncle's parsimony, is linked to a text both physically corrupt and of questionable value. The manuscript is in turn associated with the painting of the Wanderer. John Melmoth's experience of the Stanton text is compelling. Although he originally opens the manuscript with "some reluctance" (27), like that pause on the Gothic threshold noted by Eugenia C. DeLamotte,[62] he reads it through in one sitting, and his reading indulges none of the interruptions that would have plagued manuscript readings in Radcliffean Gothics. And, contrary to the misreadings of several critics, young Melmoth apparently does *not* burn the Stanton manuscript.[63] This is a curious misreading, although the wording of the text is highly ambiguous. Here is the passage in full:

> Such was the conclusion of the manuscript which Melmoth found in his uncle's closet. When he had finished it, he sunk down on the table near which he had been reading it, his face hid in his folded arms, his senses reeling, his mind in a mingled state of stupor and excitement. After a few moments, he raised himself with an involuntary start, and saw the picture gazing at him from its canvas. He was within ten inches of it as he sat, and the proximity appeared increased by the strong light that was accidentally thrown on it, and its being the only representation

of a human figure in the room. Melmoth felt for a moment as if he were about to receive an explanation from its lips.

He gazed on it in return,—all was silent in the house,—they were alone together. The illusion subsided at length; and as the mind rapidly passes to opposite extremes, he remembered the injunction of his uncle to destroy the portrait. He seized it;—his hand shook at first, but the mouldering canvas appeared to assist him in the effort. He tore it from the frame with a cry half terrific, half triumphant;—it fell at his feet, and he shuddered as it fell. He expected to hear some fearful sounds, some unimaginable breathings of prophetic horror, follow this act of sacrilege, for such he felt it, to tear the portrait of his ancestor from his native walls. He paused and listened:—"There was no voice, nor any that answered;"—but as the wrinkled and torn canvas fell to the floor, its undulations gave the portrait the appearance of smiling. Melmoth felt horror indescribable at this transient and imaginary resuscitation of the figure. He caught it up, rushed into the next room, tore, cut, and hacked it in every direction, and eagerly watched the fragments that burned like tinder in the turf-fire which had been lit in his room. As Melmoth saw the last blaze, he threw himself into bed, in hope of a deep and intense sleep. . . . (59–60)[64]

The only thing that is explicitly reported by the text to have been burned was the portrait itself, after it was hacked to pieces. The manuscript is not mentioned at all in the burning passage; nor is its fate mentioned later in the novel. The painting and the manuscript, both representations of Melmoth the Wanderer, seem inextricably linked. The notion that the manuscript was burned seems to have been supplied by the reader, perhaps in an unconscious desire to supply the coherence missing in the passage, a process similar to Hayden White's "emplotment." Specifically, emplotment is a strategy that results from the desire "to make a plausible story out of a congeries of 'facts,' which, in their unprocessed form, make no sense at all."[65] Indeed, the text seems almost to demand such a reading. The conflation of manuscript and painting in this passage, Uncle Melmoth's earlier admonition to burn both of them, the ambiguity of Maturin's descriptive language, his apparent failure to explicitly dispose of the manuscript later and our expectations about the novel's fulfillment of romantic conventions seem to combine to suggest that the manuscript was burned when it was not, and even careful readers are not immune to this confluence of factors.

Young John Melmoth's uninterrupted absorption by the Stanton manuscript introduces a theme that persists throughout the novel, that of compulsive reading or listening, a theme often present amid the text's frequent images of those activities. In the Stanton manuscript, in a possible parody of contemporary critical anxieties about the dangers of addiction to romance reading, Stanton is trapped in the madhouse because he "as usual seized the first book near him, and began to read," and, even though this book's "first lines struck him as indicating insanity in the writer," and the book's proposals and illustrations are variously characterized as "wild," "grotesque" and "insane," Stanton "read on without suspicion of his own danger, quite absorbed in *the album of a mad-house,* without ever reflecting on the place where he was" (46–47). He fails to apply the interpolated text to his own circumstances, to let the narrative inform his own reality. Monçada, too, is captivated by the strange manuscript in Adonijah's possession, despite the bizarre surroundings of manuscripts and skeletons, and a "night of storms" whose winds remind him of "the voices of the departed . . . the pleadings of the dead." Monçada informs John Melmoth that "[i]nvoluntarily I fixed my eye on the manuscript I was to copy and never withdrew till I had finished its extraordinary contents" (272), despite the fact that the manuscript in question occupies some 262 published pages, nearly a third of the novel! And Monçada narrates his story with only two interruptions (130, 173), rarely even pausing to draw breath or drink water, although as I have noted previously, the narrator has edited out an implied series of interruptions, to spare the reader. In other words, the narrator enables the reader to receive the story whole—a textual manipulation that constitutes a form of emplotment.

Especially intriguing are Adonijah's hybrid Greek-Spanish manuscripts. These manuscripts represent a kind of fake *polyglossia,* to use Bakhtin's term. Bakhtin's illustration of languages "interanimating" each other in a multilingual culture is from Latin literature: "From start to finish, the creative literary consciousness of the Romans functioned against the background of the Greek language and Greek forms. From its very first steps, the Latin literary world viewed itself in the light of the Greek word, *through the eyes* of the Greek word; it was from the very beginning a word 'with a sideways glance,' a stylized word enclosing itself as it were, in its own piously stylized quotation marks."[66] Yet here in *Melmoth* no interanimation occurs. The purpose of Adonijah's peculiar use of Greek and Spanish is to function as a code, a way of preventing, or sealing off, access, except to those who know both languages, like the two "keys," a public and a private key, that comprise modern computer encryption systems. There is in this strange hybridization a tension between transmission and secrecy. Victor Sage sees in *Melmoth*'s "focus on written documents" a "parody of legal process," to which the authority of first-hand oral testimony—of which I will have more to say below—stands in opposition to "dead legalistic procedures—documents relying on documents, hidden, inaccessible authority, handed down by blind repetition."[67] If so, then Adonijah's manuscripts represent the supreme example of the legal system's incomprehensibility (except by a specialist, one who possesses multiple discursive skills) and calls to mind Monçada's earlier, voluminous, and unsuccessful appeal to the civil authorities regarding his confinement in the convent. Adonijah's manuscript can be preserved and physically transmitted, but its meaning can only be discerned and retransmitted by one who knows the code. As we have seen, the Adonijah scrolls are surprisingly intact, in defiance of Gothic convention whereby old manuscripts, like old castles, bear all the marks of the passage of time; these scrolls represent a kind of anti-Gothic manuscript. The hybridization of the manuscript's languages seems to fuse the ancient and modern worlds, modern Spanish written using ancient characters on scrolls. Adonijah's subterfuge of writing in Spanish with Greek characters fools the Inquisitors, who do not inquire further into them. This alone is peculiar, given the Inquisition's authority over, and the Inquisitors' willingness to involve themselves in, almost all aspects of life in Spain. The Inquisitors' lack of inquisitiveness about the strange manuscript is especially troubling in light of Monçada's earlier response to a Hebrew Bible when he encountered it in his flight from the Inquisition: because Monçada "could not make out a single letter" of this book, he "therefore wisely took it for a book of magic, and closed it with a feeling of exculpatory horror" (245). The Hebrew Bible functions as an ironic double of Adonijah's manuscripts, the survival of which seems to exist as a metaphor for the Protestant Reformation and the survival of the printed Bible in defiance of Catholic ecclesiastical power.[68] But why did the Inquisitors not see Adonijah's manuscripts as magic? Monçada's somewhat unconvincing explanation is that the unintelligible writing was ignored due to the Inquisitors' "ignorance, sheltered by their pride, and that still more strongly fortified by the impenetrable secrecy attached to their most minute proceedings," all of which combine to make them "hesitate to entrust to anyone the circumstances of their being in possession of manuscript which they could not decypher" (270). Adonijah's stories are preserved, along with stuffed animals, the bones of various creatures including a mammoth, and the four skeletons of those to whom the tales are related, two of them belonging to Adonijah's wife and child (268), one of them apparently that of Immalee (271), and one unidentified, but probably belonging to a tale that is not contained in this novel.

But despite the integrity of the Adonijah manuscripts, texts do not always survive in pristine condition. As we have seen, the Stanton manuscript is marred by ellipses and lacunae, usually at strategic moments. After Stanton, traveling through Spain, encounters two young lovers struck by lightning and Melmoth the Wanderer laughing maniacally as the bodies are carried away, Stanton spends the night in a nearby house. There an old Spanish woman narrates a tale about a wedding feast and two of Melmoth's victims, the bride and a much-beloved priest. This embedded tale in turn transmits the Inquisition's report on the interrogation of the monk who had dared to condemn Father Olavida at his funeral, which in turn includes the prisoner's remarkable confession under torture—or at least it would have, except that the manuscript becomes "blotted and illegible" at this point (39). This missing confession, this absent sacrament, is the unreachable center of the interpolated narrative structure, what would be the fifth narrative level. Even before Monçada narrates the "Tale of the Indians," his own tale includes his brother's written narrative, smuggled into his convent, and written on "many a defaced page" (122), papers "received in fragments, and from time to time, by the hands of the porter" (130). Later communications from his brother are also defaced (175), so once again, as was the case with the Stanton manuscript, the reader must attempt to assemble a coherent narrative from non-contiguous segments. Monçada swallows the fragments of his brother's letter in order to destroy them, another parody of contemporary critical concerns about the consumption of texts. We also hear about, but do not read, Monçada's written appeal to the civil magistrates, the writing of which—represented to the brothers in the convent as his "confession"—occupies "[h]our after hour" (132) and consumes "quires of paper" (132), an appeal that is eventually copied (138), and subsequently rejected (173), perhaps a metaphor for the fate of Maturin's early novels (his own quires of paper), that were both financial failures and may have prevented his advancement in the Anglican Church in Ireland.[69]

Narrative, then, is not without its limitations. Besides the textual corruption, an image of aporetic inarticulability, the limits of narratibility are represented by the presence of literal aporias in many of the tales. Father Olavida, confronted at the wedding feast by Melmoth the Wanderer, is unable to pronounce his benediction on the wine and the wedding party (34), and dies trying to pronounce Melmoth's name—he can only point to him and drop dead (35).

Melmoth's name is so inarticulable that Father Olavida's rhetorical hesitation spreads to the processes of life itself.

While this is one of the most dramatic aporias in the novel, it is echoed by others. When Monçada first realizes that John Melmoth is related to Melmoth the Wanderer, he falls "to the ground convulsed." Several days later he is still so agitated that he has difficulty speaking: "He began—hesitated—stopped; tried in vain to arrange his ideas, or rather his language." Monçada finally confesses, in response to young Melmoth's queries about his motives for traveling to Ireland, that only a few days previously he thought it beyond mortal power to disclose, as "incommunicable as it was incredible" (72). His subsequent lengthy narrative, however, transcends this incommunicability, setting a pattern of narrative resolution of aporias in the novel. In the same vein, the "something inexplicable" in Monçada's heritage (his illegitimacy) is resolved (not the illegitimacy itself, but the inexplicability of it) when he forces his mother to explain (narrate) it (80, 90). Narrative, then, becomes a means of reconciling the aporetic void in these cases.

Elsewhere, there is the "agony unutterable, *unuttered*" suffered by the widow Sandal as Margaret Mortimer lies dying in childbirth (492); the "*uncommunicable condition*" that constitutes Melmoth's price for freeing Standon and Monçada from their respective prisons (237), and Walberg from poverty and starvation (427); and the "withering monosyllable, not to be told" that is the answer to Isidora's question of where Melmoth's possessions are held (355). Certainly some of these inarticulabilities can be readily surmised by the reader—the withering monosyllable that names the location of Melmoth's possessions, for example, is obvious enough, even if it cannot be stated, just as the skeletons in Adonijah's chamber are "speechless, yet speak" (271). These textual aporias exist in tension with the novel's images of transmission of tales. They frustrate the progress of the tales, constituting a dialectic, like the *tick-tock* of the clock that alternates hope and fear, heaven and hell.

The novel's emphasis on the narrating act itself and its relationship to temporal aporias, such as time's being and nonbeing, or the relationship between mortality and eternity, bring us back to Paul Ricoeur's claim about the circular relationship between time and narrative. "[T]ime becomes human time to the extent that it is organized after the manner of a narrative; narrative, in turn, is meaningful to the extent that it portrays the features of temporal experience." The key to this circular relationship is Ricoeur's analysis of Aristotle's mimetic activity, which Ricoeur subdivides into three parts or phases: Ricoeur calls the first phase *mimesis*$_1$, the "pre-understanding of the world of action, its meaningful structures, its symbolic resources, and its temporal character." The artist already *knows* something of the nature of the world, based on experience; she knows how to articulate and narrate human action. *Mimesis*$_2$ fulfills a mediating function between "the individual events or incidents and a story taken as a whole," imposing a "structural function of closure" on the work. This is the plotting or *configuring* function, the kind of organization of events that Aristotle refers to as *muthos*. *Mimesis*$_3$ represents "the intersection of the world of the text and the world of the hearer or reader." As readers, we refigure the plot based on its "capacity to model our experience."[70] It is mimesis$_2$, the emplotment function, mediating between the world of things and the world of the reader, that is most relevant to our analysis of *Melmoth the Wanderer*. Mimesis$_2$ structures incidents episodically (and therefore temporally) and integrates them into a story, a whole. Frank Kermode observes in his famous study that we make sense of our lives through "fictive concords with origins and ends" because we are born, and we die, in medias res. Because we cannot gain a perspective of the whole of our lives, we do this fictively, so as to "see the structure whole."[71] It is this act of narrating, of following a story, Ricoeur says, that makes Augustine's temporal paradoxes productive, because the repetition of a story allows us to "read the ending in the beginning and the beginning in the ending . . . to read time itself backwards, as the recapitulation of the initial conditions of a course of action in its terminal consequences,"[72] much as we saw in the climactic image of the gigantic "clock of eternity" in "The Wanderer's Dream" (539). The many interpolations of *Melmoth the Wanderer* call attention to this process of emplotment and mediation. Dale Kramer is exactly correct when he says that the tales all have a set of common elements ("religion, monasticism, madness, responsibility, money, vanity") and that "[i]n each story [Maturin] shifts the emphasis among these elements so that quite different configurations emerge."[73] The key word here is *configurations*—the configuring act (emplotment, mimesis$_2$) is ever visible, even while, as Regina B. Oost points out, "Maturin steadfastly refuses to romanticize authorship in his depiction of characters such as Biddy Brannigan and the Walberg narrator," and in fact represents the narrators as "distasteful."[74] These acts of narrating seem to continue ad infinitum, the reader moving "steadily into the interior of a labyrinth."[75]

We seem to have reached another paradox in applying Kermode's meditation to this text. How can the fragmentary nature of some of the tales, and the lack of closure of most of them, suggest the kind of coherence that makes narrative satisfying to us, that enables narrative to impose some sense of order on our chaotic existences? Kathleen Fowler suggests that *Melmoth the Wanderer* "is not formed in the conventional manner, nor yet unformed," but is "intentionally de-formed. The reader must herself wrest its integrity from apparent chaos; Maturin thereby generates a tension which . . . serves his essential artistic and thematic purposes."[76]

I want to argue that what makes *Melmoth the Wanderer* unique in its approach to time and narrative is its dialectical nature with respect to coherence. Order is and is not imposed on chaos; closure is and is not attained; our desire for it is and is not fulfilled. As we have seen, we reach closure in some of the tales, such as the Walbergs' and Immalee's, while some, such as Stanton's or Monçada's, remain unfinished. We would expect the result of this to be unsatisfying, but the novel's repetition of the phrase "there are other narratives" (by the writer/stranger [434]; by Monçada's reference to "his intention" to disclose "the fates of the other victims, whose skeletons were preserved in the vault of the Jew Adonijah in Madrid" [534]), suggests also a desire for continuance. While narratives are supposed by theorists such as Kermode to provide closure, here the closure remains elusive: Adonijah's life is prolonged until he completes the act of narration he has vowed to accomplish, until "written in a book and sealed" (269–70). Closure, completion of that task, would bring that life to an end. Like Godwin's perfectibility as a progressive movement toward a perfection that is never achieved,[77] writing is a movement toward closure, even if that is ultimately not achieved, an apparent paradox. It is the act of writing, the configuring, emplotting activity in the midst of chaos, that is important.

Also paradoxical is Charles Maturin's reversal of the usual effects of the interpolated tale and the fragmented manuscript. Such a plot device often contributes to the sense of archaism, as critics such as David Punter have pointed out in the context of Horace Walpole's *The Castle of Otranto*. This device not only serves to detach the author from his text (he's now only an editor), but it distances the reader from the text as well, because the reader now comes to it through the filtering of multiple editorial and/or narratorial voices.[78] (Of course, in Maturin's case, these voices are "irritatingly consistent.") Leigh A. Ehlers has perceptively observed that Maturin undercuts these detachments between the narrators and the events they describe because "[a]s each becomes a forced participant in horrible events, Maturin creates a paradigm for the fusing of event and narrator."[79] Maturin's use of footnotes in the printed text also yields contradictory results. On the one hand, these notes "collapse the distance between reader and victim," as when they remind us of similarities between details of the Inquisition fire or the mob murder of the parricide and actual episodes in recent Irish history. The horrors are not remote in time and space, as is common to most Gothic novels set in the distant past (and usually other countries). We are drawn into the text, and identify with the observers of the scenes. In the most grisly example, Maturin watches as the parricide who betrayed him is torn to pieces before his eyes and his identification with the victim is strong: "I actually for a moment believed myself the object of their cruelty" (257). Maturin then further twists the narrative knife by means of a footnote describing Lord Kilwarden's murder at the hands of a mob in Dublin in 1803, and a shoemaker who becomes so fascinated watching the horrid spectacle that he becomes "an *idiot for life*" (257n, emphasis original). In this incident, Maturin manages to over-identify with, first, the victim of the mob's brutality, and then, in a dizzying shift of perspective, with the acutely fascinated observer, internalizing both positions to the point of hysteria.

At the same time, the presence of such notes in a narrated tale "implies mistrust of the narrative imagination, of storytelling, that does not conform to the dictates of science and reason, [and] introduces between text and commentary a tension that remains unresolved."[80] In fact, on one of these occasions, Maturin speaks to his critics—alluding to their response to his play *Bertram*—by disavowing the theological views he has put "into the mouth of an agent of the enemy of mankind" (303n). The footnotes are further evidence of a fusion of the two temporalities of past and present, much as we saw in the example of the Greek-Spanish manuscript: the footnotes remind us of the presence of a modern author-editor, interjecting scholarly comments; this is both a narrative and a narrating instance.

Given this level of involvement, a hyperawareness of one's position, simultaneously inside and outside the text, it is no surprise that witnessing events or listening to narratives in the novel can become a contagion. Stanton picks up the book in the madhouse and is ensnared by it. Monçada, subject of his own interpolated tale and narrator of others, is "promoted" up the narrative hierarchy to the world of the frame tale and joins John Melmoth as an equal. He has transcended his fictive level. Thus, narrative does not remain merely narrative; it has the power to make all the world a text.

This collapsing of the distance between reader and narrator or observer takes place in the temporal realm as well. If "time becomes human time to the extent that it is organized after the manner of a narrative," then narrative *models* temporality for us. We refigure the plot to the extent that it conforms to our own experience of the world of time, a function of what Ricoeur calls mimesis$_3$. The emplotment function (mimesis$_2$) that is made so visible in *Melmoth* is more complex than the simple imposition of order on chaos. Emplotment, as Ricoeur reads Aristotle, is "the triumph of concordance over discordance," but the discordance must have some room for expression.[81] Classical theories of tragedy emphasize the *peripeteia*, the reversals that add complexity to what would otherwise be an overly simplistic plot. *Melmoth* uses interpolated tales to provide this additional complexity, this "special kind of middle" between *tick* and *tock,* in Kermode's analysis, although a middle not uniform in duration, for time speeds up and slows down in response to the narrative's demands.

As for the stories that have not been told, Ricoeur notes that we are "inclined to see in a given sequence of the episodes of our lives '(as yet) untold' stories, stories that demand to be told, stories that offer anchorage points for narrative." He provides two examples in which these "'(as yet) untold stor[ies]" have particular "force": the patient in psychoanalysis who must assemble from "bits and pieces of lived stories, of dreams, of 'primitive scenes,' [and] conflictual episodes . . . a narrative that will be both more supportable and more intelligible"; and the example of a judge attempting to understand one's course of actions, who must construct one's character by "unravelling the tangle of plots the subject is caught up in," a background from which the told stories emerge.[82] In *Melmoth the Wanderer* we see stories emerging from a background that holds additional stories never told. The physicist Stephen Hawking speaks of "virtual particles" that emerge from nothingness and disappear again, but whose effects can be measured in high energy particle accelerators. Computers have "virtual memory" or function as "virtual machines" among different users, each of whom has the illusion of an entire machine to himself.[83] Here in *Melmoth* a kind of "virtual coherence" results from stories told and untold.

ORAL AND WRITTEN NARRATIVES

I have said that *Melmoth the Wanderer* is obsessed with descriptions of narrating acts, and a substantial number of its tales are represented as oral narratives. Except for the Stanton manuscript, most of the tales are told rather than written. Victor Sage explains this emphasis by placing the issue in the context of Maturin's Calvinistic background, referring to the "authority of the living witness which is a powerful Reformation principle, constantly brought against the corruption of 'authority', derived from dead legalistic procedures."[84] And indeed, a passage in "The Lovers' Tale" emphasizes the superior authority of oral accounts: "When Mrs Ann told these and other thrilling tales of the magnanimity, the loyalty, and the sufferings of her high ancestry, in a voice that alternately swelled with energy, and trembled with emotion, and as she told them, pointed to the spot where each had happened,—her young hearers felt a deep stirring of the heart,—a proud yet mellowed elation that never yet was felt by the reader of a written history, though its pages were as legitimate as any sanctioned by the royal licenser at Madrid" (455).

While I find Sage's argument compelling, there is a temporal dimension to this issue that Sage does not explore. We tend to regard these two narrative modes (oral and written) as largely interchangeable, but there are important, fundamental differences. In his fascinating study of the development of our awareness of time, G. J. Whitrow, discussing the concept of time at the dawn of history, observes that "language itself inevitably introduced an element of permanence into a vanishing world. For, although speech itself is transitory, the conventionalized sound symbols of language transcended time. At the level of oral language, however, permanence depended solely on memory. To obtain a greater degree of permanence the time symbols of oral speech had to be converted into the space symbols of written speech."[85] Monçada's oral narration of the material from the Adonijah manuscripts effectively reverses this historical development. Monçada has converted the spatial symbols of writing (emphasized *as* writing in all its texture and graphemic attributes, Greek characters in the Spanish language) into temporal symbols. Space has been converted into time. Of course, all of this is in turn packaged into novel form, reconverting it into a spatial organization. As we saw in our discussion of *The Mysteries of Udolpho,* the reader must then spend time traversing this space as Genette contends when he suggests that "written narrative exists in space as space, and the time needed for 'consuming' it is the time needed for *crossing* or *traversing* it, like a road or a field."[86]

These constant conversions between temporal (oral) and spatial (written) narratives emphasize the metonymic relationship between space and time. Time and space become intertwined, and texts and acts of narration become blurred. The intertwining of time and space appears in the figure of the Wanderer himself, who possesses not just extraordinary temporal "powers," but can move freely in space and dissolve distances, (much as Maturin dissolves the space between the reader and the writer). Seen in this way, the mistaken ellipses in the oral narrative make sense. These particular ellipses that trouble critics such as Kathleen Fowler are probably not noticed by the average reader, who may accept them as a standard plot device in a Gothic romance, and has probably forgotten whether the narrative in question is supposed to be oral or written.[87] It is less a case of the author's losing track among so many layers of telling and retelling, than, more significantly, that *we* lose track. The incoherence (violation of convention) of the ellipses is elided, just as even the careful reader mistakenly assumes the Stanton manuscript was burned along with the portrait. Both the ellipses and the burned manuscript are among the untold stories that are assembled into a narrative. It does not really matter, strictly speaking, whether these anomalies are the result of authorial oversight or haste. There is certainly ample evidence that Maturin's particular economic circumstances, and consequent decisions made by his publisher, helped determine the shape of the novel as finally published. For example, Kramer notes that, while Maturin was writing the novel, his wife delivered their fourth child, he was harassed by creditors, and was caring for his elderly father. Maturin even failed to number the pages of his manuscript, and his publisher, Archibald Constable, had much difficulty ascertaining his intentions. The firm's correspondence attests to the publisher's aporetic hesitation:

> We received by our Clerk a considerable quantity [of manuscript], but strange to say it was so unconnected, that with great difficulty, we found part of it belonging to the first Tale [presumably the "frame" story], and a part of it to the second [Stanton's tale], at least we thought so, so little however appeared to connect with the first Tale, that we could not make up the *third sheet* . . . in one Word we are wholly at a stand, and it is utterly impossible that the work can proceed except some plan is pursued whereby the *connection* of the various portions of the MS. is kept up—there is no paging, no connecting words, nothing to guide us—and after corresponding for two months there are only two sheets set up and that without a title. . . .[88]

Rather than answer the queries from his publisher, Maturin's usual response was to "send copy more rapidly than before."[89]

Regardless of Maturin's original intentions, the text becomes ours to shape. To consider again the most vivid scene in the novel, when Monçada is stuck in the tunnel underneath the convent—his body a literal aporia—and time dilates, a story provides both the means of his entrapment and the means of his escape. Monçada recalls that the body of the traveler stuck in a passage in an Egyptian pyramid swelled due to his terror and he experiences a similar sensation. But hearing of his companions' proposal to dismember him so that they can escape causes the traveler's body to contract in a "strong muscular spasm" (192), and Monçada once again emulates the figure in the tale: "I tried to crawl backwards,—I succeeded. I believe the story I recollected had an effect on me, I felt a contraction of muscles corresponding to what I had read of" (193).

Strictly speaking, the text does not say that Monçada *himself* swells up in the passage from terror, but the figure in the story does, and Monçada has strongly identified with that character whose situation he has "*appl[ied]*" (his emphasis) to himself. While this incident is rich with interpretive possibilities (including a birth metaphor replete with matricidal cannibalism, and Monçada's escape from the passage by a process of contraction and backing out, a kind of un-birth or temporal reversal), what is more important to our analysis is his assertion that "I believe the story I recollected had an effect on me." The recollection of the story is manifested physically in the contraction of his muscles and subsequent escape. Ultimately we are left with an image of storytelling. Linda Bayer-Berenbaum's intriguing analysis of the novel emphasizes the degree to which it demonstrates the infinitely convoluted and repeating Gothic line, convolutions and repetitions that are conveyed through characterization, setting, imagery (Bayer-Berenbaum notes that "[i]n volume 3 alone there are twelve pages exclusively devoted to descriptions of tapestry"), framing, plot progressions, syntax, and word choice. In the previous chapter, we saw how the Gothic line, with its infinite recursions, is a figure for the tangle of genealogical relationships that *Udolpho*'s Emily St. Aubert must untangle to solve the riddle of her heritage and identity. In *Melmoth the Wanderer,* this convoluted Gothic line, "the tortured struggle that fruitlessly repeats itself, the driven, compulsive energy that increases with frustration, and the empty quality of the line that does not circumscribe a space but dissects it in endless tangles,"[90] is expressed in a narrative tangle that involves, not just the structure of the narrative itself, but its twin obsessions with time and acts of narration.

These tangled repetitions, as figures for eternity, stand in marked contrast to the clock-watching, mechanistic, now-saying existence that has become the norm for those who are increasingly subject to institutional control over their lives and their time, transforming them into mechanisms. It is not by accident that clocks and storytelling co-exist in *Melmoth*. Rather, they converge. In the aporetics of temporality—of time's being and nonbeing, of our desire to reconcile our own human existence with the gulf of eternity, our desire to pass the baton to another like ourselves—we find ourselves literally stuck, down in that narrow passage with Monçada. What seems to get us out of this passage (although I suspect part of us always remains stuck within it) is not clock-watching, but storytelling, our only means to refigure the infinite in human terms, to humanize that space between tick and tock. While individual stories may achieve climax and closure, there is really no end to the storytelling acts themselves, which persist until we perish. As Stuart Sherman notes, "clocks pursue a constant, running correspondence between numerical index and passing moment, whereas texts virtually always move away from the momentary towards permanence."[91] Seen from a loftier perspective than we can attain, Maturin's stories would appear to go on, infinitely embedded within themselves, twisting and turning ever inward, endlessly convoluted. Exactly the phenomenon we experience in Charles Robert Maturin's *Melmoth the Wanderer*.

If narrative provides the means for Alonzo di Monçada to free himself from his spatial confinement, it can also allow us to imaginatively free ourselves from our confinement in time. Through the power of narrative, we can seem to reverse time's arrow, or even stand at the end of human history and survey all that has gone before. Narrative's power to accomplish such feats forms the subject of the next chapter.

3

Transcending Time: Mary Shelley and the Power of Narrative

In the literary twilight of the mid 1820s, *The Last Man* appeared
as a poem by Thomas Campbell (1823), an unfinished drama
by Thomas Lovell Beddoes (1823–5), a novel by Mary Shelley
(1826), a satirical ballad by Thomas Hood (1826), a painting by
John Martin (1826), and an anonymous prose fragment in
Blackwood's Magazine (1826). Each dealt with universal disaster and focused on the last surviving human being, a figure peculiarly attractive to writers who felt they had outlived their
cultural milieu and were left stranded in an uncongenial age.
— Fiona J. Stafford, *The Last of the Race*

But I am chained to Time, and cannot thence depart!
— Percy Shelley, *Adonais*

MARY WOLLSTONECRAFT SHELLEY WAS VERY MUCH A PRODUCT OF HER
time, and yet she spent much of her life trying to escape the limitations of time. There are two major obstacles to a critical appraisal
of her writing, both of them—one literary and one personal—
involving the relationship between past and present. Having written, at the age of nineteen, one of the most famous novels of the
century in consequence of a ghost story writing contest involving
some of the key figures of British Romanticism, a novel that both
articulates and critiques the ideology of the Romantic movement of
which it is a key text, her other work received surprisingly little critical attention prior to the years leading up to her bicentenary year,
in 1997. Many students and even critics are surprised to learn that
she was much more than a one-novel writer. "As a child," she tells
us, she "scribbled."[1] In a literary career that spanned four decades,
she produced five more novels, a novella, at least two dozen tales,
two travel books, two plays, numerous essays, reviews, translations,
and poems, and contributions to five volumes of biographies, as
well as editing her husband's poetry and essays for publication. Yet

in many ways her past—the success of her first novel—haunted her literary career, just as it has continued to haunt her literary reputation for nearly two centuries.

The second major problem with Mary Shelley criticism also turns on the relationship between past and present. Her own origins are as mythic as those of her famous first novel. Born of the union of radical philosophers Mary Wollstonecraft and William Godwin, two of the most important radical philosophers of the late eighteenth century, she was "destined," as Diane Long Hoeveler put it, "to be an overdetermined personality."[2] It is as if she were the offspring, not of two human beings, but of the coition of *An Enquiry Concerning Political Justice* and *A Vindication of the Rights of Woman.* Her elopement with the radical poet Percy Bysshe Shelley and her membership in an intellectual and social circle that also included Lord Byron and Leigh and Marianne Hunt further renders her life and letters nearly inseparable in the mind. Add to this mix a life characterized by personal tragedies almost equally mythic (including the death of her mother as a consequence of bearing her, the loss of her husband by drowning, the deaths of three of her four children, a miscarriage shortly before her husband's death, the death of her half-sister by suicide, a lengthy estrangement from her father, and prolonged poverty as she struggled to support herself and her sole remaining child), and the urge to interpret her writing in biographical terms, to "reduce Shelley's writing to a coda on her life" is nearly irresistible.[3] It would be extraordinary indeed if her writing were *not* marked by the presence of the figures who peopled her life, beginning in her early childhood when such luminaries as Samuel Taylor Coleridge and Sir Humphry Davy visited her father's home.[4] But the long tradition of reading her fiction as almost entirely biographical is ultimately reductive.[5] It also overlooks the degree to which her personal preoccupations, and those of her cultural moment, frequently coalesce. Her third novel in particular, *The Last Man,* has often been read either as a roman à clef—with the author's late husband, Percy Bysshe Shelley, and Lord Byron among the contemporary figures modelled—or as a projection of Mary Shelley's own guilt, anger and emotional loss onto the novel. While there may be some truth to these readings, they usually fail to note her novel's relationship to a whole series of poems and novels dealing with the "last of the race" theme.

I suggest that Mary Shelley made use of her relationships and experiences as catalysts for her fiction, and that her life experiences resonate in her writing to the extent that she sometimes drew upon them to impart a sense of authenticity to the events and descriptions of her narratives. But she also drew upon the issues of her day—including politics, scientific developments, and theories of history and literature—and she approached her writing for reasons other than the mimetic or therapeutic. As Maggie Kilgour observes, "Her art draws on her life not because she is narcissistic or literal minded, but because she sees art and life intertwined—not surprising in a girl who was raised in a literary household, and who encountered her own mother only as a text."[6] Shelley was, I maintain, in dialogue with her personal circumstances, but also with her contemporary world. She was a prodigious reader, as the Shelleys' detailed reading lists reveal, and she was excited by the world of ideas in which she lived most of her life. For much of her life, she was self-consciously a writer, and her trajectory as an author reflects both her wide-ranging interests and her fascination with the writer's craft.

Mary Shelley experimented with a multitude of genres, temporal settings and narrative strategies, as evidenced by the diversity of her five novels after *Frankenstein*. Her second novel, *Valperga; or, the Life and Adventure of Castruccio, Prince of Lucca* (1823), is an historical romance set in medieval Italy; *The Last Man* (1826) is an apocalyptic tale of a worldwide plague at the end of the twenty-first century; *The Fortunes of Perkin Warbeck, A Romance* (1830) is another historical romance, this one set in late fifteenth-century England; and her last two novels, *Lodore* (1835), and *Falkner* (1837) are "domestic" novels set in her own time.

Despite such wide variations in genre and setting, there are more similarities among Mary Shelley's novels than the echoes of incidents from her own life that so preoccupy the critics. Shelley was fascinated with the problem of negotiating past and present, as was nineteenth-century Britain, and this theme pervades much of her fiction. Much has been said about *Frankenstein*'s topicality, such as its incorporation of discourses clearly drawn from the vitalist debate that began in 1814 and the theories and experiments of Erasmus Darwin, Humphry Davy, and Luigi Galvani.[7] Yet Victor Frankenstein's early exposure to the writings of Cornelius Agrippa, Paracelsus, and Albertus Magnus sets him on his fateful path of scientific exploration. When Victor's father dismisses such writings as "sad trash," it only hardens his resolve to learn more. His natural philosophy tutor at Ingolstadt, M. Krempe, denounces the books of these authors as "nonsense," but his chemistry professor, M. Waldman, after delivering a paean to modern science's miracles, does not express "contempt" for Victor's choice of reading material, praising instead the "indefatigable zeal" of these early figures. He states that "[t]he labours of men of genius, however erroneously directed, scarcely ever fail in ultimately turning to the solid advantage of mankind."[8] Despite the irony of Waldman's claim about the advantages to mankind, Victor's quest depends on his being able to reconcile these competing scientific world views—the medieval and the modern, the two sides of Robert Miles's "Gothic cusp"[9]—and it is Waldman's dialectical approach that inspires him. Victor is influenced by both the ancient and modern masters of science. His "success" stands in marked contrast to the failure of the protagonist in Shelley's *The Fortunes of Perkin Warbeck* to achieve such a reconciliation. Perkin Warbeck is a relic of a chivalrous age (the Plantagenet dynasty) who wishes to turn back time, to undo the emerging modern (Tudor) era, and bring back a medieval society, but it is too late. Perkin Warbeck's desire, and his code of conduct, are seen as increasingly anachronistic. At the same time, however, Shelley is sharply critical of the "commercial spirit" of the early modern period.[10] The novel seems to suggest that one must negotiate past and present if one is to survive in a changing world.

Much of Shelley's fiction examines the relationship—analogous to the aporetic relationship between time and eternity—between an individual and one's cultural epoch, a theme that we see her exploring most explicitly in three of her "tales" and in her third novel, *The Last Man*. Shelley's narrative probing of the dynamics of this relationship forms the subject of this chapter. Each of these works features a character who, by means of an assortment of time travel-like devices, finds himself outside his own time, thus experiencing "the sense of having outlived one's cultural moment."[11] Valerius, a Roman republican, and Rodger Dodsworth, an Englishman, are the reanimated heroes of two tales, both of them living anachronisms who are out of place in the modern world. Winzy, the protagonist in "The Mortal Immortal," obtains the secret of immortality, but in so doing becomes detached from humanity, and the blessing of immortality becomes a curse; and Lionel Verney, the narrator of *The Last Man,* is the sole survivor of a worldwide plague at the end of the twenty-first century, living in a world where, without human society, time has lost all meaning.

I want to argue that Shelley, in approaching the subject of what Augustine would have referred to as "the time of the soul and the time of the world"[12] from several different perspectives, returns always to the social construction of time, not time as constructed by physics. Time is shaped and given meaning by human relationships with one's intimates, as well as with the wider world of society. One is part of one's cultural moment, and, absent a network of human relationships, not only do her characters and the narratives they inhabit become aporias, but time itself can become inarticulable. In some ways, this view is not far removed from Burke's narrative of generations, in which he draws an analogy between the state and the family as a preserver and transmitter of values: "In this choice of inheritance we have given to our frame of polity the image of a relation in blood; binding up the constitution of our country with our dearest domestic ties; adopting our fundamental laws into the bosom of our family affections; keeping inseparable, and cherishing with the warmth of all their combined and mutually reflected charities, our state, our hearths, our sepulchres, and our altars."[13]

At the same time that she seems to affirm the Burkean model, however, Shelley's apparent fascination with characters who are able to transcend their own epoch (and narrative devices that, as we shall see, fictively arrest and reverse the flow of time) suggests a desire to be unconstrained by the Burkean flow of time. Part of this desire is personal, for her own views of temporality underwent a dramatic shift in the years after her husband's death in 1822.[14] Calendar time had ceased to have as much relevance as it did when Mary, Percy, and Claire Clairmont set out on their *Six Weeks' Tour*, and it was important to connect each exciting event with a specific point in time. Her journal entry from April 26, 1823 reflects an attitude toward time that she frequently expressed during the period in which she was writing *The Last Man:* "Time is to me null. It strikes me as an impertinence to talk of its passing—there is but one moment, one date for me; since then I have embarked on Eternity—when emotions & feelings are our time pieces—& time is finished." Although this journal entry expresses her sense of being outside time, elsewhere she frequently uses Promethean images of herself chained to time, on several occasions quoting Percy's line from *Adonais,* "But I am chained to time, & cannot thence depart." A journal entry from October 26, 1824 typifies her frustration at being constrained by time as well as bearing the marks of its passage: "Time rolls on! Time! And what does it bring? I live in a desart—its barren sands feed my hour-glass and they come out fruitless as they went in. I write without hope. . . . What can I do? How change my destiny? Months change their names—years their cyphers—my brow is sadly trenched—the blossom of youth faded—my mind gathers wrinkles. . . ."

This is a sentiment not unlike that expressed on May 15, 1824, when she wrote that "At the age of twenty six I am in the condition of an aged person."[15]

Shelley's conflicted personal sentiments resonate with her cultural epoch's "widespread sense of degeneration," which fueled its fascination with "last of the race" narratives.[16] A few months after she began *The Last Man*, Shelley wrote, "The last man! Yes I may well describe that solitary being's feelings, feeling myself as the last relic of a beloved race, my companions, extinct before me."[17] Burke's narrative of generations, however desirable its promise of order and symmetry, can also be constraining when we are "chained to time." Chained thus, we are unable to "see the structure whole"[18]—in terms of the life of humanity, as well as our own individual lives—to attain the perspective that Augustine attributes to God, who is "outside time in eternity . . . see[ing] in time the things that occur in it."[19] Shelley's own sense of personal loss and her fears of aging and the decline of her imaginative powers are strikingly similar to Fiona J. Stafford's characterization of the decade of the 1820s, which she discusses in Kermodean terms:

> The desire for definition or for the "sense of an ending", so characteristic of a "transitional" period had become highly ambivalent by the 1820s. In a moribund culture, where creative energy seemed to be dwindling inexorably, leaving nothing new to say, the desire for a new beginning was strong. . . . The desire for definition can thus be seen turning backwards towards a lost origin. . . . But for those whose desire for the origin was thwarted by the undeniable knowledge that linear time made any return impossible, the only point of absolute definition was the Last Man. And it is this particularly modern realization that emerged for the first time in chilling clarity in the literature of the 1820s.[20]

As Frank Kermode argues, narrative provides a means to transcend our limitation of perspective. Shelley not only exploits this capability in her fiction, but ultimately tests the ability of narrative to transcend linear time, and even to reverse the direction of time's arrow, in order that "the Past could be unacted."[21]

THE TALES: "VALERIUS," "ROGER DODSWORTH," AND "THE MORTAL IMMORTAL"

When Percy Shelley drowned in Italy in 1822, Mary Shelley began receiving a limited allowance from Shelley's father, Sir Timothy, for the support of her only remaining child (and his heir), Percy Florence Shelley. But Shelley also found herself providing financial assistance to her father, who was always hounded by creditors, so she often felt compelled to write for economic, as well as

artistic, reasons. Shelley increasingly turned to periodical publication for financial support. She wrote a number of reviews and essays and was a frequent contributor to the annual "gift books," the
most prominent of which was *The Keepsake,* for which she published fifteen tales between 1828 and 1839, sometimes two or three
tales per issue.[22] Shelley's magazine work could certainly be regarded as "hack writing," and indeed, Shelley herself derisively referred on at least one occasion to "the mud of the magazines," a
prejudice she may have inherited from her father, who always refused to write for periodicals. And she certainly felt that the strict
spatial limitations cramped her style, but regarded the annuals as a
source of ready cash.[23] These annuals, published in November for
the Christmas market, featured costly engravings and lavish bind-
ings and were the coffee table books of their day.[24] Although she
was well aware of the way the annuals—the very term suggests
ephemerality—were regarded by critics and aspirants of serious literature, Shelley reconciled herself to her times.

Despite writing for money, she obviously found in the annuals an
opportunity to experiment with different narrative strategies, particularly in the interaction between text and illustrations. Usually
the engravings were commissioned first. As Gregory O'Dea describes the process, "[t]he tale, then, must elaborate and extenuate
the moment depicted in the engravings by narrating events that
lead to and away from that moment." The author must construct a
narrative that "originates in a non-narrative object."[25] But even
limited by the constraints of the medium (and the need to work in
that medium in the first place), she was able to exercise considerable imagination, as O'Dea points out in his discussion of the way
Shelley integrates the image into her tales. Sometimes the image
represents a climactic moment in the story ("The Trial of Love,"
1834); sometimes the engraving does not illustrate a scene from
the tale but is "an object available to Shelley's narrator, . . . the
painting becom[ing] for him, as the engraving is for Shelley, a fragment in need of fulfillment, something that will bring forth a tale"
("The Invisible Girl," 1832); or sometimes even by making the
scene part of, not the tale itself, but its narrative frame ("The Swiss
Peasant," 1830). Shelley's choices of subjects also reflect her freely
ranging imagination, and often parallel themes in her novels, some
drawn from history, and some drawn from contemporary events.
Family feuds and factional strife, central to *Valperga,* are key
themes in at least four of her tales ("A Tale of the Passions" [1823],
"The Dream" [1831], "The Brother and Sister: An Italian Story"
[1832], and "The Pilgrims" [1837]). Problems of inheritance, legiti-

macy, and usurpation characterize her novel *Perkin Warbeck* and another four tales ("Ferdinando Eboli: A Tale" [1828], "The Evil Eye" [1829], "The Elder Son" [1834] and "The Heir of Mondolfo" [mid-1820s, published 1877).[26] The conflict between Greece and Turkey that appeared in her 1826 novel, *The Last Man,* also provides the setting for 1838's "Euphrasia: A Tale of Greece."

Shelley uses her tales to experiment with narrative techniques such as various framing devices, and with different genres such as the "Jacobin antiromance," the Oriental tale, the Gothic, the fairy tale, domestic-sentimental fiction, and the fantasy or science fiction tale.[27] It is with three of these latter tales that we are concerned, because their treatment of the themes of immortality and reanimation involve protagonists who have outlived their times—times that have been socially and culturally derived. Fiona J. Stafford associates the concern about such temporal displacements with writers during the 1820s.[28]

In "Valerius: the Reanimated Roman," "Roger Dodsworth: the Reanimated Englishman," and "The Mortal Immortal," Shelley uses elements from her father's 1799 novel, *St. Leon,* to articulate her own temporal anxieties. According to Charles E. Robinson, "Valerius: The Reanimated Roman," an originally untitled tale of the reanimation of a Roman of Cicero's time, is believed to date from 1819, although it was not published until 1976.[29] If this story does in fact date from 1819, it also anticipates some of the temporal experimentation that Shelley will conduct a few years in her future, in *The Last Man.* "Valerius" is unfinished, consisting of two fragments, the first largely told in Valerius's own words, and the other fragment from the point of view of a second narrator, Isabell Harley.[30] In contrast to *Frankenstein,* which offers a form of reanimation (although only in the sense of revivifying body parts, and not the consciousness of any of the creature's donors), the details of "reanimation" never form a part of the tale in "Valerius." Shelley never describes how her hero was revived. Instead, the fact of his reanimation is a given, and her tale revolves around the *response* of Valerius to the world around him, as he tours the ruins of the city he once knew, a displaced person. He is "a being cut off from our world; the links that had bound him to it had been snapped many ages before."[31]

Shelley's juxtaposition of past and present is rendered from the unusual perspective of a man whose present is our past, and for whom all that we know as the present is the distant future. He is an aporetic hesitation in the flow of time. His temporally anomalous status allows Shelley to produce ironic inversions of temporal perspectives. For example, Valerius characterizes Rome as "fallen, torn, degraded by a hateful superstition" (335). The "hateful superstition" is of course Catholicism, a familiar characterization in Radcliffean Gothic.[32] But this tale does not situate the superstition of Catholicism in opposition to the spirit of a purer Protestant form of Christianity. Instead, Christianity is contrasted to the ancient Roman gods (and secondarily, to Isabell Harley's "Pantheic Love with which Nature is penetrated" [342]), a contrast intensified when the experience of the Pantheon's beauty is disrupted by the sight of a cross, this apprehension causing Valerius to become "embittered" (343).

The architecture of Rome performs a complex temporal function in the tale. To the nineteenth-century reader, these are simply ruins, but Shelley manages to "decompress" them from a homogeneously distant past by separating those belonging to the republican era from the imperial period. From the viewpoint of Valerius, an avowed republican, some ruins, such as the Forum, are in his past, and he laments their ruined glory, but others—from our viewpoint equally decayed—are from the imperial period, which still lay in Valerius's future. This juxtaposition results in another ironic temporal inversion when Valerius, lamenting the ruin of the Forum, finds unexpected comfort in the Coliseum, "that noble relic of imperial greatness," erected after his time, a ruin "imperial it is true, but Roman." Despite the different political ideologies the ruins represent, they have more in common with each other than with the nineteenth century. When Valerius sees in the moonlight "a glory around the fallen walls, crowned as they are by weeds and brambles," he is "seized" by "a holy awe," perceiving that "[t]he seal of Eternity was on this building" (335). The problem for Valerius is that he is out of place in this time, perceiving the Italians as having dared to "usurp the name of Romans" (333) and being as out of place in the nineteenth century as his body in the clothing he now wears, modern dress "now common all over Europe, but . . . unsuited to him" (332). His doubled awareness—remembering, "as it were but yesterday," ancient Rome, his memories superimposed on nineteenth-century ruins—produces a "feeling of utter solitude" (336). In a way, he becomes a living version of Ozymandias.

"Valerius" also provides an ironic commentary on William Godwin's doctrine of perfectibility, because at the moment when Valerius originally died, he "was possessed by the strong persuasion that, since philosophy and letters were now joined to a virtue unparalleled upon earth, Rome was approaching that perfection from which there was no fall," but when he awakens in the nineteenth century, "[t]hat light, which [he] had hailed as the forerunner of perfection, became the torches that added splendour to her funeral" (336). Instead of progress, there has been a noticeable decline of civilization, a rather pessimistic view of the future that contests both Godwin's progressivism and Burke's conservatism.

Valerius's peculiar temporal status, floating outside time, having existed in two different timescapes but no longer belonging to either, is anticipated by the tale's beginning at a point that is simultaneously specific and vague—"About eleven o'clock before noon in the month of September" (332). And owing at least in part to the incompleteness of the tale, there is no final closure. What happens to Valerius? Unlinked as he is to either past or present, Isabell Harley is convinced that he will "soon perish" if she is unsuccessful at "joining at least one" of the links that bound him to the world (340). Without strong social ties, he is as much an inhuman freak as Godwin's St. Leon,[33] but a kind of anti-St. Leon, doomed not to live but to die, although we never learn his fate. He is left as an aporia, an inarticulable contradiction between two fragmented perspectives and episodes.

In "Roger Dodsworth: The Reanimated Englishman," Mary Shelley presents another anachronistic character, this time exploiting the comic possibilities of reanimation. This tale, apparently written in 1826, but not published until 1863, "demonstrates that [Shelley] had a greater sense of humor than her modern critics allow."[34] Beginning with the premise of a humorous account of a hoax carried in several newspapers, which described an Englishman frozen in an avalanche in Italy in 1654 and reawakening some 150 years later, Shelley at least accounts for the means of reanimation this time. Still, she focuses on her hero's *response* to his reanimation, rather than on the details of it. While revisiting the theme of reanimation in a much lighter spirit, Shelley also explores a few other temporal matters not considered in the tale of Valerius. Particularly intriguing is her discussion of the implications of Dodsworth's state of suspended animation. (Her exact phrase is "a human being whose animation had been suspended by action of the frost.")[35] She describes his period of stasis in terms that emphasize his imperviousness to change:

> Animation (I believe physiologists agree) can as easily be suspended for an hundred years, as for as many seconds. A body hermetically sealed up by the frost, is of necessity preserved in its pristine entireness. That which is totally secluded from the action of external agency, can neither have any thing added to nor taken away from it: no decay can take

place, for something can never become nothing; under the influence of that state of being which we call death, change but not annihilation removes from our sight the corporeal atoma; the earth receives sustenance from them, the air is fed by them, each element takes its own, thus seizing forcible repayment of what it had lent. But the elements that hovered round Mr. Dodsworth's icy shroud had no power to overcome the obstacle it presented. No zephyr could gather a hair from his head, nor could the influence of dewy night or genial morn penetrate his more than adamantine panoply. The story of the Seven Sleepers rests on a miraculous interposition—they slept. Mr. Dodsworth did not sleep; his breast never heaved, his pulses were stopped; death had his finger pressed on his lips which no breath might pass. He has removed it now, the grim shadow is vanquished, and stands wondering. His victim has cast from him the frost spell, and arises as perfect a man as he had lain down an hundred and fifty years before. (44)

Like Valerius, Roger Dodsworth is an aporia in both senses: an inarticulable contradiction, as well as—even more dramatically—a moment of hesitation. The stasis in which Dodsworth passes his century and a half is a prolonged hesitation. With such a scientific explanation for this suspended animation, Shelley blurs the boundaries between Todorov's categories of the uncanny ("the supernatural explained") and the marvelous ("the supernatural accepted"). In Todorov's scheme, while we remain suspended between the two categories, we are in the realm of the fantastic. "The fantastic . . . lasts only as long as a certain hesitation: a hesitation common to reader and character, who must decide whether or not what they perceive derives from 'reality' as it exists in the common opinion."[36]

Curiously, Dodsworth's 170-year extension corresponds to the (actual, as opposed to stated) period of Melmoth the Wanderer's lengthened existence, although the tale, while written after *Melmoth*'s publication, was evidently based on news reports, rather than Maturin's novel. In Dodsworth's case, rather than having been experienced directly, the intervening years are condensed into a point, from which Dodsworth emerges transformed by the time that has passed, not within, but without him. This period of stasis, during which nothing happens to him, is nevertheless impermanent, and when it expires, Roger Dodsworth is as out of place as Valerius, although here Shelley's juxtaposition of past and present is more gently comic than tragic. Indeed, the alterations of fashion are the first changes remarked upon: "His dress has already excited Doctor Hotham's astonishment—the peaked beard—the love locks—the frill, which, until it was thawed, stood stiff under the mingled influence of starch and frost; his dress fashioned like that of one of Vandyke's portraits, or (a more familiar similitude) Mr. Sapio's costume in Winter's Opera of the Oracle, his pointed shoes—all spoke of other times" (44).

But equally strange are political fashions. "[I]ndulg[ing] in conjecture," because the celebrated Dodsworth of the many newspaper accounts refuses to appear in person, Shelley's narrator imagines the first conversation between the newly thawed Dodsworth and the Doctor who has revived him. All the queries and responses as they try to discern each other's political views are couched in ambiguity. Shelley exploits Dodsworth's association with the time of Charles I to comic effect. The elder asks if there is any news from England, whether " 'any change for better or worse occurred in that poor distracted country?' " Dr. Hotham, "suspect [ing] a Radical" answers "coldly" and asserts England's prosperity to be the highest in history. "Mr. Dodsworth now more than suspects the Republican," although this supposition is confounded when in the ensuing conversation, Dr. Hotham blesses the king. " 'The King!' ejaculates Mr. Dodsworth," but he recovers as "his loyalty late a tiny bud suddenly expands into full flower," and they go on misunderstanding one another about the "despicable race of the Stuarts" and the "worth[y] . . . house of Hanover" (45–46). Royal houses have their time as well, it seems.

In one of the more sobering passages of the tale, Shelley invokes the familiar Gothic anxiety about inheritance when her narrator wonders about the whereabouts of Dodsworth's "patrimony," his "co-heirs, executors, and fellow legatees." Other hands "have tilled his acres, and then become clods beneath them," to such an extent that "the youthful soil would of itself reject the antique clay of its claimant" (45). Because the Burkean principle of inheritance has been allowed to operate, he no longer has a claim to his own land. He has been transformed into a usurper of his own property. Shortly after this realization, the narrator surmises that his patrimony "is sunk into the thirsty gulph that gapes ever greedy to swallow the past" (47). In fact, Roger Dodsworth, along with "his learning, his acquirements," is "probably obsolete," and the tale closes with the words on his gravestone:

To the Memory of R. Dodsworth,
An Englishman,
Born April 1, 1617; Died July 16, 1826; Aged 209 (50)

But this is an *imagined* inscription; the narrator allows that he might be alive.

Both "Valerius" and "Roger Dodsworth" reveal that lives are strongly shaped by cultural forces. Both tales reinforce the concept of one's "own" time, that is, the time of our contemporaries, our families and friends, our heroes and villains; outside our own time, life isn't really life, as it has no meaning. It is instead a kind of ghostly afterlife. If the notion of one's own time gives us a sense of place and meaning in the vast gulf of eternity, then Shelley dramatizes in these two tales—first tragically, then comically—the notion that one's "own time" is a social construct rather than a law of physics.

Even more outside his own time, and more like Godwin's *St. Leon*, is the protagonist of "The Mortal Immortal," a tale whose title expresses the aporia of time and eternity. This tale, which appeared in the *Keepsake* for 1834, has proven to be the most widely anthologized of Shelley's tales (though not the most often reprinted during her lifetime).[37] Winzy, the young apprentice to Cornelius Agrippa (one of the authors whom Victor Frankenstein had studied prior to Ingolstadt), secretly quaffs his master's elixir of immortality. Like Victor Frankenstein's efforts to create his monster, development of Agrippa's elixir was a "mighty work"—what the philosopher calls "the labour of my life"—the actual extraction of the substance involving more than three days and nights of continuous effort.[38] The boy does not know that the potion is an elixir of immortality because his master has told him it is "a philter to cure love" (222). Agrippa based this falsehood on the mistaken belief that his apprentice would never wish to cease loving his Bertha (the subject of the tale's engraving, depicting a scene that gives no hint of the tale's fancifulness) and would therefore leave the elixir alone, but he has misjudged the degree to which Winzy feels frustrated by Bertha's coquetry. In contrast to his miserable failure in love, the fruits of scientific labor are seductive from the moment Agrippa gives his instructions to his apprentice: "Look at that glass vessel. The liquid it contains is of a soft rose-colour; the moment it begins to change its hue, awaken me—till then I may close my eyes. First, it will turn white, and then emit golden flashes. . . ." And indeed Winzy's perception of the success of his master's experiment engages almost all the senses, for when he awakens from the reverie into which he has fallen, he "gazed on it with wonder: flashes of admirable beauty, more bright than those which the diamond emits when the sun's rays are on it, glanced from the surface of the liquid; an odour the most fragrant and grateful stole over my sense; the vessel seemed one globe of living radiance, lovely to the eye, and most inviting to the taste" (222).

The lure of scientific knowledge is the lure of beauty, described in rapturous and poetic terms, and Winzy cannot resist, quaffing almost without thought, "the most delicious liquor ever tasted by the palate of man." Still unaware of the elixir's true purpose, when Winzy subsequently falls asleep under its influence, the experience is ecstatic: "I will not attempt to describe the sleep of glory and bliss which bathed my soul in paradise during the remaining hours of that memorable night. Words would be faint and shallow types of my enjoyment, or of the gladness that possessed my bosom when I woke. I trod air—my thoughts were in heaven. Earth appeared heaven, and my inheritance upon it was to be one trance of delight" (223). This description is reminiscent of Godwin's *St. Leon*, during the first and only instance in the novel in which he partakes of the "prescription of the stranger," the *elixir vitae* given him by a Wandering Jew-like figure: "I fell asleep almost instantly . . . but in no long time I was visited with the pleasantest dreams imaginable. Nothing was distinct; nothing was attended with the consciousness of my former identity; but everything was gay, cheerful, invigorating, and delicious. I wandered amidst verdant lawns, and flower-enamelled gardens. I was saluted with the singing of a thousand birds, and the murmuring of a thousand fountains. Kids, fawns, and lambs frisked and gamboled before me."[39]

But Godwin's version is more rooted in the imagery of Greek mythology than Shelley's, as St. Leon, in his dream, ultimately joins a Bacchanalian revel, the subject of chants by "nymphs and their swains," who "ascribed to [him] the beauty of Apollo, the strength of Hercules, the invention of Mercury, and the youth of Bacchus." When he awakes, he finds himself to be "all elasticity and life."[40] Just as St. Leon becomes separated from humanity as a consequence of his strange gift, and comes to regard his gift as a curse, Winzy becomes disenchanted with immortality for the same reason. And while Godwin's version of the tale is ultimately more tragic on a grander scale, because St. Leon loses his wife, is estranged from his daughters, and, most painful of all, becomes alienated from his son, Shelley's version is the more poignant for being painted on a smaller canvas. Her Bertha (by now Winzy's wife) is considerably less virtuous than Godwin's Marguerite, and becomes both "jealous and peevish" (227) as she grows visibly older while her husband does not. He sadly remembers her youthful loveliness while he contemplates her in her old age, superimposing two images of her (much as *Udolpho*'s Dorothée juxtaposes two mental images of the Marchioness's chamber, twenty years apart): "the dark-eyed, dark-haired girl, with smiles of enchanting archness and a step like a fawn—this mincing, simpering, jealous old woman" (228). Still, Winzy remains loyal to her. Eventually she becomes "bed-rid and paralytic" but Winzy nurses her faithfully, "as a mother might a child," assuming the traditional female role of the caregiver, and taking consolation in the fact that he "performed [his] duty scrupulously toward her" until her death, at which time he weeps "to feel [he] had lost all that really bound [him] to humanity." Winzy is the fusion of the poet and the scientist, more so than St. Leon; certainly more so than Victor Frankenstein. But in the end, he's still unhappy, characterizing his life after Bertha as that of "a sailor without rudder or compass, tossed on a stormy sea—a traveller lost on a wide-spread heath, without landmark or star to guide him . . ." (229). Human relationships provide our means of reconciling ourselves to the gulf of time.

Three centuries later, with no sign that his immortality has lessened, Winzy's existence has become the embodiment of opposites: "alone, and weary of myself—desirous of death, yet never dying—a mortal immortal." In despair, he determines to embark on an undescribed expedition (presumably to the polar regions, to "war[] with the powers of frost in their home") to put his immortality to the test once and for all, hoping that "by scattering and annihilating the atoms that compose my frame, [to] set at liberty the life imprisoned within, and so cruelly prevented from soaring from this dim earth to a sphere more congenial to its immortal essence" (230).[41] To be truly immortal requires abandoning corporeality. Winzy is "stuck" (Derrida's translation of Aristotle's *diaporeo*)[42] between time and eternity, neither truly mortal nor immortal.

Immortality severs the ties that bind Winzy, like St. Leon, to humanity, and he is set adrift. Unlike St. Leon, Winzy and Bertha never participate in the genealogical alternative to immortality (although St. Leon's children were all born prior to his meeting the stranger who disclosed to him the secrets of the philosopher's stone). Winzy and Bertha never have children, for the depth of their devotion to each other appears to have precluded offspring: "we were all in all to each other; and though, as she grew older, her vivacious spirit became a little allied to ill-temper, and her beauty sadly diminished, I cherished her in my heart as the mistress I had idolized, the wife I had sought and won with such perfect love" (227). This "ideal" union is perversely even more of a false solution than St. Leon's fate, because, while St. Leon suffers the alienation of his children, he knows that they still exist, and are happier without him. His line goes on, but Winzy is cut off from humanity without any issue to carry on after him. Shelley here seems to be suggesting that there are limits to the virtues of domesticity, although given the true state of Winzy's marriage to Bertha, it is hardly an ideal domestic arrangement. At one point, Winzy says that their "situation became intolerable: Bertha was fifty—I twenty years of age" (227); he said that when he "looked at the faded beauty of Bertha—I seemed more like her son" (226), and the neighbors make similar remarks. They become almost as much a mockery of generational succession as Victor Frankenstein's attempts to father a new race of creatures, and in the end, there is a similar desire for dissolution. Immortality also seems a false solution, and Winzy's existence is as much a ghostly afterlife as is that of Valerius.

PROPHETIC RETROSPECTIVE: *THE LAST MAN*

A ghostly afterlife is exactly the kind of existence experienced by Lionel Verney, the hero of Shelley's 1826 novel, *The Last Man*. The novel is strongly marked by a sense of inexorable movement toward Verney's status as the last man alive on earth after a worldwide plague in the late twenty-first century, even though the plague does not make its first appearance until a third of the way through the novel.[43]

Mary Shelley's novel was one of a series of futuristic romances from the late eighteenth and early nineteenth centuries that made use of the "Last Man" theme. Louis-Sébastien Mercier's *L'An 2440* (1770) and Jean-Baptiste François Cousin de Grainville's *Le dernier homme* (1805, translated into English a year later as *The Last Man, or Omegarus and Syderia, A Romance of Futurity*), were a few popular apocalyptic precursors, along with Byron's 1816 poem, "Darkness," itself influenced by Pope's *The Dunciad*.[44] In a unique narrative twist that accounts for how we might be reading such a future apocalyptic account in the first place—always a difficult explanation with such narratives—Shelley frames her novel as an ancient prophecy by the Cumæan Sybil, written on Sibylline leaves (in various ancient and modern languages) found in a hidden cave in 1818 by an anonymous "author" (who may or may not be Mary Shelley, as Audrey A. Fisch has observed.)[45] It falls to this "author" to translate the Sibyl's account, which is "scattered and unconnected," to fill in gaps, and to "transform" the leaves into a coherent account, because "they were unintelligible in their pristine condition" (3–4). This transformation—"mak[ing] a plausible story out of a congeries of 'facts,' which, in their unprocessed form, make no sense at all"—is exactly the process that Hayden White calls "emplotment."[46]

Shelley's version of emplotment interposes both the Sibyl herself and an anonymous author/editor, and in the process imposes a dizzying temporal perspective on the narrative.[47] It is an ancient prophecy of a future apocalypse written retrospectively by its lone survivor, who looks back upon the final decades of the human race's existence from the year 2100. By narrating the close of human history, the novel reconfigures and humanizes time. Since history is now complete, we can perceive it in its entirety.

Some of *The Last Man*'s elaborate temporal framing seems to penetrate the narrator's consciousness. At one point, he refers to a feeling of "some past real existence," imagining that all his "sensations were a duplex mirror of a former revelation."[48] After all, Verney's account consists of his recollection of events (from a point when time has already lost its former meaning), a series of events prophesied by the Sibyl, recorded as she remembered her prophecy, translated and edited by the frame narrator, and finally interpreted by the reader. Even the individual who entered the cave and scattered the Sibylline leaves has influenced the narrative, which has been only imperfectly reconstructed. This framing process allows Shelley, absent the time machine that H. G. Wells would not "invent" until nearly seventy years later, to use the past tense and establish what Giovanna Franci has termed "one of the most widely used models in science fiction; the use of the past in the narration to describe things which are supposedly to happen in the future." In Gérard Genette's typology, the narrating instances of such prophetic narratives actually represent occurrences of the classical *subsequent* narrative which characterizes the vast majority of written narratives.[49] Especially interesting here is the fact that, while the interval between the moment of narrating and the time of a story's events is usually not a significant consideration, Lionel Verney's temporal perspective, as he writes from what is essentially the end of human time, casts a shadow over his entire narrative. As Verney remarks midway through the novel: "Time and experience have placed me on an height from which I can comprehend the past as a whole; and in this way I must describe it, bringing forward the leading incidents, and disposing light and shade so as to form a picture in whose very darkness there will be harmony" (192–93).

Paul A. Cantor argues that the appeal of the "last man" theme in nineteenth-century literature lies in the text's ability "to stand at the final moment of human history and thus to be able to survey the whole of human cultural achievement," a desire which Cantor attributes to "the developing historicist sense of the age."[50] The perspective itself becomes the theme. As Jane Blumberg has put it, "Lionel Verney, the Last Man, begins his narration as if looking through the wrong end of a telescope. With this experience of global annihilation he looks back at what was once thought to be all-encompassing and commanding, now infinitely tiny and far away."[51] As we have seen in our discussion of *Melmoth the Wanderer*, Frank Kermode has articulated the human desire to make sense of our lives through "fictive concords with origins and ends" exactly because we lack the ability to "see the structure whole." Fiona J. Stafford sees the nineteenth century's abundance of "last man" narratives as part of a process that began with the mid-eighteenth century's preoccupation with "last of the race" myths, such as Thomas Gray's "The Bard" (1757), Oliver Goldsmith's "The History of Carolan, the Last Irish Bard" (1760), and James Macpherson's *Ossian* poems (1760–63), all depicting legendary Celtic bards. As Stafford points out, each of these "last bard" myths was "directly related to the widespread sense of degeneration and, as the sole survivor of a once-vigorous race, intensified the anxiety by introducing a specific, individual tragedy." In a figure such as Carolan, however, " 'the last and greatest' is the climax and culmination of his tradition, rather than the decaying remains."[52] This representation of lastness as culmination is more akin to the concept of time as *kairos,* "a point in time filled with significance, charged with a meaning derived from its relation to the end," than to the more familiar concept of chronological time, or *chronos,* " 'passing time' or 'waiting time'—that which, according to Revelation, 'shall be no more.' "[53] Shelley's *The Last Man* is consistent with this thematic tradition of "climax and culmination," but it also moves beyond it by transcending the world of time and narrative. Burke's claim for inheritance, in his discussion of the hereditary crown of England, is that it is secure "to the end of time"[54]—a point conceived to be so far distant that it will never be reached. Shelley's novel takes us there.

Chronos

Although the novel's ending in the year 2100 provides a round number for the year in which civilization comes to a close, if Shelley had a particular event in mind when she chose the year 2073 as the year in which England becomes a republic (for example, three hundred years after a particular political event or set of events in England or pre-revolutionary France), it is not obvious. A more likely explanation is that this date is two hundred fifty years distant from 1823, the year in which she first began to write *The Last Man*. Two hundred fifty years would seem to be far enough in the future to provide sufficient distance from the contemporary political scene, while still being close enough to the year 2100 to form a narrative within the span of an individual's life. Muriel Spark observes that *The Last Man* fuses fantasy and realism; the year 2073 provides "a precise fixture in time" and Spark notes that Shelley "does not pay more than passing regard" to the date once she establishes it, "since its purpose is fulfilled,"[55] much as the "historical" settings of Gothic novels have no real historicity. By making reference to a date at the outset and then largely neglecting a consistent chronology, Shelley is following the pattern set by Radcliffe in *The Mysteries of Udolpho*.

Shelley's vagueness about objective time contributes to a distancing effect while it also reinforces the concept of time emptied of meaning. Except for the "Author's Introduction," which fixes the time and place definitely and immediately (Naples, December 8, 1818), she rarely cites specific dates. In fact, there are only four specific occurrences in Verney's narration where the month, day, and year are all provided: (1) June 20, 2094, the date of Verney's son Alfred's birthday party, when Verney has his vision of death and it is revealed that the plague *is* in London; (2) January 1, 2098, when Adrian and his three hundred followers leave for Paris; (3) December 30, 2097, which appears as the date of the letter sent from Lucy Martin to Idris, just before the departure; and (4) January 1, 2100, the date when Verney climbs St. Peter's and carves the year 2100 on the topmost stone—although this last example is somewhat qualified, as Verney had previously stopped keeping track of time and had made a "rough calculation" by the stars to determine the date.

Events in *The Last Man* are identified most frequently by season or month, in some cases by month and day, or season and year, or by the number of days, weeks or months elapsed since a previous event. Sometimes an event is dated, not when it occurs, but in retrospect. For example, November 20, the date when Alfred dies and Verney contracts the plague, is mentioned on at least three occasions, but only *after* the fact. And in one particularly notable case she emphasizes that the anniversary of Lord Raymond's election as Protector took place on October 19, but, curiously, the date is not mentioned at the point in the narrative when the event occurs, and the year is never mentioned at all. We are reminded of this anniversary date twice (92, 94). It is on that night that Lord Raymond fails to attend the anniversary party because he is tending to Evadne, and, although his wife, Perdita, had learned of his association with Evadne somewhat earlier, the anniversary party really marks the end of her idyllic relationship with Raymond. Shelley does not date the pivotal event of Raymond's election—surely the kind of event which might be considered worthy of recording due to its historical importance, an event associated with public time. Instead, she only marks it on its anniversary, and then its real significance is associated, not with his ascension to the highest office in the land, but with the end of his relationship with Perdita—an apparent statement of Shelley's perception of the relative values of political power and familial relationships. It is not public time with which she is concerned. Nor does Shelley make much of the details of Lord Raymond's election to the Protectorship, which are heavily condensed into some five pages, from his first declaration of intent to his election. Although Verney is an observer of the proceedings, few details are given and most of the action occurs off-stage. The philosophical and political arguments that form the debate are not represented at all, Lord Raymond's eloquence is only described, the content of his speech only summarized, and the election itself is disposed of anticlimactically. Eve Tavor Bannet notes that the plague "exposes Man and History to women's time . . . confin[ing] him to a present whose value and meaning come to depend entirely on the presence and companionship of other human beings." This is underscored by the plague's bringing to an end "Man's great time-filler . . . civilization itself. Without a public sphere and all the 'adornments of humanity' to produce, govern, and squabble over," men have "little or nothing to do."[56] Shelley's representation of the date of Lord Raymond's election as being important only because it marks a change in his relationship with Perdita anticipates the ultimate devaluation of the public sphere that the plague will bring.

Another example of specific dating occurs in the month of June. Several important events take place during this month, and it is a tumultuous month in *The Last Man*, filled with cosmic phenomena and portents, particularly around the time of the solstice. This celestial event has traditionally been endowed with cosmic significance from the time of the Druids—an invocation of what Heidegger would term primordial time. The "dark sun" of 2093 which heralds the spreading of the plague from the east is seen on the 21st of June. And Verney's prophetic vision on the occasion of his son's birthday takes place on June 20, 2094. Indeed, the plague began "early in June to raise its serpent-head on the shores of the Nile" (127). And sometime during the week of June 16–23, 1816, at the Villa Diodati, Shelley had had the dream that precipitated *Frankenstein*, during a summer of violent thunderstorms, while Byron, the Shelleys, Claire Clairmont, and Dr. Polidori passed the time telling ghost stories.

But seasonal references in the novel are most striking for their being indicators that all is not as it should be, that time is somehow out of joint (as is the departure from daily routine, such as when the consumptive Idris wanders through the house by night and sleeps fitfully during the day). This pattern is set in the "Author's Introduction," where the December is spring-like. Shortly after Verney returns to England following the deaths of Lord Raymond and Perdita, and as the plague begins its march across Asia and Europe, chapter 5 of volume 2 begins, "Some disorder had surely crept into the course of the elements, destroying their benignant influence" (166). That winter is characterized by four months of violent winds and storms. The following year, as plague ravages England, the autumn is unnaturally warm and rainy, causing the people to hope for winter. But the winter months bring only more rainstorms, floods, and no frost until February, which is followed by three days of winter and then an early thaw. Spring comes amid fear of balmy weather. This spring is exceptionally beautiful, with the lanes full of violets, but soon, "The Destroyer of man brooded again over the earth" (198) and by June, "the paths were deformed by unburied corpses" (200), a grim counterpoint to the violet-filled lanes only a few months before.

It is most difficult to construct a chronology of the events of the novel from the specific date, season, and durational references, and the task becomes virtually impossible when one attempts to correlate other factors such as references to ages of characters at various points in Shelley's novel; calculating forward from 2073 and backward from 2100 results in a discrepancy of at least a year in the dating. This discrepancy may indicate errors in Verney's accounting of events in flashback, or in the "Author's" process of piecing together the scattered Sibylline leaves, or errors on the part of Shelley herself, particularly as there is evidence that Charles Colburn rushed the novel into print on January 23, 1826 before Shelley had a chance to make all the corrections she wished to make.[57] Shelley's own altered attitude toward time subsequent to her husband's death, as discussed previously, may have contributed to her being less vigilant where the novel's timeline is concerned.

As was the case in *Udolpho*, the world of public, calendar time is not particularly important here. If Shelley felt herself to be "chained to time," the novel at least imaginatively frees her, in positing a no-time outside narrative and history. And indeed, at the end of the novel, Verney has apparently abandoned writing and sails away to the south; yet he has achieved a measure of happiness in seeking perception and experience, what Coleridge would call the Primary Imagination, without the need to recreate. As Verney puts it, "I form no expectation of alteration for the better; but the monotonous present is intolerable to me" (342). His awareness has shifted from the retrospection that occupied him while he narrated his history, and from the present, toward his future potential. Even while he disavows any expectation of improvement, his future-directed orientation is an aspect of Heidegger's *Care*, the self-awareness that looks to one's future potential. Verney reverses the "levelling down" of Care to the preoccupation with minutiae that Heidegger condemns.[58] He is going to create his own future, through a triumph of the will, but the narrative ends with this as a potentiality. In this context, the assessments of the novel's vision that some critics have made (Muriel Spark, who considered it the best of Shelley's novels, nevertheless called it "ruthlessly pessimistic," while Robert Lance Snyder asserted that it is "characterized by an austerity and brooding related to the inability to discern any rationale within human destiny"), seem to miss the point.[59] Even in the wake of universal cataclysm, the individual survives—and manages to improve himself. Unlike the ending of *The Dunciad* or "Darkness," all is not night, all is not stillness, and perhaps a form of Godwinian perfectibility still lives at the end of the twenty-first century.

Another apparent sign of the Radcliffean influence on the novel is Shelley's emphasis on the time of evening, particularly sunset. As we saw in *Udolpho*, the sunset marked a time of transition, a time characterized as looking backward (memory) as well as forward (expectation). Such a time is significant in *The Last Man* as well. Not only is it the time when Verney and Idris declare their love for each other, but Evadne's death takes place at sunset and sets the tone for other events that will occur at that hour: "This hour, melancholy yet sweet, has always seemed to me the time when we are most naturally led to commune with higher powers; our mortal sternness departs, and gentle complacency invests the soul" (130).

Sometimes Shelley associates the imagination with this time of communion with higher powers, as does Radcliffe. When Lord Raymond dies in the ruin of the collapsing building after entering Constantinople, Verney searches well into the evening: "The sun set" and he sees in the ruins "weird shapes . . . for a moment I could yield to the creative power of the imagination" (145). Two contrasting apparitions that haunt the band of survivors journeying across France are associated with this time of the day:

> Once, at the dusk of the evening, we saw a figure all in white, apparently of more than human stature, flourishing about the road, now throwing up its arms, now leaping to an astonishing height in the air, then turning round several times successively, then raising itself to its full height and gesticulating violently . . . as it became darker, there was something appalling even to the incredulous, in the lonely spectre, whose gambols, if they hardly accorded with spiritual dignity, were beyond human powers. (298)

In yet another Radcliffean association, this one a case of the "supernatural explained," this "goblin" turns out to be a former opera-dancer, stricken with the plague, who, "in an access of delirium . . . had fancied himself on the stage" (299). Another example of the supernatural explained speaks directly to the way our perceptions shift under the influence of different times of day. This apparition stands in opposition to the white figure:

> At another time we were haunted for several days by an apparition, to which our people gave the appellation of the Black Spectre. We never saw it except at evening, when his coal black steed, his mourning dress, and plume of black feathers, had a majestic and awe-striking appearance; his face, one said, who had seen it for a moment, was ashy pale. . . . Sometimes at dead of night, as we watched the sick, we heard one galloping through the town; it was the Black Spectre come in token of inevitable death. He grew giant tall to vulgar eyes; an icy atmosphere, they said, surrounded him. . . . It was Death himself, they declared. . . . One day at noon, we saw a dark mass on the road before us, and, coming up, beheld the Black Spectre fallen from his horse, lying in the agonies of disease upon the ground. He did not survive many hours; and his last words disclosed the secret of his mysterious conduct. He was a French noble of distinction, who, from the effects of plague, had been left alone in his district; during many months he had wandered from town to town, from province to province, seeking some survivor for a companion. . . . (299)

In evening, this figure is "majestic and awe-striking"; in the "dead of night," he is Death itself; at noon, he is just "a dark mass on the road," a man "fallen from his horse, lying in the agonies of disease upon the ground."

The theme of sunset-related communion with higher powers is

reinforced in volume 3, chapter 7, when the pitiful remnant of fifty human beings traveling through Switzerland arrives at Jura at noon, but ascends the mountain at sunset. All behold in wonder the "glorious Alps, clothed in dazzling robes by the setting sun" (305). Their reaction is significant, even those who had been overwhelmed by death:

> By degrees, our whole party surmounting the steep, joined us, not one among them, but gave visible tokens of admiration, surpassing any before experienced. One cried, "God reveals his heaven to us; we may die blessed." Another and another, with broken exclamations, and extravagant phrases, endeavoured to express the intoxicating effect of this wonder of nature. So we remained awhile, lightened of the pressing burthen of fate, forgetful of death, into whose night we were about to plunge; no longer reflecting that our eyes now and for ever were and would be the only ones which might perceive the divine magnificence of this terrestrial exhibition. An enthusiastic transport, akin to happiness, burst, like a sudden ray from the sun, on our darkened life. (305–6)

The time of transition from day to night marks a similar transition in the life of the human race.

Rhythms of the Narrative

Despite the obvious similarities to Radcliffean Gothic, Shelley's narrative pacing seems more deliberately planned and is linked to the novel's three-volume structure. Both Brian Aldiss and Muriel Spark have likened *The Last Man* to a musical composition, which provides an appropriate metaphor for examining the novel's larger structure and tempo. Brian Aldiss has said of *The Last Man* that "[l]ike a concerto, it comes in three movements, and the movements are at odds with each other. The first movement is of great length, almost a social novel in itself; the second movement concerns the coming of the plague and the liberation of Constantinople by Lord Raymond; and the third is almost a travel diary coupled with the alarming mathematics of diminishing numbers."[60] Spark observes that the novel's opening theme is "pastoral domesticity," until Lord Raymond's death leaves a vacancy for the Protectorate. That vacancy and the fact he died in a city devastated by plague provide two "stray factors, subsidiary to the opening theme, which are taken up and developed to prominence in the next phase," the theme that Spark characterizes as "political intrigue attempting to justify itself in the face of encroaching disaster." The political, social, and ideological concepts are eventually discarded, leaving a solitary protagonist. "Structurally," Spark notes, "it is a symphonic technique—a pattern composed of movements, evolving one from the other."[61] This pattern of movements is echoed by Hugh J. Luke, who sees the three phases of the novel—and the corresponding phases of Verney's life, as "a kind of inversion of the Wordsworthian idea of the three ages of man. . . . But where Wordsworth perceives a progression from unity to alienation back to a heightened sense of unity, Mary Shelley presents us with a pattern of life beginning in alienation, temporarily achieving a sense of union, and then returning to an intensified isolation."[62]

Shelley's treatment of specific temporal references (months, seasons, and times of day) differs among the three volumes of the novel. Volume 1 spans the longest period (at least the first eighteen years of England's history as a republic, and Verney's early childhood), but contains the fewest temporal references. Only a few months—May, September, and October—are mentioned. There are few references to time of day, almost all either at night or evening. Most of the first volume is of the nature of the five-year idyll in Windsor in chapter 6, which contains no specific time references at all and gives the impression of a long summer afternoon. The following passage is typical: "Sometimes we passed whole days under the leafy covert of the forest with our books and music. . . . When the clouds veiled the sky, and the wind scattered them there and here, rending their woof, and strewing its fragments through the aërial plains—then we rode out, and sought new spots of beauty and repose. When the frequent rains shut us within doors, evening recreation followed morning study, ushered in by music and song. . . . Then we were as gay as summer insects, playful as children" (64). Volume 1 is thus a long, slow, pastoral movement.

Volume 2, spanning some four years, contains many more references to time (and to the future, as the majority of the most dramatic prophetic incidents occur during this volume). The pace begins to accelerate about midway through the volume as the plague traverses Europe and reaches England. From the time of Alfred's birthday on June 20, 2094, we seem to *feel* the time passing in a catalog of months: August, September, October, then the autumn followed by the unnatural winter, then in quick succession, February, March, May, June, July, August, September, October, November, and another winter. The effect is similar to what Shelley referred to as the perception that "every moment of the day is divided, felt, and counted,"[63] the kind of "now-saying" that we have seen in *Melmoth the Wanderer*.

Volume 3, spanning four or five years, contains *many* more references to months and times of the day, four times the number of
references to sunset as volume 2, and more than double the number of night and morning references. The pace of this volume is
rapid, a musical rondo, heightened by what Aldiss has called the
"alarming mathematics of diminishing numbers."[64] The geographi-
cal movement adds a vividness to the passage of time and the
shrinking human population, space, and arithmetic making time
visible.[65] Thus, from Paris to Versailles ("fifteen hundred souls . . .
the eighteenth of June") to Dijon ("end of July," "just eighty of us
in number" [297].) An exceptionally compact passage at the beginning of chapter 7 sets the pace and contrasts the perception of time
in recollection to that actually experienced. It also alludes to the
different time perceptions of the two Verneys, who are on multiple
time tracks:

> It is strange, after an interval of time, to look back on a period, which,
> though short in itself, appeared, when in actual progress, to be drawn
> out interminably. By the end of July we entered Dijon; by the end of
> July those hours, days, and weeks had mingled with the ocean of forgot-
> ten time, which in their passage teemed with fatal events and agonizing
> sorrow. By the end of July, little more than a month had gone by, if
> man's life were measured by the rising and setting of the sun: but, alas!
> in that interval ardent youth had become grey-haired; furrows deep and
> uneraseable were trenched in the blooming cheek of the young mother;
> the elastic limbs of early manhood, paralyzed as by the burthen of years,
> assumed the decrepitude of age. Nights passed, during whose fatal
> darkness the sun grew old before it rose; and burning days, to cool
> whose baleful heat the balmy eve, lingering far in eastern climes, came
> lagging and ineffectual; days, in which the dial, radiant in its noon-day
> station, moved not its shadow the space of a little hour, until a whole
> life of sorrow had brought the sufferer to an untimely grave. (297)

The remnant experiences what Shelley herself called "the tyranny
of the present,"[66] a kind of Augustinian present with a vengeance.
And only a few pages after the July passage, a week has elapsed and,
"After remaining a week at Dijon . . . we arrived at the foot of Jura
. . . fifty human beings" (303). Chapter 8 begins with the survivors
having reached Switzerland at last, but the reader is shocked to realize, only a page later, that: "Near the sources of the Arveiron we
performed the rites for, four only excepted, the last of the species"
(309). Given the almost agonizingly slow pace of the first half the
novel, events begin to move rapidly indeed in the second half.
    The three "movements" of this novel are indeed at odds with one

another, much as a concerto is comprised of multiple musical themes and keys, and varying tempos (usually fast-slow-fast, but inverted to slow-fast-fast in *The Last Man,* to emphasize the loss of the pastoral). The novel's structure is also consistent with the conventions of the sonata form during the Classical period, as perfected by Mozart and Haydn,[67] in which exposition of a theme (for example, the pastoral, presented initially by Verney's solitude as a shepherd boy with a dog for a companion), leads to development of that theme, usually in a different key (as Verney is educated, becomes involved in a family, society, politics, and the events of the world) and ultimately to recapitulation (Verney again alone, with a shepherd dog for a companion). The endings of the three volumes can be seen as forming a dialectic. Volume 1 ends on a note of hope, with a sea journey, in May, to reunite Perdita with Raymond; Volume 2 ends with the death of hope, on a wintry February day amid the leafless trees of Windsor: "Can the madman, as he clanks his chains, hope? Can the wretch, led to the scaffold, who when he lays his head on the block, marks the double shadow of himself and the executioner, whose uplifted arm bears the axe, hope? Can the ship-wrecked mariner, who spent with swimming, hears close behind the splashing waters divided by a shark which pursues him through the Atlantic, hope? Such hope as theirs, we may also entertain!" (226) Volume 3 ends in January, but in genial Italy rather than gloomy England, as Verney and his dog prepare to sail southward into Homeric myth. Once again, the season is unseasonable, but this former anomaly has now been transformed, synthesized, and it no longer foretells disaster.

In addition to the larger rhythms that structure the novel and the temporal framing of ancient prophecy/future events/recollection in flashback, the novel is permeated by narrative rhythms that work to constantly complicate the reader's perception of time. Consider Verney's auspicious beginning: "I AM the native of a sea-surrounded nook, a cloud-enshadowed land, which, when the surface of the globe, with its shoreless ocean and trackless continents, presents itself to my mind, appears only as an inconsiderable speck in the immense whole; and yet, when balanced in the scale of mental power, far outweighed countries of larger extent and more numerous population." (5)

Shelley's use of "I AM" (in small capitals) to begin Verney's narrative, though due at least in part to typographical conventions, suggests the ancient Hebrew name for God.[68] Verney has created this history, his own as well as his country's, and in fact has created this entire world, symbolically dividing the waters from the land. His view of space is vast enough that England is a mere speck to him (when it presents itself to his mind) and his perspective of time is comparably vast. His "I AM" affirmation also calls to mind Coleridge's concept of the imagination in book 13 of the *Biographia Literaria:*

> The IMAGINATION then, I consider either as primary, or secondary. The primary IMAGINATION I hold to be the living Power and prime Agent of all human Perception, and as a repetition in the finite mind of the eternal act of creation in the infinite I AM. The secondary imagination I consider as an echo of the former, co-existing with the conscious will. . . . It dissolves, diffuses, dissipates, in order to recreate; or where this process is rendered impossible, yet still at all events it struggles to idealize and to unify.[69]

In *The Last Man* we see multiple levels of primary and secondary imagination at work: Verney's acts of perception and then recreation are enclosed within the Sibyl's perception and recreation, which in turn are enclosed within the author's perception of the tale written on the Sibylline leaves and his or her efforts to "model the work into a consistent form" (4); the modeling efforts are equivalent to Coleridge's "struggles to idealize and to unify."[70]

From his view of eternity, Verney quickly narrows his spatial perspective and returns to his youth ("In my boyish days she [England] was the universe to me") before, in the second paragraph of the novel, beginning his own history by describing his father's origins, youth, and downfall, and the birth of Verney and his sister, Perdita, thus narrowing his temporal perspective as well. He has entered his own history, the Word made flesh. In her first, brief chapter, Shelley establishes a narrative rhythm that she employs throughout the novel. Her narrator repeatedly employs the technique of taking up an account from a particular point in time, perhaps several months or a year after a previous major event in the novel, briefly summarizing what has occurred in the interim, and then providing greater detail through analepsis; sometimes these detailed accounts involve multiple characters' viewpoints. Instead of employing what Gérard Genette calls the classical rhythm of detailed *scene* for strong, dramatic portions of the narrative, alternated with *summary* for the weaker, nondramatic actions, Shelley uses *both* summary and scene for many of her particularly dramatic events.[71] This narrative rhythm represents a dialectic of progress and regress in which the reader moves forward and backward at varying tempos— quickly forward for a summary, then quickly backward to the previous milestone in the narrative before moving slowly forward again, in more detail. The repetition of the same events in different levels retards the progress of the narrative. While Ann Radcliffe used embedded lyric poetry to slow the pace of her narrative, Shelley employs a rhythmic strategy that echoes the pattern of the novel as a whole. We know from the outset that the narrator stands at the end of history. The narrative tells us how he arrived there, but it lingers on the way.

A good example of this technique occurs in chapter 9 of volume 1, a temporally complicated chapter. The preceding chapter concluded on the night of the celebration of the anniversary of Lord Raymond's election as Lord Protector, October 19. On that fateful night Lord Raymond forsook the celebration (and hence his official duties) and remained by the side of the stricken Evadne. Chapter 9 begins "soon after the festival" (98) and it is noted that "We" (i.e., Verney, Idris, and Adrian) "in our retirement, remained long in ignorance of [Perdita's] misfortune." The phrase "long in ignorance" implies some length of time, perhaps several months. A visit of Lord Raymond and Perdita to Windsor is arranged, but "it was May before they arrived," thus, some seven months after the night of the anniversary. On the occasion of the May visit, Perdita and her daughter arrive first, early in the morning, and Raymond arrives soon after. Idris and Perdita spend the day with the children while Raymond talks of his plans as Lord Protector to Adrian and Verney. In the evening Perdita plays and sings the music of Mozart, then suddenly, while Idris is playing a "passionate and sorrowful air in Figaro" (99), she leaves the group, sobbing. Verney follows her and Perdita subsequently confides in her brother, recounting the weeks immediately following the October anniversary, and the exchange of letters between Raymond and herself that seemed to spell an end to their relationship. We then return to the "present" (i.e., May), and learn that "in the mean time, Raymond had remained with Adrian and Idris" (104). We have returned to the time just after Verney left the group to hear Perdita's tale, which itself was an analepsis, all enclosed within Verney's extended flashback. Raymond proceeds to narrate the events of the preceding October from *his* viewpoint, a discussion "which lasted for several hours," and he subsequently departs alone, leaving Perdita "to follow him with her child" (106). An unspecified amount of time then passes as Raymond seeks consolation in a dissolute lifestyle, while Perdita endeavors to fulfill his duties as Lord Protector in his place. Verney and Adrian eventually confront Raymond, who reveals that he is about to return to Greece as a soldier and asks Adrian to accompany him. He goes on to say that he has reflected on this step "the live-long summer," so obviously several months have passed since the May meeting.

Some 140 changes of position in story time, more than twice the number of shifts per page of narrative than most other chapters in the novel, occur in this chapter.[72] The number of temporal shifts and the multiplicity of viewpoints (Verney's, Lord Raymond's, Perdita's) are disconcerting and produce a sense of fragmentation that contrasts with the unity of the idyllic period three chapters earlier, five years that Verney describes iteratively in the "gay as summer insects, playful as children" selection cited previously. The narrative structure of volume 1, chapter 9, pointedly dramatizes what has been lost. Where there had been one viewpoint, one temporal perspective, and a sense of timelessness conveyed through the use of the iterative, there is now confusion conveyed by multiple perspectives and a rapidly shifting time line. We are a long way from the Burkean narrative of "order" and "symmetry" in which transmission is accomplished in a sequential fashion and events unfold from one omniscient perspective. At this point in *The Last Man*, time has become plastic and unreliable, tainted by the narrator's own position at the end of history. Ricoeur states that there is a "difference between the retained past and the represented past." Verney's present, i.e., the point at which he writes his narrative (the year 2100), is inscribed in memory and "retroactively gives a particular coloring to the [narrated] reproduction."[73] He reproduces the events in memory at a point when public time has effectively ceased to exist and his altered temporal conditions affect the temporality of the representation.

Another example of Shelley's summary/scene rhythm occurs in the subsequent chapter, chapter 10 of volume 1. Verney, Idris, and Perdita spend a year traveling around England, Scotland, and Ireland to take Perdita's mind off her husband's flight. Adrian returns from Greece, "after the lapse of more than a year" (the same year, presumably that Verney, Idris, and Perdita were traveling [115]). Adrian now proceeds to narrate the intervening events since he and Raymond had left England—the truce that had existed when he and Raymond arrived in Greece, the subsequent attacks of the Turks, and the horror and brutality of a Greek massacre of a Turkish city. Back in the primary narrative's "present," more time passes as the four await tidings from Greece, and they learn of Raymond's heroic exploits before he is captured by the Turks. Perdita and Verney resolve to travel to Greece, and they depart in May.

The Last Man also contains a series of stories embedded within Verney's account, that interrupt the flow of the narrative, but, unlike Radcliffe's use of embedded lyrics to simply stall forward progress, Shelley's interpolated narratives draw us backward. Most prominent of these is the poignant story of Juliet, whom we meet several times. We first learn of her history, and that of her family's, in volume 2, chapter 8, where she is reunited with a lost lover after the deaths of everyone in her family. She reappears early in volume 3 as the rescuer of Idris, who had been wandering the streets of London, distraught by the death of her son. Later, we are drawn back to her story yet again; at this point, her husband has died of the plague, and both she and her infant daughter become the victims of the impostor-prophet in France.

A similar pattern is employed in volume 3, chapter 3, where Verney tells the story of Lucy Martin, whose lost first love returns to find her unhappily married, but who dies before they can be reunited when Lucy's husband deserts her. She is nearly left behind in England as a result of nursing her invalid mother, and Verney and Idris are on their way to rescue her when Idris dies. We are reminded of Lucy's story several chapters later, when she in turn succumbs to the plague.

These narrative rhythms mirror the larger structure of the novel within which they are enclosed; we already know from the outset that it is a story of the last man alive on earth and any suspense can only be associated with the intermediate events. By using the rhythm of flashbacks within the larger flashback ("In the mean time, what did Perdita?" 118), Shelley continually reminds us, on a subliminal level, that the ultimate outcome has already been fixed, even before we arrive at Verney's speculations on fate which occur with increasing frequency during the final chapters of the novel. Occasional intrusions by the narrator from his vantage point at the end of time, as I will show, also reinforce the tragic conclusion.[74] This narrative rhythm exemplifies Ricoeur's "living dialectic" that makes a story "followable." The episodes of a narrative draw the reader forward "in the direction of the linear representation of time." But at the same time, the configuration of the plot effectively reverses this temporal direction. The "end point" must provide "the point of view from which the story can be perceived as forming a whole." The episodes must be seen as leading to the end, even if the conclusion has not been foreseen.

A new quality of time emerges from this understanding . . . the repetition of a story, governed as a whole by its way of ending, constitutes an alternative to the representation of time as flowing from the past toward the future, following the well-known metaphor of the "arrow of time."

It is as though recollection inverted the so-called "natural" order of time. In reading the ending in the beginning and the beginning in the ending, we also learn to read time itself backwards, as the recapitulation of the initial conditions of a course of action in its terminal consequences.[75]

While nearly all narratives function in this manner, Shelley's narrative rhythms and temporal framing (Verney's recollection enclosed in the Sybil's prophecy), and her appropriation of the "Last Man" theme for her subject, make this "living dialectic" visible to the reader.

Superimposed upon the rhythm that leads the reader inexorably toward the future, there is a theme of "turning back" that occurs throughout *The Last Man*. Some of these reversals are physical. For example, after they have left Windsor, presumably never to return, Verney and Idris turn back toward Datchet to rescue Lucy Martin and her ailing mother, and, when Idris dies, Verney returns to Windsor to inter her with her ancestors. Later, when Adrian is detained in Versailles in an attempt to prevent the "accursed Impostors" (292) from seducing any more of Adrian's people to their cause, the officers refuse to obey Verney when he wants to return to Versailles. Despite the fact that at this point the plague has resumed its deadly toll with the advent of warmer weather and their only salvation seems to lie in reaching Switzerland, Verney denounces the refusal of the officers to go *backward* in the strongest terms, calling them "dastards" and "selfish and lawless men" (293). He alone returns to Versailles in a night-long ride (killing his horse in the process) and arrives just as the false prophet shoots himself.

These reversals of physical direction mirror a temporal reversal. We have previously seen that time in *The Mysteries of Udolpho* seems to run in circles. In *The Last Man,* it seems to run backward. Brian Nellist has pointed out that in *The Last Man* "history goes into reverse. Survivors from the U. S. A. land in Ireland and the Irish savagely invade England. The few English survivors muster under Adrian to seek warmer lands to die in and in effect invade Normandy."[76] Yet the temporal reversal is far more extensive, constituting a "rolling back" of the tides of civilization, as the plague progresses and the population declines. Distinctions of economic class are lost when the plague renders rich and poor equal, for "The grave yawned beneath us all . . ." (231). The declining population causes the survivors to become equal also in the labor that must be done—in fact, where the tasks of daily life are concerned, "the poor were the superior, since they entered on such tasks with alacrity and experience" (223). The dissolution of economic classes is echoed in references to rich and poor exchanging stations in death, in yet another reversal: "The wretched female, loveless victim of vulgar brutality, had wandered to the toilet of high-born beauty, and, arraying herself in the garb of splendour, had died before the mirror which reflected to herself alone her altered appearance. Women whose delicate feet had seldom touched the earth in their luxury, had fled in fright and horror from their homes, till, losing themselves in the squalid streets of the metropolis, they had died on the threshold of poverty" (232).

Shelley's representation of the unraveling of civilization (and the reversal of the progress of time) is depicted especially dramatically in two chapters that contain a series of "farewell to" statements in which civilization appears to lose attributes approximately in the reverse order of their acquisition. First comes the farewell to "the patriotic scene" and to nationalism; then to "the giant powers of man—to knowledge that could pilot the deep-drawing bark through the opposing waters of shoreless ocean,—to science that directed the silken balloon through the pathless air,—to the power that could put a barrier to mighty waters, and set in motion wheels, and beams, and vast machinery, that could divide rocks of granite or marble, and make the mountains plain!" (233) Verney bids farewell to "the arts,—to eloquence . . . to poetry and deep philosophy" and to architecture, sculpture, music, drama, and finally to joy. Later, Verney states that: "We had bidden adieu to the state of things, which, having existed many thousand years, seemed eternal . . . government, obedience, traffic, and domestic intercourse . . . patriotic zeal, to the arts, to reputation, to enduring fame, to the name of country . . . all expectation, except the feeble one of saving our individual lives from the wreck of the past" (300). There appears to be a definite sequence in what is lost: nationalism (when all her inhabitants have left her, Verney observes that "England remained, though England was dead" [264]), then scientific knowledge, then the arts. Poetry, sculpture, music, and drama, presumably being the most "primitive" of civilization's attributes (or at any rate the longest held), the arts are the last to disappear. While the sequence of attributes lost in Pope's apocalyptic vision at the end of *The Dunciad* is Fancy, Wit, Art, Truth, Philosophy, Metaphysics, Mathematics, Religion, Morality, until finally, "Nor *human* spark is left, nor glimpse *divine!*", in Shelley's version, the arts continue with Verney's recording of his history, before he abandons writing altogether at the end of the novel.[77]

Also lost in this great unraveling of civilization are generational distinctions: "The world has grown old, and all its inmates partook of the decrepitude. Why talk of infancy, manhood, and old age? We all stood equal sharers of the last throes of time-worn nature. Arrived at the same point of the world's age . . ." (231). Such a loss of generational distinctions, stands in marked contrast to Burke's vision, when, later in the same sentence as his "just correspondence and symmetry" statement, he asserts, "by the disposition of a stupendous wisdom, moulding together the great mysterious incorporation of the human race, the whole, at one time, is never old, or middle-aged, or young, but in a condition of unchangeable constancy, moves on through the varied tenor of perpetual decay, fall, renovation, and progression."[78] In effect, all have arrived at what Verney called "the abyss of the present" (337). Without the openness to the future that characterizes Heidegger's Care, without the prospect of generational succession, the present is an abyss indeed. The looming prospect of everyone's death would, in one sense, seem to exemplify Heidegger's assertion that "Care is being-toward-death." Yet, Heidegger goes on to ask, "in spite of my no longer being there, 'does time not go on?'" and he answers "in the affirmative."[79] Clearly, Shelley is challenging this affirmative response, or at least positing a situation in which it might be negated. If the imagined future does not include the existence of civilization—the society that shapes and gives meaning to time—it could be argued that time in fact does not go on. Burke refers to inheritance (specifically the binding of the British people to the *"heirs"* and *"posterity"* of William and Mary) as having been secured "to the end of time."[80] In Shelley's novel, we reach that point. We actually reach it twice, because the novel begins with England's transformation into a republic in 2073.

In *The Last Man,* civilization evaporates as the remnant of humanity reverts to primitivism, although there is a kind of Wordsworthian celebration of this simpler life. During a long and particularly cruel winter, society reverts to what Verney calls "patriarchal modes," "as in ancient times":

Youths, nobles of the land, performed for the sake of mother or sister, the services of menials with amiable cheerfulness. They went to the river to break the ice, and draw water: they assembled on foraging expeditions, or axe in hand felled the trees for fuel. The females received them on their return with the simple and affectionate welcome known before only to the lowly cottage—a clean hearth and bright fire; the supper ready cooked by beloved hands; gratitude for the provision for to-morrow's meal: strange enjoyments for the high-born English, yet they were now their sole, hard earned, and dearly prized luxuries. (223)

Wandering across the continent, the declining remnant of humanity is reminiscent of the biblical Israelites wandering in the wilderness, but as if they were returning to slavery, rather than escaping it. Moses-like,[81] Adrian is referred to as "our lawgiver and our preserver" (272). Their "tribe" is organized into "bands" and "at each of the large towns before mentioned, we were all to assemble; and a conclave of the principal officers would hold council for the general weal" (288), which is again reminiscent of the gatherings of the congregation of the Israelites. As they continue to wander and their numbers continue to dwindle, they dream more and more of a kind of Eden: "In the beginning of time, when, as now, man lived by families and not by tribes or nations, they were placed in a genial clime, where earth fed them untilled, and the balmy air enwrapt their reposing limbs with warmth more pleasant than beds of down. The south is the native place of the human race" (235). Their hope is to find a place on earth that has not been touched by the plague, and as this concept lays hold of their minds, their visions grow increasingly romantic and utopian: "Perhaps in some secluded nook, amidst eternal spring, and waving trees, and purling streams, we may find Life" (237). The Tree of Life, one might almost say.

As the human population in *The Last Man* continues to dwindle, societal concepts disappear. Time itself loses its meaning as the four survivors of the plague wander through Italy, although they do establish daily routines. Verney notes that the four survivors "made laws for ourselves, dividing our day, and fixing distinct occupations for each hour" (313). Even gender disappears as an attribute, once Clara, who was the last to have all the "feminine and maiden virtues" (328), is dead.

The ultimate unraveling of time occurs when Verney is left alone on earth. As William Lomax has observed, "as the Last Man, he is also automatically the First Man."[82] Once alone, Verney, who compares his situation to Robinson Crusoe's, attempts to keep a record of the passage of time by marking the days on a willow wand, but gives up only twenty-five days after the deaths of the others. In the absence of all human society, there is no longer any need for public time, which he decisively rejects when he breaks his willow wand in despair. His own voice begins to sound strange to his ears, so little does he use it, and eventually all discourse ceases, including writing, once he has committed his history to paper. In a sense he has returned to a time before Adam could "write."

The turning back of time occurs also at a physiological level for Verney. He first experiences an interruption in the progress of time when, "on the third night" of his illness, "animation was suspended" (249). In effect, he has died and has been reborn, Christ-like, after three days. His recovery, remarkable for his being the only person in the novel who contracts the plague and does not die, is the more miraculous in that it results in his health being significantly *improved* in comparison to what it had been before his illness. The illness fatal to everyone else becomes Verney's *elixir vitae*, and not only is his recovery itself reminiscent of St. Leon's rejuvenation, he even uses Godwin's terms: "the wheels and springs of my life, once again set in motion, acquired *elasticity* from their short suspension" (250, emphasis added). Verney prospers in recovery, with "renewed vigour" and "cheerful current" of blood, even while Idris's health fades alarmingly.[83] Verney had previously used the same mechanical imagery to describe Idris's consumption: "she felt, she said, as if all the wheels and springs of the animal machine worked at double rate, and were fast consuming themselves" (219). But for Verney, the plague seems to have renewed him by first stopping the progress of his life and subsequently resetting his biological clock to a younger and more vigorous age. He is almost a superman: "[M]ethought I could emulate the speed of the racehorse, discern through the air objects at a blinding distance, hear the operations of nature in her mute abodes; my senses had become so refined and susceptible after my recovery from mortal disease" (250–51).

At the end of the novel, he describes his project to write the history of the Last Man as an "occupation best fitted to discipline my melancholy thoughts, which had strayed backwards, over many a ruin, and through many a flowery glade, even to the mountain recess, from which in early youth I had first emerged" (339). Thus Verney's narrative itself constitutes a reversal of time. While all narrative at least figuratively accomplishes this temporal reversal— "the past is . . . read as present . . . in relation to a future we know to be already in place, already in wait for us to reach it"[84]—what is figurative in most narratives is explicit in *The Last Man*. At the end of the novel Verney is in a state quite similar to his early, rebellious youth as a shepherd, as he prepares to roam, not the fields and valleys of England, but the oceans of the world, once again accompanied by a faithful shepherd dog. Even the dog, whom Verney had discovered still tending sheep long after its master had died, has participated in the temporal reversal as he too has reacquired a

companion.[85] For Verney and his new companion, the "time after
. . . is an image of the time before."[86]

In one of the many paradoxes that add dramatic tension to *The
Last Man,* all these incidents of the apparent reversal in the flow of
time occur in opposition to repeated statements that time cannot
be rolled back. That notion of mortal man's inability to reverse time
is first introduced in the context of interpersonal relationships, specifically when Lord Raymond realizes that he is in love with
Evadne: "Genius, devotion, and courage; the adornments of his
mind, and the energies of his soul, all exerted to their uttermost
stretch, could not roll back one hair's breadth the wheel of time's
chariot; that which had been was written with the adamantine pen
of reality, on the everlasting volume of the past; nor could agony
and tears suffice to wash out one iota from the act fulfilled" (87).
After Lord Raymond departs suddenly for Greece, Verney attempts
to console Perdita: "[U]ntil I could persuade her that the Past could
be unacted, that maturity could go back to the cradle, and that all
that was could become as though it had never been, it was useless
to assure her that no real change had taken place in her fate"
(112). Later, man's inability to reverse the flow of time is demonstrated even more dramatically when Perdita drowns herself and
her body is pulled aboard the vessel: "No care could re-animate
her, no medicine cause her dear eyes to open, and the blood to flow
again from her pulseless heart" (155). Similar echoes of this frustration occur as loved ones die throughout the novel. When Idris
dies, Verney lifts her from the carriage where she had slumped over
and observes that "her heart was pulseless, her faded lips unfanned
by the slighted breath." Yet he still brings her into the cottage, lights
a fire and chafes her "stiffening limbs . . . for two long hours" in a
futile attempt to revive her (258).[87]

In a sense, what Verney achieves by the end of the novel is a temporal reversal, a qualified version of what he had earlier used as an
example of the impossible, that "the Past could be unacted, that
maturity could go back to the cradle, and that all that was could
become as though it had never been" (112). But the reversal is a
limited one, for Verney is no longer the rebellious shepherd boy he
was. His hair is "nearly grey" (340) and he has the full and painful
knowledge ("self-knowledge . . . tenfold sadness" [337]) of what he
has lost, much as Wordsworth does upon revisiting Tintern Abbey.

Even nature participates in this temporal reversal. As I have previously noted, the seasons rarely behave as they should, from the
first moment of the "Author's Introduction," where the winter is
actually spring-like. Phenomena such as a black sun that rises in

the west and sets in the east depict occasional reversals of the normal progress of the celestial bodies, mirroring the unraveling of civilization as its forward progress is halted and reversed, and eventually, when only Verney is left alive, all social groups and meanings have disappeared.

Just as Carolan and the ancient Celtic bards are seen as the fulfillment of their races in the eighteenth-century's "last of the race" myths, at several points in the novel, *The Last Man*'s narrator achieves an ultimate perspective that encompasses all of time and history. This first occurs shortly after his first encounter with a plague victim, a solitary cottager, and again later, while looking out over England on a wintry midnight following the discovery of the plague among Idris's servants. Verney's narration, from a vantage point that takes in all of history, yet is actually a prophecy from ancient times, (a subsequent narrative embedded within a prior narrative) represents still another reversal of perspective. The numerous temporal and spatial reversals are held in tension against the signs of time's inexorable forward movement: deaths, recurrent descriptions of ruins, and small details, such as the rotting meal in the deserted Italian cottage or the discovery of Lord Ryland's body devoured by insects.

It is tempting to assert that *The Last Man*'s emphasis on the desire to reverse time despite overwhelming evidence that time cannot be rolled back owes much to Mary Shelley's own circumstances, including the losses of her husband, three children, and half-sister during the preceding years. Time continued to bring fresh tragedies, and the desire to master it, to stand it on its head, is hardly surprising. But it is so easy to see Mary Shelley's life in her fiction that one can lose sight of her skills as a writer. As Gregory O'Dea has observed, purely biographical readings of *The Last Man* "tend to ignore the novel's philosophical and thematic content, and implicitly resist the thought that Shelley had ideas to examine independent of her circumstances and acquaintances." And Lee Sterrenburg, calling the novel "intellectually ambitious," sees in it and its disease metaphors an "encyclopedic survey of a number of political positions, including utopianism, Bonapartism, and revolutionary enthusiasms of various kinds."[88] On the other hand, Shelley's life and her fiction were clearly interrelated, and the lives and deaths of Percy Shelley and Lord Byron may have served as catalysts for what became a comprehensive exploration into the nature of time and narrative.

Lionel Verney admits that he has used the writing of his history "as an opiate; while it described my beloved friends, fresh with life and glowing with hope; active assistants on the scene, I was soothed" (192), much as *Udolpho* is haunted by the spectralized presence of the departed. The limbs of Verney's friends have been chafed by the fire and they have lived, but their reanimation is transitory, ending at the very moment in which he concludes his task and, as Genette would express it, the narrative approaches the story: "I . . . recorded with sacred zeal the virtues of my companions. They have been with me during the fulfilment of my task. I have brought it to an end—I lift my eyes from my paper—again they are lost to me. Again I feel that I am alone" (339).[89]

Verney's use of the word "opiate" and the dramatic rendering of the moment at which his narrative ends and he experiences his loss afresh—significant departures from Radcliffe's approach—strongly suggest Shelley's awareness that the consolation offered by narrative is limited. Yet despite its limitations as an emotional outlet, she clearly had a fascination with the power and limitations of narrative. Depressed after her return to England subsequent to her husband's death, her depression deepened by her inability to write, she recorded in her journal on June 8, 1824, just three weeks after learning of Lord Byron's death in Greece:

> The lamp of thought is again illumined in my heart—& the fire descends from heaven that kindles it . . .
> I feel my powers again—& this is of itself happiness—the eclipse of winter is passing from my mind—I shall again feel the enthusiastic glow of composition—again as I pour forth my soul upon paper, feel the winged ideas arise, & enjoy the delight of expressing them—study & occupation will be a pleasure not a task—& this I shall owe to sight & companionship of trees & meadows flowers & sunshine. . . .[90]

This Promethean entry reveals that for Mary Shelley, narrative is not an opiate to assuage personal grief but a *power,* and there is pleasure in its exercise. At this point, she had already begun *The Last Man,* in which she wove together the work of grieving, the cultural preoccupation with apocalyptic narratives, and the exploration of new novelistic techniques. Where she experimented with the "Chinese box" narrative structure in *Frankenstein,* in *The Last Man,* Shelley was more ambitious: Instead of a symmetrical structure of interlocked narratives, she experimented with multiple timescapes, with her own recent past enclosing a remote past that in turn enclosed a distant future, a temporal schema that explodes the concept of linear time.

But *The Last Man*'s framing is curiously asymmetrical (much as *Melmoth the Wanderer*'s is) and all of its narratives are open-ended.

Verney's account ends with his preparation to embark on his sea voyage; we never return either to the time of the Sibyl or to the time of the "Author." In fact, the Introduction has emphasized the possible unreliability of the pattern formed by the Author's arrangement of the leaves, rendering the "future . . . already in wait for us to reach it" uncertain.[91] The closest we come to narrative symmetry is Verney's experience of what we would call *déjà vu* as he gazes over the once familiar, now deserted, landscape of Windsor to which he has returned so that Idris could be entombed with her royal ancestors: "To this painful recognition of familiar places, was added a feeling experienced by all, understood by none—a feeling as if in some state, less visionary than a dream, in some past real existence, I had seen all I saw, with precisely the same feelings as I now beheld them—*as if all my sensations were a duplex mirror of a former revelation*" (264, emphasis added). Verney's experience is exactly the phenomenon that Heidegger described as the " 'Moment' " of vision ("Augen*blick*") that unifies the "*ecstasies* of temporality." Verney has introduced "expectation into memory . . . as the future of what is remembered,"[92] so in that moment of vision, the novel's temporal framing is laid bare to the protagonist.

The temporal framing that characterizes *The Last Man,* the tendency to embed stories such as Lucy Martin's and Juliet's, and the framing in *Frankenstein* all suggest a Maturin-like fascination with embedded narratives; there is always one more level of embedding to be discovered. A clue to this fascination may lie in Shelley's 1829 review of Anna Brownell Jameson's *The Loves of the Poets:* "[A Poet's] soul is like one of the pools in the Ilex woods of the Maremma, it reflects the surrounding universe, but it beautifies, groupes, and mellows their tints, making a little world within itself, the copy of the outer one; but more entire, more faultless."[93] The monster's narrative in *Frankenstein* is more "idealized" (as Coleridge would have put it), more "faultless" or true, than Victor's (and Safie's letters are even more so).[94] Verney's narrative in *The Last Man,* and the stories it encloses, may themselves be faultless, but the medium on which they are recorded, and the process of ordering the events are corruptible, because they belong to "the surrounding universe." This corruptibility may be what Coleridge had in mind when he said that the secondary imagination *struggles* ("to idealize and to unify").[95] But despite such limitations, the "Author" notes that her "labours" to "model the work into a consistent form"—to fashion coherence by idealizing and unifying—have transported her from her own world "to one glowing with imagination and power" (Author's Introduction 4). The ability to enter that

world of imagination and power—whether as a reader or a writer—
is, after all, one of narrative's most enduring qualities. We recall
Ricoeur's three phases of mimesis: the artist's "pre-understanding
of the world of action, . . . [including] its temporal character" (*mimesis*$_1$); the plotting or configuring function (*mimesis*$_2$); and "the
intersection of the world of the text and the world of the hearer or
reader; the intersection, therefore, of the world configured by the
poem and the world wherein real action occurs and unfolds its specific temporality" (*mimesis*$_3$).[96]

Kairos

Even though *The Last Man* is itself an extended flashback, for
the most part the narrator tells his story within the timeline of his
narration, occasionally moving forward and backward a few months
or a year. Superimposed upon this rhythm, and providing another
of the novel's experiments with historical perspective, is the intrusion by the narrator—the Lionel Verney of c. 2100, at various points
throughout the text. This device is particularly effective in propelling *The Last Man* toward its conclusion. Thus, at the moment
when Verney begins his history with his archetypal "I AM," he splits
into two Verneys, one who is in a sense omniscient (and omni-temporal), and the other, whose knowledge is limited to that which he
himself possessed as he experienced the events that form the
novel. At significant points in the novel, the "2100-Verney" makes
his presence known, usually, but not always, at the beginning of a
chapter. With the exception of his introductory paragraph, which
sets the stage for his history, the first intrusion of the 2100-Verney
occurs midway through volume 1, shortly after Verney first meets
Idris, in the course of describing a number of visits by Adrian and
Idris to his cottage. He suddenly interjects: "Oh my pen! Haste
thou to write what was, before the thought of what is, arrests the
hand that guides thee. If I lift up my eyes and see the desart earth,
and feel that those dear eyes have spent their mortal lustre, and
that those beauteous lips are silent, their 'crimson leaves' faded, for
ever I am mute!" (57) After describing the declaration of love between Verney and Idris as they contemplate the evening star, the
2100-Verney reflects on the power of memory, in terms reminiscent of Wordsworth's "spots of time."[97] "Veiled for ever to the
world's callous eye must be the transport of that moment. Still do I
feel her graceful form press against my full-fraught heart—still
does sight, and pulse, and breath sicken and fail, at the remembrance of that first kiss" (58). Following this interjection, we do not

hear from the 2100-Verney for some time, until about halfway through volume 2, when chapter 6 begins, "I have lingered thus long on the extreme bank, the wasting shoal that stretched into the stream of life, dallying with the shadow of death. Thus long, I have cradled my heart in retrospection of past happiness, when hope was. . . . But the same sentiment that first led me to portray scenes replete with tender recollections, now bids me hurry on" (173). This chapter in particular contains a curious mixture of tenses that lends an immediacy to the recounting of events. At one point Verney states, "The plague was in London! Fools that we were not long ago to have foreseen this" (179), but on the next page, he uses the present tense: "But we are awake now. The plague is in London; the air of England is tainted, and her sons and daughters strew the unwholesome earth."

The 2100-Verney's intrusions now begin to take place more frequently. Chapter 8 of volume 2 begins:

> After a long interval, I am again impelled by the restless spirit within me to continue my narration; but I must alter the mode which I have hitherto adopted. . . . I had used this history as an opiate; while it described my beloved friends, fresh with life and glowing with hope; active assistants on the scene, I was soothed; there will be a more melancholy pleasure in painting the end of all. But the intermediate steps, the climbing the wall, raised up between what was and is, while I still looked back nor saw the concealed desert beyond, is a labour past my strength. Time and experience have placed me on an height from which I can comprehend the past as a whole; and in this way I must describe it, bringing forward the leading incidents, and disposing light and shade so as to form a picture in whose very darkness there will be harmony. (192–93)

Here is the "retrospectively synoptic view of human history" that Cantor described, the future "already in place, already in wait for us to reach it."[98] Shelley has made the object of her narration the story of the human race itself, the heroism and pathos of its dying hours.

But just as time demands human society to give it meaning, narratives demand readers. While describing the labors of tending the sick and comforting the sorrowing in chapter 1 of volume 3, the 2100-Verney suddenly addresses his readers: "Have any of you, my readers, observed the ruins of an anthill immediately after its destruction?" (230). This is his first direct address to his presumed readers *as* readers, who, at the time he begins his history, do not seem to exist, but whom he seems compelled to invent,[99] because narrative "seems ever to imagine in advance the act of its transmission, the moment of reading and understanding that it cannot itself ever know, since this act always comes after the writing, in a posthumous moment."[100]

The 2100-Verney's intrusions are sometimes darkly prophetic, as, early in volume 3, when he refers to Adrian's energy and cheerfulness, and first uses the phrase "LAST MAN": "[Y]ou could not guess that he was about to lead forth from their native country, the numbered remnant of the English nation, into the tenantless realms of the south, there to die, one by one, till the LAST MAN should remain in a voiceless, empty world" (240). By the time the reader arrives at volume 3, the pace of the novel accelerates dramatically, as we have already seen in our discussion of the progress of the remnant of humanity across the landscape. The narrator's intrusions add to this effect. In sharp contrast to the slow lingering over events in volume 1, the 2100-Verney's intrusions occur more rapidly and reinforce the effect of haste. As he notes, "hours charioted us towards the chasm" (197). Even the pace of diurnal cycles seems strangely altered: "But it was winter now . . . we became ephemera, to whom the interval between the rising and setting sun was as a long drawn year of common time. We should never see our children ripen into maturity . . ." (198). Part of the accelerating effect stems from a conscious decision by the 2100-Verney to alter his narrative technique and to compress events (perhaps to alleviate his own grief as well as out of consideration for his invented audience), and, in so doing, strengthening the connection between time and narrative. Of the journey across France, he says: "If I were to dissect each incident, every small fragment of a second would contain an harrowing tale, whose minutest word would curdle the blood in thy young veins. It is right that I should erect for thy instruction this monument of the foregone race; but not that I should drag thee through the wards of an hospital, nor the secret chambers of the charnel-house. This tale, therefore, shall be rapidly unfolded" (291). But not rapidly enough for the critics, one of whom complained about the "sickening repetition of horrors," which were viewed as a "strange misapplication of considerable talent," a theme echoed by another reviewer, who thought the novel bore "the impress of genius, though perverted and spoiled by morbid affectation," and generally characterized it as "the offspring of a diseased imagination, and of a most polluted taste."[101]

Later, in chapter 8, as the time lines of the two Verneys begin to converge, it becomes difficult to separate their respective knowledge, as the fatal knowledge of the 2100-Verney infects the consciousness of the Verney character. At the burial service for the last plague victim, leaving only Adrian, Verney, Clara, and Evelyn surviving, he observes that, "From this moment I saw plague no more" and goes on to reflect, "My present feelings are so mingled with the past, that I cannot say whether the knowledge of this change visited us, as we stood on this sterile spot. It seems to me that it did; that a cloud seemed to pass from over us, that a weight was taken from the air" (309–10). It is now no longer possible for 2100-Verney to maintain a distinction between his own perspective (the time of the narration) and what the Verney in the time line of the story knows, hence the knowledge that none of the four were to die of the plague. The "time of the signified and the time of the signifier" begin to converge.[102]

And only a short time later, Verney begins the next-to-last chapter of the novel by explicitly reminding us what lies ahead: "Now— soft awhile—have I arrived so near the end? Yes! *It is all over now*—a step or two over those new made graves, and the wearisome way is done" (318, emphasis added.) Writing has at last become a mixed blessing. Like the memories of Shelley's loved ones, who seem to live and breathe again as she reads the old letters found in her desk, and like Valerius and Roger Dodsworth, humanity has temporarily been reanimated. But bringing back Verney's loved ones has also caused him to experience anew the pain of losing them, and he expresses this pain in a rage that the disaster that has destroyed humanity has left nature untouched and has also stripped him of an audience. Indeed, he becomes his own final audience/auditor/reader:

> Arise, black Melancholy! Quit thy Cimmerian solitude! Bring with thee murky fogs from hell, which may drink up the day; bring blight and pestiferous exhalations, which, entering the hollow caverns and breathing places of earth, may fill her stony veins with corruption, so that not only herbage may no longer flourish, the trees may rot, and the rivers run with gall—but the everlasting mountains be decomposed, and the mighty deep putrify, and the the genial atmosphere which clips the globe, lose all powers of generation and sustenance. Do this, sad visaged power, while I write, while eyes read these pages.
> And who will read them? (318)

Despite the extreme melancholy of this passage, the characters in *The Last Man* sometimes reflect a capacity for joy that seems extraordinary, given their circumstances. Although Verney, Adrian, Clara, and Evelyn are alone, they have complete freedom, including the freedom to shape their daily rhythms, and thus control time. Verney notes that the four survivors "made laws for ourselves, dividing our day, and fixing distinct occupations for each hour" (313). And they seem satisfied by the small scope of their society: "Of what consequence was it to our four hearts, that they alone were the fountains of life in the wide world?" (312). This passage, along with the five-year idyll discussed earlier, confounds Anne Mellor's thesis that this novel, and indeed all of Shelley's fiction, idealizes the bourgeois family, for in both occasions in which the author rhapsodizes about those particular intervals, the group is an oddly configured "family."[103] And at the end of the novel, Lionel Verney is determined to face his future and improve himself through study, much as Shelley in 1823 was determined to continue to improve herself in the face of widowhood, financial difficulties, and her rejection by polite society. Resolving to "sit amidst the ruins and smile" (290–91), to create his own future, and accompanied only by his dog and his books, Verney sails away on the same ocean that took his companions from him, a way of confronting and transcending his fears that was characteristic of Mary Shelley as well, an attitude that Heidegger would characterize as "anticipatory resoluteness." In *The Last Man,* Shelley envisions a world stripped of all human relationships, and through Verney, she even allows herself to imagine a future without her "powers." To live authentically means to confront our own "being-toward-death."[104]

When Verney abandons writing and sails away into myth, he also abandons the secondary imagination. It has served its purpose. All that remains, all that he needs, it would seem, is Imagination in its pure and primary form: "I shall witness all the variety of appearance, that the elements can assume" (342). But he will not write of it. Writing is an act of remembering, of *re*-creating. It is oriented toward the past, but at this point in the novel, because human history has been remembered and narrated, it is essentially complete. Verney's thoughts turn toward the future. Heidegger notes that "the future has priority in the ecstatic unity of primordial and authentic temporality," because *Da-sein,* or "being-in-the-world," involves a self-awareness that looks toward its own future—including its own non-existence. It is "being-toward-the end."[105] Verney is not preoccupied by the minutiae of the present, and he is no longer burdened with remembering.

Therefore, when he abandons discourse, Verney re-emerges from history and also abandons the past tense. Time for Verney is *kairos,* "charged with a meaning derived from its relation to the end."[106] His plan to sail away to the south is yet to happen at the time of his last writing—it is the future tense, the tense of the Sibyl, and hence one more representation of the myriad uncertainties which permeate the novel. During the sea voyage that claimed the lives of Adrian and Clara, Verney was terrified by his vision of the smallness of their craft upon the vast ocean: "The vast universe, its myriad worlds, and the plains of boundless earth which we had left—the extent of shoreless sea around—contracted to my view— they and all that they contained, shrunk up to one point, even to our tossing bark, freighted with glorious humanity" (321). This vision of humanity "tossing" amid the vastness of space is also a figure for the gulf of time in which we find ourselves similarly afloat. The contraction of Verney's universe to a single point hauntingly anticipates the twentieth-century cosomological view of the universe in the moments before the Big Bang—the *ultimate* unraveling of space *and* time, and thus the ultimate dissolution, much as "The Mortal Immortal"'s Winzy hopes, "by scattering and annihilating the atoms that compose my frame, [to] set at liberty the life imprisoned within," so that his spirit can "soar[] from this dim earth to a sphere more congenial to its immortal essence."[107] Yet another cycle of creation is implied here; now Verney *embraces* what he then feared, using the same terms. Abandoning his "height from which [he] can comprehend the past as a whole" (192–93) in favor of sea level and a future he comprehends not at all, no longer "I AM," he is only the "freight" of a "tiny bark," beneath the "ever-open eye of the Supreme."

Yet is not that Supreme known as "I AM" in the Judeo-Christian mythos? Again, we are returned to the words that begin the narrative, reminding us once again that this is "a duplex mirror of a former revelation." Peter Brooks's statement that the end of a narrative leads us to "a time after which is an image of the time before," comes in the sense of our having "reached the non-narratable." What can be after the end, which lies outside Ricoeur's "circle of narrativity," in which "[t]ime becomes human time to the extent that it is organized after the manner of a narrative; [and] narrative, in turn, is meaningful to the extent that it portrays the features of temporal existence"?[108] At the end of *The Last Man*, neither narrative nor human time applies, so the Burkean model has been demolished. There is only an inarticulable and aporetic no-time. Paradoxically, however, Shelley has narrated us to the brink of the un-narratable where it seems somehow almost within our grasp.

In attaining this perspective, Shelley uses narrative, with all its temporal trappings, to suggest the transcendence of the world of time and narrative. But the paradoxical is the norm in *The Last Man,* which constructs a temporal dialectic, just as cultural fears of degeneration lead to the construction of myths of a "Last Man" who represents, not the end of civilization, but its fulfillment, a Last Man who is also a First Man, a dialectic of origins and ends, "the ending in the beginning and the beginning in the end." The novel's numerous apparent reversals of time, mirrored by the metaphorical reversals in physical space, occur in opposition to what we "know" to be time's one-way arrow, as if we are looking through the wrong end of a telescope. Indeed, our intrinsic knowledge of the nature of time is affirmed by the novel's constant images of death, ruin, and decay. Nor can we fail to be perplexed by the uncertainties that multiply as rapidly as the temporal reversals. Verney's narration, from a vantage point which takes in all of history ("an height from which I can comprehend the past as a whole" [192]), yet framed by a prophecy that is of doubtful accuracy and may or may not come true, represents yet another aporetic uncertainty.[109]

TABLE 2
Time Shifts and Temporal Positions in Selected Chapters of Mary Shelley's **The Last Man.**

Volume/ Chapter	Description of Events	# of Time Shifts	# of Temporal Positions	# of Pages	Shifts per Page
1.9	Marital Troubles	140	49	13.25	10.57
2.6	Alfred's Birthday/Plague in London	58	24	12.75	4.55
3.10	Final chapter	72	30	14.50	4.97

4

Aporia in the House: Three Sensation Novels

The progress of geological and paleontological studies in the first half of the nineteenth century, climaxed by Alfred Wallace's and Charles Darwin's simultaneous announcement of the theory of biological evolution (1858) . . . made it evident that "the past" had to be measured not in centuries or millennia but by geological ages stretching back hundreds of thousands of years. The nebular hypothesis of the origin of the solar system— that the sun and its planets resulted from the cooling of superheated gaseous masses in space—had a similar effect. Although the hypothesis itself, the product of eighteenth-century speculation, now was rejected by most astronomers, it continued to have a powerful impact on the popular mind. The human imagination had to adjust itself to staggering new concepts of time derived not only from the age of the earth but from the even more immense spans involved in the nebular process.

The adjustment profoundly affected the Victorians' view of their own place in the cosmic sequence.

—Richard D. Altick, *Victorian People and Ideas*

In 1859, the year that Wilkie Collins began writing *The Woman in White*, Karl Marx published *A Contribution to the Critique of Political Economy*, John Stuart Mill published *An Essay on Liberty*, and Charles Darwin published *The Origin of Species*. Like Collins's novel, each of these texts mounts an elaborate investigation into the past that produces a radical reinterpretation of the present.

—Ronald R. Thomas, "Wilkie Collins and the Sensation Novel"

BY THE 1860s, THE BURKEAN MODEL OF COHERENT TRANSMISSION across generations was under assault on a number of fronts. Cultural attitudes toward time had shifted markedly since the eighteenth century, as a consequence of both revolutionary and evolutionary forces. If the French Revolution brought a new awareness of the present as a rupture between past and future, continuing developments in the sciences, religion, and history only exacerbated this phenomenon. Some milestones include Jean-

Baptiste de Lamarck's *Philosophie zoologique,* published in 1809, and Sir Charles Lyell's *Principles of Geology* in 1830,[1] and the so-called Higher Criticism of Germans such as David Friedrich Strauss, whose *Das Leben Jesu* (*Life of Jesus*), published in Germany in 1835 (and translated into English by George Eliot in 1846). Such publications, along with technological developments—the communications revolution brought about by the advent of the railway, the telegraph, and the cheap postal system[2]—contributed to a profound temporal hyperawareness and self-consciousness about the period's uniqueness. The sciences continued to emphasize the earth's great age, as well as the notion that the human race was the product of the inexorable processes of time. Victorian society was characterized by "the oscillations of an existence torn between the sense of its mortality and the silent presence of the immensity of time enveloping all things."[3] Nor were all these new ideas confined to the disciplines from which they emerged.

Nineteenth-century periodicals had a large readership and covered a wide range of subjects; and such ideas found their way into popular literature as well. Tennyson's 1850 elegy, *In Memoriam, A. H. H.* refers at least twice to the nebular hypothesis of the origin of the solar system, and in this passage also addresses emerging evolutionary theory:

> They say,
> The solid earth whereon we tread
> In tracts of fluent heat began,
>   And grew to seeming-random forms,
>   The seeming prey of cyclic storms,
> Till at the last arose the man
>
>   (118. 7–12)

And of course Tennyson's memorable phrase, "Nature, red in tooth and claw,"[4] wonderfully captured the anxiety and even horror that accompanied the revolution in thinking about the processes that became known as natural selection. Indeed, one of the consequences of the nineteenth century's scientific discoveries was an increase in "fears of racial, national, and biological degeneration spawned by Charles Darwin's theories of evolution,"[5] a narrative of history that competes with Burke's. These fears mark a significant reversal of the Burkean optimism about the "sure principle of transmission," or, for that matter, at the opposite end of the eighteenth-century political spectrum, Godwin's doctrine of perfectibility. We have seen in the previous chapter that the popularity of "last of the race" themes reflected growing anxieties about degeneration. As the nineteenth century progressed, the future increasingly came to be seen as at least potentially threatening. If evolutionary processes can work progressively, they might work regressively as well, and threaten cherished institutions such as the church and the family. Rebecca Stern notes that, "[a]lthough evolutionary theory provided soothing answers to questions of human nature, the threat of degeneration spawned new and different fears about the future of humankind, most especially about the future of the nuclear family."[6] These fears were exacerbated by the advent of legalized divorce in 1857 and the lurid accounts of Divorce Court proceedings in the popular press.

Nor was evolutionary theory the only concern engendered by scientific research. "According to the second law of thermodynamics, announced in 1850 and immediately adopted by Dickens for the running imagery of *Bleak House,* the irreversible conversion of energy to heat in the cosmos will ultimately turn it into a lifeless mass of incandescence."[7] Clearly, emerging scientific theories captured the imagination of the public through popular literature.

In addition to the mixed blessings afforded by the pace of Victorian scientific developments in the theoretical realm were those similarly mixed blessings that constituted the fruits of developments in the realm of applied technology, particularly the advent of the railroad, at once the pride of Britain, and the source of a whole new set of anxieties. Nicholas Daly points out that the railways brought with them "a heightened consciousness of time . . . transform[ing] the Victorian experience of time as well as space" because "the train brought with it standard time. Before the railway's advent numerous local times flourished. . . . Standardized time and the strict time-tabling of trains ushered in time-consciousness. The modern traveler needed to have a watch, and anxiety about missing trains became a recognizable medical complaint, as the title of a contemporary monograph, *Hurried to Death,* suggests." Note that what began as a means to improve linear travel, to render the traversing of space less time consuming, transformed the very concept of time itself. One had to conform to this newly standardized time. In Heideggerian terms, public time assumes ever more control over the individual. The public time of the clock and calendar originally served as a means of reconciling the time of the individual to the time of the universe by using the movements of celestial bodies to divide the vastness of time into digestible segments. In a way, it functioned on the temporal plane as a medium of exchange, like a monetary system. But, as standard, public time begins to assume increasing importance, it ceases to function as a means of reconciliation and requires that the individual reconcile his own existence to its demands. Its degree of control increases in direct relationship to one's perception of it as a commodity that can only decrease. If the railways made England smaller, they also compressed time, a temporal transformation that informs popular literature of the period. As Daly observes,"the sensation novel came to play a part in the transformation of human experience of time and space which was being effected by the railways (and by the telegraph and the cheap postal system, the principal elements of the communications revolution that accompanied the railways)."[8]

The phenomenon of serial publication was seen as both a consequence and a contributing cause of the harried and hurried pace of everyday life; in an 1862 review of three sensation novels, Margaret Oliphant complained about "[t]he violent stimulant of serial publication—of *weekly* publication—with its necessity for frequent and rapid recurrence of piquant incident and startling situation."[9]

The decade of the 1860s was the decade of sensation fiction. The sensation novel seems to have burst onto the scene, experienced a brief, dizzying period of popularity, and then, at least according to some critics, it began to fade from fashion, although its influence would continue to be felt for years to come.[10] The three novels often regarded as having established the sensation fiction genre, Wilkie Collins's *The Woman in White,* (serialized 1859–60), Mrs. Henry Wood's *East Lynne* (serialized 1860–61), and Mary Elizabeth Braddon's *Lady Audley's Secret* (serialized 1861–62), are the subject of this chapter.[11] While much as been written about these novels in recent years, their embedded discourses on temporality have been largely ignored by most critics. In fact, I will argue that temporal discourse, far from being just an interesting footnote, forms a major plot element in these novels and contributes to their popularity by encoding a series of concerns about the ways time becomes socially constructed in the 1860s. The novels' discourses on time are part of the timeliness (in both senses of the word) that critics saw as characteristic of the genre, for they reflect prevailing developments in society. A series of legislative initiatives occurred alongside the scientific and technological developments already mentioned. The British Parliament began to take an increasingly active role in legislating social change, from the first Reform Bill of 1832 through the Child Custody Act of 1839, the Matrimonial Causes Act of 1857, the second Reform Bill of 1867, and the Married Women's Property Act of 1870.[12] This legislation helped to transform individuals' social identities and relationships, particularly that of marriage. Marriage had formerly been associated with closure and finality; it was the traditional plot device that resolved discontinuities and ensured the orderly transmission of property to the next generation. Now it seemed more problematic.

Also transforming identity was the rapid increase in the middle class and in consumer culture, leading to "anxieties about the breakdown of established class relationships and the mutability of social roles" and "debates about the nature of identity and the limits of the inner self."[13] All three novels that I will discuss depict assumptions of identities that create aporetic situations, situations that the texts have difficulty articulating. *The Woman in White*'s Percival Glyde attempts to alter the circumstances of his birth by fabricating a marriage between his parents (retroactively resolving the discontinuities in the "narrative" of his life); the title character in *Lady Audley's Secret* changes her name and marries a baronet, even though she is already married; and *East Lynne*'s Isabel Vane rises from her deathbed and takes another name so that she can return to her home and children as their governess. In all three cases, as we shall see, narrative plays a significant role in attempting to resolve the contradictions that have been created, for the desire to make sense of our lives in time by constructing a coherent narrative is as strong as ever; yet the contradictions threaten to overwhelm the ability of narrative to achieve coherence. And in all three cases, even death fails to provide a complete resolution of the aporia. In fact, the only "resolution" that can be achieved is through the imposition of a social taboo—a prohibition against speaking of the matter (by not speaking the offending name). This results in a social constraint against articulating the inarticulable. If we *cannot* articulate it, then we *will* not.

In the sensation novel of the 1860s, the past is the source of a secret transgression such as bigamy or murder that threatens to undermine stability in the present, just as the debate over evolutionary theory creates public awareness of a "deep time" that haunts the present. "Sensation novels, . . . consistently obsessed with some historical threat, repeatedly manifest an anxiety about some dangerous secret from the past, something volatile and destructive to the present that has been repressed and will certainly burst forth with violence into the present. By so doing, they narrate and resolve the very historical anxieties that were manifested in the emerging economic, political, and scientific theories with which this literature was contemporary."[14] Although these secret transgressions have been concealed, the past will not stay buried. Sometimes the secret is revealed in a deathbed confession (such as in Wilkie Collins's *The Dead Secret*), and sometimes it is discovered by a detective, who reconstructs the narrative of past events based on fragmentary evidence. In this way, the Gothic themes of usurpation become particularized, individualized, and domesticated. No longer buried in the distant past, the sensation novel's secrets lie in the more immediate past. They are private transgressions, but they still threaten the orderly transmission of property, titles, and values. *The Woman in White, Lady Audley's Secret,* and *East Lynne* deal with Burkean issues of descent and inheritance in the age of Darwin.

The contemporary settings of the sensation novel were often remarked upon by reviewers at the time. In H. L. Mansel's famous 1863 review of twenty-four sensation novels, he states, "[t]he sensation novel, be it mere trash or something worse, is usually a tale of our own times." Henry James also noted the contemporaneity of the genre in his review of *Lady Audley's Secret,* saying that "[t]he novelty lay in the heroine being, not a picturesque Italian of the fourteenth century, but an English gentlewoman of the current year, familiar with the use of the railway and the telegraph. The intense probability of the story is constantly reiterated. Modern England—the England of to-day's newspaper—crops up at every step."[15] James's use of the term *probability* refers to more than an adherence to realistic detail. Christopher Kent has described the intense interest in statistical theory that took place at this time, noting that "thinking about probability underwent a significant reorientation" as phenomena traditionally regarded as random events showed patterns of regularity. The publication in 1857 of Henry Thomas Buckle's *History of Civilization* "proclaimed the advent of a truly scientific history" and, among other things, called attention to "the law-like regularity of the suicide rate," a phenomenon which had hitherto been regarded as entirely random. Such details apparently fascinated Charles Dickens; quoting Percy Fitzgerald's 1905 biography of Dickens, Kent notes that the author would "often dwell on the dreadfully tyrannical power of the law of average."[16] Thus, James's reference to probability in his Braddon review is in accord with the contemporary interest in applying scientific principles to the study of society.

James's invocation of "the England of to-day's newspaper" is also more significant than it first appears. During the first third of the nineteenth century there was an increasing demand for fiction about contemporary life, and, according to Richard D. Altick, "[b]y the middle of the century, a novel was virtually assumed to be a story of the present day." In case there could possibly be any lingering doubts, authors often emphasized a novel's modernity in their subtitles; thus, for example, Caroline Norton's *Stuart of Dunleath: A Story of Modern Times* (1851), Wilkie Collins's *Basil: A Story of Modern Life* (1852), Dickens's *Hard Times, For These Times* (1854), Charles Reade's *A Terrible Temptation: A Story of the Day* (1871), and Trollope's *The Way We live Now* (1875). "Authors of sensational novels were particularly grateful for the credibility that newspapers supplied to their accounts of murder, bigamy, forgery, white collar crimes of other descriptions, elaborate deceptions, the discovery of lost wills."[17] The published proceedings of the divorce courts provided additional fodder for novelists of sensation, as did "accounts in newspapers and magazines [that] described instances of 'personation' or identities remodelled across boundaries of class, gender, and ethnicity." Bigamy, a common theme in sensation fiction, "signifies the threat of multi-lineal descent and consequently of uncertain paternal origins,"[18] and is thus a threat to Burke's orderly generational narrative. Although the three novels with which we are concerned lack the subtitles that call attention to their modernity, their plots are clearly the stuff of their times.

In the review previously cited, Margaret Oliphant begins by contrasting her own time (the eve of the second Great Exhibition in 1862) and the moment of the Crystal Palace exhibition in 1851. This is particularly apropos of our discussion, because, at one point late in the novel, *The Woman in White*'s narrator comments, "The year of which I am now writing, was the year of the famous Crystal Palace Exhibition in Hyde Park." Oliphant refers to Britain in 1851 as a world "lost in self-admiration," but goes on to draw a distinction between that "world" and the "changed world in which we are standing," noting the "distant roar" of guns from across the Atlantic (the American Civil War). Ronald R. Thomas accounts for this shift in world view by observing that, by 1862, as the sensation novel is in its ascendancy,"the 'mechanism' of ordinary life replace[d] the machinery of industry as a source of wonder and amazement."[19] *Mechanism* is the word used frequently by Maturin in *Melmoth the Wanderer,* a word that in 1820 connotes monotony and Gothic oppression, but by 1860 it is machinery—whether cogs and springs or the intricacies of human social interaction—to be taken apart and examined with fascination. All three of our chosen sensation novels exemplify this fascination. *The Woman in White* and *Lady Audley's Secret* each "take apart" and examine a woman's movements in space and time to discern the relationships inscribed in those movements, while *East Lynne* examines the

mechanism of daily domestic (and emotional) life from two temporal perspectives.

In examining the intricacies of human interaction, one way that
these novels explore the increasing importance of time—situating
one's identity in time by narrating the past—is through their examination of some of life's transition moments. It is our passage across
certain boundaries that redefines our identity in the eyes of the law.
When one crosses such a boundary, her legal status changes. This
alteration in legal status makes such transformations temporally
significant because the passage separates the time before from the
time after. Yet in the Victorian era such boundaries are revealed
to be disconcertingly permeable or vague, so that one's status with
respect to them may be uncertain.[20] A-poria literally means "without passage," yet here we face the opposite problem; the passage
across boundaries or borders is too easy. When The Woman in
White's Laura Fairlie marries Sir Percival Glyde, which forms an
important separation point in the text, hers is a kind of life/death
passage, for Laura Fairlie legally "dies" (i.e., ceases to exist) when
she marries, according to the legal concept of coverture. Later in
the novel, when her death is faked, she is biologically alive but legally dead, and her legal death is attested to by a number of written
documents and inscriptions—dated and thus bound up with public
time—all of which constitute false narratives that must be systematically overwritten by a new narrative before she can be accepted
as her living self. These false narratives expose the fiction of the
Burkean narrative of inheritance, even while they demonstrate its
desirability. In his discussion of the Glorious Revolution of 1688,
Burke had been able to gloss over the apparent interruption in the
hereditary succession of kings, making it seem no discontinuity at
all.[21] Walter Hartright and Marian Halcombe must undertake a
similar task, to cover the gaps and discontinuities in Laura's own
fragmented tale and construct a coherent narrative of events. But
in the process of doing so, narrative is revealed for the construct
that it is.

The plot of Lady Audley's Secret also turns on a false report of
death, but the boundary that this novel really explores is the one
separating sanity from insanity, and this, too, is disturbingly vague.
Lady Audley seems sane, but carries latent madness that may be
awakened under certain circumstances. Her mental health is uncertain, even to a knowledgeable authority in such matters, but she
may appear sane at times and act at other times in ways that the
law would characterize as insane. Thus, there is no clear demarca-
tion between before and after, and she seems able to move back and

forth across this boundary. Braddon's narrator even extends this potential to Robert Audley, her barrister and amateur detective. She notes near the end of the novel that, "There is nothing so delicate, so fragile, as that invisible balance upon which the mind is always trembling. Mad to-day and sane to-morrow."[22] Note the reversal in the expected sequence in this last sentence. One does not "go mad"; one "goes sane," as if causality has been inverted. The boundary between sanity and insanity is a permeable one from both directions.

East Lynne explores the boundaries between past and present, and those that define the home, separating the public and private spheres, the inside from the outside. Wood takes her readers inside the household and reveals what goes on there, using a character whose moral status is problematical. As Andrew Maunder observes, "she is one of the few authors writing in 1860 who writes about married life itself rather than, as most were doing, using marriage as a means of tying up the plot at the end. Most controversially perhaps, the novel points to the ambivalence of the fundamental Victorian middle-class feminine ideals of 'good' wife and 'good' mother, exposing the pharisaical attitude which divided women into two camps—the angel and the demon."[23] Isabel is multiply-transformed by time. She is born to a nobility that has faded through profligacy and a rising merchant class. She is transformed not just by marriage but by two phenomena that are increasingly common in the 1860s but could not have existed only a few decades earlier: divorce and a railway crash. These transform the angel in the house into something decidedly aporetic. Isabel can return to the house where she once was a wife but is no longer, because marriage is no longer permanent. It does not provide closure; nor does Isabel's subsequent death.

All three of these novels involve an investigation of the past and the construction of a narrative that seeks to make sense of that past, and therefore the present, much as Victorian science tried to make sense of the earth's past. But such an effort produces as many anomalies as it attempts to resolve. Indeed, all three novels reach a state of narrative—and even linguistic—failure, suggesting that narrative may no longer be able to "contain" the aporias of time; its chaotic nature resists our attempts to "humanize" it.

THE WOMAN IN WHITE

Collins's three-decker novel is strikingly organized, not into three books, but three "*epochs*."[24] The choice of words is rich with meanings. The *Oxford English Dictionary*'s definition of *epoch* contains two divisions, the first denoting "[a] fixed point in the reckoning of time" (seven definitions dealing with systems of chronology, historical or natural events and astronomy, all examples dating from the seventeenth and eighteenth centuries, and all emphasizing the idea of a "moment"); and the second division denoting "[a] period of time" (four definitions, all suggesting a "continuous process," including *epoch* in the geological sense, all examples but one [applicable to the physics of harmonic motion] predating Collins's life, with the geological example dating from 1802). The division of the novel into epochs calls attention to the temporal aspects of narrative. It also juxtaposes the story of one family, or more specifically, "the story of what a Woman's patience can endure, and what a Man's resolution can achieve"[25]—itself a statement characterized by a multiplicity of meanings, as Jonathan Loesberg and Lillian Nayder have both argued[26]—against the age of the earth. This juxtaposition reflects the growing Victorian consciousness of the scope of time. Collins ironically inserts this term having so many overtones of geological time (*epoch*) into a narrative that bears all the characteristics of contemporaneity noted by Mansel, James, and other critics.

But there is also a fascinating slippage between the two major senses of the term, one denoting a moment in time, and one a continuous process, for the text supports both meanings. Not only is the length of a human life, however important to us, only a moment in the grand scale of the earth's geological processes, but even the stories of the lives as narrated partake of both the momentary and the continuous. The first epoch sees the process of transforming Laura Fairlie into Lady Glyde, the actual transformation of woman into wife (which includes the loss of her legal identity according to the law of coverture, as described by Lenora Ledwon and Lillian Nayder), seeming to take only a literal moment.[27] The clergyman's pronouncement is unnarrated, taking place, according to Marian's journal, on December 22 sometime between 10:00 ("She is dressed . . .") and 11:00 ("It is all over. They are married.") It is as if narrative, with its symbiotic relationship to time, cannot narrate what lies outside the realm of temporal experience. Upon this pronouncement, except for one brief entry at 3:00 marking their departure, "The First Epoch of the Story closes here" (216–17). The second epoch is similarly both a process (the progressive ill-treatment of Lady Glyde, leading to her "death") and a dramatic, transformative moment (her apparent resurrection as she looks at Hartright over the inscription on her own tombstone), while the third epoch represents the painstaking process of restoring her identity through a process by which the events of the first two epochs are repeatedly narrated until the gaps are filled. It is as if we are dealing with the temporal paradox of movement and non-movement with which both Aristotle and Augustine struggled. Laura moves inexorably toward becoming Sir Percival Glyde's wife, but her actual transition is somehow outside time, a transition marked by no movement. She is changed, at least legally, from a state of being to one of non-being in what Deleuze and Guattari term an "instantaneous incorporeal transformation," as a judge transforms the accused into a convict or a hijacker transforms an airplane's passengers into hostages through a speech act.[28]

While the first epoch simply begins on "the last day of July" (34), meaning it could be almost any year for Collins's readers (including the present one), the novel's explicit dating begins with the second epoch. This epoch begins with the inscription *"June 11th, 1850."* It is nearly a year after the opening of the novel. Why does Collins wait until the second epoch to give us the full date? Probably because it is the precise dating of events in the second epoch that is key to the mystery's solution. The first epoch does not contain any of the links in what Robert Audley will call the "wonderful chain" of "circumstantial evidence,"[29] while the second epoch not only is marked by the presence of dated narratives, but by repeated reminders as to the importance of dates, usually at the beginning of each of the assembled narratives, a pattern that continues into the early part of the third epoch. Until the second epoch, dates are of no more importance to the reader than they are to the narrator, but this changes once Laura is transformed into Lady Glyde and her husband's plot to obtain her money is put into action. Events now have particular temporal significance; they must be correctly situated in linear sequence. Thus Frederick Fairlie notes "I am told to remember dates" (361); the housekeeper, Eliza Michelson, early in her own account apologizes for not having made a note of the date: "I made no memorandum at the time, and I cannot therefore be sure to a day of the date" (379), and later comments "I am told that it is of the last importance to ascertain the exact date of that lamentable journey, and I have anxiously taxed my memory to recall it." (419); Count Fosco's cook, Hester Pinhorn, states (in a narrative noted to have been "[t]aken down from her own statement"), "I am sorry to say it's no use asking me about days of the month, and such-like" (420); the gardener at Blackwater Park "knew that his master had driven away, at night, 'some time in July, the last fortnight or the last ten days of the month'—and knew no more" (473); the attorney Mr. Kyrle reminds Hartright that "If you could show a discrepancy between the date of the doctor's certificate and the date of Lady Glyde's journey to London, the matter would wear a totally different aspect" (464), and Hartright insists to Marian that "We must persist to the last in hunting down the date of Laura's journey. The one weak point in the conspiracy, and probably the one chance of proving that she is a living woman, centre in the discovery of that date" (470), an assertion reiterated twice during Hartright's final interview with Fosco (614, 627). The third epoch is more often than not marked by expressions of frustration concerning the *absence* of accurate dates, noted on at least eight occasions.[30]

A fascinating detail that has been overlooked by critics is that the narrative systematically indicts the characters who are depicted as out of touch with "the times," in both senses of the term. The lack of awareness of what we have come to call public time (the missing dates) by Eliza Michelson, Hester Pinhorn, and the gardener makes them anachronisms in an age characterized by a heightened consciousness of time. They do not carry watches, they are not "hurried to death," and there is something a bit odd about them as a result. But this deficiency is not solely an attribute of class. Laura is subtly criticized for having "omitted to make a memorandum beforehand of the date on which she took the journey" (to London), and the voice of Hartright-as-narrator declares, with some frustration, "All hope of fixing that important date by any evidence of hers, or of Mrs Michelson's, must be given up for lost" (445). In fact, "[t]he terrible story of the conspiracy" that Marian was able to obtain from Laura shortly after their escape from the asylum, "was presented in fragments, sadly incoherent in themselves, and widely detached from each other" (445). The doctor, normally conscious of dates, but "having been ill at the time, had omitted to make his usual entry of the day of the week and month" during the events in question (472). Thus, those who lack what we might call "temporal competence" are either from servant classes or ill. Laura, with a particularly delicate constitution, and under the influence of stress and drugs, falls under the latter category, but her repeated failure to be able to demonstrate competence in both temporality and the temporal attributes of narrative is a persistent frustration for Walter and Marian. Laura did not just fail to remember the date; she "omitted to make a memorandum beforehand," an anticipatory narrative. In her letter to Mrs. Vesey, "no date was mentioned—not even the day of the week" (457). Worse, Laura cannot produce more than a fragmented, "sadly incoherent" narrative of the events of her journey, so her temporal and narrative incompetence come to the same thing, emphasizing Ricoeur's "circle of narrativity" in the breach.

By contrast, both Walter and Marian are especially competent in matters temporal and narratological, Walter in constructing a coherent, temporally sound narrative of Laura's movements, and Marian in supplying details from the authority of her journal. Marian's diary is often consulted as a source of details. It is, in fact, in the midst of her narrative, that the first, undated epoch ends, and the second, dated one, begins. Marian herself uses her journal to recall the location of the asylum in which Anne Catherick had been confined as well as "all the other particulars of the interview [between Catherick and Hartright] exactly as she heard them from Mr Hartright's own lips." Her retrieval of this information is accomplished with computer-like efficiency: "Accordingly she looked back at her entry and extracted the address" (439). When Walter begins his investigation "by gathering together as many facts as could be collected," he states that "[t]he first source of information to which I applied was the journal kept at Blackwater Park by Marian Halcombe" (456). Shortly after, he notes that "[t]he information derived from Marian's diary made it a matter of certainty that Count Fosco had opened her first letter from Blackwater Park to Mr Kyrle, and had, by means of his wife, intercepted the second" (460). And still later, "The considerations thus presented to me in the diary, joined to certain surmises of my own that grew out of them, suggested a conclusion which I wondered I had not arrived at before . . . the Count is a spy!" (584). Marian's narrative establishes the coherence of the narrative of events that Walter is trying to construct.

Fosco, that master plotter, is also adept at both time and narrative and quickly realizes there is a temporal anomaly in the false narrative. As soon as Hartright asks for the date on which Laura travels to London, he replies, "So! So! You can lay your finger, I see, on the weak place" (610). Moreover, he demonstrates his worldly mastery of temporality by developing a detailed, hour-by-hour "programme" under which he will draft, arrange and revise his contribution to the narrative, as proof of Hartright's assertions, including time for a "snooze of restoration," and he follows his programme almost exactly. Nicholas Daly argues that this scene demonstrates that, for Fosco, "time itself rather than Hartright has become the enemy," emphasizing the motif of the dramatic deadline by which Hartright "extract[s] a date from Fosco . . . [by] us[ing] a time," a literal deadline "before the clock strikes and the seal is broken."[31]

While I do not dispute Daly's assertion, I would argue that Fosco makes his enemy serve his purpose, by transforming his temporal constraints into a performance that is nothing short of a tour de force. He is able to turn time to his own ends in a way that is unmatched by anyone else in the novel. Of course, it can be argued that time does eventually run out for him when he is assassinated by the Brotherhood he had betrayed.

I have stated that these missing dates represent what we have come to call public time, and events often turn on a public record of a temporal event. The importance of accurate dating makes time essential to the novel's plot in at least three ways. For one, Walter Hartright's construction of a timetable that depicts the movements of Laura, as documented by several witnesses and public records, is the means by which he is finally able to prove that the woman buried in the grave that bears Lady Glyde's name cannot in fact be "Lady Glyde." (And it is the "weak point," both in the conspiracy and in the composition of the novel itself, for Collins got this date scheme wrong in the serial version of 1859–60, and perpetuated the errors in the first edition of 1860, as J. A. Sutherland and Walter M. Kendrick have both pointed out.)[32] What Hartright sets out to do is to prove that the false narrative crafted by the plot of Fosco and Glyde is false because it violates a narrative's required adherence to temporal laws. In other words, it is judged a failure according to the conventions of narrative, which requires that the account be in accord with what we know of time. The false narrative, once analyzed to its lowest level of detail, would assert that Laura died and then left Limmerick alive, which we know to be an impossibility (unless we want to move into the realms of fantasy or science fiction, which are clearly beyond the limits of this genre).

Hartright's detective work serendipitously uncovers another temporal anomaly in Glyde's alteration of the parish marriage register to make his own birth legitimate. Mrs. Catherick's description of the process by which Percival mimicked the handwriting and ink color of the register calls attention to the absurdity of his action: "[H]e succeeded in the end, and made an honest woman of his mother, after she was dead in her grave!" (552). He has attempted to "marry" his parents. Once this fact of history is revealed to be demonstrably false, another "fact" is disproven, for not only is Lady Glyde not dead, but she is not Lady Glyde at all, because her husband, the reputed Sir Percival Glyde, is really illegitimate. His legal status is as inexplicable as that of Juan di Monçada in *Melmoth the Wanderer*. Percival has tried to repair his own "weak point," rewriting the authorized narrative of inheritance by inserting his parents' names in the church's marriage registry, inventing a false genealogy, much as John Sandal's mother attempted to manipulate genealogy for her own greedy motives.[33] Percival has attempted to alter the details of his own birth.

These absurdities are aporias, unutterable contradictions that Glyde and Fosco have attempted to utter, making their entire "plot" a failed attempt to construct a coherent narrative in the face of an aporia, while, on the other side, Peter Thoms suggests that Walter, Marian, and Laura seek "the providential . . . closure which resolves events into a cohesive whole."[34] And it is upon small details that coherence often depends, a fact of which Collins was both aware and concerned, when he requested that reviewers not reveal any of the "hundreds of little 'connecting links,' of trifling value in themselves, but of the utmost importance in maintaining the smoothness, the reality, and the probability of the entire narrative." As Walter Kendrick argues,

> These little links are trifling and crucial at once. They do not guarantee the novel's correspondence to some structure outside of itself; rather, they guarantee that the novel will form a system which is consistent in all its parts. The reader will be able to validate the novel's coherence, but not by comparing it to something he has felt or seen elsewhere. Rather, he will be able to compare one part of the novel with another, using as his standard the novel's own scale of dates and durations.[35]

The novel is "transformed into an intelligible story with a beginning, a middle, and an end"[36] through a process of almost incessant repetition. Peter Brooks reminds us that it is "a condition of all classic detective fiction, that the detective repeat, go over again, the ground that has been covered by his predecessor, the criminal." The detective repeats the past, experiencing it again, in order to reconstruct it and give it a formal coherence in the present context. He resolves the narrative discontinuities. As Brooks points out, in a discussion of a Sherlock Holmes story, "Todorov identifies the two orders of story, inquest and crime, as *sjužet* and *fabula*. He thus makes the detective story the narrative of narratives, its classical structure a laying-bare of the structure of all narrative in that it dramatizes the role of *sjužet* and *fabula* and the nature of their relation." What is especially striking in Brooks's analysis is his assertion that the detective's narrative of the criminal act "need not mean that it did in fact happen," because "the story is after all a construction made by the reader, and the detective, from the implications of the narrative discourse . . . verification of the *fabula* lies in its plausibility, its fitting the needs of explanation."[37] What is important is the plausibility, or coherence, of the narrative repetition: Does it fit the pattern of the evidence? The same goal applies to the Darwinian "narrative" of the human race.

The frequent recounting of earlier events in the third epoch of *The Woman in White*, which, Walter M. Kendrick has argued, is not so much a sequel to the first two epochs as much as it is a retelling of earlier events, provides continuity in both space and time, achieving the plausibility that Brooks described: "The complex doings at Blackwater Park between June 20 and July 26 involve the simultaneous activity of several characters in different places. The apparent fullness of the early narratives conceals tricks with space behind a pretense of fidelity to time. Only when Count Fosco's confession reveals where he was during the many gaps in Marian's vision of him does spatial continuity match its temporal counterpart." Kendrick points out that, by the end of the novel, "when the same time period has been narrated eight times, the reader is at last able to construct a full narrative from the omniscient perspective which Hartright has enjoyed since the beginning—including not only how time passed during that busy month but also where each character passed it. Only at the end of the novel does its complex mosaic of corrupted words, violated spaces, broken time, and splintered space make the coherent whole which the 'Preamble' promised."[38] Now the incoherent fragments—Laura's confused account—make sense and represent an ordered narrative.[39]

Repetition also functions on a psychological level in the novel. Ann Cvetkovich has focused on the "shock of [the] physical event" of Anne Catherick's touch upon Hartright's arm at night in the beginning of the novel, a shock that "resonates forward and backwards across the text." He continues to be haunted by doubts about whether he acted rightly or not: "The writing of the past causes him to reexperience his earlier sensations, while the future contaminates his account so much that 'the shadows of after-events [darken] the very paper' he writes on." Cvetkovich argues that "[p]ast and present grow confused, and the affect the episode conjures seems to be produced as much by subsequent events as by the encounter itself. Is Anne Catherick's significance present to Walter when he meets her, or is it only constructed retrospectively, in light of 'after-events'?"[40] According to Cvetkovich, Walter later experiences what he characterizes as "[a] thrill of the same feeling which ran through me when the touch was laid upon my shoulder on the lonely high-road" (*The Woman in White*, 86) when he watches Laura Fairlie, dressed in white, walking in the moonlight. It is the repetition that is important here: "That original event acquires significance because of its relation to subsequent events, even though Walter has attempted to describe it as shocking in and of itself. Two primal moments with these women merge in this one."[41] This is exactly the phenomenon we have discussed in connection with *Udolpho*: repetition unifies the temporal dimensions because it "opens potentialities that went unnoticed, were aborted, or were repressed in the past," coloring memory with expectation.[42] The past is retroactively infused with new potential.

Hartright's repetitive and detailed analysis of the timeframe in which Laura was supposed to have died exemplifies the methods of the emerging discipline of forensic science. Hartright's detective work consists largely of a minute comparison of multiple accounts and dated public records, seemingly a triumph of empiricism consistent with what Richard D. Altick calls "the prevailing temper of the time," which he characterizes as "positivistic, scientific, rationalist," noting for example, the Victorian interest in physiognomy and phrenology.[43] Yet at the same time, Hartright's analysis undercuts any confidence we may have in really *knowing* the world. Just as madness was increasingly seen in Victorian times as a malady to which almost anyone might be subject—the "line" dividing sanity and insanity was increasingly being viewed as tenuous—so too do time and memory seem increasingly indeterminate in *The Woman in White*. As we have discussed in the context of the detective story, verification is not as important as plausibility. Further, there is an implication here that *any* narrative of events, if examined so minutely and exhaustively, might not withstand scrutiny, particularly if we are unable, as Laura was, to recreate a logical, temporal sequence of events. Nor is Hartright's detective work a matter only of detached observation. In some ways it anticipates Heisenberg's Uncertainty Principle, which asserts that we cannot know the exact position of a sub-atomic particle at a particular moment in time, because the very act of observation would affect its position.[44] Even a disinterested observer (and Hartright clearly is not) cannot observe a phenomenon without changing it. "The narrative deciphers the shifting traces of the past, but then seems to present that past as a reconstruction of what really happened, written from the point of view of the order that the initial absence questioned, and the ideological contradictions that this engenders are negotiated by juggling with narrative focus and voice and the way that narrative time is organised."[45] The novel's "epochs" of the recent past, like the geological epochs they invoke, do not have sharply defined edges.

It is difficult to establish a definitive, precise chronology. The text thus undermines the very positivism that it seems to endorse.

One of the fascinating ways that the novel subverts its own positivism is through Collins's famous error in the time scheme of the novel, which effectively calls into question his own temporal and narrative competence. J. A. Sutherland describes Collins's attention to the details of plot composition and his tendency to carefully plan his novels well in advance, a characteristic noted by Trollope, and a characteristic quite different from Dickens, who often improvised during serial publication. But in the midst of the serialization of *The Woman in White,* Collins apparently decided that, as he had originally envisioned it, the novel's denouement—which would have turned on the postmarks of some letters sent by Mrs. Michelson in her otherwise undated account—would have been too "efficient," too "open-and-shut," with about a third of the novel yet "to spin out." Collins therefore tried to adjust the details to prolong the suspense, but some embarrassing incongruities remained in the serial publication and in the first, three-volume edition of 1860, as Sutherland notes. "Reviewing the third edition in *The Times,* 30 October 1860, E. S. Dallas made the well-known objection about the impossibility of the novel's time scheme (reckoning from Marian's diary Laura must have gone up to London a fortnight later than the narrative asserts her to have done . . .)." Kendrick apparently quotes the same reviewer, who complained that the third volume of the first edition of the novel is "a mockery, a delusion, and a snare." But Kendrick goes on to note that, in the course of his correction of these errors for the 1861 edition, Collins set

> all relevant dates back sixteen days. In doing so, however, he passed over Mrs. Clement's testimony . . . [pp. 479–85 of the Penguin edition] which contains no numerical dating but which can be coordinated with the other narratives by phrases like "the next day" and "a fortnight later." This brief section of Volume III had been "true" according to Hartright's discovery, but in the second edition it puts Anne Catherick in London sixteen days too early. The second edition, therefore, and all subsequent editions based on it, continue to mock, delude, and snare their readers—although for more than a century no one seems to have been disturbed by the fact.[46]

Wilkie Collins's inability to completely control the temporality of his narrative—his corrective efforts have still left a discontinuity in place—oddly mirrors the "weak point," the temporal anomaly in Fosco's plot. Time itself has a peculiarly chaotic aspect that seems to resist our efforts to humanize it, to impose our own form of coherence on it. Each narrator imparts a version of reality, but all have been filtered through the narrator's consciousness or further adapted by Hartright's editorial efforts to suit his own purposes. In the Preamble, Hartright promises that he will "trace the course of one complete series of events by making the persons who have been most closely connected with them, at each successive stage, relate their own experience, word for word" (33). But Hartright himself sequences the narratives temporally, organizing them into a form that a judge in a court of law "*might* once have heard" (33, emphasis added), just as the "author" of *The Last Man* must "transform" the Sybilline leaves in the cave into a coherent narrative, because "they were unintelligible in their pristine condition."[47] Hartright's task is a process of emplotment, what Ricoeur terms *mimesis*₂, as we saw in our discussion of *Melmoth the Wanderer*. Hartright claims that truth is his object, but "truth always in its most direct and intelligible aspect" (33). "Intelligible" is an important qualification to make, and therefore, Marian Halcombe's story is presented "in Extracts from her Diary," which, Hartright explains, omits "only those [passages] which bear no reference to Miss Fairlie or to any of the persons with whom she is associated in these pages" (184). He therefore "learns to control the past and hence the present and future through the manipulation of time and memory."[48]

The multiple marriage registers, for example, each narrate a version of reality, just as each narrator does.[49] The inarticulability of Glyde's identity (what do we call him now? Certainly not *Sir* Percival, but is his surname still valid?) would remain had not the novel elided it. No one but the reader is told about "Glyde's" alteration of the marriage register, apparently not even Marian or Laura (563, 571). In fact, it is emphasized by the difficulty in identifying his body. His servant affirms that the dead man is Glyde, but, as one onlooker puts it, "he's struck stupid-like, and the police don't believe him" (540), which Hartright-as-narrator affirms a few pages later when he says "the helpless condition of the servant had made the police distrustful of his asserted recognition of his master" (542). Prior to the fire, the same servant had mistaken Hartright for his master in the darkness (534). Hartright himself had never before seen Glyde, so he could not identify him either, and until reliable witnesses who were familiar with his appearance could be sent for, he is identified—appropriately enough for our discussion—by his watch and its inscription (542).

The inability of anyone to articulate Glyde's name, and the "scrupulous manner" in which Marian, Walter, and Laura avoid all mention of this name from that point on (571) ironically articulate his aporetic identity. Glyde is not unmasked, except by the flames that strip away his life and assumed identity, but these flames simultaneously destroy the evidence of his forgery. The fact of his death, then, is the only truth—at least the fact that *someone* is dead, although no one knows who he really is. As Rebecca Stern states, "The semiotics of sensation fiction reflect the increasingly confusing milieu of Victorian life. These novels are rife with contradictions between signifiers and signifieds, operating on symbolic systems in which appearances rarely correspond with actualities, in which it is nearly impossible to construe 'truth' or 'nature' from exterior signs. In *The Woman in White,* for example, Laura Fairlie's tombstone marks Anne Catherick's grave; [and] Sir Percival Glyde proves to be neither a Sir nor a Glyde."[50]

Death itself may be the ultimate truth, but the confusion surrounding its signs opens up more perplexities than it resolves, which itself raises troubling questions about mechanisms such as inheritance. Burke's "sure principle of transmission" seems so orderly and lineal. One is born, lives, marries, dies, and transmits life, property, and values to the next generation. Questions of identity, such as Glyde's, never seem to have arisen.[51] And Burke's implied assumption that time can be organized like a narrative leaves out the possibility that such an undertaking may be beyond the power of narrative, a possibility that *The Woman in White* articulates. Faced with what Hartright at one point calls "the ways of our unintelligible world" (546), neither Fosco nor Collins seemed able to construct a perfectly "intelligible" and coherent narrative. Of course, Fosco's inability to do so was a deliberate plot device on Collins's part, but it is ironic that Collins himself experienced the same kind of narrative failure. The task of narrativizing time seems too difficult, which suggests that science's goal of constructing a coherent narrative of the Earth's, and the human race's, past—an extension of Ricoeur's "bridge" of ancestral memories between our own time and the historical past[52]—is fraught with similar anomalies. To illustrate the difficulty of the effort to "narrativize" humanity's past, consider Darwin's *The Origin of Species*—one of many scientific works that attempted to write the narrative of the past. *The Origin* alone underwent six distinct editions between 1859 and 1872. Morse Peckham notes that about seventy-five percent of the sentences that comprised the first edition were rewritten—some of them as many as five times during the subsequent versions. Moreover, the length of the work expanded nearly by over 1500 sentences—increasing the original number by nearly forty percent.[53]

Organizing time like a narrative is a repetitive process involving a series of successive approximations, but, like Godwin's perfectibility, perfection—in this case, a perfect narrative representation of time—is never achieved.

LADY AUDLEY'S SECRET

Similar temporal dilemmas and questions of identity permeate *Lady Audley's Secret*. Mary Elizabeth Braddon's most renowned novel shares many important characteristics with Collins's *The Woman in White*. Both deal with issues such as marriage (and how that is defined) and the ownership and transmission of property, and both feature young women confined in mental institutions. Both *The Woman in White* and *Lady Audley's Secret* present mysteries that are resolved by amateur detectives, and, in both cases, the resolution turns on the establishment of one's movements in the world of public time, a project that will transform Robert Audley from "a lump of torpidity"[54] into a train schedule-obsessed bundle of fatigue and anxiety, a fair representation of the transformation of Victorian society to a state of "temporal hyperawareness." But, as Jenny Bourne Taylor has noted, Braddon has "brilliantly" reversed the situation of *The Woman in White*: "Helen Maldon, the abandoned wife, manipulates her own image to become Lucy Graham and then 'Lady Audley' and substitutes another body for her own place in the grave to sustain her social position; it is she who is finally placed in an asylum to protect the upper-class family." In accomplishing this reversal, Braddon also transforms the traditional Victorian ideal of "the angel in the house" into something far more ominous. As a contemporary reviewer noted, "Lady Audley is at once the heroine and the monstrosity of the novel."[55] Thus Braddon's Lady Audley is a more complicated character than Collins's Laura Fairlie, and we are made to feel considerable sympathy for her plight. However villainously she acted, she *is* an abandoned wife, as Taylor pointed out, because she and her infant were deserted by her husband for more than three years without so much as a letter from him.[56] She was forced to live with her alcoholic father and later to seek domestic situations. If that is not "baggage" enough—and Lady Audley has plenty of baggage to indict her, including the labels on her hatbox—we discover that she has the "hereditary taint [of madness] in her blood," having inherited it, like mitochondrial DNA, from her mother, whose own madness "was an hereditary disease transmitted to her from her mother, who had died mad" (372, 344). There is a certain pathetic inevitability to her plight, for no matter how normal she might appear, the "hereditary taint" lies waiting to strike at any moment. Lucy 's mother "had been, or had appeared, sane up to the hour of [her] birth, but from that hour her intellect had decayed . . ." (344–45). Taylor observes that "[p]uerperal, or post-natal, insanity, was considered to be one of the main causes of female insanity and accounted for between 7 and 10 per cent of female asylum admissions."[57] Lady Audley is doubly the victim of heredity. Not only does her mother transmit latent madness to her, but the very act of bringing forth a new generation herself—another life passage—awakens the sleeping demons within. Jill Matus states that, "If Lady Audley is mad because she has a mad mother, she is also mad by virtue of becoming a mother." Lady Audley is a living vehicle of transmission, but of madness, a state that would interrupt the legal transmission of property. In a cruelly ironic inversion of Burke's "sure principle of transmission," the novel is saying that "[we transmit our madness], in the same manner in which we enjoy and transmit our property and our lives."[58] There is a fatality about Lady Audley, and it may help explain her desire to console herself with luxury.

Robert Audley's relentless pursuit of Lady Audley by investigating the "paper trail" of her movements in space and time anticipates our postmodern anxieties about privacy.[59] Robert vows to "trace the life of my uncle's wife backwards, minutely and carefully, from this night to a period of six years ago. This is the twenty-fourth of February, fifty-nine. I want to know every record of her life between tonight and the February of the year fifty-three" (220). Lady Audley's past movements have left their trace in the present, even as, as we have seen, "A scar is the sign not of a past wound but of 'the present fact of having been wounded.' "[60] Robert's pursuit of Lady Audley is nearly obsessive—there is a hint of truth after all in her accusation that Robert suffers from monomania, and even before she levels this charge, Robert has considered it himself.[61] Note that Lady Audley's justification of her claim to Sir Michael that his nephew suffers from monomania emphasizes stagnation, due to the repetition of mental and linguistic processes:

> What is one of the strongest diagnostics of madness—what is the first appalling sign of mental aberration? The mind becomes stationary; the brain stagnates; the even current of the mind is interrupted; the thinking power of the brain resolves itself into a monotone. As the waters of a tideless pool putrefy by reason of their stagnation, the mind becomes turbid and corrupt through lack of action; and perpetual reflection

upon one subject resolves itself into monomania. Robert Audley is a monomaniac. The disappearance of his friend, George Talboys, grieved and bewildered him. He dwelt upon this one idea until he lost the power of thinking of anything else. The one idea looked at perpetually became distorted to his mental vision. Repeat the commonest word in the English language twenty times, and before the twentieth repetition you will have begun to wonder whether the word which you repeat is really the word you mean to utter. Robert Audley has thought of his friend's disappearance until the one idea has done its fatal and unhealthy work. He looks at a common event with a vision that is diseased, and he distorts it into a gloomy horror engendered of his own monomania. (284)

Robert does indeed suffer from a certain fixity of habit. His is a life of stasis; where there is movement at all, it is without apparent purpose. He has spent five years as a barrister who has never argued a case, who, after "exhausting himself with the exertion of smoking his German pipe and reading French novels," lies about in the shady Temple Gardens to rest (35): "The usual lazy monotony of his life had been broken as it had never been broken before" by George's disappearance (99). Indeed, Aeron Haynie notes that Robert is sleeping by a stream when George is supposedly murdered.[62] Robert characterizes himself as an "idle *flaneur*" (427). After the interview with George Talboys's father, he is prepared to abandon his quest to bring George's killer to justice until George's sister Clara asks him, "Shall you or I find my brother's murderer?" and insists that he must "[c]hoose between the two alternatives" (201).

Clara must prod Robert again near the end of the novel. At this point, Robert has determined that George is alive and living in Australia, but Robert still remains for five weeks at Grange Heath, the home of the Talboys family, where he enjoys Clara's lectures to him "on the purposeless life he had led so long" (427). Even then, he only commits to go to Australia to search for George when Clara vows, "If I were a man, I would go to Australia, and find him, and bring him back" (430). Robert complains that women cause mischief because the "are *never lazy*" (208, emphasis original), and he is constantly contrasted with his cousin Alicia, to whom he appeals at one point that she not "unsettle" him (73), and to whom he nearly always refers by using some variant on the word "bouncing," clearly suggesting activity to excess. Thus, he advises her to "be patient, and take life easily, and try and reform yourself of banging doors, bouncing in and out of rooms, talking of the stables, and riding across country," upon which Alicia "bounced out of the drawing-room," and Robert "murmured thoughtfully" that she would be "[s]uch a nice girl, too, if she didn't bounce!" (129).[63] It is no wonder that they clash; Alicia complains that the "slow lump of torpidity he calls his heart can beat, I suppose, once in a quarter of a century: but it seems that nothing but a blue-eyed wax-doll can set it going" (262). She refuses to believe Lady Audley's theory of Robert's madness: "He's not at all the sort of person to go mad. How should such a sluggish ditchpond of an intellect as his ever work itself into a tempest? He may moon about for the rest of his life, perhaps in a tranquil state of semi-idiotcy . . . but he'll never go mad" (325).

Thus it is quite against his purposeless nature for Robert to embark on a "minutely and carefully" conducted investigation into "every record" of his aunt's life for a six-year period, as this investigation is conducted by means of unceasing motion, usually on the train. As Nicholas Daly has characterized Robert's quest: "Robert Audley shuttles between London, Audley Place, Southhampton, Portsmouth, Liverpool, Dorsetshire, and Yorkshire, in search of clues, taking expresses wherever possible, and fretting when he has to take a slower train. The temporal frame of reference of the story is filled out with references to the 10:50 (express), the 3:00, 3:30, and 6:15 trains."[64] *Lady Audley's Secret* is filled with references to train schedules, clocks, and the fatigue and anxiety that accompany Robert's frenetic pace.[65] Like the "stupid, bewildering clock" in the clock-tower at Audley Court, a clock "which had only one hand; and which jumped straight from one hour to the next, and was therefore always in extremes" (7), Robert Audley seems to be constantly in a state of temporal extremis, jumping from one train to the next, and one hour to the next. Indeed, the clock at Audley Court may not have been broken, as modern readers may assume. According to Stuart Sherman, "[b]efore the advent of the pendulum, the vast majority of timepieces sported only a single hand, delegated to mark the hour." Sherman dates Huygens's invention of the pendulum clock in 1656.[66] Thus, the old clock is "stupid" only because it is out of date, lacking the precision, the "now-saying" that modern life demands of its timepieces. It jumps to "keep up" just as the people of the 1860s found themselves "hurried to death," and just as Robert jumps to keep up, in the present, with his aunt's past movements.

Audley Court's irregularities exist in both the spatial and temporal dimensions, which inform each other. It is spatially irregular because its building (linguistically both a noun and a verb, a signifier of space as well as time) has occupied an exceedingly long interval of time. We are told early in the novel that Audley Court is

> a house that could never have been planned by any mortal architect, but must have been the handiwork of that good old builder—Time, who, adding a room one year, and knocking down a room another year, toppling over now a chimney coeval with the Plantagenets, and setting up one in the style of the Tudors; shaking down a bit of Saxon wall there, and allowing a Norman arch to stand here; throwing in a row of high narrow windows in the reign of Queen Anne, and joining on a dining-room after the fashion of the time of Hanoverian George I. to a refectory that had been standing since the Conquest, had contrived, in some eleven centuries, to run up such a mansion as was not elsewhere to be met with throughout the county of Essex. (8)

Audley Court, like the castles of Gothic novels, is a "material survivor of a powerful lineage."[67] But unlike those Gothic relics of a past age, this one seems to be a work in progress, a product of evolutionary forces in a kind of architectural version of deep time. It seems to have been a building eleven hundred years in the making, rather than a castle from a particular era that may have seen additions in a later era. Audley Court is more like the earth itself, like *epoch* in the sense of the *OED*'s second division of definitions, as a "continuous process."

Robert Audley's decision to "trace the life of [his] uncle's wife backwards, minutely and carefully, from this night to a period of six years ago," is undertaken in order to "set [his] doubts at rest, or—or to confirm [his] fears" (219), noting that it is the "one manner in which [he] can do this" (220). Robert's backward tracing of the life of Lady Audley echoes Ricoeur's image of our traveling back the chain of ancestral memories in order to situate ourselves in time. Robert's "retrograde investigation," as Braddon titles volume 2, chapter 7, not only solves the crime, but it moves Robert from the position of stasis that he has occupied for at least the past five years. The George Talboys affair sets him in motion. Curiously, the direction of his movement is backward, although as the novel progresses the narrative is really moving in two directions simultaneously. He moves backward into his aunt's past, and forward, with ever increasing speed, in the train whose "shrieking engine bore him on the dreary northward journey, whirling him over desert wastes of flat meadow-land and bare corn-fields" (volume 2, chapter 9, "Beginning at the other end," 239) moving inexorably, and increasingly rapidly, toward a confrontation with Lady Audley, and toward her ultimate confinement, which will restrict her movements and impose the kind of stasis that characterized Robert's former existence.

This frantic pace takes its toll on Robert. Soon after George's disappearance near Audley Court, the narrator informs us that "[t]he young barrister was worn out by a long day spent in hurrying from place to place" (99). Much later, almost the same words are used: "He soon fell asleep, worn out with the fatigue of hurrying from place to place during the last two days" (243).

There are other negative consequences of Robert's ultramodern pace. One is his sense of being increasingly bound by time, to the degree that he impatiently awaits a specific time, and is apparently unable to live meaningfully when in this state of forced, prolonged, anticipation. Robert's anticipation, though, is in marked contrast with the Augustinian anticipation that permeates Emily St. Aubert's awareness in *Udolpho,* a "present of the future." Rather than contributing to a rich, thick present, Robert's anticipation is characterized by anxiety. At one point, "He had a long time to wait before it would be necessary to leave the Temple on his way to Shoreditch, and he sat brooding darkly over the fire and wondering at the strange events that had filled his life within the last year and a half, coming like angry shadows between his lazy inclinations and himself, and investing him with purposes that were not his own"(393).

His anxiety and weariness continue to mount, and time begins to control his life. On occasion it is the enemy, something to be disposed of: "Mr. Audley walked wearily up and down the room, *trying to get rid of the time.* It was no use leaving the Temple until eleven o'clock, and even then he would be sure to reach the station half an hour too early" (395, emphasis added). As is the case for *Melmoth*'s Donna Clara, time has been levelled down to Heidegger's "now-saying," but while Donna Clara's behavior seems only neurotically obsessive, Robert Audley's is infused with mid-Victorian anxiety. Dominated by the mechanism of time, he has become a mechanism too, like Maturin's Fra Paolo. He seems helpless, unable to function outside the bounds of the railway timetable. If he is late, he misses his train. But being early seems just as undesirable as being late, and even more incomprehensible to him. What would he do in a train station if he arrived early?

An even more disturbing consequence of this sort of temporal "conditioning" is Robert's sense of existential angst, expressed at two different points in the novel. The first occurs when he dines alone: "Robert ate his dinner, and drank a pint of Moselle; but he had poor appreciation for the excellence of the viands or the delicate fragrance of the wine. The mental monologue still went on, and the young philosopher of the modern school was arguing the favourite modern question of the nothingness of everything and the folly of taking too much trouble to walk upon a road that led nowhere, or to compass a work that meant nothing" (207). And later, the futility of life casts an even longer looming shadow, during a conversation with Clara Talboys: " 'Do you think I can read French novels and smoke mild Turkish until I am three-score-and-ten, Miss Talboys?' he asked. 'Do you think that there will not come a day in which my meerschaums will be foul, and the French novels more than usually stupid, and life altogether such a dismal monotony that I shall want to get rid of it somehow or other?' " (428). Robert is suffering from the malady of modernity. It is as if life is now, as time was, something to be gotten rid of, something to do while we anticipate . . . what? That question seems unanswerable. Robert is in a state of anticipation, but doesn't know exactly what he anticipates. Uncomfortable with anticipation, he occupies himself with a retrograde investigation, just as *The Origin of Species, Principles of Geology,* and the nebular hypothesis constitute retrograde investigations that attempt to make sense of an increasingly frantic contemporary world by narrating its origins.

We could very well argue that all of the trouble in *Lady Audley's Secret* occurs because of a temporal problem, Sir Michael's inability to gracefully accept the aging process, his "cruel fears that his age was an insurmountable barrier to his happiness; this sick hatred of his white beard; this frenzied wish to be young again, with glistening raven hair, and a slim waist, such as he had had twenty years before" (12). These fears of aging make Sir Michael susceptible to "the terrible fever called love," to which he succumbs "at the sober age of fifty-five" (13). There's even a whiff of something forbidden in Sir Michael's doting behavior toward Lucy. Alicia relates in an "indignant letter" to her cousin Robert that "her father had just married a wax-dollish young person, no older than Alicia herself, with flaxen ringlets and a perpetual giggle" (36). Sir Michael's misfortunes can be seen as punishment for his foolishness in attempting to bridge the generations. While an older man's marrying a younger woman would not have been at all unusual in Victorian England, Alicia's reference to a woman "no older than Alicia herself" raises the specter of something faintly incestuous. Sir Michael attempts to assuage his "frenzied wish to be young again" by marrying someone his daughter's age, but who looks and acts even more childlike. Helen Talboys's obituary says she is "twenty-two" (40), but she "looked little more than twenty" (13). Later, the narrator remarks upon her "extreme youth and freshness," noting that Lady Audley "owned to twenty years of age, but it was hard to believe her more than seventeen" (55), and "[a]ll her amusements were childish." It's almost as if she is getting younger as the novel progresses, a retrograde journey through time that parallels Robert's retrograde investigation. She seems to violate the laws of temporality, and indeed her own story of her past does not "add up." As "unnatural" as Sir Michael's pathetic attempt to reverse his own aging process, Lady Audley's is an implausible narrative, as Robert will learn when he reads the traces of her passage through time.

Robert's retrograde investigation also mirrors Victorian society's attempts to render the texts that give conflicting accounts of humanity's own expanding past into a coherent, plausible narrative. This collision of past and present can be seen elsewhere in the novel as well. We have already noted the emphasis on the railway and the telegraph, the setting in, as James put it, "the England of to-day's newspaper," yet there are recurring reminders of both the past—Lady Audley's own past haunts the novel, of course—and the ephemerality of the present, a present quickly discarded. George first learns of his wife's alleged death in "a greasy *Times* newspaper of the day before," lying on "a heap of journals" (39). Both the greasiness and the date are testimonials to decay. And the fatal link in the chain of circumstantial evidence that definitively establishes that Lucy Audley is Helen Maldon is her handwriting in the faded and mildewed pages of an *annual* from 1845, "the costumes grotesque and outlandish; the simpering beauties faded and commonplace" (160), all signs of decay and the fading of fashion,[68] all metaphorically suggesting the fears of degeneration raised by evolutionary theory.

But Robert's desire to reconstruct and narrate Lady Audley's past produces as many anomalies as it attempts to resolve. One of the consequences of his "retrograde investigation" is that we are never quite sure what to call Lady Audley, just as we are never sure what to call Sir Percival Glyde once his origin has been revealed. The narrator consistently refers to Lady Audley as "my lady," which becomes increasingly ironic as the novel progresses (and I have therefore continued to refer to her as "Lady Audley" for consistency's sake, in keeping with that convention). Lady Audley's true name is difficult to discern, beneath the various layers of her identity. Not only are we not sure *who* she is, but *what* she is is similarly in doubt. She is a maze of paradoxes, a wife who cannot be a wife, because she is already a wife, a murderer who is not really a murderer, a madwoman who may or may not be mad. Our inability to name who or what she is renders her aporetically inarticulable. The noted specialist, Dr. Mosgrave, "experienced in cases of mania" (362), finds, after his initial examination of Lady Audley, "no evidence of madness in anything she has done" (370). It is only after Robert informs him of "the story of George's disappearance, and of his own doubts and fears"—curiously, he omits all mention of her starting the fire that nearly killed several people—and after Robert appeals to Dr. Mosgrove "to save our stainless name from degradation and shame" (371), that Dr. Mosgrove conducts a second interview, lasting ten minutes, and announces:

> I have talked to the lady . . . and we understand each other very well. There is latent insanity! Insanity which might never appear; or which might appear only once or twice in a life-time. It would be *dementia* in its worst phase perhaps: acute mania; but its duration would be very brief, and it would only arise under extreme mental pressure. The lady is not mad; but she has the hereditary taint in her blood. She has the cunning of madness with the prudence of intelligence. I will tell you what she is, Mr. Audley. She is dangerous. (372)

Not surprisingly, the ambiguities associated with contemporary definitions of insanity have fascinated a number of critics. Jenny Bourne Taylor refers to "the absence of any stable reference point for defining insanity," noting that "Lucy's 'insanity' is both the revelation of a truth and an extension of her ability to continually transform herself, confound the distinction between appearance and reality." Nicholas Rance says that the revelation of Lady Audley's madness comes as a surprise to the reader, because she has been presented as "the triumph of cool calculation." Upholding Doctor Mosgrove's initial assessment, Ann Cvetkovich states that "[t]he secret that lies behind the novel's sensational mystery is that Lady Audley is neither insane nor criminal, but instead acts out of rational self-interest to protect her livelihood." Elaine Showalter agrees, claiming that "Lady Audley is not mad, but she is dangerous. . . . She is devious and perfidious not because she is a criminal and mad, but because she is a lady and sane."[69] In any event, just as we saw in the case of Sir Percival Glyde, the aporetic identity is kept secret. Lady Audley is committed to a Belgian asylum.

What ultimately convicts Lady Audley is the same phenomenon that "convicts" Collins's Fosco: one's passage through a world increasingly governed by public time leaves traces. Sir Percival's July 25 letter to Fosco indicating that Laura will travel to London on July 26 proves the falsehood of the death certificate dated July 25, when it is combined with the dated record in the livery stable register corroborating her arrival in London on the 26th.[70] Lady Audley's past movements are reconstructed by the labels on her luggage and the inscriptions in a gift book. Even where human memories are involved, there are often connections to the clock or calendar that make such testimony compelling as evidence. *Lady Audley's Secret*'s Miss Tonks asserts that "Lucy Graham" "came in August, 1854" and zeroes in on the date when she is able to recall the day of the week: "I think it was the eighteenth of August, but I'm not quite sure that it wasn't the seventeenth. I know it was on a Tuesday" (234). Robert is able to ascertain that Luke Marks's assistance of a badly injured man took place on the same day as George's disappearance when Luke states "I rek'lect the date because Farmer Atkinson paid me my wages all of a lump on that day, and I'd had to sign a bit of a receipt for the money he give me." He can determine the time because Luke recalls that "Audley church clock struck nine as I was crossin' the meadows between Atkinson's and the Court" (414). We have seen that *The Woman in White*'s Hartright privileges those who maintain a heightened awareness of public time, carefully dating their letters and journals. If we are to function in society increasingly governed by public time, we must be conversant with it.

Conversant with time, perhaps, but not with a complete narrative of Lady Audley's crime, or even her name. As was the case in *The Woman in White*, the aporia's marriage partner is spared a number of the details. Once Lady Audley has confessed to her husband that she has married him under false pretenses, Sir Michael declares, "I cannot hear any more . . . if there is any more to be told, I cannot hear it" (352). Robert only tells Alicia that her father's "grief . . . [i]s connected with Lady Audley," at which she blushes crimson at the realization that "[t]his sorrow must surely then have arisen from some sudden discovery; it was, no doubt, a sorrow associated with disgrace" (356). Preparing to depart Audley Court and leaving his nephew in charge of the disposition of Lady Audley, Sir Michael reiterates his unwillingness to hear the whole story of his wife's misadventures and is unable even to speak her name: "'I leave all in your hands, Robert,' he said, as he turned to leave the house in which he had lived so long. "I may not have heard the end; but I have heard enough. Heaven knows I have no need to hear more. I leave all to you, but you will not be cruel—you will remember how much I loved—'

His voice broke huskily before he could finish the sentence" (361).

Just as we do not know what to call her, neither does her "husband." She has become the rhetorical figure of hesitation.

EAST LYNNE

While *Lady Audley's Secret* reverses some elements of *The Woman in White*'s situation, both novels turn on the the problem of plausibly narrating an individual's movements in space and time, in order to separate a true narrative from a false one. Our third sensation novel, Mrs. Henry Wood's *East Lynne,* takes a dramatically different approach to its representation of the "England of today's newspaper." To be sure, there is a crime to be solved (the Hallijohn murder, and Richard Hare's guilt or innocence), but Wood relegates this mystery to a subplot. Another kind of "crime"—a moral transgression—is the subject of the main plot. *East Lynne* is just as preoccupied as *The Woman in White* and *Lady Audley's Secret* with the ways that actions taken in the past shape the present and the future. In this case, it is the decision of a moment that transforms Isabel Vane's fate.

Perhaps in no other sensation novel are the aporias of time so singularly naked (like the naked singularity of twentieth-century physicists). We have already seen that, in addition to the calendars that reconcile the time of our lives to the movements of celestial objects, and the human generations that provide ways for us to link ourselves to our ancestors and their memories, we also divide our lives by means of rituals or moments of transformation (such as marriage or death). These transformations create boundaries that separate the time before the event from the time after. At the moment of the completion of the marriage ceremony, a woman in Victorian times changes, not just her marital status, but her name, her legal identity, probably her home, and, in some cases, her social class. It is a profoundly transformative event. Prior to 1857, except by act of Parliament, this change was permanent until one of the partners was transformed by death. For all practical purposes the border between the two states (unmarried/married) could only be crossed in one direction, as was the case with death. The Matrimonial Causes Act of 1857 changed all that, creating the possibility of another transforming event that reverses the marriage ceremony, introducing an "after the after" that is not quite a repetition of the "before" state, but a kind of ghostly double of it. The divorced person's status is the same, but not the same. Of course, even before 1857, there were separations, as well as various extra-legal remedies for an untenable domestic situation—one partner could change her identity, perhaps even fake her death, and marry again, but such "solutions" lay outside the legal system. But, after 1857, it was possible to divorce and marry again, adding a new life-transforming event to the short list of marriage and death, thereby introducing a whole new range of possibilities. One's former spouse could therefore come back in the present, revealing that one has "a past." Wood exploits this possibility quite dramatically in *East Lynne,* where it is not just a buried secret that comes back to haunt the present, but the past itself in the person of Isabel Vane, who becomes quite literally an aporia of time.

Matters begin conventionally enough—for the sensation novel, that is—when Lady Isabel Vane, jealous of her husband and misunderstanding his attentions to another woman, Barbara Hare, attentions that involve Archibald's assistance in clearing Barbara's brother of a murder he's been falsely accused of committing, succumbs to the attentions of a villainous suitor. Isabel abandons her husband and children, eloping with Francis Levison to Grenoble. But Wood intensifies Victorian melodrama when Isabel, who has been disfigured in a railway accident in France and mistakenly reported dead, returns to her own home, disguised as the grotesque Madame Vine. There she is employed as governess to her own children, her husband having subsequently married Barbara. In the first half of the novel, Barbara, who has been in love with Archibald all along, must witness his life with Isabel with frustration and unfulfilled desire; in the second half of the novel, it is Isabel who must watch tender domestic scenes between Archibald and Barbara. In her doubling back to the household where she formerly ruled, Lady Isabel becomes a döppelganger, dead but not dead.[71] Archibald unknowingly has two wives under the same roof, his "once, and future" (made-present) wife. Isabel is the other who was wife, and Barbara is the wife who was other. Like a spectre, the undead Isabel haunts East Lynne: Archibald, upon meeting her, feels she reminds him of someone, and the text twice refers to him as "dreamy."[72] His sister Cornelia sees Madame Vine briefly without her glasses and remarks that "one would think it's the ghost" of Isabel (532); and the housekeeper, Joyce, is sufficiently startled by the apparition during a midnight fire alarm that she accidentally drops one of the children on the floor (622). But Isabel, herself a spectre, is similarly haunted by the spectre of her past that renders her unable to "forget the dreadful present" (502). Her life consists of two epochs, separated by a chasm of choice.

From the moment of her entry into the hall at East Lynne, Isabel is haunted by her uncanny perceptions. Her past is superimposed upon her present, a phenomenon that we saw when Emily St. Aubert and Dorothée entered the Marchioness's chamber in *The Mysteries of Udolpho*. Here, however, the uncanniness derives not from the entry into a chamber that seems just as the occupant had left it or from the striking resemblance between Emily and her aunt. In *East Lynne*, the uncanniness involves the same person returning to a particular place with a new identity that is insufficiently overlaid upon the old, so that the former identity keeps intruding. Worse, she must be on her guard, lest she give herself away by knowing too much. Isabel first recognizes a familiar servant. "As she ascended to the hall she recognised old Peter: strange, indeed, did it seem, not to say, 'How are you, Peter?' but to meet him as a stranger" (457). The effect is even more pronounced as she is shown to her new room:

> Joyce rang the bell, ordered the refreshment to be made ready, and then preceded Lady Isabel up-stairs. On she followed, her heart palpitating: past the rooms that used to be hers, along the corridor, towards the second staircase. The doors of her old bed and dressing-rooms stood open, and she glanced in with a yearning look. No, never more, never more could they be hers: she had put them from her by her own free act and deed. Not less comfortable did they look now, than in former days: but they had passed into another's occupancy. The fire threw its blaze on the furniture: there were the little ornaments on the large dressing-table, as they used to be in her time, and the cut glass of the crystal essence bottles was glittering in the fire-light. On the sofa lay a shawl and a book, and on the bed a silk dress, as if thrown there after being taken off. No: these rooms were not for her now; and she followed Joyce up the other staircase. (458)

Her second life at East Lynne is a constant pattern of these doubled memories, usually serving to remind her that Barbara now has what was once hers, and would be still, but for her ill-fated choice:

> From the inner room, however, came the sound of the piano, and the tones of Mr. Carlyle's voice. She recognised the chords of the music: they were those of the accompaniment to the song he had so loved when she sang it to him. Who was about to sing it to him now?
> Lady Isabel stole across the drawing-room to the other door, which was ajar. Barbara was seated at the piano, and Mr. Carlyle stood by her, his arm on her chair, and bending his face on a level with hers, possibly to look at the music. So, once had stolen, so, once had peeped the unhappy Barbara, to hear this self-same song. She had been his wife then;

she had received his kisses when it was over. Their positions were reversed.

   . . . Terribly, indeed, were their positions reversed; most terribly was
she feeling it. (489–90)

The novel operates on a constant dialectic of repetition and difference. Even the simplest objects awaken painful memories, such as
the occasion when Barbara asks Madame Vine to repair a piece of
jewelry that had once belonged to Isabel:

> Madame Vine . . . returned with her cement. Barbara watched her, as
> she took the pieces in her hand, to see how the one must fit on to the
> other.
>   "This has been broken once before, Joyce tells me," Barbara said.
> "But it must have been imperceptibly joined, for I have looked in vain
> for the damage. Mr. Carlyle bought it for his first wife when they were
> in London after their marriage. She broke it. You will never do it, Ma-
> dame Vine, if your hand shakes like that. What is the matter?"
>   A great deal was the matter. First, the ominous words had been upon
> her tongue. "It was broken here, where the stem joins the flower:" but
> she recollected herself in time. Next, came up the past vision of the
> place and hour when the accident occurred. Her sleeve had swept it off
> the table; Mr. Carlyle was in the room, this very room, and he had
> soothed her sorrow, her almost childish sorrow, with kisses sweet. Ah
> me! poor thing! I think our hands would have shaken as hers did. The
> ornament and the kisses were Barbara's now. (616)

Another source of the novel's melodrama is the pattern by which
Isabel constantly hears people discussing her as if she were dead.
Of course, to the other characters, she *is* dead, and so Isabel can
satisfy our archetypal curiosity about what people will say about us
when we are gone. This proves to be a mixed blessing, indeed. Isabel must endure "sharp lances perpetually thrust upon her memory—the Lady Isabel's memory—from all sides, [which] were full of
cruel stings, unintentionally though they were hurled" (656–57).
Thus, it is not just the past that haunts the present. The "dreadful
present," as Isabel terms it (502), thrusts itself upon her memories.
Many of these "cruel stings," predictably, are harsh, as in Madame
Vine's initial interview with Barbara, now Mrs. Carlyle:

> "Mr. Carlyle married Lady Isabel Vane, the late Lord Mount Severn's
> daughter. She was attractive and beautiful, but I do not fancy she cared
> very much for her husband. However that may have been, she ran away
> from him."

"It was very sad," observed Lady Isabel, feeling that she was expected to say something. Besides, she had her rôle to play.

"Sad? It was wicked, it was infamous," returned Mrs. Carlyle, giving way to some excitement. "Of all men living, of all husbands, Mr. Carlyle least deserved such a requital. You will say so when you come to know him. And the affair altogether was a mystery: for it never was observed or suspected, by any one, that Lady Isabel entertained a liking for another. She eloped with Francis Levison—Sir Francis, he is now. He had been staying at East Lynne, but no one detected any undue intimacy between them, not even Mr. Carlyle. To him, as to others, her conduct must always remain a mystery."

As Isabel/Madame Vine conceals her emotions by adjusting her spectacles, Barbara continues to twist the knife:

"Of course the disgrace is reflected on the children, and always will be; the shame of having a divorced mother—"

"Is she not dead?" interrupted Lady Isabel.

"She is dead. Oh yes. But they will not be the less pointed at, the girl especially, as I say. They allude to their mother now and then, in conversation, Wilson tells me: but I would recommend you, Madame Vine, not to encourage them in that. They had better forget her."

"Mr. Carlyle would naturally wish them to do so."

"Most certainly. There is little doubt that Mr. Carlyle would blot out all recollection of her, were it possible. But unfortunately she was the children's mother, and, for that, there is no help. I trust you will be able to instil principles into the little girl which will keep her from a like fate." (463)

But on occasion, Isabel hears more sympathetic portrayals of her character that are no less painful. Mrs. Hare, the mother of Barbara, informs Madame Vine that "she was the sweetest woman, that unfortunate Lady Isabel. I loved her then, and I cannot help loving her still. Others blamed her, but I pitied." Mrs. Hare is certain that Lady Isabel must have experienced the most profound regret and wretchedness after her elopement, and even acknowledges that, while Archibald undoubtedly loves her daughter "with a true, a fervent, a lasting love," she wonders if "there perhaps was more romantic sentiment in the early passion felt for Lady Isabel. Poor thing! she gave up a sincere heart, a happy home" (487–89). And Isabel's young cousin, William Vane, refuses to adhere to the household prohibition against speaking of Isabel, and expresses to Madame Vine how much he loved Isabel (664). All these incidents force Isabel to constantly confront the implications of her decision to elope with Sir Francis Levison. In a sense, she must repeatedly narrate her own past, just as *The Woman in White* and *Lady Audley's Secret* repeatedly narrate the movements of Laura Fairlie and Lady Audley. And Isabel's narration, like those others, forces "a radical reinterpretation of the present."[73] But here the similarities end in that it is Isabel who conducts the retrograde investigation of her life herself, constantly considering the consequences of her past action to her present life.

East Lynne was written just a few years after the passage of the Matrimonial Causes Act, so it is topical that Archibald, who is a lawyer, had "not lost a moment in seeking a divorce" (336). Yet he has not entirely become a creature of his changing times. He still clings to his old beliefs, by refusing to remarry while "She—who was my wife—lives" (372), citing the Biblical injunction against adultery.[74] Despite the law's newly temporalized construction of the definition of wife, Archibald seems unwilling to confront the possibility of doubleness. It is only when Lord Mount Severn, Isabel's nearest relative (who does not trust the newspapers [379]), receives from the French authorities confirmation of the report of her death, that Archibald proposes to Barbara (422). Isabel Vane transgresses the border between life and death—a boundary between before and after—and this renders her status (and therefore her identity) problematic. In accordance with the Matrimonial Causes Act, she *was* Archibald's wife, but *is* no longer; his divorce was perfectly legal, because she committed adultery.[75] But Archibald clearly holds to a different standard. He divorced Isabel under the terms of civil law, but continues to adhere to traditional Christian teachings that one commits adultery if one remarries while one's wife still lives, which was why he waited until he believed Isabel to be dead before he agreed to marry Barbara. The two "laws" are in conflict here. By the definition of civil law, Barbara, not Isabel, is his legal wife; but by the strict definition of the New Testament, the reverse is true. In effect, both women are his wives. Equally, both women are not. The law—or at least, the coexistence of two laws with competing definitions—has created a contradiction.

Two definitions. Two wives, the before and the after. In them, the past and present collide, just as Britain's past and present collide in the mid-Victorian period. Isabel is of noble birth, but sadly fallen in fortune due to the prodigal life-style of her father (the past glory of England's nobility now faded—a potent symbol of evolutionary degeneration), while Barbara springs from a wealthy household of the middle class (the emerging merchant class, and hence the future). Archibald Carlyle is also wealthy. He not only buys East Lynne from Isabel's father—the property transmitted not through

Burkean inheritance, but through a sales transaction—in a sense he buys *her,* as the only solution to her poverty and her virtual imprisonment in the household of a relative—"There is but one way . . ." (164). As a result of her wealthy middle-class origins, Barbara's life is relatively carefree—except for her longing for Archibald and her anguish about her brother, Richard—while Isabel's is a life of suffering and hardship that is not just emotional, but involves poverty, hunger, illness, deforming injury, physical pain, and humiliation.

The contrasting physical appearance of the two women mirrors their temporal irreconcilability, with Wood employing the light/ dark opposition common to many Victorian novels, including both *Lady Audley's Secret* and *The Woman in White.*[76] Isabel has "dark shining curls" and "soft dark eyes" (49), while Barbara is "very fair, with blue eyes, light hair, [and] a bright complexion" (61). Isabel's health is delicate, suggesting consumption. She is long to recover from illness after the birth of her first child (223), suffers a relapse a year after her third child was born (245), and Archibald sends her to Boulogne to recover her health. Like Lady Audley's latent insanity, Isabel's consumptive tendency is apparently inherited from her mother (581) and Isabel passes it on to her son, William, who dies of the illness. Conversely, Barbara has, in Dr Martin's words, "a thoroughly good constitution: a far stronger one than . . . Lady Isabel" (583)—the vigor of the middle class. Indeed, Isabel's first impression of Barbara upon her return to East Lynne is of a woman more beautiful than ever, and not a day older than when Isabel first saw her, at least nine years before[77]—a vision of arrested time.

Barbara is ostentatious and extravagant about her wardrobe— which is based on the latest fashion—while Isabel's natural tastes are simpler than her station; indeed, the irascible Miss Cornelia tells Barbara shortly after Isabel's marriage to Archibald that "I had expected airs and graces and pretence, and I must say she is free from them" (207). Isabel dresses up only with some reluctance. In fact, one of the rare occasions when her attire is consistent with her social status is at the benefit concert she has organized for Mr Kane (122), the organist of St Jude's Church who has a wife and seven children to support on a salary of thirty pounds (111–13).

The contrast between the two women is demonstrated very pointedly in the first encounter between the two, on the occasion of Isabel and her father, the Earl Mount Severn, going to church after a long absence from the village of West Lynne. Wood's third-person narration skillfully shifts the point of view to accentuate the

contrast. Here is the description of Barbara, from the austere Miss
Carlyle's perspective:

> Miss Carlyle completed her dinner preparations, all she did not choose
> to trust to Joyce, and was ready for church at the usual time, plainly but
> well-dressed. As she and Archibald were leaving their house, they saw
> something looming up the street, flashing and gleaming in the sun. A
> pink parasol came first, a pink bonnet and feather came behind it, a
> grey brocaded dress, and white gloves.
>
> "The little vain idiot!" ejaculated Miss Carlyle. But Barbara sailed up
> the street towards them, unconscious of the apostrophe.
>
> "Well done, Barbara!" was the salutation of Miss Carlyle. "The jus-
> tice might well call out! you are finer than a sunbeam." (106)

Miss Corny's initial impression is not even of a person, but of
"*something* looming up the street, flashing and gleaming in the
sun" (emphasis added), followed by "a pink parasol . . . a pink bon-
net and feather . . . a grey brocaded dress, and white gloves," doubt-
less the current style. In contrast, note Wood's description of
Isabel's entry into the church, this time from Barbara's point of
view:

> Scarcely were they seated, when some strangers came quietly up the
> aisle; a gentleman who limped as he walked, with a furrowed brow, and
> grey hair; and a young lady. Barbara looked round with eagerness, but
> looked away again: they could not be the expected strangers, the young
> lady's dress was too plain. A clear muslin dress with small lilac sprigs
> upon it, and a straw bonnet: Miss Corny might have worn it herself on
> a week day, and not have found herself too smart; but it was a pleasant
> dress for a hot summer's day. But the old beadle, in his many-caped
> coat, was walking before them sideways with his marshalling bâton, and
> he marshalled them into the East Lynne pew, unoccupied for so many
> years.
>
> "Who in the world can they be?" whispered Barbara to Miss Carlyle.
>
> "The earl and Lady Isabel."
>
> The colour flushed into Barbara's face, and she stared at Miss Corny.
> "Why—she has no silks, and no feathers, and no anything!" cried Bar-
> bara. "She's plainer than anybody in the church!"
>
> "Plainer than any of the fine ones—than you, for instance. The earl
> is much altered, but I should have known them both anywhere. I
> should have known her from her likeness to her poor mother; just the
> same eyes, and sweet expression." (107)

Isabel and Barbara, both to become Mrs. Carlyle in turn, are thus
anti-doubles of each other, as are the two nearly-equal halves of

the novel. Isabel Vane's elopement with Francis Levison occurs at virtually the mid-point. The first half is characterized by Isabel's relationship with Archibald Carlyle up to that point—her father's death, Archibald's proposal, their marriage and the births of their children, her growing jealousy of Barbara Hare, and Francis Levison's attentions. The second half deals with the consequences of Isabel's flight, her breakup with Levison, her poverty, the nearly fatal railway crash, her return to East Lynne as governess of her children, her illness and death. (The Richard Hare plot is interwoven throughout both halves.) Isabel's elopement with Levison splits the novel in two, and shatters her own life, alienating her from her family as much as St. Leon's acceptance of the stranger's gift of immortality does. Indeed, Wood titles one of her chapters, "Alone For Evermore." Victorian mores permit no return from her fall, which occurs "in a moment"—much as Laura Fairlie's transformation by marriage is momentary. And Isabel's realization of the enormity of what she has done is almost equally instantaneous:

> She had taken a blind leap in a moment of wild passion; when, instead of the garden of roses it had been her persuader's pleasure to promise her, (but which, in truth, she had barely glanced at, for that had not been her moving motive), she had found herself plunged into an abyss of horror, from which there was never more any escape; never more, never more. The very hour of her departure she awoke to what she had done: the guilt, whose aspect had been shunned in the prospective, assumed at once its true, frightful colour, the blackness of darkness; and a lively remorse, a never dying anguish, took possession of her soul for ever. (334)

As we have seen, the novel's two halves are mirror images of one another. In the first half, it is Barbara Hare who pines for Archibald and suffers to see him giving his love to another, and this situation is almost exactly reversed in the second half, with Isabel having to endure the displays of affection between Archibald and Barbara. Yet despite this mirror effect, there are distinct differences between the two halves, and the respective situations of Isabel and Barbara. For one thing, we feel differently disposed toward the two women. Margaret Oliphant's response to the two is typical: "From first to last, it is she alone [i.e., Isabel] in whom the reader feels any interest. Her virtuous rival we should like to bundle to the door and be rid of anyhow."[78] Nowhere is this contrast more obvious than in Wood's use of the heartbeat as a metaphor that helps to explain Oliphant's response (and ours) to the two heroines, and is a figure for temporality—the counting out of our existence in time. In the first half of the novel, Wood makes repeated references to Barbara's beating heart, particularly in her encounters with Archibald. In the second half, it is more often Isabel's heart that is beating. Yet, again, there are important differences. Barbara's heatbeat episodes are limited to situations in which she feels anxiety on behalf of her brother Richard (two of eleven references), or in which she must suppress her passion for Archibald (eight of her eleven specific heartbeat references). The episodes with Archibald usually involve her being in his presence and unable to express her emotions— either prior to his marriage to Isabel, when his attitude toward her is based strictly on friendship and he is unaware of her love for him (and hence it is not appropriate for her to express her love for him), or subsequent to his marriage to Isabel, when expressing her love would be even more unwelcome.[79]

In contrast, Lady Isabel's beating heart is referred to at least twenty-three times and beats in response to a much wider range of emotional experiences. In some cases, like Barbara, forbidden passion is involved, with Sir Francis Levison often the object, as Isabel encounters him in situations when she is either engaged, or married to Archibald. But Isabel's heart also beats in anger or frustration, as a result of jealousy, in response to grief, embarrassment, fear of her disguise being discovered, and as a result of maternal longing. On several occasions her heart is referred to as "rebellious" for beating strongly (263, 591).[80]

In its associations with the body—the animal nature—Wood obviously uses the beating of the heart to represent biological life (she makes a point of emphasizing that young William's "busy little heart had ceased to beat" when he dies of consumption [652]). But, more importantly, the heartbeat represents the emotional life of the characters. Except for the two women, only three other characters have this attribute: Of Isabel's father, Lord Mount Severn, it is said that "a better heart or more generous spirit never beat in human form" (42). There is a single reference to Richard Hare's beating pulses when he finally sees Sir Francis Levison (566), and Archibald's heart beats on three occasions: once as he gazes upon the sleeping Isabel, early in their marriage (198); once when his "pulses—for Richard Hare's sake—beat a shade quicker," as he begins to unravel the first threads of the murder plot (299); and once while standing at William's deathbed (651). To some extent, Archibald Carlyle is indeed heartless, as we perceive his singular inability to grasp the source of Isabel's anxieties. As Andrew Maunder observes, "[m]any nineteenth-century readers . . . must have considered Carlyle insensitive in his neglect of his wife." A contemporary reviewer stated that Carlyle's "character is consistent with the serious preoccupations which render him so unobservant of the love of Barbara on the one hand, and on the other of the jealousy and suffering of his devoted wife."[81] Carlyle is a man of his times, perhaps—a professional with a thriving practice and "serious preoccupations." But Wood's heartbeat motif also perfectly explains Oliphant's lack of interest in Barbara. Besides having considerably less emotional range than Isabel, she is effectively dead—and therefore more or less outside time—from the point that Isabel takes flight from East Lynne. The last time Barbara's heart beats—in fear for her brother being discovered—occurs on the night that Isabel runs away with Levison. We never see such emotion from her again. Significantly, on the occasion of Archibald's marriage proposal, after he has received the (false) news of Isabel's death, the scene lacks any mention of Barbara's heart beating. On the contrary, at the point when she murmurs her love and acceptance of his proposal, the text states that "Barbara's heart was at length at rest" (422). Her desires have been domesticated. And her heart seems to be at rest for the next 270 pages, but for the brief confession of Barbara's "feeling in my heart against your children [i.e., Archibald's children with Isabel], a sort of jealous feeling" in the final scene of the novel (690). No wonder Barbara seems ageless; it is as if she has been embalmed. In contrast, Isabel's heart beating episodes increase in frequency after she returns to East Lynne.

Curiously, with all these references to hearts beating, Wood refers to the *tempo* of the beats less than one time in five.[82] More often, she simply mentions the *fact* of the beating. For example, "[Barbara's] heart beat as she stood there silently, looking up at him in the moonlight" (65). Occasionally Wood refers to the strength of this pulse: "[Barbara's] heart beat as if it would burst its bounds" (324); "you might have heard Barbara's heart beating" (77); "Lady Isabel laid her hand upon her beating heart. But for that delectable 'loose-jacket', Afy might have detected her bosom's rise and fall" (451). Perhaps Wood's comparative lack of interest in the tempo of the pulse is consistent with her narrative tempo, which agonizingly prolongs her melodrama.

Wood's text seems to keep the two wives apart as much as possible, even allowing for the (assumed) class differences between governess and mistress. They do meet a few times in the course of Isabel's domestic duties, but such meetings are brief and awkward. And the final revelation of Isabel's true identity, as she lies dying, occurs while Barbara is away, the text preventing Isabel and Barbara from meeting as themselves, as if matter and anti-matter could not be brought together without mutual annihilation. Language itself breaks down in the scene between Isabel and Archibald, a linguistic dissolution that is figured in the temporal dimension. When she is finally revealed to her former husband without the ridiculous glasses, hat, and scarf that facilitated her disguise, neither language nor social custom has the means to represent such an unthinkable situation: " 'Isabel? Are you—were you Madame Vine?' he cried, scarcely conscious of what he said" (680). "Are you—were you . . ."; he literally cannot situate her identity in time, and his aporetic hesitation reveals that he does not know how to react to her. "The first clear thought that came thumping through his brain was, that he must be a man of two wives." In the deathbed scene that follows, one moment Archibald bends forward to kiss Isabel goodbye, "until his breath nearly mingled with hers," and the next moment "suddenly, his face grew red with a scarlet flush, and he lifted it again," Wood's text asking whether it is the image of the man who stole Isabel away or his "absent and unconscious wife" (683) that causes this reaction. Past and present have collided; Isabel herself is an aporia of time, an aporia that baffles the attempts of other characters to comprehend. Lord Mount Severn, being summoned to Archibald's house had "[n]ever . . . been so utterly astonished. At first he could not really understand the tale.

'Did she—did she—come back to your house to die?' he blundered. 'You never took her in? I don't comprehend.' " (685)

Mount Severn repeats Archibald's rhetorical hesitation.

Nor can Archibald's second wife, Barbara, fathom what has taken place, much less articulate it. She can only echo her husband's words, and then cannot speak at all, her confusion written with her body's reaction:

> "I went into her room, and I found that she was dying. But I found something else, Barbara. She was not Madame Vine."
>
> "Not Madame Vine!" echoed Barbara.
>
> "It was my former wife, Isabel Vane."
>
> Barbara's face flushed crimson, and then grew white as marble; and she drew her hand from Mr. Carlyle's. He did not appear to notice the movement, but stood with his elbow on the mantelpiece while he talked, giving her a rapid summary of the interview; not its details. (689)

East Lynne ends on a peculiar note, almost immediately after this revelation. Archibald reassures a tearful Barbara that he still loves her and proposes to solve the dilemma by refusing to speak of that which seems unable to be articulated: "Never . . . need her name be mentioned again between us. A barred name it has hitherto been: let it so continue" (690).[83] Barbara accepts this with a pledge that she only wishes to please her husband, then blushes, confessing that she has sometimes felt jealous of his children by Isabel, despite trying to suppress these feelings (Isabel had predicted earlier that a second wife would be jealous of Isabel's children, when, suffering from a fever, she had begged Archibald not to marry Barbara [229]). Archibald resorts to cliché ("Every good thing will come with time that we earnestly seek . . . the only way to ensure peace in the end is, to strive always to be doing right, unselfishly, under God" [691]), and the novel abruptly ends. Despite the words of consolation, Wood seems to have left her readers hanging. While Barbara's confused reaction is understandable, and blended families were not unknown (consider William Godwin's household, for example, with five children to four different fathers), the novel certainly foregrounds Barbara's anxieties about the issue of *issue*, because the novel ends on that note. Instead of the generations coming together, as we saw in the person of Emily St. Aubert, the generations seem to disperse, to be rendered discontinuous, in the family of Archibald, Isabel, and Barbara Carlyle. The apparent emptiness of Archibald's platitudes—his seeking to close the aporetic gap by echoing the "master narrative" of Victorian morality—might be a consequence of our twenty-first-century sensibilities, but it does seem that the novel's ending lacks closure, as if the enormity of Isabel's transgression has left not only Archibald and Barbara, but Wood herself, at a loss for words. Not being able to speak the forbidden name again, and hence having nothing else to say, we will say nothing. But we end on a note of discontinuity, just as Burke might have feared. The aporia remains, in its singular nakedness, despite Isabel's death. Instead of death being the only certainty, the inexplicable and inarticulable situation—its *wrongness*—continues to haunt the present.

Isabel calls into question the definition of marriage, which, as we have seen, depends on who is defining it. In returning to East Lynne, as if from the dead, she is what Derrida would call "the *revenant* (the ghost, he, she, or that which returns)," perfectly in keeping with both Miss Cornelia's assessment ("ghost" [532]) as well as Joyce's ("spectre" [622]). Perhaps more perplexing, however, with repercussions beyond that of the ghost story, is the way that Isabel complicates our perception of important social boundaries. Sarah Bernstein has described the 1860s as a decade preoccupied by anxieties about the blurring of boundaries: between species, in the debate fueled by Darwin's 1859 publication of *The Origin of Species* and "contemporary fears of evolutionary transformation not as progress but as degeneration"; and between identities, "whether the social borders of identities within the novels themselves or genre distinctions between types of fiction circulating in British culture."[84] I want to extend this argument to the realm of the legal and temporal transformations that take place outside time, in the space of a moment. The experience of the marriage ceremony separates the married from the unmarried, but it also transforms the unmarried into the married, as I noted in my discussion of Collins's Laura Fairlie. The marriage ceremony carries with it, for the female, the transformation of identity under the legal concept of coverture. It is a temporal boundary: before and after. It also has a spatial component that involves the household: inside and outside, the private and the public. Isabel seems to transgress all these boundaries when she returns to East Lynne from the dead. She *sees,* as an outsider, what an outsider should not see—the tender love scenes between Archibald and his new wife. The aporias that surround her contribute not just to melodrama but to a sense of the uncanny. In his discussion of the uncanniness of the *arrivant* (a word that can mean "'arrival,' 'newcomer,' or 'arriving'"), Derrida notes, in a passage that uncannily describes the situation of Isabel Vane/Madame Vine:

> What we could here call the *arrivant,* the most *arrivant* among all *arrivants,* the *arrivant* par excellence, is whatever, whoever, in arriving, does not cross a threshold separating two identifiable places, the proper and the foreign . . . , as one would say that the citizen of a given identifiable country crosses the border of another country. . . . I am talking about the absolute *arrivant,* who is not even a guest. He surprises the host—who is not yet a host or an inviting power—enough to call into question, to the point of annihilating or rendering indeterminate, all the distinctive signs of a prior identity, beginning with the very border that delineated a legitimate home and assured lineage, names and language, nations, families and genealogies. The absolute *arrivant* does not yet have a name or an identity.[85]

Isabel has crossed a border, in coming back, not just from Switzerland, but from the dead. Her name is as inarticulable as Sir Percival Glyde's or Lady Audley's (for different reasons), but the fact of her presence in body cannot be denied. Hers is a transgression that seems to violate more than social mores; it is as if she has upset the natural order of things. The past should have stayed buried!

The *wrongness* of her return is expressed by both Joyce ("Indeed, my lady, you never ought to have come" [653]) and Archibald ("It was wrong. Wrong in all ways" [682]). It is wrong because her time has passed. She has made her choice, she has been transformed, and she cannot be as she once was. Isabel is as unable to reconnect with her family as Godwin's St. Leon was with his, and she has become the same sort of wanderer, although, despite the length of the novel, she is not doomed to suffer this alienation for long. Archibald has tried to reconcile her inexplicable flight by refusing to utter her name, or hear it spoken. He has refused to articulate the inarticulable, subsituting a linguistic void, as if he could negate the signified by deleting the signifier from the lexicon, as he does when he changes the name of his first-born from "Isabel Lucy" to "Lucy" (333)—just as Marian and the Hartrights do not speak Percival Glyde's name and Sir Michael Audley does not speak the name of Helen/Lucy. But in *East Lynne,* the signified, the *arrivant,* confronts the household with her presence.

But only for awhile, for her anti-matter cannot long survive in our universe. Her time, after all, like the time of the nobility, is past. She is almost a "last of the race" figure. Soon Isabel will recross that boundary between life and death. In her death-bed interview with Archibald, she pleads for a word of forgiveness and love, "for I am as one dead now to this world, hovering on the brink of the next" (682). At this point, Isabel is neither Lady Isabel Vane, nor Mrs. Archibald Carlyle, nor even Madame Vine. She is nameless, so it is perhaps fitting that "Isabel ends without a name, without a past, with only initials carved on her tombstone."[86]

MARRIAGE, DEATH, NARRATIVE, AND MATHEMATICS

We return, like *revenants* ourselves, to the concept of closure and coherence. All three of these sensation novels depict the reading public's fascination with "the 'mechanism' of ordinary life,"[87] in part by exploring the boundaries of identity, marriage, and death and the transformative events with which they are associated. These boundaries are curiously intertwined, like the workings of an intricate timepiece. Marriage and death traditionally provided the resolution of plot discontinuities that assured narrative coherence. Let us consider to what extent such plot devices provide coherence and closure in these novels.

The numbers of such events alone are suggestive. There are eight marriages among the three novels that involve either major characters or characters who figure significantly in the plot (Laura and Sir Percival, Laura and Walter, and the non-marriage of Sir Percival's parents, in *The Woman in White;* George and Helen Talboys, Lucy Audley and Sir Michael Audley, and Robert and Clara in *Lady Audley's Secret;* Isabel and Archibald, and Archibald and Barbara in *East Lynne*). And there are no fewer than twelve deaths (actual or false) among the three novels, according to the same criteria. These are Laura Fairlie, Sir Percival Glyde, Count Fosco, and Frederick Fairlie in *The Woman in White;* Helen Talboys, George Talboys, and "Madame Taylor" in *Lady Audley's Secret;* and Isabel's father (the Earl of Mount Severn), Lady Isabel, William Carlyle, Isabel/Madame Vine, and Hallijohn (the man of whose murder Richard Hare was falsely accused) in *East Lynne*. One third of these deaths involve false reports, either intentional—by the "deceased" or by other parties (Laura Fairlie, Helen Talboys); unintentional (Isabel Vane); or a disappearance that was believed to be a death (George Talboys; Helen/Lady Audley believes, along with the reader, that she has caused her husband's death, a fact that we later learn to be untrue). False reports of death seemed sufficiently common that, upon reading of Isabel's death in the newspaper, Lord Mount Severn decided to make further inquiries, because he "knew what mistakes are often made in these reports from a distance" (*East Lynne* 379). A third of the twelve deaths among the novels—half the actual deaths—also involve some question of identity, with the deceased "not himself/herself" at the time of death (Count Fosco, whose real identity in the "Brotherhood" remains a mystery; Sir Percival Glyde, who has no right to that name or title since his parents were not married; "Madame Taylor"/Lady Audley; and "Madame Vine"/Isabel Vane). To these we might add that Hallijohn's death was an undisputed fact, but the identity of his murderer was long in doubt. The townspeople of West Lynne believed it to have been Richard Hare; Richard Hare believed it to have been the mysterious Thorn; and it was actually Francis Levison (who had used "Thorn" as an alias).

Questions of identity also contribute to confusion about the legitimacy of several of the marriages. Lady Audley and Sir Michael Audley's marriage is invalid because of Lady Audley's prior marriage to George Talboys. Laura Fairlie's marriage to Sir Percival may be legal in one sense—neither party was married before—but her husband is certainly not Sir Percival Glyde. And Archibald Carlyle's marriage to Barbara Hare, while valid in the eyes of the law, is questionable in Archibald's mind, as I have previously discussed, because of his belief in the Biblical definition of marriage. Such questions about identity and the legitimacy of marriage undermine Burke's "sure principle of transmission." If we cannot know who the parties are, or the legal status of their marriages, how can property, values, and life be transmitted coherently across generations? Death in these novels is surrounded by similar questions and paradoxes.

Heidegger also saw Death as paradoxical, calling it "the possibility of the absolute impossibility of *Da-sein*." In other words, being-in-the-world (*Da-sein*) means living with the possibility of one's death ever present. In Heidegger's scheme, this anticipation of one's end—which can occur at any moment, and which one can see occurring to others—gives meaning to our existence. Heidegger drew an analogy to an unripe fruit in the process of ripening. "[R]ipening, it *is* the unripeness. The not-yet is already included in its own being."[88] Da-sein is similarly unfulfilled up to the moment of death, yet paradoxically, the death that would fulfill Da-sein ends it. Being-in-the-world cannot experience its own negation. It is a passage that cannot be passed, a "stuckness"—an aporia.

The relationship between death and narrative, like that between marriage and narrative, is twofold. Death or marriage can resolve plot discontinuities, providing closure. But throughout these three novels we see bodies of written evidence in support of deaths or marriages that are false—*The Woman in White*'s "The Narrative of the Tombstone" is a lie in almost every respect. The prevalence of false narratives has implications for how we view temporality, because of the circular relationship between time and narrative that Ricoeur describes, in which narrative "humanizes" time. If events such as marriage and death symbolically structure or segment time, thus also humanizing it, the questionable truth value of such events, their uncertainty, meant that, far from being the ultimate solution (re-solution), death and marriage have a disturbingly paradoxical character. Rather than resolving aporias, they introduce their own. And we have already seen that narrative's ability to resolve these aporias is questionable, for narrative can be manipulated. Thus Kermode's "fictive concords with origins and ends" are fictive, indeed.[89]

At its lowest level, language is a system of binary opposites—black marks on a white page (spatial organization), or a pattern of sounds and silences (temporal organization). Curiously, the way that narrative is used to resolve the discontinuities in these novels often involves a process of denial or negation. Laura Fairlie's name is erased from her tombstone; the marriage register forged by Percival Glyde is burned and his name is never mentioned to his widow;

Lady Audley is spirited out of the country in secret, to live and die in an asylum as "a certain Madame Taylor,"[90] the text just as unable to articulate a name for her as her "husband" is; and Isabel Vane's name will not be spoken in the Carlyle household, although her presence continues to be felt in the household, both in the bodies of her children and in the absence of the signifier of her name (her presence is never so real as in the reinforced prohibition against speaking her name).

Neither death nor marriage can resolve all the discontinuities introduced in these novels. All three conclude on a strangely discordant domestic note. *The Woman in White* ends with Hartright saying, "let Marian end our Story" (646)—and she does not. There is a narrative void. *Lady Audley's Secret*'s final, "At peace" chapter seems to provide a happy ending, but it possesses an unreal quality of dreams realized (and unrealized), a fantasy resolution. "Mr. Audley's dream of a fairy cottage has been realised" in "a fantastical dwelling-place of rustic woodwork." This is a place to which others come (a succession of visitors is mentioned, including Master George Talboys, "a bright, merry-hearted girl, and a grey-bearded gentleman," and Sir Harry Towers [435–36]). The fairy cottage is in sharp contrast to "the familiar dwelling-place in which [Sir Michael Audley] once dreamed a brief dream of impossible happiness" (436): Audley Court is shut up, ruled over by "a grim old housekeeper." One enters faerie, and one is expelled from it, by a strange economy. Unlike Audley Court, that handiwork of Time, the fairy cottage of the concluding chapter seems to lie outside time. If time is involved at all, it is the realm of anticipation. Sir Michael "remains in London until Alicia shall be Lady Towers, when he is to remove to a house he has lately bought in Hertfordshire" (436). We are poised in the moment before Alicia becomes Lady Towers, in a land where the past—for George Talboys, at least—"fades little by little every day," a fairyland where one forgets his past life. Memory is not the present of things past, as it was for Emily St. Aubert. And *East Lynne* concludes with the nameless grave and another "interdicted" name, yet another narrative void. We have moved in the opposite direction from *Melmoth*'s multiplying of narrative incidents to an elimination of them.

At the same time we see the motif of narrative or linguistic erasure, a form of subtraction, as a strategy to achieve coherence, we see—perhaps in compensation for the subtraction—a different form of multiplication. The strangely wrought coherence of these three novels is mirrored by the peculiarly configured families, all of which seem to possess a surplus of members. Laura and Walter

Hartright also have Marian living with them. Indeed, during the long quest to restore Laura's identity earlier in the novel, while they lived in hiding in London, Walter and Marian seemed more like the parents of the childlike Laura than as equals. (They combine their funds and divide up their labors, with Marian doing the housework and Walter earning a living by painting. They painstakingly reeducate Laura, "amus[ing] her in the evenings with children's games at cards, with scrap-books full of prints" [452–56]. Laura, in turn, "spoke as a child might have spoken, . . . showed me her thoughts as a child might have shown them" [458].) A similar spouse-cum-sibling relationship exists at the end of *Lady Audley's Secret*. Robert and Clara Audley live with Clara's brother George in the "fairy cottage" (435), and little Georgey is often present. While Archibald and Barbara Carlyle's partnership seems unencumbered by additional members, two of Isabel's children live in the household—some of Barbara's last words in the novel are of them—and, barred name or no, Isabel's memory and the enormity of what she had done continue to haunt the present. In all three of these concluding situations, therefore, it is as if the harmony contains too many notes.

We have moved from *Udolpho*'s concluding domestic scene where the two lovers are united in marriage but no children are present, to situations where these scenes include children of multiple marriages, as if the fears of the degeneration of the family mandate reinforcements. But the surplus of family members complicates the single narrative thread of inheritance suggested by Burke's hereditary metaphor. (It should be noted that in *East Lynne*, the patriarchal descent is not threatened. As I have previously discussed, such a threat produced some of the anxiety associated with bigamy—the children of multiple fathers complicating the hereditary lines. Indeed, the illegitimate son of Isabel and Francis Levison is conveniently killed in the railway crash that nearly killed Isabel [374]. His death not only makes it possible for her to return to East Lynne without the complication of a child, it also conveniently disposes of any [patriarchal] hereditary complications.)

Burke's *Reflections on the Revolution in France* articulates the desire for a coherent narrative in the face of a sense of historical dislocation, a victory for concordance over discordance. But in the face of what Walter Hartright termed "our unintelligible world,"[91] a world of rapid change, the triumph of concordance over discordance grows increasingly challenging. Life's milestones afford the means of structuring our existence, by creating ritualized boundaries that segment our lives into a series of befores and afters. But these boundaries have become more permeable in the nineteenth century, and existence is not so neatly segmented. Time is not so easily humanized, as both it, and human existence, become increasingly complicated in the age of Darwin, the railway, the telegraph, and the divorce court. The "Victorians' view of their own place in the cosmic sequence"[92] is exceedingly difficult to determine, much less articulate, and one possible solution is just not to speak of it.

The angel in the house, who, as part of the "sure principle of inheritance," served to transmit moral values to the next generation, has herself been transformed by her times. She may have become, like Laura Fairlie, childish and feeble-minded, a victim of crafty schemers. She may have become, like Lady Audley, an hereditary madwoman, "a designing and infamous woman." Or she may have become, like Isabel Vane, an aporia in the house. It is indeed, as Margaret Oliphant put it, a "changed world" in which she stands.[93] No longer a matter only for philosophers, the aporetic nature of time has reached the inner sanctum.

5

Conclusion

AWARENESS OF THE APORETIC CHARACTER OF TIME IS NOT PECULIAR TO the eighteenth or nineteenth centuries. Aristotle wrestled with it in the fourth century, B.C.[1] and Augustine struggled with it some 700 hundred years later,[2] still more than 1400 years before the time we are considering here. But there seems little question that the various historical, scientific, technological, and cultural developments that I have been discussing, as well as the increase in the size of the reading public, have resulted in the anomalies of time's aspect being brought home to a wider audience. It is no longer a concern that is confined to philosophers, as evidenced by the temporal discourses encoded in a number of popular novels from the period of the French Revolution to the age of Darwin.

We have seen that both revolution and evolution have left their marks upon public perceptions of temporality, and new anxieties have accompanied new developments in the theories of science and history, in applied technology, and in law. If there are recognizable trends during the period we have examined, we may say that public time has assumed greater importance, and that popular conceptions of time have simultaneously expanded and become foreshortened. They have expanded, or lengthened, because there is now a growing realization that there is so much more time for which to account—the "deep time" of the astronomers, geologists, and biologists. Ricoeur stated that human existence is "torn between the sense of its mortality and the silent presence of the immensity of time enveloping all things,"[3] and during the period I have been examining, enveloping time has grown more immense indeed. Yet, paradoxically, time has become foreshortened in the public awareness during the same period, because railway travel and the telegraph have sharply reduced the time required to travel or communicate, resulting in a heightened consciousness of the present moment. The present of the 1860s is not a rich, thick three-fold present as Augustine theorized, but a more anxious, "now-saying" moment.

Another way of stating that public time has assumed greater importance is to say that there has been an increase in the extent to which time has become socially constructed during this period, a temporal phenomenon that the novels on my list have certainly demonstrated. Largely absent from *The Mysteries of Udolpho,* socially constructed time has begun to emerge by the time *Melmoth the Wanderer* appeared in 1820. We see this in the novel's preoccupation with clocks and bells, and more dramatically with its anxieties about humans being transformed into mechanisms by industrialization. Some of Mary Shelley's short fiction and in particular her novel *The Last Man,* expresses an apparent desire to escape from linear time altogether—to view it from a vantage point that encompasses all of history, to fictively reverse its direction, and even to render it "null" (as Shelley referred to it in her journals). Finally, in *The Woman in White, Lady Audley's Secret,* and *East Lynne,* we see society further standardizing time through the railway timetable and demanding that its members be conversant with this new definition of time. But we also see social changes such as divorce, a growing middle class and more permeable class boundaries altering notions of identity. These changes occur even as scientific developments such as evolutionary theory and the laws of thermodynamics spark widespread fears of degeneration. Evolution provides a narrative of generations that contests the Burkean model of preservation through inheritance. But despite the emergence of this competing narrative, and despite growing evidence that the ability to construct a coherent account of "origins and ends" is beyond the power of narrative, the desire to do so shows no sign of diminishing. If anything, the advent of the sensation novel, and the detective novel that will follow, reflect an increased desire to fashion narratives that fit the pattern of the evidence at hand.

In the Introduction chapter, I noted the human desire to situate ourselves and our own experience of time in the context of the time of the universe, and Ricoeur's claim that we reconcile the gap between these two kinds of time in three ways: through the mechanisms of the calendar and clock (belonging to both the human and astronomical universes), through the succession of generations that permits us to travel back in time along a chain of ancestral memories, and through narrative, which has the power to reconfigure the time of the world in human terms, to "organize" time "after the manner of a narrative."[4] The calendar and the clock certainly assume a greater importance during the period we have considered, but this development has not always been a positive one, because it has produced a hyperawareness of the present moment and a new set of anxieties.

The series of human generations continues to be an important mechanism by which we bridge "the time of the soul and the time of the world,"[5] but generational succession is an imperfect solution to time's aporias. It is often regulated by institutions that can become corrupt. Of even more concern, closer examination reveals that the narrative of generations is often not as orderly and coherent as Burke's model seems to suggest, and this problem is exacerbated by the magnitude of the gulf of time to be bridged. In fact, the hope of progress that the generational model offers can just as easily be inverted to the fear of degeneration.

Nor is narrative a perfect means of reconciling time's aporias. It is not without its own limitations in a world that often seems, in the words of Collins's Hartright, "unintelligible."[6] Narrative certainly has not *repaired* the rupture that the French Revolution and eighteenth-century notions of progress created, offering instead only imagined solutions. But narrative still offers us a vision of "origins and ends," which is one reason why new narratives such as Darwin's continue to emerge. In one sense, Darwin's *Origin* seems to reinvoke the Burkean vision of a continuous chronicle of generations—Ricoeur's chain of memories—uniting it to a vision of progress, "of endless forms most beautiful and most wonderful."[7] But progress means change, and there is no change without loss, which is why Darwin's narrative could just as easily become a degenerative model, a reversal of Burke.

We recall Peter Brooks's assertion that a narrative is a "construction" whose verification "lies in its plausibility, its fitting the needs of explanation."[8] It is a representation of reality that attempts to account for the available evidence in a plausible fashion, but even an imperfect representation affords some consolation. By "organizing" time, narrative—whether Burke's or Darwin's—gives meaning to the interval of human existence. Compared to the time of the cosmos, the span of a human life seems no more than the interval between *tick* and *tock*. However inadequate to the task, narrative is ultimately the best solution that we have to reconcile temporal aporias and humanize the world of time.

Notes

INTRODUCTION

The epigraphs to this chapter are drawn from Edmund Burke, *Reflections on the Revolution in France* (Amherst, NY: Prometheus Books, 1987), 37–38; Paul Ricoeur, *Time and Narrative,* trans. Kathleen Blamey and David Pallauer, 3 vols. (Chicago: University of Chicago Press, 1984–88), 3: 114; Jacques Derrida, *Aporias: Dying—awaiting (one another at) the "limits of truth,"* trans. Thomas Dutoit (Stanford, CA: Stanford University Press, 1993), 13; respectively.

1. Aristotle, *Physics,* trans. Robin Waterfield (Oxford: Oxford University Press, 1996), 102–3 (217b) and 105 (219a).
2. Augustine, *Confessions,* trans. R. S. Pine-Coffin (London: Penguin Books, 1961), 270 (book 11, sec. 22) and 261 (11: 10). Augustine assures us that his answer is not, "He was preparing Hell for people who pry into mysteries" (262; 11: 12), but rather that there was no "before" until time was created (263; 11: 13).
3. Burke, *Reflections on the Revolution in France,* 28, 82, and 84–85; Robert Miles, *Gothic Writing 1750–1820: A Genealogy* (London: Routledge, 1993), 33.
4. Hayden White, *Tropics of Discourse: Essays in Cultural Criticism* (Baltimore: The Johns Hopkins University Press, 1985), 83–84.
5. It should be noted here that the phenomenon of emplotment is certainly not unique to the Gothic genre. But the Gothic's preoccupation with themes of inheritance, usurpation, and identity, and its compulsion to narrate and resolve discontinuities between past and present (all to be discussed momentarily) *are,* I would argue, characteristics peculiar to the genre.
6. Ann Radcliffe, *The Mysteries of Udolpho,* ed. Bonamy Dobrée (Oxford: Oxford University Press, 1998), 26.
7. William Godwin, *Enquiry Concerning Political Justice and its Influence on Morals and Happiness,* 3rd ed., 2 vols (1798, facsimile ed., Toronto: The University of Toronto Press, 1946), 1: 92–93.
8. See Ellen Moers, *Literary Women* (Garden City, NY: Doubleday & Company, 1976), in particular her chapter entitled "Female Gothic," 90–110.
9. Ian Watt, *The Rise of the Novel: Studies in Defoe, Richardson and Fielding* (Berkeley: University of California Press, 1957), 290. Watt allows "several novelists, such as Smollett, Sterne and . . . Burney" to rise above this level of mediocrity.
10. Jacqueline Howard, *Reading Gothic Fiction: A Bakhtinian Approach* (Oxford: Oxford Clarendon Press, 1994). Howard is critical of feminist "appropriations" (17, 53) of the Gothic, especially where such critical approaches rely on post-structuralist models (Sassurean linguistics and Lacanian psychoanalysis) to view the language and culture of Gothic fiction, rather than eighteenth and nineteenth century institutions and ideologies (51–53). Howard bases her critical approach on situating Gothic novels in their historical and cultural context, using

Bakhtin's *heteroglossia,* or "multi-voicedness" as a means of exploring various discourses in Gothic novels (1–5).

11. See Howard, *Reading Gothic Fiction,* 113–17, and Radcliffe, *The Mysteries of Udolpho,* 13, for this particular example.

12. Diana Long Hoeveler, *Gothic Feminism: The Professionalism of Gender from Charlotte Smith to the Brontës* (University Park: Pennsylvania State University Press, 1998), 148. A full exploration of gender-based critical views of the Gothic is beyond the scope of this project. However, for some fine studies, see David Punter, *The Literature of Terror: A History of Gothic Fiction from 1765 to the Present Day* (London: Longman, 1980), who sees the Gothic as having been, from "its inception a 'woman's fiction,' written by and for women" (411); Kate Ferguson Ellis, *The Contested Castle: Gothic Novels and the Subversion of Domestic Ideology* (Urbana: University of Illinois Press, 1989), who divides the genre into (female) "insider narratives" (e.g., Radcliffe) and (male) "outsider narratives" (e.g., Godwin, Lewis, and Maturin); Eugenia C. DeLamotte, *Perils of the Night: A Feminist Study of Nineteenth-Century Gothic* (New York: Oxford University Press, 1990); and Anne Williams, *Art of Darkness: A Poetics of Gothic* (Chicago: University of Chicago Press, 1995), who states "'Gothic' is not one, but two; like the human race, it has a 'male' and a 'female' genre" (1). As to Charlotte Dacre, at least Hoeveler discusses her; neither Ellis nor Williams mentions her at all (the latter not even in a chapter devoted to *The Monk* entitled "Demon Lovers"), and Punter identifies *Zofloya* as a derivative of *The Monk* and briefly mentions its influence on Percy Shelley's Gothic romances, *Zastrozzi* and *St. Irvine* (Punter, *The Literature of Terror,* 106).

13. Punter, *The Literature of Terror,* 52. Punter is speaking specifically of Horace Walpole's *The Castle of Otranto* in this quotation, but he goes on to characterize much of the fiction of the 1790s as often rejecting the present "in favour of geographically and historically remote actions and settings" (61). Raymond Chapman makes virtually the same claim about the "carelessness" of Gothic writers toward the reality of the past, specifically the Middle Ages; see Raymond Chapman, *The Sense of the Past in Victorian Literature* (New York: St. Martin's Press, 1986), 34. Earlier, J. M. S. Tompkins had attributed the "nominally historic" interest in the past that characterized much of the fiction of the last three decades of the eighteenth century as "an elaboration of the impressions made by Gothic architecture on modern sensibility." See J. M. S. Tompkins, *The Popular Novel in England, 1770–1800* (London: Methuen, 1932), 227.

14. Samuel Taylor Coleridge, *Biographia Literaria* (London: J. M. Dent, 1997), bk. 14, 179.

15. The term "explained supernatural" has become so commonplace in discussions of Ann Radcliffe's fiction, particularly *The Mysteries of Udolpho,* that it is difficult to determine where the phrase originated. Critics frequently use the term in quotation marks but without attribution; among them are Terry Castle, "The Spectralization of the Other in *The Mysteries of Udolpho,*" in *The New Eighteenth Century: Theory, Politics, English Literature,* ed. Felicity Nussbaum and Laura Brown (New York: Methuen, 1987), 231–53, citation at 231; Robert Miles, *Ann Radcliffe: The Great Enchantress* (Manchester, UK: Manchester University Press, 1995), 129, 132–33; and E. J. Clery, whose *The Rise of Supernatural Fiction, 1762–1800* (Cambridge, UK: Cambridge University Press, 1995) contains a chapter on Radcliffe entitled "The Supernatural Explained," in which the term is used at least six times without attribution. Perhaps the earliest references to the term itself were an August 1794 review of *Udolpho* in *British Critic,* whose anonymous

reviewer stated, "[t]he endeavour to explain supernatural appearances and incidents, by plain and simple facts, is not always happy . . ." quoted in Deborah D. Rogers, *The Critical Response to Ann Radcliffe* (Westwood, CT: Greenwood Press, 1994), 21; and a *Critical Review* article, also from August 1794, which stated, "mysterious terrors are continually exciting in the mind the idea of a supernatural appearance, keeping us, as it were, upon the very edge and confines of the world of spirits, and yet are ingeniously explained by familiar causes," quoted in Nicola Trott, "Wordsworth's Gothic Quandary," *Charles Lamb Bulletin* 110 (2000): 47. Certainly the objection to the practice itself, whatever the terminology used, was much discussed. Mrs. Anna Barbauld and Sir Walter Scott, both writing in 1810, refer to the practice, Barbauld giving at least a qualified justification of the device. She states, "though [Radcliffe] gives, as it were, a glimpse of the world of terrible shadows, she yet stops short of anything really supernatural: for all the strange and alarming circumstances brought forward in the narrative are explained in the winding up of the story by natural causes; but in the mean time the reader has felt their full impression" (quoted in Rogers, *The Critical Response to Ann Radcliffe,* 96–97). Scott takes exception to the practice, saying "[w]e disapprove of the mode introduced by Mrs Radcliffe and followed by Mr. Murphy [actually Charles Robert Maturin] and her other imitators, of winding up their story with a solution by which all the incidents appearing to partake of the mystic and the marvellous are resolved by very simple and natural causes" (*Quarterly Review* 3 [May 1810]: 344, quoted in Clery, *The Rise of Supernatural Fiction,* 193n). In his 1824 memoir, "Mrs Ann Radcliffe," Scott claims that Radcliffe's "rule" of accounting for the "mysterious, and apparently superhuman" elements of her narrative by natural explanations "has not been done with uniform success." See *The Complete Works of Sir Walter Scott,* 10 vols. (Philadelphia: Parry & McMillan, 1857), 8: 70–71.

16. Tzvetan Todorov, *The Fantastic: A Structural Approach to a Literary Genre,* trans. Richard Howard (Ithaca, NY: Cornell University Press, 1975), 41–42.

17. "Preface to *Lyrical Ballads,*" in *Literary Criticism of William Wordsworth,* ed. Paul M. Zall (Lincoln: University of Nebraska Press, 1966), 40.

18. H. L. Mansel, "Sensation Novels," *Quarterly Review* 113 (1863): 489; Henry James, "Miss Braddon," *The Nation,* 9 November 1865, repr. in *Notes and Reviews* (Cambridge, MA: Dunster House, 1921), 112–13.

19. Mansel, "Sensation Novels," 482–83.

20. "Our Female Sensation Novelists," *Christian Remembrancer* n.s. 46 (1863): 210, quoted in Kate Flint, *The Woman Reader 1837–1914* (New York: Oxford University Press, 1993), 277.

21. White, *Tropics of Discourse,* 83–84.

22. Burke, *Reflections on the Revolution in France,* 37–38.

23. Ricoeur, *Time and Narrative,* 3: 182, 3: 183–86, and 1: 3, respectively.

24. Frank Kermode, *The Sense of an Ending: Studies in the Theory of Fiction* (New York: Oxford University Press, 1967), 8.

25. Fiona J. Stafford, *The Last of the Race: The Growth of a Myth from Milton to Darwin* (Oxford: Clarendon Press, 1994) 83–109.

26. A. J. Sambrook, "A Romantic Theme: The Last Man," *Forum for Modern Language Studies* 2 (1966): 28.

27. George Gordon, Baron Byron, "Darkness," in *Lord Byron: The Major Works,* ed. Jerome J. McGann (Oxford: Oxford University Press, 2000), 272–73.

28. Sambrook, "A Romantic Theme: The Last Man," 27.

29. To be sure, the notion of a six thousand-year old universe did not always

exist: for example, the creation myth in Plato's *Timaeus* is not dated, because it would not have occurred to him to do so; and Aristotle argued that time was boundless and the universe had no precise beginning point at all, but has always existed, with a cyclic perspective on history. (Troy's fall was in Aristotle's future as well as his past.) See Stephen Toulmin and June Goodfield, *The Discovery of Time* (Chicago: University of Chicago Press, 1977), 43–46. Toulmin and Goodfield discuss the Protestant Reformation's literalist reaction to the Catholic church's centuries-old tradition of allegorical interpretation of the Bible on p. 75.

30. Immanuel Kant, *Universal Natural History and Theory of the Heavens,* trans. W. Hastie (Ann Arbor: The University of Michigan Press, 1969), 144–45. Also quoted in Toulmin and Goodfield, *The Discovery of Time,* 131–32. In fact, Kant maintained that this process of creation was ongoing.

31. Milton K. Munitz, introduction to *Universal Natural History and Theory of the Heavens* (Ann Arbor: The University of Michigan Press, 1969), vii–viii. Also referred to by Toulmin and Goodfield, *The Discovery of Time,* 133.

32. Toulmin and Goodfield, *The Discovery of Time,* 146–49.

33. Ricoeur, *Time and Narrative,* 3: 183.

34. Stafford, *The Last of the Race,* 118.

35. Ricoeur, *Time and Narrative,* 3: 12.

36. DeLamotte summarizes the views of eight critics who discuss this issue from various perspectives. See *Perils of the Night,* 188.

37. Reinhart Koselleck, *Futures Past: On the Semantics of Historical Time,* trans. Keith Tribe (Cambridge, Massachusetts: The MIT Press, 1985), 27, 246–50, 145, 28–29.

38. Aristotle, *Physics,* 105 (219a); Augustine, *Confessions* 261 (11: 11).

39. Koselleck, *Futures Past,* 256–57. Koselleck does not provide the identity of the German word. He only states, "Toward the end of the century, the collective singular 'progress' was coined in the German language, opening up all domains of life with the questions of 'earlier than' or 'later than,' not just 'before' and 'after.'"

40. M. M. Bakhtin, "Discourse in the Novel," in *The Dialogic Imagination,* ed. Michael Holquist, trans. Caryl Emerson and Michael Holquist (Austin: University of Texas Press, 1998), 279.

41. Miles, *Ann Radcliffe: The Great Enchantress,* 38.

42. Koselleck, *Futures Past,* 142.

43. Benedict Anderson, *Imagined Communities: Reflections on the Origin and Spread of Nationalism* (London: Verso, 1991), 193–94.

44. Richard D. Altick, *Victorian People and Ideas* (New York: W. W. Norton & Company, 1973), 73.

45. Altick, *Victorian People and Ideas,* 226.

46. Charles Darwin, *The Origin of Species,* in *Darwin,* ed. Philip Appleman (New York: W. W. Norton & Company, Inc., 1970), 199.

47. Altick, *Victorian People and Ideas,* 228.

48. Earlier, I referred to both Burke and Godwin as emphasizing movement. My view here is not inconsistent with that position. Godwin sees the essence of humanity improving over time (perfectibility). Burke, however, sees the movement of the generations in time as transmitting the essence of British civilization, but this essence remains largely unchanged. He does not "exclud[e] a principle of improvement" (*Reflections,* 38), but he does not emphasize it as much as Godwin, so Burke's narrative is "conservative" in this sense. Nowhere is this more evident than in Burke's discussion of the Glorious Revolution of 1688 and Parliament's change in the royal succession. "A state without the means of some change is

without the means of its conservation." Burke argues quite forcefully that the Glorious Revolution does not represent the right of the people to choose their kings. On the contrary, he claims that the legislature never "manifest[ed] a more tender regard for that constitutional policy [of conservation], than at the time of the Revolution, when it deviated from the direct line of hereditary succession." He asserts that the hereditary descent remained "in the same blood," and was only "qualified with Protestantism," noting that the legislature "altered the direction but kept the principle" (26). Paradoxically, for Burke, the "deviat[ion]" does not represent a deviation. This dialectic of movement (the alteration of the line of succession) and non-movement (the preservation of the line) is consistent with Aristotle's meditations on the movement and non-movement of time.

49. Bakhtin, "Forms of Time and of the Chronotope in the Novel," in *The Dialogic Imagination*, 84.

50. Ricoeur, *Time and Narrative*, 1: 72.

51. Kermode, *The Sense of an Ending*, 44–45.

52. Ricoeur, *Time and Narrative*, 1: 3.

53. Ibid.

54. *The Journals of Mary Shelley, 1814–1844*, ed. Paula R. Feldman and Diana Scott-Kilvert (Baltimore: Johns Hopkins University Press, 1987), 463.

55. White, *Tropics of Discourse*, 83–84.

56. Wilkie Collins, *The Woman in White*, ed. Julian Symons (New York: Penguin Books, 1985), 546.

CHAPTER 1.   NO TIME LIKE THE PRESENT

Portions of this chapter originally appeared in *Journal for Early Modern Cultural Studies* 5.1 (2005): 49–75 and are reprinted with permission.

The epigraphs to this chapter are drawn from Augustine, *Confessions,* trans. R. S. Pine-Coffin (London: Penguin Books, 1961), 278 (bk. 11, sec. 28); Ann Radcliffe, *The Mysteries of Udolpho,* ed. Bonamy Dobrée (Oxford: Oxford University Press, 1998), 634; Paul Ricoeur, *Time and Narrative,* trans. Kathleen Blamey and David Pallauer, 3 vols. (Chicago: University of Chicago Press, 1984–1988), 3: 140; respectively.

1. Robert Miles, *Ann Radcliffe: The Great Enchantress* (Manchester, UK: Manchester University Press, 1995), 38.

2. Reinhart Koselleck, *Futures Past: On the Semantics of Historical Time,* trans. Keith Tribe (Cambridge, Massachusetts: The MIT Press, 1985), 257; Frank Kermode, *The Sense of an Ending: Studies in the Theory of Fiction* (New York: Oxford University Press, 1967), 96.

3. I am aware of, and agree with, James Watt's contention that the Gothic genre as we know it is "a relatively modern construct" and that, notwithstanding Walpole's subtitle added to the second edition of *Otranto*—"a Gothic story"—and Clara Reeve's emulation of this convention in *The Old English Baron: A Gothic Story* (1778), the novels that we today regard as constituting the Gothic genre were considered to be "romances." See James Watt, *Contesting the Gothic: Fiction, Genre and Cultural Conflict, 1764–1832* (Cambridge, UK: Cambridge University Press, 1999), 1–3. Still, whatever the label, and whatever the literary moment in which it was first applied, Radcliffe's romances were widely recognized

as foremost among a class of fictions that we now regard as a genre. We see evidence of this in Coleridge's letter to Wordsworth in October 1810, when he notes: "I amused myself a day or two ago on reading a romance in Mrs. Radcliff's [sic] style with making out a scheme, which was to serve for all romances a priori—only varying the proportions." Quoted in Deborah D. Rogers, *The Critical Response to Ann Radcliffe* (Westwood, CT: Greenwood Press, 1994), 99. And Sir Walter Scott is one of a number of critics who referred to Radcliffe's "imitators," quoted in E. J. Clery, *The Rise of Supernatural Fiction, 1762–1800* (Cambridge, UK: Cambridge University Press, 1995), 108–9.

4. See, for example, George Lukács, who notes that "in the most famous 'historical novel' of the eighteenth century, Walpole's *Castle of Otranto,* history is . . . treated as mere costumery," *The Historical Novel,* trans. Hannah and Stanley Mitchell (London: Merlin Press, 1962), 19; David Punter, who observes of *The Castle of Otranto,* that "Walpole is quite unconcerned with the details of life in the Middle Ages; what he is concerned with is conjuring a general sense of 'pastness,'" *The Literature of Terror: A History of Gothic Fictions from 1765 to the Present Day* (London: Longman, 1980), 52; and Terry Castle, notes to *The Mysteries of Udolpho,* by Ann Radcliffe, ed. Bonamy Dobrée (Oxford: Oxford University Press, 1998), 686.

5. Ann Radcliffe, *The Mysteries of Udolpho,* ed. Bonamy Dobrée (Oxford: Oxford University Press, 1998), 94, 97. Subsequent references to this edition will be parenthetical; Castle, notes to *The Mysteries of Udolpho,* 681.

6. Castle, notes to *The Mysteries of Udolpho,* 692.

7. Miles, *The Great Enchantress,* 175, 87–88, 144–45.

8. Edmund Burke, *Reflections on the Revolution in France* (Amherst, NY: Prometheus Books, 1987), 24, 38.

9. M. M. Bakhtin, "Epic and Novel: Toward a Methodology for the Study of the Novel," in *The Dialogic Imagination,* ed. Michael Holquist, trans. Caryl Emerson and Michael Holquist (Austin: University of Texas Press, 1998), 13.

10. David Punter, *The Literature of Terror: A History of Gothic Fictions from 1765 to the Present Day* (London: Longman, 1980), 6.

11. Bakhtin, "Epic and Novel," 17, 13, 15.

12. Miles, *The Great Enchantress,* 38.

13. Among the most provocative treatments of the novel's dreamlike affect is Terry Castle's "The Spectralization of the Other in *The Mysteries of Udolpho,*" in *The New Eighteenth Century: Theory, Politics, English Literature,* ed. Felicity Nussbaum and Laura Brown (New York: Methuen, 1987), 231–53, especially 232, 239. Ian P. Watt's "Time and Family in the Gothic Novel: *The Castle of Otranto,*" *Eighteenth Century Life* 10.3 (1986): 159–71, also refers to dreams in a temporal context (164). Both articles will be discussed below.

14. Although Emily herself does not use this term in connection with the wedding, it is clear that what occurs is a usurpation from the language of Emily's aunt: "'I shall now celebrate my marriage with some splendour,' continued Madame Montoni, 'and to save time I shall avail myself of the preparation that has been made for yours, which will, of course, be delayed a little while'" (142). But Emily does, on more than one occasion, refer to Montoni's "usurped authority" over her (240, 379).

15. Castle, notes to *Udolpho,* 683.

16. See Rhoda L. Flaxman, "Radcliffe's Dual Modes of Vision," in *Fetter'd or free? British Women Novelists, 1670–1815,* ed. Mary Anne Schofield and Cecilia Macheski (Athens, OH: Ohio University Press, 1986), 124–33, for a discussion of Radcliffe's cinematic descriptive technique.

17. M. M. Bakhtin, "Forms of Time and of the Chronotope in the Novel: Notes toward a Historical Poetics," in *The Dialogic Imagination*, 155, emphasis original.

18. Ricoeur, *Time and Narrative*, 3: 182.

19. Aristotle, *Physics*, trans. Robin Waterfield (Oxford: Oxford University Press, 1996), 105 (219a), 109 (221b).

20. See Castle, notes to *Udolpho*, 674–75, for a discussion of Radcliffe's preference for the lyrical side of Milton; see Rictor Norton, *Mistress of Udolpho: The Life of Ann Radcliffe* (London: Leicester University Press, 1999), 49–50, for a discussion of Radcliffe's use of poetical quotations, in which Norton cites a study by Warren Hunting Smith, *Architecture in English Fiction*. The total of twenty-one includes one poem referred to by the narrator as "that beautiful exhortation of an English poet" (184), but which is unidentified and may be by Radcliffe herself, according to Castle, notes to *Udolpho*, 684. I have not been able to identify this poem either.

21. I consider as exceptions the "sonnet" Du Pont inscribed to Emily (7), the stanzas of Emily's father about the celestial chorus bearing the soul to heaven (175), the fragment of Du Pont's song (446), "The Mariner" (463), and "Shipwreck" (558–59), for a total of five.

22. The four explicit seasonal references are as follows: (a) Spring: "The First Hour of Morning" ("breath of May" [74]), "The Sea Nymph" (179–81), "The Mariner" (463–64), and "The Butter-fly to His Love" ("April buds" [477–79]); (b) Summer: "The Glow-Worm" (16–17); (c) Autumn: "To Autumn" (592).

23. M. M. Bakhtin, "Discourse in the Novel," in *The Dialogic Imagination*, 320–21.

24. Miles, *Great Enchantress*, 51. For a general overview of eighteenth-century notions of the sublime, the beautiful, and the picturesque, Miles's chapter, "The aesthetic context" (34–56) is helpful. For contemporary sources on the sublime and the beautiful, see Edmund Burke, *A Philosophical Enquiry into the Origin of Our Ideas of the Sublime and Beautiful*, ed. David Womersley (London: Penguin Books, 1998). For contemporary sources on the picturesque, see William Gilpin, *Observations, Relative Chiefly to Picturesque Beauty, Made in the Year 1772, on Several Parts of England; Particularly the Mountains, and Lakes of Cumberland, and Westmorland*, 2 vols (London: R. Blaimire, 1786).

25. Flaxman, "Radcliffe's Dual Modes of Vision," 125.

26. D. L. Macdonald, "Bathos and Repetition: The Uncanny in Radcliffe," *Journal of Narrative Technique* 19.2 (1989): 199.

27. Bakhtin, "Forms of Time and of the Chronotope in the Novel," 247–48.

28. Aristotle. *Physics*, 105 (219a); Augustine, *Confessions*, 261 (bk. 11, sec. 11).

29. Watt, "Time and Family in the Gothic Novel," 164.

30. Linda Bayer-Berenbaum, *The Gothic Imagination: Expansion in Gothic Literature and Art* (Rutherfurd, NJ: Fairleigh Dickinson University Press, 1982), 29.

31. Scott Paul Gordon notes that the novel "stages a competition between two vocabularies (economic vs. sentimental)" and argues that Quesnel's ownership of the tree "ensures that his economic evaluation of this object triumphs over St. Aubert's sentimental evaluation of it." However, "by insisting that Quesnel is blind when it comes to taste, *Udolpho* itself awards St. Aubert the victory he cannot achieve within the novel." See Scott Paul Gordon, *The Practice of Quixotism: Postmodern Theory and Eighteenth-Century Women's Writing* (New York: Palgrave Macmillian, 2006), 158–59.

32. Bakhtin, "Forms of Time and of the Chronotope in the Novel," 84.

33. For discussions of the castle as a representation of the body, see Clare Kahane's essay, "The Gothic Mirror," in *The (M)other Tongue: Essays in Feminist Psychoanalytic Interpretation,* ed. Shirley Nelson Garner, Claire Kahane, and Madelon Sprengnether (Ithaca, NY: Cornell University Press, 1985), 334–51, in which Kahane cites some earlier critics, including Norman Holland and Leona Sherman. For discussions of oppressive, enclosing spaces, see Kate Ferguson Ellis, *The Contested Castle: Gothic Novels and the Subversion of Domestic Ideology* (Urbana: University of Illinois Press, 1989) and Eugenia C. DeLamotte, *Perils of the Night: A Feminist Study of Nineteenth-Century Gothic* (New York: Oxford University Press, 1990). There have been a few notable exceptions to my claim that little attention has been paid to the castle as a trope of time: one of these is Bayer-Berenbaum, who observes, "When the walls that outlast generations crumble, the powers of time appear even more awesome. In the face of decaying material, we sense the eternal forces of destruction, and the eternity of time is contrasted by the temporality of matter" (*The Gothic Imagination,* 27). DeLamotte also mentions the fact that Gothic buildings are associated with the historic past (*Perils of the Night,* 15). Ian P. Watt's "Time and the Family in the Gothic Novel" is also an exception that will be discussed momentarily. And James Watt observes that "[t]hough the Gothic castle has provided a powerful metaphor for psychoanalytic literary criticism in recent decades, it is important to recognize the more literal role which the castle played in the political discourse and in the fiction of the late eighteenth and early nineteenth centuries" (*Contesting the Gothic,* 64).

34. Quoted in Castle, notes to *Udolpho,* 686.

35. Ian P. Watt, "Time and Family in the Gothic Novel," 163.

36. Ricoeur, *Time and Narrative,* 3: 114.

37. Bakhtin, "Forms of Time and of the Chronotope in the Novel," 246.

38. There do seem to be limits to this apparent tolerance, however. In *The Italian,* Ellena is forced to sleep in a "miserable mattress, over which hung the tattered curtains of what had once been a canopy." See Ann Radcliffe, *The Italian,* ed. Frederick Garber (Oxford: Oxford University Press, 1981), 211.

39. Eugenia C. DeLamotte notes that lingering on the threshold, accompanied by terror, is a standard Gothic motif (*Perils of the Night,* 16, 19).

40. Gérard Genette, *Narrative Discourse: An Essay in Method,* trans. Jane E. Lewin (Ithaca, NY: Cornell University Press, 1983), 34, emphasis original.

41. See Tzvetan Todorov, *The Fantastic: A Structural Approach to a Literary Genre,* trans. Richard Howard (Ithaca, NY: Cornell University Press, 1975), 41–42, for a discussion of Radcliffe's novels as examples of the uncanny; and Castle, "Spectralization" 251 (and, in fact, much of her essay).

42. Sigmund Freud, "The Uncanny," in *Collected Papers.* 5 vols. (New York: Basic Books, 1959), 4: 387–89.

43. The same passage is quoted by Castle, "Spectralization," 239. No one seems to have mentioned the odd syntax of Laurentini's exclamation. Whose is the fascination? Presumably Laurentini's fascination with the Marchioness, but the construction opens this up to question.

44. William Wordsworth, "Lines Written a Few Miles above Tintern Abbey, On Revisiting the Banks of the Wye during a Tour, July 13, 1798," in *Lyrical Ballads and Other Poems, 1797–1800,* ed. James Butler and Karen Green (Ithaca, NY: Cornell University Press, 1992) 116–20; quotations from lines 62, 76–77. For Radcliffe's influence on Wordsworth and the Romantic poets, see Norton, *Mistress of Udolpho,* 250–53.

45. Ricoeur, *Time and Narrative,* 3: 76.

46. Ibid., 3: 76, 3: 36–37. Wordsworth does go on to imagine the future, at least Dorothy's future, in which she is remembering being with him in that time and place.

47. Gilles Deleuze, *Difference and Repetition,* trans. Paul Patton (New York: Columbia University Press, 1994), 81.

48. Castle, "Spectralization," 238–39.

49. Robert Miles, *Gothic Writing 1750–1820: A Genealogy* (London: Routledge, 1993), 76.

50. Bayer-Berenbaum, *The Gothic Imagination,* 70. It is worth noting that Edmund Burke identifies infinity as one of the sources of the sublime. See *A Philosophical Enquiry,* 115.

51. Terry Castle, in her "Spectralization of the Other" essay, states that "modern critics devote themselves almost without exception solely to those episodes in the novel involving the villainous Montoni and the castle of Udolpho—even though these make up barely a third of the narrative" (232); Punter, *The Literature of Terror,* 67. Punter does, however, go on to acknowledge that Ann Radcliffe's "symbolism reaches a high point in the scene at Le Blanc where the servant Ludovico, locked for a night in a haunted room, reads a ghost story which eventually shades into reality" (68).

52. Castle, notes to *Udolpho,* 690–91.

53. Carolyn Dinshaw, "Reading Like a Man: The Critics, the Narrator, Troilus, and Pandarus" in *Chaucer's* Troilus and Criseyde: *"Subgit to alle Poesye"; Essays in Criticism,* ed. R. A. Shoaf (Binghamton, NY: Medieval and Renaissance Texts and Studies, 1992), 68.

54. For example, when Annette begins to tell the story of "the strange accident that made the Signor [Montoni] lord of this castle [Udolpho]," Annette interrupts her narrative because she imagines she hears a sound (236–37); later, Emily is "awakened by a noise which seemed to arise within her chamber," but decides the sound was only a dream (260); and one night, while listening intently for the "mysterious strains of music" she has sometimes heard, Emily seems to hear "the low mourning of some person in distress," but can't be sure whether the sound is real or imagined (355).

55. See Todorov, *The Fantastic:* "The fantastic . . . lasts only as long as a certain hesitation: a hesitation common to reader and character, who must decide whether or not what they perceive derives from 'reality' as it exists in the common opinion" (41).

56. Elizabeth MacAndrew, *The Gothic Tradition in Fiction* (New York: Columbia University Press, 1979), 110. Also quoted in Jacqueline Howard, *Reading Gothic Fiction: A Bakhtinian Approach* (Oxford: Oxford Clarendon Press, 1994), 22.

57. Genette, *Narrative Discourse,* 234–35, 228n.

58. Review of *The Mysteries of Udolpho,* by Ann Radcliffe, in *British Critic* 4 (August 1794): 110–21, reprinted in Rogers, *The Critical Response to Ann Radcliffe,* 19–21.

59. Mrs. Anna Letitia Barbauld, "Mrs Radcliffe," Introductory Preface in *The British Novelists,* 50 vols (London: Rivington and others, 1810), 43: i–ii.

60. E. J. Clery, *The Rise of Supernatural Fiction, 1762–1800* (Cambridge, UK: Cambridge University Press, 1995), 118.

61. Castle, "Spectralization," 234–35.

62. In fact, James Watt makes just such a point when he states that "[c]onser-

vative critics, in particular, praised this technique [of the explained supernatural], drawing attention to the parallel between credulity or superstition and revolutionary idealism, and implicitly equating rationalizing explanation with a recovery of the rule of law." One critic, fed up with the fact that the reading public was "much more delighted with stories about raw heads and bloody bones," than with more legitimate writers such as Henry Fielding, saw Radcliffe as an exception to the popular trend because she "*has not introduced ghosts,* but the effects of the belief of ghosts on the human imagination" (Watt, *Contesting the Gothic,* 116–17, emphasis original). Terry Castle would take this a bit further, with her claim about the world being "metaphorically suffused with a new spiritual aura" in the passage previously cited. Scott Paul Gordon provides a fascinating reading of *Udolpho* in the context of perception in his chapter entitled "Ann Radcliffe's *The Mysteries of Udolpho* and the Practice of Quixotism," arguing that, while the novel "discipline[s] Emily's overactive imagination" (mainly through Emily's father) and "ridicule[s] Emily's superstition, it does not establish as its alternative a clear-sighted perception of the 'real,' or objects as they 'really are.' Instead, *Udolpho* moves readers from one filter . . . to another. The filter it advocates spiritualizes the landscape." See Gordon,*The Practice of Quixotism,* 141–66, quotation at 149.

63. [Sir Walter Scott], *Quarterly Review* 3 (May 1810), 344, quoted in Clery, *The Rise of Supernatural Fiction,* 108–9.

64. Hayden White, *Tropics of Discourse: Essays in Cultural Criticism* (Baltimore: The Johns Hopkins University Press, 1985), 83–84.

65. Castle, "Spectralization," 234–35.

66. Deleuze, *Difference and Repetition,* 77.

67. Genette, *Narrative Discourse,* 116.

68. Martin Heidegger, *Being and Time,* trans. Joan Stambaugh (Albany: State University of New York Press, 1996), 300–303 (§65); Ricoeur, *Time and Narrative,* 3: 76.

69. Joan Stambaugh, translator's preface to *Being and Time,* by Martin Heidegger, trans. Joan Stambaugh (Albany: State University of New York Press, 1996), xv–xvi.

70. Wordsworth, "Tintern Abbey," lines 92, 85–86.

71. Augustine, *Confessions,* 278 (bk. 11, sec. 28).

72. Ricoeur, *Time and Narrative,* 3: 141, 140.

73. Burke, *Philosophical Enquiry,* 101–2, 108.

74. Ann Radcliffe, "On the Supernatural in Poetry," *New Monthly Magazine* (1826): 149.

75. Robert D. Hume, "Gothic Versus Romantic: A Revaluation of the Gothic Novel," *PMLA* (1969): 282–83.

76. Heidegger, *Being and Time,* 302.

77. Augustine, *Confessions,* 274 (bk. 11, sec. 26), 269 (bk. 11, sec. 20). This project was well under way when I read Gregory Sean O'Dea's dissertation, *The Temporal Sublime: Time and History in the British Gothic Novel* (University of North Carolina at Chapel Hill, 1991; Ann Arbor: University Microfilms International, 1991). While O'Dea cites the same excerpt from Augustine's *Confessions,* his analysis of Augustine's meditation as applied to Ann Radcliffe's novels is more concerned with time as a psychological construct in a fleeting present than as an extension of the mind (94–99).

78. Koselleck, *Futures Past,* 272.

79. Ian P. Watt, "Time and Family in the Gothic Novel," 164; Ricoeur, *Time and Narrative,* 3: 133; Bakhtin, "Forms of Time and of the Chronotope in the Novel," 84.

80. Augustine, *Confessions,* 263 (bk. 11, sec. 13), emphasis original.

81. Donald Williams Bruce, "Ann Radcliffe and the Extended Imagination," *Contemporary Review* 258 (1991): 302.

82. Scott Mackenzie, "Ann Radcliffe's Gothic Narrative and the Readers at Home," *Studies in the Novel* 31.4 (1999): 416–17. Mackenzie's use of *aporia*'s dual connotations—hesitation and "inarticulable contradiction" (which he attributes to the French translation of *aporia*)—exactly corresponds to my own, as described in my introduction.

83. Todorov, *The Fantastic,* 41. Macdonald argues that "[t]he *fantastic,* in Todorov's sense, is strictly excluded from Radcliffe," because the supernatural is always "undercut" by Emily's descriptions of her superstitions (Macdonald, "Bathos and Repetition: The Uncanny in Radcliffe," 198). While I do not necessarily disagree with this assessment, in the strict Todorovian sense, there is nevertheless for the reader *some* kind of hesitation that occurs, *some* element of suspense that falls between memory and expectation.

84. Mackenzie, "Ann Radcliffe's Gothic Narrative," 416.

85. Norton, *Mistress of Udolpho,* 275n.

86. Ibid., 37.

87. It is safe to say, however, that, had the fateful lines in fact contained any confirmation of the theory that the Marchioness was Emily's mother, all could not have been so satisfactorily resolved in Emily's mind at the end of the novel.

88. Ellis, *The Contested Castle,* 123–24. Norton also asserts that "[w]omen are the real sources of power and wealth in the novel" and notes that the novel emphasizes female ownership of property (*Mistress of Udolpho,* 101–2).

89. Bayer-Berenbaum, *The Gothic Imagination,* 48, quoting Andrew Martindale, *Gothic Art,* 140; and "Lamprecht, quoted in [Wilhelm] Worringer, *Form in Gothic,*" 41 (Bayer-Berenbaum, 72n).

90. Burke, *Reflections,* 38. Just as Burke argues that the apparent "depart[ure] from the strict order of inheritance" (22) of the crown at the time of the Glorious Revolution was in fact not a discontinuity but an affirmation of the principle of hereditary succession (21–28).

91. Bakhtin, "Forms of Time and of the Chronotope in the Novel," 89, emphasis original.

92. Macdonald, "Bathos and Repetition," 199.

93. Castle, "Spectralization," 249.

94. Koselleck, *Futures Past,* 257.

95. Punter, *The Literature of Terror,* 61, 59.

96. Rictor Norton concludes that "the only manuscript in Ann Radcliffe's own handwriting to have escaped oblivion" is a commonplace book recording the progress of her health (and her final illness) from May through November 1822, ending a few months before her death (*Mistress of Udolpho,* 238). The Talfourd memoir takes up the first 132 pages of volume one of the four-volume *Posthumous Works.* Approximately 74 of the 132 pages of Talfourd's memoir is taken up by travel journals, covering ten tours throughout England.

97. Benedict Anderson, *Imagined Communities: Reflections on the Origin and Spread of Nationalism* (London: Verso, 1991), 193–94.

98. Norton, *Mistress of Udolpho,* 94–95, 8, 90–91.

99. Miles, *Great Enchantress,* 58–62.

100. Bakhtin, "Discourse in the Novel," 416, 419–20.

101. Ibid., 420. And not only the novel genre. In "Traversing Regions of Terror: The Revolutionary Traveller as Gothic Reader," Jan Wellington notes that travel

writing has long been "recognised as an important progenitor of Gothic fiction" but goes on to analyze "how the Gothic 'returned the favor' and influenced the experience and discourse of travel" (*Studies in Travel Writing* 7 [2003]: 145–67, quotation at 146). Wellington cites numerous examples from the letter-journal of an English woman who traveled in France during the late 1790s, whose travel writing owes much to the discourses of terror common to Gothic novels.

102. Miles, *Great Enchantress*, 38, 49–50.

103. The wave of imitations was remarked upon by Scott (*Quarterly Review*, 344), and by a famous letter to a 1798 journal, "Terrorist Novel Writing," quoted in E. J. Clery and Robert Miles, eds., *Gothic Documents: A Sourcebook 1700–1820* (Manchester, NH: Manchester University Press, 2000): 183–84, among others. The Radcliffe imitators and associations with Jacobinism are discussed by both Norton, *Mistress of Udolpho,* 156–59, and Clery, *The Rise of Supernatural Fiction,* 134–45.

104. Norton, *Mistress of Udolpho,* 102–5.

105. Ricoeur, *Time and Narrative,* 1: 83.

106. Bakhtin, "Forms of Time and of the Chronotope in the Novel," 247–48.

107. Norton notes that Sir Walter Scott was an exception, Scott having commented that he could not imagine undertaking a second reading of the novel. Norton, *Mistress of Udolpho,* 107.

108. Ricoeur, *Time and Narrative,* 1: 67–68.

109. Ibid., 1: 31.

110. Ibid., 1: 72; Bayer-Berenbaum, *The Gothic Imagination,* 11.

111. Deleuze, *Difference and Repetition,* 77.

112. Ricoeur, *Time and Narrative,* 3: 36.

CHAPTER 2: THE CLOCK IS TICKING

The epigraphs to this chapter are drawn from Frank Kermode, *The Sense of an Ending: Studies in the Theory of Fiction* (New York: Oxford University Press, 1967), 44–45; and Aristotle, *De Anima,* trans. J. A. Smith, in *The Basic Works of Aristotle,* ed. Richard McKeon (New York: Random House, 1941), 561 (415b).

1. Both Robert Kiely and Chris Baldick refer to such a claim being sufficiently widespread that neither cites any critics by name: "*Melmoth the Wanderer* is a late—some have said the last—Gothic novel." See Robert Kiely, *The Romantic Novel in England* (Cambridge, MA: Harvard University Press, 1972), 189. "There are two kinds of account given of Maturin's place in Gothic fiction, both of them potentially misleading. The first, adopted in several standard literary histories, speaks of *Melmoth the Wanderer* as the last—and possibly the greatest—of the Gothic novels in the line from Walpole through Radcliffe and Lewis." See Chris Baldick, introduction to *Melmoth the Wanderer,* by Charles Robert Maturin (Oxford: Oxford University Press, 1998), ix.

2. Jack Null discusses *Melmoth's* structure and chronology in the context of prior critical misreadings, while G. St. John Stott provides a graphic depiction of *Melmoth's* tale structure which is accurate, though some lesser embedded accounts that perhaps do not reach the status of "tales" are omitted. See Jack Null, "Structure and Theme in *Melmoth the Wanderer*" *Papers on Language and Literature* 13.2 (1977): 136–39; and G. St. John Stott, "The Structure of *Melmoth the Wanderer,*" *Études Irlandaises* 12.1 (1987): 42. I should point out that Monçada

does tell John Melmoth that "we are all beads strung on the same string" (298), when John exclaims at Monçada's passing reference to Stanton (see Charles Maturin, *Melmoth the Wanderer,* ed. Douglas Grant [Oxford: Oxford University Press, 1998], 298), but my position is that this metaphor has more to do with individuals being subject to the Wanderer's manipulations than with the structure of the novel itself. Further references to the *Melmoth* text will be parenthetical.

3. Baldick, introduction to *Melmoth,* x.

4. Linda Bayer-Berenbaum, *The Gothic Imagination: Expansion in Gothic Literature and Art* (Rutherford, NJ: Fairleigh Dickinson University Press, 1982), 77, 82.

5. Paul Ricoeur, *Time and Narrative,* 3 vols., trans. Kathleen Blamey and David Pallauer (Chicago: University of Chicago Press, 1984–88), 1: 3.

6. Jacques Derrida, *Aporias: Dying—awaiting (one another at) the "limits of truth,"* trans. Thomas Dutoit (Stanford, CA: Stanford University Press, 1993), 13.

7. G. J. Whitrow, *Time in History: The Evolution of Our General Awareness of Time and Temporal Perspective* (Oxford: Oxford University Press, 1988), 158–59.

8. Stuart Sherman, *Telling Time: Clocks, Diaries and English Diurnal Form, 1660–1785* (Chicago: The University of Chicago Press, 1996), 2–5. Sherman provides a concise summary of Harrison's quest on pp. 163–70, while Whitrow provides more technical details (*Time in History,* 139–46). Sherman gives a humorous account of Samuel Pepys's fascination with his new pocket watch that featured a minute hand, and makes the point that "[i]n 1665 [the year Pepys acquired his new watch], a minute watch was rare, expensive, and horologically hubristic" (80).

9. David S. Landes, *Revolution in Time: Clocks and the Making of the Modern World* (New York: Barnes and Noble Books, 1983), 171.

10. Ricoeur, *Time and Narrative,* 1: 3.

11. M. M. Bakhtin, "Forms of Time and of the Chronotope in the Novel: Notes toward a Historical Poetics," in *The Dialogic Imagination,* ed. Michael Holquist, trans. Caryl Emerson and Michael Holquist (Austin: University of Texas Press, 1998), 155.

12. Null points out what any careful reader quickly discerns within the first dozen pages of the novel: that there is a twenty-year discrepancy between the 150 years repeatedly referred to and the novel's 1816 setting, vs. the portrait's date of 1646, even while Null argues that "Maturin does have a definite and consistent chronology in mind, which suggests careful planning." See *Melmoth* 7, 18; Null, "Structure and Theme in *Melmoth the Wanderer,*" 137–40. This anomaly is never explained by Maturin.

13. Stott discusses the reader's changing conceptions of the Wanderer in his essay, referring to the first three figures specifically. See Stott, "The Structure of *Melmoth the Wanderer,*" 44–50. Dale Kramer identifies characteristics of Satan, Adam and Eve, Cain, and Faust (both Goethe's and Marlowe's versions) as well as the Wandering Jew. See Dale Kramer, *Charles Robert Maturin* (New York: Twayne Publishers, Inc., 1973), 97. Kathleen Fowler explores the connections to the book of Job in more detail. See Kathleen Fowler, "Hieroglyphics of Fire: *Melmoth the Wanderer,*" *Studies in Romanticism* 25.4 (1986): 527–28. As the Wanderer seems at one point to "die" and then is subsequently resurrected, I've added the Lazarus analogy.

14. William Godwin, *St. Leon: A Tale of the Sixteenth Century* (1799), ed. Pamela Clemit (Oxford: Oxford University Press, 1994).

15. The emphasis is the author's. Maturin is unsparing in his use of emphasis, and, unless otherwise noted, all italics are the author's.

16. Young John Melmoth inherits property from his uncle; Stanton has no lineal heirs and is imprisoned by a "grasping relative"; Monçada's legitimate brother dies trying to free him, Monçada himself flees to England, and there are no apparent heirs; Immalee and her brother both die, their family presumably coming to an end; the Walbergs inherit her brother's property, and the Mortimer family property ultimately passes to a distant relative.

17. Baldick, introduction to *Melmoth the Wanderer*, xii; Fowler, "Hieroglyphics of Fire," 521.

18. There are at least five narrative levels. By numbers of pages, 39 percent of the novel is at the second level (a tale embedded within a frame tale, such as the Stanton manuscript or Monçada's tale), 29 percent at the third (a tale within a tale within a tale, such as Immalee's tale), and 17 percent at the fourth (such as the Lovers' Tale).

19. M. M. Bakhtin, "Discourse in the Novel," 308.

20. Peter Brooks, *Reading for the Plot: Design and Intention in Narrative* (Cambridge, MA: Harvard University Press, 1992), 28.

21. Kathleen Fowler has also mentioned this. See Fowler, "Hieroglyphics of Fire," 525.

22. Balzac is quoted in Victor Sage, introduction to *Melmoth the Wanderer* (London: Penguin Books, 2000), xiii. The *Monthly Review* article is from January 1821 (pp. 81–85), reprinted in Rictor Norton, *Gothic Readings: The First Wave, 1764–1820* (London: Leicester University Press, 2000), 333–34. Fowler asserts that the Wanderer's failure to find a replacement is a mark of the strength of faith of those whom he has tempted. See Fowler, "Hieroglyphics of Fire," 527–28.

23. Kramer, *Charles Robert Maturin*, 125. Jack Null has summarized the novel's tales somewhat differently, seeing in them the motif of family disintegration, viewed as a pattern of betrayals. See Jack Null, "Structure and Theme in *Melmoth the Wanderer*, 140–41.

24. It has been generally assumed that this character is Stanton's heir and is motivated to commit him to a madhouse out of greed. For example, Dale Kramer states, "An unprincipled relative, Stanton's natural heir, arranges to trap Stanton in a mad house." See Kramer, *Charles Robert Maturin*, 103. This may well be an accurate assessment, although it should be noted that Maturin's text is somewhat vague on this point. The novel refers to him as "Stanton's next relative, a needy unprincipled man." Later in the paragraph, he is referred to as a "kinsman," and as "the younger Stanton" when he addresses the elder Stanton twice as "cousin"; his older relative uses the same title in return (45–46). That Stanton's younger kinsman is needy and unprincipled is the apparent source for the assumption that greed motivates his betrayal.

25. I use the term loosely here. In the Catholic tradition (according to *The New Catholic Encyclopedia*), the figure termed the "promoter of the faith" (popularly called "devil's advocate") opposes the "saint's advocate" and patrons of candidates for beatification or sanctification. One of his functions is to ensure a more rigorous examination of the candidate by "prepar[ing] in writing all possible arguments, even at times seemingly slight, against the raising of any one to the honours of the altar." *The Catholic Encyclopedia*, Charles G. Herbermann and others, eds., 15 vols. (New York: Robert Appleton Company, 1907–12), s.v. *advocatus diaboli*.

26. Null describes some of the problems of precisely dating Stanton's chronology. See Jack Null, "Structure and Theme in *Melmoth the Wanderer*, 138–39n.

27. Despite the fact that most of the published criticism on *Melmoth the Wan-derer* refers to the tales by their "official" names, I find them more than a little confusing. The "Tale of the Spaniard" could be referring to any of several tales that are set in Spain; the "Tale of the Indians" is only partly set on an island off the coast of India, and Immalee is of Spanish origin and returns to Spain where much of the tale takes place; "The Tale of Guzman's Family" is perhaps most mis-leading of all, since it's really about a family whose surname is Walberg (and in fact, poor Guzman is offstage dying for the first third of the tale, and dead for the last two thirds); and there are enough lovers throughout the interpolated tales that "The Lovers' Tale" is not a helpful title. Nor is Maturin's use of the definite article consistent, as sometimes it is part of the title and sometimes not. (I have repro-duced them exactly as they are listed in the novel.) In the interests of clarity, I have therefore decided to assign "unofficial" or informal titles that more nearly reflect the principal characters in each. In making such a choice, I realize I may be exemplifying the phenomenon to which Gilles Deleuze refers in his analysis of Lewis Carroll's *Through the Looking-Glass and What Alice Found There,* when Alice and the Knight discuss the song the Knight sings. Deleuze comments: "There are indeed in Carroll's classification four names: there is the name of what the song really is; the name denoting this reality, which thus denotes the song or represents what the song is called; the sense of this name, which forms a new name or a new reality; and the name which denotes this reality, which thus de-notes the sense of the name of the song, or represents what the name of the song is called." See Gilles Deleuze, *The Logic of Sense,* trans. Mark Lester (New York: Columbia University Press, 1990), 30. New reality or not, my names are easier to remember.

28. And indeed, he is forced to escape Spain altogether, after he is presumed dead. To remain would be to emphasize his aporetic status as the living dead. He has no identity, and must begin a new life in Ireland.

29. We need to consider the Wanderer's views on religion with caution. Ma-turin himself included a footnote, in an earlier passage (a theological debate be-tween Melmoth and Immalee), in which he complained that reviewers had previously attributed "the worst sentiments of my worst characters" to him, and asserting that "the sentiments ascribed to the stranger [i.e., Melmoth] are diamet-rically opposite to mine, and . . . I have purposely put them into the mouth of an agent of the enemy of mankind" (303n). Nevertheless, as Regina B. Oost has pointed out, some reviewers still disregarded the footnote and "castigated the au-thor." See Regina B. Oost, " 'Servility and command': Authorship in *Melmoth the Wanderer,*" *Papers on Language and Literature* 31.3 (1995): 302. Despite the au-thor's assertions, however, Immalee's childhood is spent in a virtual Eden, and her life as a child of nature is highly romanticized—in sharp contrast to her life as a victim, first of her parents' machinations, and ultimately, of the Inquisition.

30. Null, "Structure and Theme in *Melmoth the Wanderer,* 143. The "Tale of the Indians" begins at nearly the precise midpoint of the Oxford edition (272 of 542 pages), and this is the case with other editions, as well: p. 208 of 412 in the University of Nebraska Press edition (Lincoln, 1961); and p. 302 of 607 in the Penguin Books edition (London, 2000).

31. Baldick, introduction to *Melmoth the Wanderer,* xv–xvi.

32. See Baldick, introduction to *Melmoth the Wanderer,* xii.

33. Martin Heidegger, *Being and Time,* trans. Joan Stambaugh (Albany: State University of New York Press, 1996), 302 (§65); 379, 382 (§80), emphasis original.

34. Edmund Burke, *A Philosophical Enquiry into the Origin of Our Ideas of*

the Sublime and Beautiful (1757), ed. David Womersley (London: Penguin Books, 1998), 115.

35. Heidegger, *Being and Time,* 178–83 (§41); 297–304 (§65); and Ricoeur, *Time and Narrative,* 1: 62.

36. Douglas Grant attributes the story of the idiot to Dr. Robert Plot's *Natural History of Staffordshire,* 1686, retold in the *Spectator,* number 447. See Douglas Grant, notes to *Melmoth the Wanderer* (Oxford: Oxford University Press, 1998), 549.

37. G. J. Whitrow notes that the system of dividing hours into sixty minutes, further divided into sixty seconds, is of Babylonian origin, since the Babylonians used the sexagesimal system for astronomical computations. See Whitrow, *Time in History,* 29.

38. Roy Porter, *English Society in the Eighteenth Century* (London: Penguin Books, 1990), 315; J. H. Plumb, *England in the Eighteenth Century* (London: Penguin Books, 1990), 150; George Gordon, Baron Byron, "Frame Work Bill Speech," in the House of Lords, February 27, 1812, in *Lord Byron: The Complete Miscellaneous Prose,* ed. Andrew Nicholson (Oxford: Clarendon Press, 1991), 22–27.

39. Kramer observes that "[l]ittle concrete information about Charles Maturin's life is available," noting that his own research revealed "a fair amount of previously unknown detail, but much of it is trivial and none is deeply revelatory of his character." See Kramer, *Charles Robert Maturin,* 11.

40. According to Douglas Grant, this quotation is from Edward Young, *The Complaint: or, Night Thoughts,* "Night the First." (Grant, notes to *Melmoth the Wanderer,* 553n.)

41. Paul Ricoeur refers to "the relational structure of primordial time." Ricoeur, *Time and Narrative,* 3: 82.

42. The scene may be Maturin's homage to Ann Radcliffe's "*God hears thee!*" above the confessional in *The Italian,* where Marchesa di Vivaldi is plotting with Schedoni for the murder of Ellena. See Ann Radcliffe, *The Italian,* ed. Frederick Garber (Oxford: Oxford University Press, 1981), 176.

43. Ann Radcliffe, "On the Supernatural in Poetry," *New Monthly Magazine* (1826): 149.

44. Ricoeur, *Time and Narrative,* 3: 140.

45. Ibid., 1: 3.

46. Augustine, *Confessions,* trans. R. S. Pine-Coffin (London: Penguin Books, 1961), 253, 261 (bk. 11, secs. 1, 11).

47. Bayer-Berenbaum, *The Gothic Imagination,* 81.

48. This scene closely resembles Ludovico's reading of the Provençal tale in *The Mysteries of Udolpho*'s, in that the boundary between dreaming and wakefulness is blurred and the reading of an embedded narrative informs the reality in which it is enclosed. But Maturin further doubles this uncanny effect by depicting both points of view—the letter writer's as well as the letter readers'. Don Francisco has been traveling in the company of strangers who have passed the time by telling tales that have disturbed his Catholic sensibilities. He retires to his chamber "full of sad and heavy thoughts," seeking consolation in reading "a tome containing legends of departed spirits . . . the revivification of the departed"—ghost stories, apparently, though "in nowise contradictive to the doctrine of the holy Catholic church"—from which he falls into a waking dream of his daughter pleading with him to save her, is awakened by a sound, and sees the figure from his dream wave to him and utter "It is too late" before disappearing just as the clock strikes three

(381–83). As they are reading Don Francisco's letter, Fra Jose and Donna Clara at several points imagine that they hear noises in the house (381), just as *Udolpho*'s Ludovico kept looking up from his book. The priest's echoing of the "ominious words" (spoken by Isidora, in Don Francisco's letter, just as the clock strikes three), along with the clock striking in Donna Clara's house, further seals the conflation of the two realities, the world of the letter, and the world in which the letter is read, just as the fictive levels are conflated in the Provençal Tale chapter of *Udolpho*. In fact, "all the many acts of reading, narrating, and performing before an audience in the novel create a *Doppelgänger* relationship between Maturin's own readers and the fictional audiences." See Mark M. Hennelly, Jr., "*Melmoth the Wanderer* and Gothic Existentialism," *Studies in English Literature 1500–1900* 214 (1981): 666.

49. Kramer sees in the Walbergs similarities to Maturin's own family, particularly between Mrs. Walberg and Mrs. Maturin, which may account for the sympathetic portrait. See Kramer, *Charles Robert Maturin*, 121.

50. Ricoeur, *Time and Narrative*, 1: 63.

51. Ibid., 1: 67–68.

52. Edmund Burke, *Reflections on the Revolution in France* (Amherst, NY: Prometheus Books, 1987), 38.

53. Gérard Genette,. *Narrative Discourse: An Essay in Method,* trans. Jane E. Lewin (Ithaca, NY: Cornell University Press, 1983), 234–35. Nor is this phenomenon limited to narrative representations. The image in the Wanderer's portrait seems uncannily alive to John Melmoth. It seems to gaze at him and he almost expects it to speak to him; indeed, after he burns the painting, he dreams that the figure does so (59–60).

54. Null, "Structure and Theme in *Melmoth the Wanderer,* 136. Oost gives this distinction to the parricide's tale, noting that this tale has no connection with the figure of Melmoth the Wanderer at all. The parricide's story is somewhat less than a major tale, however. Oost notes that the novel contains "digression after digression." Oost, "'Servility and command,'" 307–08.

55. Fowler, "Hieroglyphics of Fire," 525.

56. See Kramer, *Charles Robert Maturin*, 101, for a discussion of the evidence concerning this conjecture.

57. Fowler, "Hieroglyphics of Fire," 525; Baldick, introduction to *Melmoth the Wanderer*, xii; Aristotle, *De Anima*, 561 (415b).

58. David Punter, *The Literature of Terror: A History of Gothic Fiction from 1765 to the Present Day* (London: Longman, 1980), 157.

59. This point is often raised by the same critics who comment on the consistency of narrative voices. For example, Kathleen Fowler finds the elaborate recitation of all the tales beginning with Monçada's, all of which are told from memory, to be of dubious reliability (Fowler, "Hieroglyphics of Fire," 529), while Chris Baldick finds improbable the way "the story is seen to pass unimpaired through these several layers of report and recall, down to the last detail of dialogue and gesture" (Baldick, introduction to *Melmoth the Wanderer,* xi–xii).

60. Mary Shelley, *Frankenstein, or, The Modern Prometheus*, ed. J. Paul Hunter (New York: W. W. Norton & Co., 1996), 83. See Joyce Zonana," 'They Will Prove the Truth of My Tale': Safie's Letters as the Feminist Core of Mary Shelley's *Frankenstein*," *Journal of Narrative Technique* 21.2 (1991): 170–84, for an engaging interpretation of the letters.

61. Leigh A. Ehlers, "The 'Incommunicable Condition' of Melmoth," *Research Studies* 49.3 (1981): 172.

62. Eugenia C. DeLamotte, *Perils of the Night: A Feminist Study of Nineteenth-Century Gothic* (New York: Oxford University Press, 1990), 16, 19.

63. Among the critics who have misread this passage and reported the manuscript burned are Dale Kramer ("[t]he night after young John Melmoth burns the portrait and Stanton's manuscript . . .") and Victor Sage ("the reading of a manuscript in a room there, which he subsequently burns at the request of the dead man"). See Kramer, *Charles Robert Maturin*, 105; Sage, introduction to *Melmoth the Wanderer*, xvii.

64. The remainder of the passage in question provides even more direct associations to the conflation of dream and reality noted in the Provençal tale scene in *Udolpho* when John Melmoth imagines he sees the Wanderer enter the room and hears him whisper, "You have burned me, then; but those are flames I can survive.—I am alive,—I am beside you." Upon awakening, young Melmoth discovers a bruise on his wrist, "as from the recent gripe of a strong hand" (60).

65. Hayden White, *Tropics of Discourse: Essays in Cultural Criticism* (Baltimore: The Johns Hopkins University Press, 1985), 83–84.

66. M. M. Bakhtin, "From the Prehistory of Novelistic Discourse," in *The Dialogic Imagination*, 61.

67. Sage, introduction to *Melmoth the Wanderer*, xxiii–xxiv.

68. At several points in Monçada's tale, there are references to restrictions on access to the Bible. For example, in a theological dispute between the brothers of the convent and Monçada, we read: "'Where are those words?' 'In the Bible.' 'The Bible?—But we are not permitted to read it.'" (77); and, in his brother Juan's letter, his brother questions some of the practices of the church in part by saying, "I feel I am of an inquiring spirit, and if I could obtain a book they call the Bible, (which, though they say it contains the words of Jesus Christ, they never permit us to see) . . ." (129). Lacking access to the Bible as a master narrative, Maturin's Catholics must be told what to believe, as in the response to Monçada's complaint about this deprivation: "True, dear Monçada, but we have the word of our Superior and the brethren for it [i.e., the Bible], and that is enough" (77).

69. Kramer, *Charles Robert Maturin*, 13–14.

70. Ricoeur, *Time and Narrative*, 1: 3; 1: 54; 1: 64, 65, 67; 1: 71.

71. Kermode, *The Sense of an Ending*, 7–8.

72. Ricoeur, *Time and Narrative*, 1: 67–68.

73. Kramer, *Charles Robert Maturin*, 125.

74. Oost points out similarities between the postures of both Brannigan (the "withered Sybil") and the Walberg narrator in the inn, postures that suggest servitude. These two author figures also bear certain similarities to Maturin himself. See Oost, "'Servility and command,'" 294–99.

75. Fowler, "Hieroglyphics of Fire," 525.

76. Ibid., 522.

77. William Godwin, *Enquiry Concerning Political Justice and its Influence on Morals and Happiness*, 3rd ed., 2 vols. (facsimile ed., Toronto: The University of Toronto Press, 1946), 1: 92–93.

78. Punter, *The Literature of Terror*, 56.

79. Ehlers, "The 'Incommunicable Condition' of Melmoth," 176.

80. Ibid., 173–74.

81. Ricoeur, *Time and Narrative*, 1: 3, 1: 31.

82. Ibid., 1: 74–75.

83. Stephen Hawking, *A Brief History of Time* (New York: Bantam, 1998), 109–10, 164–65, 168–69; Douglas Downing and Michael Covington, *Dictionary of Computer Terms* (Woodbury, NY: Barron's, 1986), 239–40.

84. Sage, introduction to *Melmoth the Wanderer,* xxiii–xxiv.
85. Whitrow, *Time in History,* 22.
86. Genette, *Narrative Discourse,* 34.
87. Fowler, "Hieroglyphics of Fire," 525.
88. Constable Letter Books, National Library of Scotland MS 790, f. 639, September 9, 1819, quoted in Kramer, *Charles Robert Maturin,* 95. Of course, it is worth noting that there is no evidence that Maturin sought to change any of the decisions made by his publisher (although detailed biographical information about Maturin is limited [11]), so it is entirely possible that *Melmoth the Wanderer* was published just as he intended it all along.
89. Kramer, *Charles Robert Maturin,* 96.
90. Bayer-Berenbaum, *The Gothic Imagination,* 75.
91. Sherman, *Telling Time,* 9.

Chapter 3: Transcending Time

The epigraphs to this chapter are drawn from Fiona J. Stafford, *The Last of the Race: The Growth of a Myth from Milton to Darwin* (Oxford: Clarendon Press, 1994), 199; and Percy Bysshe Shelley, *Adonais: An Elegy on the Death of John Keats, Author of Endymion, Hyperion, Etc.,* in *Shelley's Poetry and Prose,* ed. Donald H. Reiman and Sharon B. Powers (New York: W. W. Norton & Co., 1977), 390–406, line 234.

1. Mary Shelley, "Introduction to *Frankenstein,* Third Edition, 1831," in *Frankenstein,* ed. J. Paul Hunter (New York: W. W. Norton & Co., 1996), 169.
2. Diane Long Hoeveler, "Mary Shelley and Gothic Feminism: The Case of the Mortal Immortal," in Syndy M. Conger, Frederick S. Frank, and Gregory O'Dea, eds., *Iconoclastic Departures: Mary Shelley After Frankenstein: Essays in Honor of the Bicentenary of Mary Shelley's Birth* (Madison: Fairleigh Dickinson University Press, 1997), 152.
3. Johanna M. Smith, *Mary Shelley* (New York: Twayne Publishers, 1996), ix.
4. Emily W. Sunstein, *Mary Shelley: Romance and Reality* (Baltimore: Johns Hopkins University Press, 1991), 40–41.
5. Lynn Wells provides an excellent synopsis of the "two critical poles" of readings of *The Last Man;* while the issues she raises are in the context of Shelley's third novel, they are also relevant to the tradition of Shelley scholarship as a whole. See Lynn Wells, "The Triumph of Death: Reading and Narrative in Mary Shelley's *The Last Man,*" in Conger, Frank, and O'Dea, *Iconoclastic Departures,* 212, 231–32n.
6. Maggie Kilgour, "'One Immortality': The Shaping of the Shelleys in *The Last Man,*" *European Romantic Review* 16.5 (2005): 567.
7. For *Frankenstein*'s relationship to the vitalist debate, see Marilyn Butler, "*Frankenstein* and Radical Science," *Times Literary Supplement,* April 4, 1993, repr. in *Frankenstein,* by Mary Shelley, ed. J. Paul Hunter (New York: W. W. Norton & Co., 1996), 302–7; for the influence of the experiments of Darwin, Davy, and Galvani, see Anne K. Mellor, *Mary Shelley: Her Life, Her Fiction, Her Monsters* (New York: Methuen, Inc., 1988), in particular her chapter entitled "A Feminist Critique of Science," 89–114.

8. Mary Shelley, *Frankenstein, or, The Modern Prometheus,* ed. J. Paul Hunter (New York: W. W. Norton & Co., 1996), 21, 26, 28.

9. As I have discussed in chapter 1.

10. Mary Shelley, *The Fortunes of Perkin Warbeck: A Romance,* ed. Doucet Devin Fischer, in *The Novels and Selected Works of Mary Shelley,* 8 vols. (London: William Pickering, 1996), 5: 306.

11. Stafford, *The Last of the Race,* 200.

12. Paul Ricoeur, *Time and Narrative,* 3 vols., trans. Kathleen Blamey and David Pallauer (Chicago: University of Chicago Press, 1984–88), 3: 12.

13. Edmund Burke, *Reflections on the Revolution in France* (Amherst, NY: Prometheus Books, 1987), 38.

14. Paula R. Feldman and Diana Scott-Kilvert, introduction to *The Journals of Mary Shelley, 1814–1844* (Baltimore: Johns Hopkins University Press, 1987), xviii.

15. Mary Shelley, *The Journals of Mary Shelley,* 463, 467, 484, 478.

16. Stafford, *The Last of the Race,* 87.

17. Shelley, *Journals,* 476–77.

18. Frank Kermode, *The Sense of an Ending: Studies in the Theory of Fiction* (New York: Oxford University Press, 1967), 7–8.

19. Augustine, *Confessions,* trans. R. S. Pine-Coffin (London: Penguin Books, 1961), 253 (bk. 11, sec. 1).

20. Stafford, *The Last of the Race,* 209–11.

21. Mary Shelley, *The Last Man,* ed. Hugh J. Luke, Jr (Lincoln, NE: University of Nebraska Press, 1993), 112.

22. Betty T. Bennett, Johanna M. Smith, and Emily Sunstein all discuss Mary Shelley's allowance from Sir Timothy Shelley and her need to write to support herself and her son. According to Bennett, this allowance began in November 1823, in the amount of £100. In August, 1824, it was increased to £200, to £250 in May of 1827, £300 in June, 1829 and finally, £400 in January, 1841. Emily Sunstein notes that the allowance was "repayable," meaning it was deducted from the estate, with interest, when it was finally settled upon Sir Timothy's death in 1844. With interest, Mary thus owed Sir Timothy's widow some £13,000. See Betty T. Bennett, *Mary Wollstonecraft Shelley: An Introduction* (Baltimore: The Johns Hopkins University Press, 1998), 70–72, 133–38; Smith, *Mary Shelley,* 119–28; Sunstein, *Romance and Reality,* 363–64. Charles E. Robinson discusses Shelley's periodical publications in particular. See Robinson, *Mary Shelley: Collected Tales and Stories* (Baltimore: The Johns Hopkins University Press, 1976), xvi, 373–400.

23. The quotation is from a letter to Leigh Hunt from February 9, 1824: "Write your Articles, write your Indicators . . . —it is thus you will make money— the grand desideratum with us groveling mortals—as for me bien mauvis gré I write bad articles which help to make me miserable—but I am going to plunge into a novel, and hope that its clear water will wash off the mud of the magazines." *The Letters of Mary Wollstonecraft Shelley,* 3 vols., ed. Betty T. Bennett (Baltimore: Johns Hopkins University Press, 1980–88), 1: 412. Shelley is here referring to "articles" rather than tales, but some of the stigma of magazine writing may attach. The novel she refers to is *The Last Man,* begun in January or February of that year. Godwin's disparagement of periodical publication is mentioned in Sunstein. See Sunstein, *Romance and Reality,* 247.

24. Robinson, *Mary Shelley: Collected Tales and Stories,* xiii; Sonia Hofkosh, "Disfiguring Economies: Mary Shelley's Short Stories," in Audrey A. Fisch, Anne

K. Mellor, and Esther H. Schor, eds., *The Other Mary Shelley: Beyond Franken-stein* (New York: Oxford University Press, 1993), 205–8.

25. Gregory O'Dea, "'Perhaps a Tale You'll Make It': Mary Shelley's Tales for *The Keepsake*," in Conger, Frank, and O'Dea, *Iconoclastic Departures,* 66. Both O'Dea and Robinson refer to these shorter fictions as "tales" rather than "short stories." Robinson notes that the short story form as we understand it came into being after these tales were written, and O'Dea expands this discussion by noting that, unlike the short story, the tale "is an ancient and amorphous narrative form [that] seems always to have been considered a genre of narrative fragmentation," often violating "the dramatic unities of time, place and action" we associate with the short story. A tale, for example, might encompass more than one incident and cover a period of years by using narrative summaries, a fragmented series of incidents (O'Dea, "Perhaps a Tale . . ." 63). I have adopted the conventions established by Robinson and O'Dea and will refer to these fictions as tales.

26. See O'Dea, "Perhaps a tale" 66–68, 71, 73. "The Swiss Peasant" (1830), also involves "the interrelation of sexual and political tyranny" (Smith, *Mary Shelley,* 62), a theme also explored in *Valperga*. In addition, "Transformation" (1830) at least figuratively represents usurpation, for the protagonist and a dwarf exchange bodies and the dwarf personality woos the protagonist's lover.

27. I am retaining Johanna M. Smith's generic classifications here. Smith cites "The False Rhyme" (1829) and "The Swiss Peasant" as two examples of the Jacobin antiromance; "The Evil Eye" and "Euphrasia: A Tale of Greece" as Oriental tales; "The Invisible Girl" as a hybrid of Gothic and fairy tale elements; and "Valerius: The Reanimated Roman" (written c. 1819, published 1976), "Roger Dodsworth: The Reanimated Englishman" (written 1826, published 1863), "Transformation" (1830) and "The Mortal Immortal: A Tale" (1833) as science fiction. See Smith, *Mary Shelley,* 61, 77, 67, and 33, respectively.

28. Stafford, *The Last of the Race,* 199.

29. Robinson, *Mary Shelley: Collected Tales and Stories,* 397

30. Smith, *Mary Shelley,* 34.

31. "Valerius: The Reanimated Roman," in Robinson, *Mary Shelley: Collected Tales and Stories,* 340. Subsequent references to this text will be parenthetical.

32. As, for example, Adeline's "several years of miserable resistance against cruelty and superstition" during her convent years. See Ann Radcliffe, *The Romance of the Forest,* ed. Chloe Chard (Oxford: Oxford University Press, 1986), 36.

33. In Godwin's novel, a mysterious stranger offers Reginald de St. Leon the secrets of immortality and unlimited wealth, provided he discloses the secret to no one else. St. Leon initially resists these conditions, arguing that his "heart was formed by nature for social ties," and he has no secrets from his wife. Eventually, however, he succumbs to temptation. St. Leon notes that "[f]rom the moment of my last interview with the stranger I was another creature." It transforms his whole attitude toward the human race, which, despite his love for his family, now "looked too insignificant in my eyes." He feels himself "alone in the world." After his beloved wife dies, St. Leon vows never to marry again, for "[a]n immortal can form no true and real attachment to the insect of an hour." He becomes alienated from his children, especially his son, who blames his father's interest in magical arts for destroying their family. See William Godwin, *St. Leon: A Tale of the Sixteenth Century,* ed. Pamela Clemit (Oxford: Oxford University Press, 1994), 126, 161, 164, and 296, respectively.

34. Robinson, *Mary Shelley: Collected Tales and Stories,* 377.

35. Mary Shelley, "Roger Dodsworth: The Reanimated Englishman," in Rob-

inson, *Mary Shelley: Collected Tales and Stories,* 43. Subsequent references to this text will be parenthetical.

36. See Tzvetan Todorov, *The Fantastic: A Structural Approach to a Literary Genre,* trans. Richard Howard (Ithaca, NY: Cornell University Press, 1975), 41–42.

37. According to Robinson, "The Mortal Immortal" has been published nine times through 1966, but only once, with certainty, during Shelley's lifetime. "The False Rhyme" was published at least five times during Shelley's lifetime, and several times since then. See Robinson, *Mary Shelley: Collected Tales and Stories,* 390–91, 380–81.

38. Mary Shelley, "The Mortal Immortal: A Tale," in Robinson, *Mary Shelley: Collected Tales and Stories,* 222. Subsequent references to this text will be parenthetical.

39. Godwin, *St. Leon,* 348–49.

40. Ibid., 349.

41. Both the choice of the polar regions and Winzy's reference to "scattering and annihilating" his atoms are reminiscent of the creature's anticipated suicide in *Frankenstein,* where the creature imagines his ashes being "swept into the sea by the winds" (Shelley, *Frankenstein,* 156).

42. As I have discussed in the introduction; see Jacques Derrida, *Aporias: Dying—awaiting (one another at) the "limits of truth,"* trans. Thomas Dutoit (Stanford, CA: Stanford University Press, 1993), 13.

43. Portions of this section were originally published in *Romanticism On the Net* and are reprinted with permission. See Richard S. Albright," 'In the mean time, what did Perdita?': Rhythms and Reversals in Mary Shelley's *The Last Man.*" *Romanticism On the Net* 13 (February 1999), http://www.erudit.org/revue/ron/1999/v/n13/005848ar.html.

44. A. J. Sambrook, "A Romantic Theme: The Last Man," *Forum for Modern Language Studies* 2 (1966): 25–28; William A. Walling, *Mary Shelley* (New York: Twayne Publishers, Inc., 1972), 88.

45. Audrey A. Fisch, "Plaguing Politics: AIDS, Deconstruction and *The Last Man,*" in Fisch, Mellor, and Schor , *The Other Mary Shelley,* 279–80.

46. Hayden White, *Tropics of Discourse: Essays in Cultural Criticism* (Baltimore: The Johns Hopkins University Press, 1985), 83–84.

47. Samantha Webb calls the device of the found manuscript "symbolically loaded" during the Romantic period because it symbolizes an editorial process that "usurps the narrative authority of the internal narrator and locates that authority within an institutional discourse." Included among the forces that contribute to this institutionalization are "the expansion of the literary marketplace, the professionalization of authorship, the practice of authorial anonymity, and the explosion of periodical publishing." She goes on to note that "In *The Last Man,* the odd temporal displacment of readers into the past troubles the question of authorial authority from the outset. Lionel's authorship is in crisis precisely because he has no readers to participate in his narrative 'transaction' or to accord him authority." See Samantha Webb, "Reading the End of the World: *The Last Man,* History, and the Agency of Romantic Authorship," in *Mary Shelley in Her Times,* ed. Betty T. Bennett and Stuart Curran (Baltimore: Johns Hopkins University Press, 2000), 122–24.

48. Shelley, *The Last Man,* 264. Subsequent references to this text will be parenthetical.

49. Giovanna Franci, "A Mirror of the Future: Vision and Apocalypse in Mary

Shelley's *The Last Man"* in *Mary Shelley: Modern Critical Views,* ed. Harold Bloom (New York: Chelsea House Publishers, 1985), 186; Gérard Genette, *Narrative Discourse: An Essay in Method,* trans. Jane E. Lewin (Ithaca, NY: Cornell University Press, 1983), 216–20. More precisely, *The Last Man* is an example of a subsequent narrative embedded in a predictive narrative that is in turn embedded in a subsequent narrative.

50. Paul A. Cantor, "The Apocalypse of Empire: Mary Shelley's *The Last Man,"* in Conger, Frank, and O'Dea, *Iconoclastic Departures,* 204.

51. Jane Blumberg, *Mary Shelley's Early Novels: "This Child of Imagination and Misery"* (Iowa City: University of Iowa Press, 1993), 135.

52. Kermode, *The Sense of an Ending,* 7–8; Stafford, *The Last of the Race,* 84, 87.

53. Kermode, *The Sense of an Ending,* 47.

54. Burke, *Reflections,* 28.

55. Muriel Spark, *Child of Light: A Reassessment of Mary Wollstonecraft Shelley* (Hadleigh, Essex, UK: Tower Bridge Publications Limited, 1951), 158.

56. Eve Tavor Bannet, "The 'Abyss of the Present' and Women's Time in Mary Shelley's *The Last Man,"* *The Eighteenth-Century Novel* 2 (2002): 364–65, 370.

57. Sunstein, *Romance and Reality,* 269.

58. Martin Heidegger, *Being and Time,* trans. Joan Stambaugh (Albany: State University of New York Press, 1996), 178–83 (§41), 297–304 (§65); and Ricoeur, *Time and Narrative,* 1: 62.

59. Spark, *Child of Light,* 150; Robert Lance Snyder, "Apocalypse and Indeterminacy in Mary Shelley's *The Last Man,"* *Studies in Romanticism* 17 (1978): 438.

60. Brian Aldiss, *The Detached Retina: Aspects of SF and Fantasy* (Syracuse: Syracuse University Press, 1995), 66.

61. Spark, *Child of Light,* 158.

62. Hugh J. Luke, Jr., *"The Last Man:* Mary Shelley's Myth of the Solitary," *Prairie Schooner* 39 (1965–66): 325–26.

63. Shelley, *Letters* 1: 187. The definite passage of linear time, marked by named months, is in contrast to the suspension of time which often characterizes Gothic novels. *The Last Man* contains a curious mixture of Gothic and non-Gothic elements. For example, the use of the narrative frame whereby an author is actually the editor of a manuscript from a remote time (a common Gothic device) is offset by long discussions of politics (not typical of Gothic novels). For every reference to a Gothic work such as William Beckford's *Vathek* (87), there is a reference to Edmund Burke's *Reflections on the Revolution in France* (165) or to *Gulliver's Travels* (168). As Lee Sterrenburg points out, Shelley's narrator even "footnotes his source, lest the reader miss the connection" (to Burke). See Lee Sterrenburg, *"The Last Man:* Anatomy of Failed Revolutions," *Nineteenth Century Fiction* 33 (1978): 331. *The Last Man*'s refusal to adhere to generic conventions may have confounded critics, as Muriel Spark noted (Spark, *Child of Light,* 150) and Lynn Wells repeats (Wells, "The Triumph of Death," 231n).

64. Aldiss, *The Detached Retina,* 66.

65. Sophie Thomas notes that "[r]eduction is, paradoxically, accomplished through multiplication, insofar as there is a potentially infinite reproduction of the very condition [i.e., the plague] that ostensibly ushers in closure." Sophie Thomas, "The Ends of the Fragment, the Problem of the Preface: Proliferation and Finality in *The Last Man,"* in *Mary Shelley's Fictions: From* Frankenstein *to* Falkner, ed. Michael Eberle-Sinatra (New York: St. Martin's Press, LLC. 2000), 23.

66. Shelley, *Journals,* 447–48.

67. It was traditional during this musical period for concerti, sonatas, and the first movements of symphonies to observe the "sonata form." See *Grove's Dictionary of Music and Musicians,* ed. Eric Blom, 10 vols., fifth ed. (New York: St. Martin's Press, Inc., 1955), s.v. "sonata form."

68. When I originally made this claim in 1999 in my article "'In the mean time, what did Perdita?' . . ." (*Romanticism on the Net* 13), Nora Crook, who edited the novel for Pickering and Chatto's *The Novels and Selected Works of Mary Shelley,* responded by noting that "capitalisation of the first or first two words of a chapter was not a matter of authorial choice but purely a typographical convention—one that was almost universal in the nineteenth-century and which still is practised by many publishing houses today." However, Crook goes on to "strongly support" my reading, arguing that "it points towards Mary Shelley's awareness of printing conventions, and her exploitation of these to give further meaning to her work. This is based on (1) my own sense of MWS's understanding of how to present an MS to the publisher (2) her lively awareness of double meanings as evidenced in *Frankenstein* (3) fondness for the trope of the hieroglyph appearing in both Shelleys." Crook stated that previous editions of the novel, edited by Hugh J. Luke, Jr., and Morton Paley, "retained the original capitalisation" and that she argued quite forcefully, though unsuccessfully, with Pickering and Chatto to do so as well. Nora Crook, "On Richard Albright's "'In the mean time, what did Perdita?'": Rhythms and Reversals in Mary Shelley's The Last Man,'" *Romanticism on the Net,* Sept. 1999, http://users.ox.ac.uk/~scat0385/forum.html#rick.

It is worth noting that Shelley also employs her knowledge of typography to good effect with regard to two other terms in the novel. The first occurrence of the word "PLAGUE" (127) is in small caps, as is the first occurrence of the term "LAST MAN" (240); and, indeed, four of the five times this phrase appears (the others are pages 324, 342, and twice on 339).

69. Samuel Taylor Coleridge, *Biographia Literaria* (London: J. M. Dent, 1997), bk. 13, (175).

70. They also represent what Peter Brooks, in his discussion of repetition as remembering, calls "a way of reorganizing a story whose connective links have been obscured and lost." See Peter Brooks, *Reading for the Plot: Design and Intention in Narrative* (Cambridge, MA: Harvard University Press, 1992), 139.

71. Genette, *Narrative Discourse,* 109–10.

72. I used Genette's methodology. See Genette, *Narrative Discourse,* 38ff. Table 2 on p. 164 depicts the temporal complexity (number of shifts in narrative time, and number of temporal positions) in this chapter (volume 1, chapter 9) in comparison to two other key chapters in the novel.

73. Ricoeur, *Time and Narrative,* 3: 35–36.

74. These elaborate temporal and narrative frames seem to have served several purposes, depending on how much weight is ascribed to biographical interpretations. Hugh J. Luke, Jr., has claimed that the frames provided Mary Shelley with a means to fictionally memorialize her dead husband while circumventing Sir Timothy Shelley's prohibition against publishing Percy's poetry or biography. Further, her desire for "the release of self-revelation without its consequences" required "a fragmentation of the complex personality of [Percy] Shelley" (among several characters, including the astronomer Merrival as well as Adrian) and a similar fragmentation "of the complexities of her attitude toward him." See Hugh J. Luke, Jr., "*The Last Man:* Mary Shelley's Myth of the Solitary," 318–20. In the same light, Anne K. Mellor believes that the framing provides sufficient distance

from Mary Shelley for her to deal with the magnitude and complexity of her pain, including her "unfinished emotional business" with her husband, her relationship with her father and others such as Byron, and even her views on conflicting political philosophies (Anne K. Mellor, *Mary Shelley: Her Life, Her Fiction, Her Monsters*, 146–64). Paradoxically, although Shelley's elaborate system of frames may have been a means for her to deal with emotional pain from a safe distance, one effect upon the reader is the relentless building of suspense toward the most ultimate of outcomes, what Giovanna Franci called "a constant awareness of an *after*, an ending" (Franci, "A Mirror of the Future," 185).

Lee Sterrenburg finds in Shelley's temporal framing the means for her to systematically consider, and reject, the political philosophies of both Godwin and Burke. "The demonic plague in *The Last Man* cancels out the utopian rationality of Godwin as surely as it cancels out the conservative organicism of Edmund Burke." (Sterrenburg, "Anatomy of Failed Revolutions," 331–35). And Paul A. Cantor characterizes the novel's politics as suggesting a fantasy of an artistocracy of artistic merit rather than birth, "going her husband one better in the imagining a state in which poets might become the *acknowledged* legislators of the world" (Cantor, "The Apocalypse of Empire," 201).

75. Ricoeur, *Time and Narrative*, 1: 66–68.

76. Brian Nellist, "Imagining the Future: Predictive Fiction in the Nineteenth Century," in *Anticipations: Essays on Early Science Fiction and its Precursors*, ed. David Seed (Syracuse: Syracuse University Press, 1995), 116.

77. Alexander Pope, *The Dunciad in Four Books* (Harlow, Essex, UK: Longman, 1999), 356–60, lines 4.631–52, quotation at line 4.652.

78. Burke, *Reflections*, 38.

79. Heidegger, *Being and Time*, 303 (§65).

80. Burke, *Reflections*, 28, emphasis original.

81. William Lomax has also noted the resemblance between Moses and Adrian. Lomax, however, calls Adrian "a Moses leading an exodus across the channel to a Promised Land." See William Lomax, "Epic Reversals in Mary Shelley's *The Last Man*: Romantic Irony and the Roots of Science Fiction" in *Contours of the Fantastic: Selected Essays from the Eighth International Conference on the Fantastic in the Arts*, ed. Michele K. Langford (New York: Greenwood Press, 1990), 9–10. My own view is that such a movement would not constitute a true reversal, and that the remnant is led from England, formerly privileged in the novel, back toward the kind of slavery implied by the plague, particularly as they perversely seek warmer climes despite the repeated associations between warm weather and the plague (see pp. 230, 233, 279, for example). Such associations are consistent with Daniel Defoe's *Journal of the Plague Year*, which Shelley read on May 26–27, 1817 (Shelley, *Journals*, 171), and it is worth noting that Shelley lost two of her children, Clara Everina and William, in Italy during the hot summer months in 1818 and 1819. Nevertheless, her *Journals* contain many references to her preference for the Italian climate. See for example her entries for January 18, 1824 and an undated entry apparently from the summer of 1825 (*Journals*, 470–71 and 489).

82. Lomax, "Epic Reversals," 11.

83. There is a clear parallel with Adrian, who loses his reason and nearly dies in consequence of his unrequited love for Evadne early in the novel, long before the advent of the plague. At this point, Adrian is ill while everyone else is healthy. Later, he is wounded by Greek soldiers in the sack of a Turkish city, and believes his wound will shorten his life. Yet, his health prospers as Lord Protector—he was "never in better health" (171) despite considerable contact with plague victims.

84. Brooks, *Reading for the Plot*, 23.

85. I am indebted to Beverly Schneller of Millersville University for this observation.

86. Brooks, *Reading for the Plot*, 139.

87. This is an example of Mary Shelley using her own experience to lend this description authenticity and power. Compare her journal entry dated March 19, 1815, less than two weeks after she finds her baby dead: "Dream that my little baby came to life again—that it had only been cold & that we rubbed it by the fire & it lived—I awake & find no baby . . ." (Shelley, *Journals*, 70).

88. O'Dea, "Prophetic History," 284; Sterrenburg, "Anatomy of Failed Revolutions," 328.

89. Genette, *Narrative Discourse*, 27; Verney's act of causing the past to live again by systematically recalling it is reminiscent of Shelley's journal entry of October 7, 1822. Her old writing desk had just been shipped to her, and in the course of reading the letters it contained, she notes: "My William, Clara, Allegra are all talked of—they lived then—They breathed this air & their voices struck on my sense, their feet trod the earth beside me—& their hands were warm with blood & life when clasped in mine. Where are they all?" (Shelley, *Journals*, 435).

90. Shelley, *Journals*, 470.

91. Brooks, *Reading for the Plot*, 23.

92. Heidegger, *Being and Time*, 302 (§65); Ricoeur, *Time and Narrative*, 3: 37.

93. Mary Shelley, "The Loves of the Poets," in *The Novels and Selected Works of Mary Shelley*, 8 vols. (London: William Pickering, 1996), 2: 196.

94. As Joyce Zonana has noted, "Safie's narrative, enclosed within the monster's tale to Frankenstein, is located at the physical, textual center of Mary Shelley's novel." See Joyce Zonana, " 'They Will Prove the Truth of My Tale': Safie's Letters as the Feminist Core of Mary Shelley's *Frankenstein*," *Journal of Narrative Technique* 21.2 (1991): 171.

95. Coleridge, *Biographia Literaria*, 175.

96. Ricoeur, *Time and Narrative*, 1: 54; 1: 64, 65, 67; and 1: 71, respectively.

97. See *The Prelude, Or, Growth of a Poet's Mind; An Autobiographical Poem*, 1850, in *The Prelude, 1799, 1805, 1850*, ed. Jonathan Wordsworth, M. H. Abrams, and Stephen Gill (New York: W. W. Norton & Company, 1979), 429 (line 12.208).

98. Cantor, "The Apocalypse of Empire," 204; Brooks, *Reading for the Plot*, 23.

99. At the end of the novel Verney declares, "I also will write a book . . . —for whom to read?—to whom dedicated?" (339). He then begins: "DEDICATION TO THE ILLUSTRIOUS DEAD. SHADOWS, ARISE, AND READ YOUR FALL!" and rationalizes that his book might be found by "the children of a saved pair of lovers, in some to me unknown and unattainable seclusion" (339).

100. Brooks, *Reading for the Plot*, 34.

101. Rev. of *The Last Man*, by Mary Shelley, *London Literary Gazette* 474 (Feb. 18, 1826): 103, repr. in *Nineteenth-Century Literature Criticism*, 14: 254; Rev. of *The Last Man*, by Mary Shelley, *The Monthly Review* Vol I, No. III (Mar., 1826): 335, repr. in *Nineteenth-Century Literature Criticism*, 14: 254.

102. Genette, *Narrative Discourse*, 33.

103. The assertion that Shelley idealizes the bourgeois family is the central thesis of Anne K. Mellor's book, *Mary Shelley: Her Life, Her Fiction, Her Monsters*, including the chapter on *The Last Man*, entitled "Love, Guilt and Reparation: *The Last Man*" (146–64). As to my claim of non-bourgeois family groupings, there are

five who comprise the circle near Windsor Castle in book 1 (Adrian, Raymond, Perdita, Verney, and Idris), and four comprise the post-apocalyptic "family" unit, which consists of two male adults, a male child, and a female adolescent. Hardly a bourgeois family, even though the more traditional family unit that Verney, Idris, and their children make up is also idealized. Perhaps Paul A. Cantor's assessment is more to the point: "For Shelley, the ultimate human good is to be found in the family, or at least in a small circle of human beings who genuinely care for each other" (Cantor, "The Apocalypse of Empire," 199).

104. Heidegger, *Being and Time,* 303 (§65).

105. Ibid., 302–3 (§65).

106. Kermode, *The Sense of an Ending,* 47.

107. Shelley, "The Mortal Immortal," 230.

108. Brooks, *Reading for the Plot,* 139; Ricoeur, *Time and Narrative,* 1: 3.

109. Betty T. Bennett has added yet another layer of uncertainty. She observes that, because Mary Shelley was prohibited by her father-in-law from using the Shelley name publicly, the title page of *The Last Man* lists the author as "The Author of *Frankenstein.*" Therefore, Bennett says, "readers know and do not know the author." See Betty T. Bennett, "Radical Imaginings: Mary Shelley's *The Last Man,*" *The Wordsworth Circle* 26.3 (1995): 149.

CHAPTER 4: APORIA IN THE HOUSE

The epigraphs to this chapter are drawn from Richard D. Altick, *Victorian People and Ideas* (New York: W. W. Norton & Company, 1973), 99; and Ronald R. Thomas, "Wilkie Collins and the Sensation Novel," in *Columbia History of the British Novel,* ed. John Richetti (New York: Columbia University Press, 1994), 506.

1. Sir Gavin de Beer, "Biology before the *Beagle,*" in *Darwin,* ed. Philip Appleman (New York: W. W. Norton & Company, Inc., 1970), 3–10.

2. Nicholas Daly, "Railway Novels: Sensation Fiction and the Modernization of the Senses," *ELH* 66 (1999): 473.

3. Paul Ricoeur, *Time and Narrative,* 3 vols., trans. Kathleen Blamey and David Pallauer (Chicago: University of Chicago Press, 1984–88), 3: 140.

4. Alfred Lord Tennyson, *In Memoriam A. H. H,* ed. Erik Gray, 2nd ed. (New York: W. W. Norton & Company, 2004), 88 (lines 118. 7–12) and 41 (line 56. 15). The other reference to the nebular hypothesis occurs on p. 65, lines 89. 47–48.

5. Rebecca Stern, " 'Personation' and 'Good Marking-Ink': Sanity, Performativity, and Biology in Victorian Sensation Fiction," *Nineteenth Century Studies* 14 (2000): 41.

6. Ibid., 41.

7. Altick, *Victorian People and Ideas,* 111.

8. Daly, "Railway Novels," 472–73.

9. Margaret Oliphant, "Sensation Novels," *Blackwood's Edinburgh Magazine* 91 (1862): 568. Jenny Bourne Taylor also quotes from this passage. See "Psychology and Sensation: The Narrative of Moral Management in *The Woman in White,*" *Critical Survey* 2.1 (1990): 49.

10. Jonathan Loesberg states that "by 1870 the genre itself seems to have lost definition and to have ceased to be controversial." See Jonathan Loesberg, "The Ideology of Narrative Form in Sensation Fiction," *Representations* 13 (1986): 115.

Ronald R. Thomas states that "[a]bout a decade . . . [after the advent of the genre], just as mysteriously, sensation fiction essentially disappeared from the literary landscape, only to resurface toward the end of the century, this time disguised as another popular genre, the detective novel." See Thomas, "Wilkie Collins and the Sensation Novel," 479. And Susan D. Bernstein argues that "by the early 1870s this insistent intonation of 'sensation fiction' had practically vanished from critical discourse." See Susan D. Bernstein, "Ape Anxiety: Sensation Fiction, Evolution, and the Genre Question," *Journal of Victorian Culture* 6.2 (2001): 254. Nevertheless, many mainsteam novels published throughout the second half of the nineteenth century contain elements regarded by readers and critics as sensational, and as Thomas points out, the sensation novel was one of the forerunners of the detective novel. This is similar to the Gothic novel's influence earlier in the century, an influence that persisted even after the genre's initial popularity had waned. David Punter, Tamar Heller, and Jenny Bourne Taylor are among many critics who view the Gothic novel as one of the precursors of the sensation novel; see David Punter, *The Literature of Terror: A History of Gothic Fiction from 1765 to the Present Day* (London: Longman, 1980), 214–38; Tamar Heller, *Dead Secrets: Wilkie Collins and the Female Gothic* (New Haven, CT: Yale University Press, 1992), 1–12; Jenny Bourne Taylor, introduction to *Lady Audley's Secret* (London: Penguin Books, Ltd., 1998), xii.

Despite Ronald R. Thomas's claim that "sensation fiction essentially disappeared from the literary landscape" after the 1860s, he goes on to note that Anthony Trollope "succumbed to writing a novel in the sensation mode with *The Eustace Diamonds* (1873)." For that matter, Thomas suggests that Dickens's *Bleak House* (1853), "in almost every way seems to anticipate the conventions of the sensation genre" (Thomas, "Wilkie Collins and the Sensation Novel" 481, 498). Andrew Maunder argues that "the sensation novel cannot be contained tidily within a single decade. . . . The genre continued in various formats for the rest of the century (the three-volume novel, the local newspaper, the cheap magazine), merging as it always had done with other modes of writing including the detective story and the 'New Woman' novel." See Andrew Maunder, General Introduction to *Varieties of Women's Sensation Fiction, 1855–1890,* 6 vols. (London: Pickering & Chatto Publishers Limited, 2004), xiii.

For her part, Margaret Oliphant included *Great Expectations* among the three sensation novels discussed in her 1862 review cited above.

11. Loesberg, "The Ideology of Narrative Form," 115.

12. Altick, *Victorian People and Ideas,* 312–15.

13. Taylor, introduction to *Lady Audley's Secret,* xvi.

14. Thomas, "Wilkie Collins and the Sensation Novel," 506.

15. H. L. Mansel, "Sensation Novels," *Quarterly Review* 113 (1863): 488; Henry James, "Miss Braddon," *The Nation,* November 9, 1865, repr. in *Notes and Reviews* (Cambridge, MA: Dunster House, 1921), 112–13. Earlier in the same review, James invokes Radcliffe in his discussion of Collins's *The Woman in White*. In an oftquoted passage, James states, "To Mr. Collins belongs the credit of having introduced into fiction those most mysterious of mysteries, the mysteries which are at our own doors." James goes on to say, "This innovation gave a new impetus to the literature of horrors. It was fatal to the authority of Mrs. Radcliffe and her everlasting castle in the Apennines. What are the Apennines to us, or we to the Apennines? Instead of the terrors of 'Udolpho', we were treated to the terrors of the cheerful country-house and the busy London lodgings. And there is no doubt that these were infinitely the more terrible. Mrs. Radcliffe's mysteries were ro-

mances pure and simple; while those of Mr. Wilkie Collins were stern reality" (110). It is interesting that, in seeming to assert that the sensation novel was "stern reality" in marked contrast to the "pure and simple" *romances* of the Gothic—as if to establish a distinction between the romantic and realistic novel, James invokes affect (horror and terror) as a common characteristic of both genres. In so doing, he actually emphasizes the sensation novel's affinity with the Gothic.

Similarly, Lillian Nayder describes the critics' anxieties about "the disturbing 'proximity' of the stories, which domesticated and modernized the horror of Gothic fiction, bringing it home to Victorian England from medieval and Renaissance Italy." See Lillian Nayder, *Wilkie Collins* (New York: Twayne Publishers, 1997), 71.

16. Christopher Kent, "Probability, Reality and Sensation in the Novels of Wilkie Collins," *Dickens Studies Annual* 20 (1991): 260.

17. Richard D. Altick, *The Presence of the Present: Topics of the Day in the Victorian Novel* (Columbus, OH: Ohio State University Press, 1991, 38, 81. Without attempting to provide an exhaustive list, Altick has noted some 107 sample titles of novels from the nineteenth century that make explicit reference to the characteristics of modernity and/or the terms *fact* and *real life,* such as *A Tale* [or *A Novel] Founded on Facts,* which particular phrase occurs thirteen times on one of his lists (36–43).

18. Bernstein, "Ape Anxiety," 267, 258.

19. Wilkie Collins, *The Woman in White,* ed. Julian Symons (New York: Penguin Books, 1985), 584; Oliphant, "Sensation Novels," 564; Thomas, "Wilkie Collins and the Sensation Novel," 484.

20. Bernstein proposes a correlation between evolutionary theory's rendering of boundaries between species as permeable, and the genres of sensation fiction, which often blurred literary taxonomies, as well as depicting a blurring of class and gender boundaries. The language in these novels often figuratively blurred racial and species boundaries as well (Bernstein, "Ape Anxiety," 250–71).

21. As I have discussed in my introduction.

22. Mary Elizabeth Braddon, *Lady Audley's Secret,* ed. Jenny Bourne Taylor (London: Penguin Books, Ltd., 1998), 396.

23. Andrew Maunder, introduction to *East Lynne,* by Mrs. Henry Wood (Peterborough, Ontario: Broadview Press Ltd., 2000), 25.

24. Mark M. Hennelly, Jr. discusses the novel's organization into epochs in the context of reader response, stating that "whether we assume the temporal metaphor of stages or the spatial metaphor of levels to discuss reader response to *The Woman in White* really makes no difference because the two approaches constantly conflate and overlap as one reads the novel." See "Reading Detection in *The Woman in White,*" *Texas Studies in Literature and Language* 22.4 (1980): 450. My treatment of the spatial/temporal aspects of the novel's parts is quite different, as will be seen.

25. *The Oxford English Dictionary,* compact edition (New York: Oxford University Press, 1971), s.v. *epoch;* Collins, *The Woman in White,* "Preamble," 33. Subsequent references to this text will be parenthetical.

26. Loesberg, "The Ideology of Narrative Form," 130–31; Nayder, *Wilkie Collins,* 80.

27. Lenora Ledwon, "Veiled Women, the Law of Coverture, and Wilkie Collins's *The Woman in White,*" *Victorian Literature and Culture* 22 (1994): 1–5; Nayder, *Wilkie Collins,* 73.

28. Gilles Deleuze and Félix Guattari, *A Thousand Plateaus: Capitalism and Schizophrenia,* trans. Brian Massumi (Minneapolis: University of Minnesota Press, 1987), 80–81.

29. Braddon, *Lady Audley's Secret,* 123.

30. These are expressed on pages 436, 437, 445, 457, 472, 473, 581, and 610, all in the third epoch.

31. Daly, "Railway Novels," 475.

32. See J. A. Sutherland, "Two Emergencies in the Writing of The Woman in White," *Yearbook of English Studies* 7 (1977): 148–56; Walter M. Kendrick, "The Sensationalism of *The Woman in White,*" *Nineteenth-Century Fiction* 32.1 (1977): 18–35. Sutherland provides a more extensive explanation of the circumstances that surrounded the anomaly, while Kendrick's is the better explanation of the nature of the narrative anomaly itself. This matter will be explored in more detail below.

33. Charles Maturin, *Melmoth the Wanderer,* ed. Douglas Grant (Oxford: Oxford University Press, 1998), 494.

34. Peter Thoms, *The Windings of the Labyrinth: Quest and Structure in the Major Novels of Wilkie Collins* (Athens, Ohio: Ohio University Press, 1992), 78. Thoms has exploited the dual meaning of the term *plot* in his chapter on *The Woman in White* (55–86). Thoms notes that Walter, Marian, and Laura must rewrite history in the third epoch, writing themselves out of the "plot" written by others and ultimately exchanging it for one written by themselves.

35. Kendrick, "The Sensationalism of *The Woman in White,*" 24.

36. Thoms, *The Windings of the Labyrinth,* 77.

37. Brooks, *Reading for the Plot,* 24–25.

38. Kendrick, "The Sensationalism of *The Woman in White,*" 33.

39. Leaving aside, of course, Kendrick's objections about the earlier gaps and other apparent discontinuities.

40. Ann Cvetkovich, "Ghostlier Determinations: The Economy of Sensation and *The Woman in White,*" *Novel* 23.1 (1989): 30–31.

41. Cvetkovich, "Ghostlier Determinations," 35–36.

42. Ricoeur, *Time and Narrative,* 3: 76, 3: 36.

43. Richard D. Altick, *Victorian Studies in Scarlet* (New York: W. W. Norton & Company, 1970), 78, 64.

44. Heisenberg had the electron in mind when he developed his theory. In this case, to be able to observe an electron would require the use of light of very short wavelengths, which would therefore be highly energetic. These high-energy quanta hitting the electron would inevitably affect it. See David C. Cassidy, *Uncertainty: The Life and Science of Werner Heisenberg* (New York: W. H. Freeman and Company, 1992), 226–29, for a very accessible explanation of the Uncertainty Principle in its historical context.

45. Taylor, "Psychology and Sensation," 51.

46. Sutherland, "Two Emergencies," 148, 155; E. S. Dallas is quoted in Kendrick, "The Sensationalism of *The Woman in White,*" 23, along with the Kendrick passage cited above.

47. Mary Shelley, *The Last Man,* ed. Hugh J. Luke, Jr (Lincoln, NE: University of Nebraska Press, 1993), 3–4.

48. Taylor, "Psychology and Sensation," 56.

49. The marriage registers are supremely ironic in two ways: first, Mr. Wansborough's *copy* of the *official* register represents the truth, because it is the original that has been altered through forgery; and second, it is the void at the bottom of

his copy of the register that articulates meaning. As Collins put it, "That space told the whole story!" (529). Glyde attempted to narrate coherence by filling that void.

50. Stern, "'Personation' and 'Good Marking-Ink,'" 39.

51. Nor the possibility of disinheritance, as when George Talboys's father assures Robert Audley that "I have no longer a son," briefly recants, and then states, "I revoke my intended forgiveness of the person who was once my son" (Braddon, *Lady Audley's Secret*, 191, 193).

52. Ricoeur, *Time and Narrative,* 3: 114.

53. Morse Peckham, "Introduction to the Variorum Edition" of *The Origin of Species,* by Charles Darwin, in *Darwin,* ed. Philip Appleman (New York: W. W. Norton & Company, Inc., 1970), 98.

54. Braddon, *Lady Audley's Secret,* 262. Subsequent references to this text will be parenthetical.

55. Taylor, introduction to *Lady Audley's Secret,* xix; David Skilton, introduction to *Lady Audley's Secret* (New York: Oxford University Press, 1987), xviii.

56. "[T]hree years and a half this very month," according to George's account to Miss Morley on the return passage to England aboard the *Argus* (23).

57. Jenny Bourne Taylor, notes to *Lady Audley's Secret,* by Mary Elizabeth Braddon (London: Penguin Books, Ltd., 1998), 450.

58. Jill Matus, "Disclosure as 'Cover-up': The Discourse of Madness in *Lady Audley's Secret," University of Toronto Quarterly* 62.3 (1993): 342; Edmund Burke, *Reflections on the Revolution in France* (Amherst, NY: Prometheus Books, 1987), 31–32.

59. Because our workplace activities, our retail and banking transactions, and even our cars' progress through intersections are video monitored, our telephone calls are monitored "to ensure quality," our computers' very mouseclicks are tracked for marketing purposes, and our most sensitive personal information can be accessed and appropriated by strangers, we can sympathize with Lady Audley in a way that Braddon probably did not expect.

60. Gilles Deleuze, *Difference and Repetition,* trans. Paul Patton (New York: Columbia University Press, 1994), 77.

61. Robert entertains these doubts on at least two occasions, on one of which he asks himself, rather early in his pursuit of the circumstances surrounding George's death, "am I to be tormented all my life by vague doubts, and wretched suspicions, which may grow upon me till I become a monomaniac? Why did she come to London?" (149). Later, he asks himself a similar question: "Why did that unaccountable terror seize upon me?" he thought. "Why was it that I saw some strange mystery in my friend's disappearance? Was it a monition or a monomania? What if I am wrong after all? What if this chain of evidence which I have constructed link by link, is woven out of my own folly? What if this edifice of horror and suspicion is a mere collection of crotchets—the nervous fancies of a hypochondriacal bachelor?" (252)

62. Aeron Haynie, "'An idle handle that was never turned, and a lazy rope so rotten': The Decay of the Country Estate in *Lady Audley's Secret,"* in *Beyond Sensation: Mary Elizabeth Braddon in Context,* ed. Marlene Tromp, Pamela K. Gilbert, and Aeron Haynie (Albany: State University of New York Press, 2000), 71.

63. Later, Robert refers to Alicia as a "dear bouncing generous thing" (209), and a "spitfire," one whose "animation of . . . manner" must be suppressed (223). "Loitering" in front of Audley Court, and wondering why Alicia has become such a nuisance to him lately, he calls her "a dear girl," "a generous-hearted, bouncing, noble English lassie" (260). And, although he never uses the word to her directly

in the course of the novel, Alicia is familiar with the characterization, for later she laments, "Perhaps Robert might care for me, if I had inflammation of the lungs. . . . He couldn't insult me by calling me a Bouncer then. Bouncers don't have inflammation of the lungs" (335).

64. Daly, "Railway Novels," 474.

65. I have counted at least fourteen specific references to train schedules, timetables or ordinal references such as "the first up-train" (204). These occur on pages 67 ("10:50 express"), 77 ("6:15" [train]), 145 ("express that left Brentwood at three o'clock"), 204 ("first up-train"), 226 ("an early train . . . reached Shoreditch a little after nine o'clock"), 239 ("an express train that started at a quarter before two"), 249 ("An express for London left Wildnernsea at a quarter-past one"), 357 ("The mail goes at twenty minutes past nine"), 367 ("The first fast train from London arrived at Audley at half-past ten o'clock"), 376 ("The mail for Dover left London Bridge at nine o'clock, and could be easily caught by Robert and his charge, as the seven o'clock up-train from Audley reached Shoreditch at a quarter past eight"), 389 ("[Robert] would fain have travelled even more rapidly than the express between Brussels and Paris could carry him"), 393 ("There was no train to Audley after the Ipswich mail, which left London at half past eight; but there was a train that left Shoreditch at eleven, and stopped at Brentwood between twelve and one"), 395 ("It was no use leaving the Temple until eleven o'clock, and even then he would be sure to reach the station half an hour too early"), 397 ("the rushing engine, in that thicket towards which the train was speeding"). Note Robert's increasing haste, impatience, and frustration as the novel progresses.

I have also noted at least 27 references to clocks, chimes and specific times. These occur on pages 7, 68, 80, 82, 83, 84, 102, 139, 147, 194, 251, 307, 310, 317, 330, 332, 334, 335, 360, 368, 373, 393, 395, 396, 401, 426, and 429; and at least eight specific references to dates. These occur on pages 161, 220, 233, 242, 247, 265, 414, and 435.

66. Stuart Sherman, *Telling Time: Clocks, Diaries and English Diurnal Form, 1660–1785* (Chicago: The University of Chicago Press, 1996), 4, 2.

67. Ian P. Watt, "Time and Family in the Gothic Novel: *The Castle of Otranto*," *Eighteenth Century Life* 10.3 (1986): 163.

68. For more on the depictions of writing in the novel, see Richard S. Albright, "'A twisted piece of paper . . . half-burned upon the hearthrug': Depictions of Writing in *Lady Audley's Secret*," *Wilkie Collins Society Journal* 4 (2001): 35–49.

69. Jenny Bourne Taylor, *In the Secret Theatre of Home: Wilkie Collins, Sensation Narrative, and Nineteenth-Century Psychology* (London: Routledge, 1988), 11–12; Nicholas Rance, *Wilkie Collins and Other Sensation Novelists: Walking the Moral Hospital* (Rutherford, N.J.: Fairleigh Dickinson University Press, 1991), 123; Ann Cvetkovich, *Mixed Feelings: Feminism, Mass Culture, and Victorian Sensationalism* (New Brunswick, NJ: Rutgers University Press, 1992), 48; Elaine Showalter, "Family Secrets and Domestic Subversion: Rebellion in the Novels of the 1860s," in *The Victorian Family: Structure and Stresses*, ed. Anthony S. Wohl (New York: St. Martin's Press, 1978), 113. Other critics such as Jill Matus have explored the Victorian concept of "moral insanity" (a defective sense of morality that left the intellect unaffected), which Matus terms "an extremely controversial notion in medical and legal discourse [at mid-century], considered by many to be a subversive and mischievous doctrine, and associated with the evasion of criminal responsibility and accountability" (Matus, "Disclosure as 'Cover-up,'" 338).

70. Collins, *The Woman in White*, 614, 633.

71. Antonia Losano examines the doppelgänger motif in "governess fiction" in a fascinating study that cites Charlotte Brontë's *Jane Eyre,* Henry James's *The Turn of the Screw,* and *East Lynne* as her primary examples, noting the uniqueness of Isabel Vane as a "chronological double" who possesses two simultaneous, and not just sequential, identities. Losano also observes that most stories with male doubles usually result in the deaths of both doubled selves, whereas stories with female doubles usually end with the second self surviving after the death of the first. See Antonia Losano, "*East Lynne, The Turn of the Screw,* and the Female Doppelgänger in Governess Fiction," *Nineteenth Century Studies* 18 (2004): 107, 115n35, 113.

72. Ellen (Mrs Henry) Wood, *East Lynne,* ed. Andrew Maunder (Peterborough, Ontario: Broadview Press Ltd., 2000.), 471. Subsequent references to this text will be parenthetical.

73. Thomas, "Wilkie Collins and the Sensation Novel," 506.

74. Luke 16:18.

75. And, according to a clause in the Divorce Act, once legally separated from her husband, she would have the same property rights as a single woman (Nayder, *Wilkie Collins,* 73).

76. *Lady Audley's Secret:* "Alicia sat with her back to the horses, and he could perceive, even in the dusk, that she was a handsome brunette; but Lady Audley was seated on the side of the carriage furthest from the inn, and he could see nothing of the fair-haired paragon of whom he had heard so much" (57).

The Woman in White (from Marian's description of herself and her half-sister): "Except that we are both orphans, we are in every respect as unlike each other as possible. My father was a poor man, and Miss Fairlie's father was a rich man. I have got nothing, and she has a fortune. I am dark and ugly, and she is fair and pretty. Everybody thinks me crabbed and odd (with perfect justice); and everybody thinks her sweet-tempered and charming (with more justice still). In short, she is an angel; and I am—Try some of that marmalade, Mr. Hartright . . ." (60–61).

77. This calculation is based upon Isabel Lucy's age being given as eight years old on the day after Lady Isabel's return to East Lynne (473), and the fact that little Isabel was born approximately one year (or possibly two) after Lady Isabel's marriage to Archibald. The uncertainty stems from the combination of several statements by the narrator. Chapter 16 describes the return of the Carlyles to East Lynne after the wedding, which we know took place on May 1 (175). Chapter 17 begins, "Another year came in" (216); on the next page is the statement, "One day—it was the month of February" (217). A few pages later, Isabel's labor takes place on "a morning early in April" (220). It is not clear whether the "another year" referred to is from the wedding to the lying in (May to April), and thus includes the February to April interval, or whether a year passes before that, which would make the period from Isabel's first sight of Barbara to the time of her return ten years, rather than nine.

78. Oliphant, "Sensation Novels," 567 .

79. Barbara's beating heart references occur on pages 65 (twice), 70, 77, 173, 174, 211, 285, and 324.

80. The references to Isabel's beating heart or pulses occur on pages 159, 167 (twice), 216, 254, 263 (twice), 342, 344, 358, 362, 448, 451, 453, 457, 460, 476, 499, 523, 577, 583, 591, and 658.

81. Maunder, introduction to *East Lynne,* 25; Samuel Lucas, rev. of *East*

Lynne, The Times (January 25, 1862): 6, repr. in *East Lynne* (Peterborough, Ontario: Broadview Press Ltd., 2000), 713.

82. On only seven occasions (out of a total of thirty-nine) does Wood refer to hearts being faster, using terms "quicker," "quickly," "rapidly," or "wildly." These occur on pages 65 and 285 for Barbara, 198 and 299 for Archibald, and on pages 167, 344, and 358 for Isabel. And of course, William's heart ceases to beat (652), as previously noted.

83. There are at least six previous references, by various characters, to the prohibition against speaking Isabel's name. These occur on pages 333, 449, 531, 551, 660, and 687. As Joyce stated, "Lady Isabel's name is an interdicted one in this house" (531).

84. Jacques Derrida, *Aporias: Dying—awaiting (one another at) the "limits of truth,"* trans. Thomas Dutoit (Stanford, CA: Stanford University Press, 1993), 35, Bernstein, "Ape Anxiety," 259, 255.

85. Derrida, *Aporias,* 87n, 33–34.

86. Showalter, "Family Secrets and Domestic Subversion," 110.

87. Thomas, "Wilkie Collins and the Sensation Novel," 484.

88. Martin Heidegger, *Being and Time,* trans. Joan Stambaugh (Albany: State University of New York Press, 1996), 232 (§50); 226 (§48).

89. Frank Kermode, *The Sense of an Ending: Studies in the Theory of Fiction* (New York: Oxford University Press, 1967), 7–8.

90. As I have argued elsewhere (see Albright, "'A twisted piece of paper'"), it is significant that Lady Audley's own death occurs offstage, is shrouded in mystery, and is documented by "a black-edged letter, written upon foreign paper . . . to announce the death of *a certain* Madame Taylor," (*LAS* 435–36, emphasis added). The stated cause of death (*maladie de langueur*) is translated by Taylor as "Anaemia, but also, more generally, listlessness" (Taylor, notes to *Lady Audley's Secret,* 454), a suggestion of inactivity that we associate with Robert Audley throughout much of the novel.

91. Collins, *The Woman in White,* 546.

92. Altick, *Victorian People and Ideas,* 99.

93. Braddon, *Lady Audley's Secret,* 237; Oliphant, "Sensation Novels," 564.

CHAPTER 5: CONCLUSION

1. The *Physics* was written some time between c. 347 B.C. and Aristotle's death in 322 B.C., but it was apparently not written all at the same time.

2. *Confessions* was written c. 397–98 A.D.

3. Paul Ricoeur, *Time and Narrative,* trans. Kathleen Blamey and David Pallauer, 3 vols. (Chicago: University of Chicago Press, 1984–88), 3: 140.

4. Ibid., 3: 183–86; 1: 3.

5. Ibid., 3: 12.

6. Wilkie Collins, *The Woman in White,* ed. Julian Symons (New York: Penguin Books, 1985), 546.

7. Charles Darwin, *The Origin of Species,* in *Darwin,* ed. Philip Appleman (New York: W. W. Norton & Company, Inc., 1970), 199.

8. Peter Brooks, *Reading for the Plot: Design and Intention in Narrative* (Cambridge, MA: Harvard University Press, 1992), 25.

Works Cited

Albright, Richard S. "'A twisted piece of paper . . . half-burned upon the hearth-rug': Depictions of Writing in *Lady Audley's Secret*." *Wilkie Collins Society Journal* 4 (2001): 35–49.

———. "'In the mean time, what did Perdita?': Rhythms and Reversals in Mary Shelley's *The Last Man*." *Romanticism On the Net* 13 (1999). http://www.erudit.org/revue/ron/1999/v/n13/005848ar.html.

———. "No Time Like the Present: *The Mysteries of Udolpho*." *Journal for Early Modern Cultural Studies* 5.1 (2005): 49–75.

Aldiss, Brian. *The Detached Retina: Aspects of SF and Fantasy*. Syracuse: Syracuse University Press, 1995.

Altick, Richard D. *The Presence of the Present: Topics of the Day in the Victorian Novel*. Columbus, OH: Ohio State University Press, 1991.

———. *Victorian People and Ideas*. New York: W. W. Norton & Company, 1973.

———. *Victorian Studies in Scarlet*. New York: W. W. Norton & Company, 1970.

Anderson, Benedict. *Imagined Communities: Reflections on the Origin and Spread of Nationalism*. 1983. London: Verso, 1991.

Aristotle. *De Anima*. Translated by J. A. Smith. In *The Basic Works of Aristotle*. Edited by Richard McKeon. New York: Random House, 1941. 535–603.

———. *Physics*. Translated by Robin Waterfield. Oxford: Oxford University Press, 1996.

Augustine. *Confessions*. Translated by R. S. Pine-Coffin. London: Penguin Books, 1961.

Bakhtin, M. M. *The Dialogic Imagination*. Edited by Michael Holquist. Translated by Caryl Emerson and Michael Holquist. Austin: University of Texas Press, 1998.

Baldick, Chris. Introduction to *Melmoth the Wanderer,* by Charles Robert Maturin. Oxford: Oxford University Press, 1998. vii–xix.

Bannet, Eve Tavor. "The 'Abyss of the Present' and Women's Time in Mary Shelley's *The Last Man*." *The Eighteenth-Century Novel* 2 (2002): 353–81.

Barbauld, Mrs. Anna Letitia. "Mrs Radcliffe," Introductory Preface. In *The British Novelists*. 50 vols. London: Printed for Rivington and others, 1810. 43: i–viii.

Bayer-Berenbaum, Linda. *The Gothic Imagination: Expansion in Gothic Literature and Art*. Rutherford, NJ: Fairleigh Dickinson University Press, 1982.

Bennett, Betty T. *Mary Wollstonecraft Shelley: An Introduction*. Baltimore: The Johns Hopkins University Press, 1998.

———. "Radical Imaginings: Mary Shelley's *The Last Man*." *The Wordsworth Circle* 26.3 (1995): 147–52.

Bernstein, Susan D. "Ape Anxiety: Sensation Fiction, Evolution, and the Genre Question." *Journal of Victorian Culture* 6.2 (2001): 250–71.

Blumberg, Jane. *Mary Shelley's Early Novels: "This Child of Imagination and Misery."* Iowa City: University of Iowa Press, 1993.

Braddon, Mary Elizabeth. *Lady Audley's Secret.* 1862. Edited by Jenny Bourne Taylor. London: Penguin Books, Ltd., 1998.

British Critic 4, review of *The Mysteries of Udolpho*, by Ann Radcliffe, August 1794: 110–21. Rogers 19–21.

Brooks, Peter. *Reading for the Plot: Design and Intention in Narrative.* Cambridge, MA: Harvard University Press, 1992.

Bruce, Donald Williams. "Ann Radcliffe and the Extended Imagination." *Contemporary Review* 258 (1991): 302.

Burke, Edmund. *A Philosophical Enquiry into the Origin of Our Ideas of the Sublime and Beautiful.* 1757. Edited by David Womersley. London: Penguin Books, 1998.

———. *Reflections on the Revolution in France.* 1790. Amherst, NY: Prometheus Books, 1987.

Butler, Marilyn. "*Frankenstein* and Radical Science." *Times Literary Supplement,* April 4,1993. Reprinted in *Frankenstein,* by Mary Shelley. Edited by J. Paul Hunter. New York: W. W. Norton & Co., 1996. 302–13.

Byron, George Gordon, Baron. "Darkness." 1816. In *Lord Byron: The Major Works.* Edited by Jerome J. McGann. Oxford: Oxford University Press, 2000. 272–73.

———. "Frame Work Bill Speech," in the House of Lords, February 27, 1812. In *Lord Byron: The Complete Miscellaneous Prose,* edited by Andrew Nicholson. Oxford: Clarendon Press, 1991. 22–27.

Cantor, Paul A. "The Apocalypse of Empire: Mary Shelley's *The Last Man.*" In Conger, Frank, and O'Dea, *Iconoclastic Departures.* 193–211.

Cassidy, David. C. *Uncertainty: The Life and Science of Werner Heisenberg.* New York: W. H. Freeman and Company, 1992.

Castle, Terry. Notes to *The Mysteries of Udolpho,* by Ann Radcliffe. Edited by Bonamy Dobrée. Oxford: Oxford University Press, 1998. 673–93.

———. "The Spectralization of the Other in *The Mysteries of Udolpho.*" *The New Eighteenth Century: Theory, Politics, English Literature.* Edited by Felicity Nussbaum and Laura Brown. New York: Methuen, 1987. 231–53.

Catholic Encyclopedia, The. 15 vols. Edited by Charles G. Herbermann, Edward A. Pace, Condé B. Pallen, Thomas J. Shahan, and John J. Wynne. New York: Robert Appleton Company, 1907–12.

Chapman, Raymond. *The Sense of the Past in Victorian Literature.* New York: St. Martin's Press, 1986.

Christian Remembrancer n.s. 46, "Our Female Sensation Novelists," 1863: 210. Flint 277.

Clery, E. J. *The Rise of Supernatural Fiction, 1762–1800.* Cambridge, UK: Cambridge University Press, 1995.

Clery, E. J., and Robert Miles, eds. *Gothic Documents: A Sourcebook 1700–1820.* Manchester, NH: Manchester University Press, 2000.

Coleridge, Samuel Taylor. *Biographia Literaria.* 1817. London: J. M. Dent, 1997.

Collins, Wilkie. *The Woman in White.* 1860. Edited by Julian Symons. New York: Penguin Books, 1985.

Conger, Syndy M., Frederick S. Frank, and Gregory O'Dea, eds. *Iconoclastic Departures: Mary Shelley After Frankenstein: Essays in Honor of the Bicentenary of Mary Shelley's Birth.* Madison: Fairleigh Dickinson University Press, 1997.

Crook, Nora. "On Richard Albright's "'In the mean time, what did Perdita?'": Rhythms and Reversals in Mary Shelley's The Last Man." *Romanticism on the Net.* http://users.ox.ac.uk/~scat0385/forum.html#rick.

Cvetkovich, Ann. "Ghostlier Determinations: The Economy of Sensation and *The Woman in White.*" *Novel* 23.1 (1989): 24–43.

———. *Mixed Feelings: Feminism, Mass Culture, and Victorian Sensationalism.* New Brunswick, NJ: Rutgers University Press, 1992.

Daly, Nicholas. "Railway Novels: Sensation Fiction and the Modernization of the Senses." *ELH* 66 (1999): 461–87.

Darwin, Charles. *The Origin of Species.* 1859. *Darwin.* Edited by Philip Appleman. New York: W. W. Norton & Company, Inc., 1970. 98–199.

de Beer, Sir Gavin. "Biology before the *Beagle.*" 1964. In *Darwin.* Edited by Philip Appleman. New York: W. W. Norton & Company, Inc., 1970. 3–10.

DeLamotte, Eugenia C. *Perils of the Night: A Feminist Study of Nineteenth-Century Gothic.* New York: Oxford University Press, 1990.

Deleuze, Gilles. *Difference and Repetition.* Translated by Paul Patton. New York: Columbia University Press, 1994.

———. *The Logic of Sense.* Translated by Mark Lester. New York: Columbia University Press, 1990.

Deleuze, Gilles, and Félix Guattari. *A Thousand Plateaus: Capitalism and Schizophrenia.* 1980. Translated by Brian Massumi. Minneapolis: University of Minnesota Press, 1987.

Derrida, Jacques. *Aporias: Dying—awaiting (one another at) the "limits of truth."* Translated by Thomas Dutoit. Stanford, CA: Stanford University Press, 1993.

Dinshaw, Carolyn. "Reading Like a Man: The Critics, the Narrator, Troilus, and Pandarus." In *Chaucer's* Troilus and Criseyde: *"Subgit to alle Poesye"; Essays in Criticism.* Edited by R. A. Shoaf. Binghamton, NY: Medieval and Renaissance Texts and Studies, 1992.

Downing, Douglas, and Michael Covington. *Dictionary of Computer Terms.* Woodbury, NY: Barron's, 1986.

Ehlers, Leigh A. "The 'Incommunicable Condition' of Melmoth." *Research Studies* 49.3 (1981): 171–82.

Ellis, Kate Ferguson. *The Contested Castle: Gothic Novels and the Subversion of Domestic Ideology.* Urbana: University of Illinois Press, 1989.

Feldman, Paula R. and Scott-Kilvert, Diana. Introduction to *The Journals of Mary Shelley, 1814–1844.* Edited by Paula R. Feldman and Diana Scott-Kilvert. Baltimore: Johns Hopkins University Press, 1987. xv–xxiii.

Fisch, Audrey A. "Plaguing Politics: AIDS, Deconstruction and *The Last Man.*" In Fisch, Mellor, and Schor, *The Other Mary Shelley.* 267–86.

Fisch, Audrey A., Anne K. Mellor, and Esther H. Schor, eds. *The Other Mary Shelley: Beyond Frankenstein.* New York: Oxford University Press, 1993.

Flaxman, Rhoda L. "Radcliffe's Dual Modes of Vision." In *Fetter'd or free? British*

Women Novelists, 1670–1815. Edited by Mary Anne Schofield and Cecilia Macheski. Athens, OH: Ohio University Press, 1986. 124–33.

Flint, Kate. *The Woman Reader 1837–1914*. New York: Oxford University Press, 1993.

Fowler, Kathleen."Hieroglyphics of Fire: *Melmoth the Wanderer.*" *Studies in Romanticism* 25.4 (1986): 521–39.

Franci, Giovanna. "A Mirror of the Future: Vision and Apocalypse in Mary Shelley's *The Last Man.*" In *Mary Shelley: Modern Critical Views*. Edited by Harold Bloom. New York: Chelsea House Publishers, 1985. 181–91.

Freud, Sigmund. "The Uncanny." In *Collected Papers*. 5 vols. New York: Basic Books, 1959. 4: 368–407.

Genette, Gérard. *Narrative Discourse: An Essay in Method*. 1972. Translated by Jane E. Lewin. Ithaca, NY: Cornell University Press, 1983.

Gilpin, William. *Observations, Relative Chiefly to Picturesque Beauty, Made in the Year 1772, on Several Parts of England; Particularly the Mountains, and Lakes of Cumberland, and Westmorland*. 2 vols. London: R. Blaimire, 1786.

Godwin, William. *Enquiry Concerning Political Justice and its Influence on Morals and Happiness*. 3rd ed. 2 vols. London, 1798. Facsim. ed. Toronto: The University of Toronto Press, 1946.

———. *St. Leon: A Tale of the Sixteenth Century*. 1799. Edited by Pamela Clemit. Oxford: Oxford University Press, 1994.

Gordon, Scott Paul. *The Practice of Quixotism: Postmodern Theory and Eighteenth-Century Women's Writing*. New York: Palgrave Macmillian, 2006.

Grant, Douglas. Notes to *Melmoth the Wanderer,* by Charles Robert Maturin. Oxford: Oxford University Press, 1998. 543–60.

Grove's Dictionary of Music and Musicians. Edited by Eric Blom. 10 vols. Fifth Edition. New York: St. Martin's Press, Inc., 1955.

Hawking, Stephen. *A Brief History of Time*. Updated and expanded tenth anniversary edition. New York: Bantam, 1998.

Haynie, Aeron. "'An idle handle that was never turned, and a lazy rope so rotten': The Decay of the Country Estate in *Lady Audley's Secret.*" In *Beyond Sensation: Mary Elizabeth Braddon in Context*. Edited by Marlene Tromp, Pamela K. Gilbert, and Aeron Haynie. Albany: State University of New York Press, 2000. 63–74.

Heidegger, Martin. *Being and Time*. Translated by Joan Stambaugh. Albany: State University of New York Press, 1996.

Heller, Tamar. *Dead Secrets: Wilkie Collins and the Female Gothic*. New Haven, CT: Yale University Press, 1992.

Hennelly, Jr., Mark M. "*Melmoth the Wanderer* and Gothic Existentialism." *Studies in English Literature 1500–1900* 214 (1981): 665–79.

———. "Reading Detection in *The Woman in White.*" *Texas Studies in Literature and Language*. 22.4 (1980): 451–65.

Hoeveler, Diane Long. *Gothic Feminism: The Professionalism of Gender from Charlotte Smith to the Brontës*. University Park, PA: Pennsylvania State University Press, 1998.

———. "Mary Shelley and Gothic Feminism: The Case of 'The Mortal Immortal'". In Conger, Frank, and O'Dea, *Iconoclastic Departures*, 150–63.

Hofkosh, Sonia. "Disfiguring Economies: Mary Shelley's Short Stories." In Fisch, Mellor, and Schor. 204–19.

Howard, Jacqueline. *Reading Gothic Fiction: A Bakhtinian Approach.* Oxford: Oxford Clarendon Press, 1994.

Hume, Robert D. "Gothic Versus Romantic: A Revaluation of the Gothic Novel." *PMLA* (1969): 282–83.

James, Henry. "Miss Braddon." *The Nation.* November 9, 1865. Reprinted in *Notes and Reviews.* Cambridge, MA: Dunster House, 1921. 108–16.

Kahane, Clare. "The Gothic Mirror." In *The (M)other Tongue: Essays in Feminist Psychoanalytic Interpretation.* Edited by Shirley Nelson Garner, Claire Kahane, and Madelon Sprengnether. Ithaca, NY: Cornell University Press, 1985. 334–51.

Kant, Immanuel. *Universal Natural History and Theory of the Heavens.* 1755. Translated by W. Hastie. Ann Arbor: The University of Michigan Press, 1969.

Kendrick, Walter M. "The Sensationalism of *The Woman in White.*" *Nineteenth-Century Fiction.* 32.1 (1977): 18–35.

Kent, Christopher. "Probability, Reality and Sensation in the Novels of Wilkie Collins." *Dickens Studies Annual* 20 (1991): 259–80.

Kermode, Frank. *The Sense of an Ending: Studies in the Theory of Fiction.* New York: Oxford University Press, 1967.

Kiely, Robert. *The Romantic Novel in England.* Cambridge, MA: Harvard University Press, 1972.

Kilgour, Maggie. "'One Immortality': The Shaping of the Shelleys in *The Last Man.*" *European Romantic Review* 16.5 (2005): 563–88.

Koselleck, Reinhart. *Futures Past: On the Semantics of Historical Time.* 1979. Translated by Keith Tribe. Cambridge, Massachusetts: The MIT Press, 1985.

Kramer, Dale. *Charles Robert Maturin.* New York: Twayne Publishers, Inc., 1973.

Landes, David S. *Revolution in Time: Clocks and the Making of the Modern World.* New York: Barnes and Noble Books, 1983.

Ledwon, Lenora. "Veiled Women, the Law of Coverture, and Wilkie Collins's *The Woman in White.*" *Victorian Literature and Culture* 22 (1994): 1–22.

Loesberg, Jonathan. "The Ideology of Narrative Form in Sensation Fiction." *Representations* 13 (1986): 115–38.

Lomax, William. "Epic Reversals in Mary Shelley's *The Last Man:* Romantic Irony and the Roots of Science Fiction." In *Contours of the Fantastic: Selected Essays from the Eighth International Conference on the Fantastic in the Arts.* Edited by Michele K. Langford. New York: Greenwood Press, 1990. 7–17.

London Literary Gazette 474, review of *The Last Man,* by Mary Shelley, 18 Feb. 1826: 103. *Nineteenth-Century Literature Criticism,* 14: 254.

Losano, Antonia. "*East Lynne, The Turn of the Screw,* and the Female Doppelgänger in Governess Fiction." *Nineteenth Century Studies* 18 (2004): 99–116.

Lucas, Samuel. Review of *East Lynne. The Times* (January 25,1862): 6. Reprinted in *East Lynne.* Edited by Andrew Maunder. Peterborough, Ontario: Broadview Press Ltd., 2000. 712–14.

Lukács, George. *The Historical Novel.* Translated by Hannah and Stanley Mitchell. London: Merlin Press, 1962.

Luke, Jr., Hugh J. "*The Last Man:* Mary Shelley's Myth of the Solitary." *Prairie Schooner* 39 (1965–66): 316–27.

MacAndrew, Elizabeth. *The Gothic Tradition in Fiction*. New York: Columbia University Press, 1979.

Macdonald, D. L. "Bathos and Repetition: The Uncanny in Radcliffe." *Journal of Narrative Technique* 19.2 (1989): 197–204.

Mackenzie, Scott. "Ann Radcliffe's Gothic Narrative and the Readers at Home." *Studies in the Novel* 31.4 (1999): 416–17.

Mansel, H. L. "Sensation Novels." *Quarterly Review*. 113 (1863): 482–514.

Maturin, Charles. *Melmoth the Wanderer*. 1822. Edited by Douglas Grant. Oxford: Oxford University Press, 1998.

Matus, Jill. "Disclosure as 'Cover-up': The Discourse of Madness in *Lady Audley's Secret*." *University of Toronto Quarterly* 62.3 (1993): 334–55.

Maunder, Andrew. General Introduction to *Varieties of Women's Sensation Fiction, 1855–1890*. 6 vols. London: Pickering & Chatto Publishers Limited, 2004. 1:vii–xxxi.

———. Introduction to *East Lynne*, by Mrs. Henry Wood. Peterborough, Ontario: Broadview Press Ltd., 2000. 9–36.

Mellor, Anne K. *Mary Shelley: Her Life, Her Fiction, Her Monsters*. New York: Methuen, Inc., 1988.

Miles, Robert. *Ann Radcliffe: The Great Enchantress*. Manchester, UK: Manchester University Press, 1995.

———. *Gothic Writing 1750–1820: A Genealogy*. London: Routledge, 1993.

Moers, Ellen. *Literary Women*. Garden City, NY: Doubleday & Company, 1976.

The Monthly Review Vol I, No. III, review of *The Last Man*, by Mary Shelley, Mar., 1826: 335. *Nineteenth-Century Literature Criticism*, 14: 254.

The Monthly Review, review of *Melmoth the Wanderer*, January 1821: 81–85. In Norton, *Gothic Readings* 333–34.

Munitz, Milton K. Introduction to *Universal Natural History and Theory of the Heavens*. Ann Arbor: The University of Michigan Press, 1969. v–xxii.

Nayder, Lillian. *Wilkie Collins*. New York: Twayne Publishers, 1997.

Nellist, Brian. "Imagining the Future: Predictive Fiction in the Nineteenth Century." In *Anticipations: Essays on Early Science Fiction and its Precursors*. Edited by David Seed. Syracuse: Syracuse University Press, 1995. 111–36.

Norton, Rictor, ed. *Gothic Readings: The First Wave, 1764–1820*. London: Leicester University Press, 2000.

———. *Mistress of Udolpho: The Life of Ann Radcliffe*. London: Leicester University Press, 1999.

Null, Jack. "Structure and Theme in *Melmoth the Wanderer*." *Papers on Language and Literature* 13.2 (1977): 136–47.

O'Dea, Gregory. "'Perhaps a Tale You'll Make It': Mary Shelley's Tales for *The Keepsake*." In Conger, Frank, and O'Dea, *Iconoclastic Departures*, 62–78.

O'Dea, Gregory Sean. *The Temporal Sublime: Time and History in the British Gothic Novel*. Diss. University of North Carolina at Chapel Hill, 1991. Ann Arbor: University Microfilms International, 1991.

Oliphant, Margaret. "Sensation Novels." *Blackwood's Edinburgh Magazine* 91 (1862): 564–84.

Oost, Regina B. "'Servility and command': Authorship in *Melmoth the Wanderer*." *Papers on Language and Literature* 31.3 (1995): 291–312.

Oxford English Dictionary. Compact edition. New York: Oxford University Press, 1971.

Peckham, Morse. "Introduction to the Variorum Edition" of *The Origin of Species,* by Charles Darwin. In *Darwin.* Edited by Philip Appleman. New York: W. W. Norton & Company, Inc., 1970. 98–100.

Plumb, J. H. *England in the Eighteenth Century.* London: Penguin Books, 1990.

Pope, Alexander. *The Dunciad in Four Books.* 1743. Harlow, Essex, UK: Longman, 1999.

Porter, Roy. *English Society in the Eighteenth Century.* London: Penguin Books, 1990.

Punter, David. *The Literature of Terror: A History of Gothic Fictions from 1765 to the Present Day.* London: Longman, 1980.

Radcliffe, Ann. *The Italian.* 1797. Edited by Frederick Garber. Oxford: Oxford University Press, 1981.

———. *The Mysteries of Udolpho.* 1794. Edited by Bonamy Dobrée. Oxford: Oxford University Press, 1998.

———. "On the Supernatural in Poetry." *New Monthly Magazine* (1826): 149.

———. *The Romance of the Forest.* Edited by Chloe Chard. 1791. Oxford: Oxford University Press, 1986.

Rance, Nicholas. *Wilkie Collins and Other Sensation Novelists: Walking the Moral Hospital.* Rutherford, NJ: Fairleigh Dickinson University Press, 1991.

Ricoeur, Paul. *Time and Narrative.* 3 vols. Translated by Kathleen Blamey and David Pallauer. Chicago: University of Chicago Press, 1984–88.

Robinson, Charles E., ed. *Mary Shelley: Collected Tales and Stories.* Baltimore: The Johns Hopkins University Press, 1976.

Rogers, Deborah D. *The Critical Response to Ann Radcliffe.* Westwood, CT: Greenwood Press, 1994.

Sage, Victor. Introduction to *Melmoth the Wanderer,* by Charles Robert Maturin. London: Penguin Books, 2000. vii–xxix.

Sambrook, A. J. "A Romantic Theme: The Last Man." *Forum for Modern Language Studies* 2 (1966): 25–33.

Scott, Sir Walter. "Mrs. Ann Radcliffe." 1824. *The Complete Works of Sir Walter Scott.* 10 vols. Philadelphia: Parry & McMillan, 1857. 8: 70–71.

[Scott, Sir Walter]. *Quarterly Review* 3 (May 1810): 344. Clery 108–9.

Shelley, Mary. *The Fortunes of Perkin Warbeck: A Romance.* 1830. Edited by Doucet Devin Fischer. In *The Novels and Selected Works of Mary Shelley.* 8 vols. London: William Pickering, 1996.

———. *Frankenstein, or, The Modern Prometheus.* 1818. Edited by J. Paul Hunter. New York: W. W. Norton & Co., 1996.

———. "Introduction to *Frankenstein,* Third Edition, 1831." *Frankenstein,* by Mary Shelley. Edited by J. Paul Hunter. New York: W. W. Norton & Co., 1996. 169.

———. *The Journals of Mary Shelley, 1814–1844.* Edited by Paula R. Feldman and Diana Scott-Kilvert. Baltimore: Johns Hopkins University Press, 1987.

———. *The Last Man.* 1826. Edited by Hugh J. Luke, Jr. Lincoln, NE: University of Nebraska Press, 1993.

———. *The Letters of Mary Wollstonecraft Shelley.* 3 vols. Edited by Betty T. Bennett. Baltimore: Johns Hopkins University Press, 1980–88.

———. "The Loves of the Poets." Edited by Pamela Clemit. In *The Novels and Selected Works of Mary Shelley.* 8 vols. London: William Pickering, 1996. London: William Pickering, 1996. 2: 195–200.

———. "The Mortal Immortal: A Tale." In Robinson, *Mary Shelley: Collected Tales and Stories.* 219–30.

———. "Roger Dodsworth: The Reanimated Englishman." In Robinson, *Mary Shelley: Collected Tales and Stories.* 43–50.

———. "Valerius: The Reanimated Roman." In Robinson, *Mary Shelley: Collected Tales and Stories.* 332–44.

Shelley, Percy Bysshe. *Adonais: An Elegy on the Death of John Keats, Author of Endymion, Hyperion, Etc.* In *Shelley's Poetry and Prose.* Edited by Donald H. Reiman and Sharon B. Powers. New York: W. W. Norton & Co., 1977. 390–406.

Sherman, Stuart. *Telling Time: Clocks, Diaries and English Diurnal Form, 1660–1785.* Chicago: The University of Chicago Press, 1996.

Showalter, Elaine. "Family Secrets and Domestic Subversion: Rebellion in the Novels of the 1860s." In *The Victorian Family: Structure and Stresses.* Edited by Anthony S. Wohl. New York: St. Martin's Press, 1978. 101–16.

Skilton, David. Introduction to *Lady Audley's Secret.* New York: Oxford University Press, 1987. vii–xxiii.

Smith, Johanna M. *Mary Shelley.* New York: Twayne Publishers, 1996.

Snyder, Robert Lance. "Apocalypse and Indeterminacy in Mary Shelley's *The Last Man.*" *Studies in Romanticism* 17 (1978): 435–52.

Spark, Muriel. *Child of Light: A Reassessment of Mary Wollstonecraft Shelley.* Hadleigh, Essex, UK: Tower Bridge Publications Limited, 1951.

Stafford, Fiona J. *The Last of the Race: The Growth of a Myth from Milton to Darwin.* Oxford: Clarendon Press, 1994.

Stambaugh, Joan. Translator's preface to *Being and Time,* by Martin Heidegger. Translated by Joan Stambaugh. Albany: State University of New York Press, 1996. xv–xvi.

Stern, Rebecca. " 'Personation' and 'Good Marking-Ink': Sanity, Performativity, and Biology in Victorian Sensation Fiction." *Nineteenth Century Studies* 14 (2000): 35–62.

Sterrenburg, Lee. "*The Last Man:* Anatomy of Failed Revolutions." *Nineteenth Century Fiction* 33 (1978): 324–47.

Stott, G. St. John. "The Structure of *Melmoth the Wanderer.*" *Études Irlandaises* 12.1 (1987): 41–52.

Sunstein, Emily W. *Mary Shelley: Romance and Reality.* Baltimore: Johns Hopkins University Press, 1991.

Sutherland, J. A. "Two Emergencies in the Writing of The Woman in White." *Yearbook of English Studies* 7 (1977): 148–56.

Taylor, Jenny Bourne. *In the Secret Theatre of Home: Wilkie Collins, Sensation Narrative, and Nineteenth-Century Psychology.* London: Routledge, 1988.

———. Introduction to *Lady Audley's Secret.* London: Penguin Books, Ltd., 1998. vii–xli.

———. Notes to *Lady Audley's Secret,* by Mary Elizabeth Braddon. London: Penguin Books, Ltd., 1998. 438–54.

————. "Psychology and Sensation: The Narrative of Moral Management in *The Woman in White." Critical Survey* 2.1 (1990): 49–56.

Tennyson, Alfred Lord. *In Memoriam A. H. H.* 1850. Edited by Erik Gray. 2nd ed. New York: W. W. Norton & Company, 2004.

Thomas, Ronald R. "Wilkie Collins and the Sensation Novel," in *Columbia History of the British Novel.* Edited by John Richetti. New York: Columbia University Press, 1994. 479–507.

Thomas, Sophie. "The Ends of the Fragment, the Problem of the Preface: Proliferation and Finality in *The Last Man.*" In *Mary Shelley's Fictions: From* Frankenstein *to* Falkner. Edited by Michael Eberle-Sinatra. New York: St. Martin's Press, LLC. 2000. 22–38.

Thoms, Peter. *The Windings of the Labyrinth: Quest and Structure in the Major Novels of Wilkie Collins.* Athens, Ohio: Ohio University Press, 1992.

Todorov, Tzvetan. *The Fantastic: A Structural Approach to a Literary Genre.* 1970. Translated by Richard Howard. Ithaca, NY: Cornell University Press, 1975.

Tompkins, J. M. S. *The Popular Novel in England, 1770–1800.* London: Methuen, 1932.

Toulmin, Stephen, and June Goodfield. *The Discovery of Time.* Chicago: University of Chicago Press, 1977.

Trott, Nicola. "Wordsworth's Gothic Quandary." *Charles Lamb Bulletin* 110 (2000): 47.

Walling, William A. *Mary Shelley.* NY: Twayne Publishers, Inc., 1972.

Watt, Ian. *The Rise of the Novel: Studies in Defoe, Richardson and Fielding.* Berkeley: University of California Press, 1957.

Watt, Ian P. "Time and Family in the Gothic Novel: *The Castle of Otranto.*" *Eighteenth Century Life* 10.3 (1986): 159–71.

Watt, James. *Contesting the Gothic: Fiction, Genre and Cultural Conflict, 1764–1832.* Cambridge, UK: Cambridge University Press, 1999.

Webb, Samantha. "Reading the End of the World: *The Last Man,* History, and the Agency of Romantic Authorship." In *Mary Shelley in Her Times.* Edited by Betty T. Bennett and Stuart Curran. Baltimore: Johns Hopkins University Press, 2000. 119–33.

Wellington, Jan. "Traversing Regions of Terror: The Revolutionary Traveller as Gothic Reader." *Studies in Travel Writing* 7 (2003): 145–67.

Wells, Lynn. "The Triumph of Death: Reading and Narrative in Mary Shelley's *The Last Man.*" In Conger, Frank, and O'Dea, *Iconoclastic Departures,* 212–34.

White, Hayden. *Tropics of Discourse: Essays in Cultural Criticism.* Baltimore: The Johns Hopkins University Press, 1985.

Whitrow, G. J. *Time in History: The Evolution of Our General Awareness of Time and Temporal Perspective.* Oxford: Oxford University Press, 1988.

Williams, Anne. *Art of Darkness: A Poetics of Gothic.* Chicago: University of Chicago Press, 1995.

Wood, Ellen (Mrs. Henry). *East Lynne.* Edited by Andrew Maunder. Peterborough, Ontario: Broadview Press Ltd., 2000.

Wordsworth, William. "Lines Written a Few Miles above Tintern Abbey, On Revisiting the Banks of the Wye during a Tour, July 13, 1798." In *Lyrical Ballads and*

Other Poems, 1797–1800. Edited by James Butler and Karen Green. Ithaca, NY: Cornell University Press, 1992. 116–20.

———. "Preface to *Lyrical Ballads.*" 1802. In *Literary Criticism of William Wordsworth.* Edited by Paul M. Zall. Lincoln: University of Nebraska Press, 1966. 38–62.

———. *The Prelude, Or, Growth of a Poet's Mind; An Autobiographical Poem.* 1850. In *The Prelude, 1799, 1805, 1850.* Edited by Jonathan Wordsworth, M. H. Abrams, and Stephen Gill. New York: W. W. Norton & Company, 1979. 29–483.

Zonana, Joyce. "'They Will Prove the Truth of My Tale': Safie's Letters as the Feminist Core of Mary Shelley's *Frankenstein.*" *Journal of Narrative Technique* 21.2 (1991): 170–84.

Index

Aldiss, Brian, 141, 143
Alison, Archibald, 41–42
Altick, Richard, 27, 165, 170–71, 181
Anderson, Benedict, 26
"angel in the house," 173, 185, 214
aporia, 13, 24, 29, 69, 71–73, 75, 116, 117, 121, 173, 179, 194–96, 207, 211, 214, 216–17; definition, 20–21, 172; as hesitation, 58, 65, 89, 125, 128, 206; as inarticulable contradiction, 42, 60, 108–9, 122, 128, 183–84, 193, 206, 208; resolution of, 28, 53
Ariosto, 63
Aristotle, 39, 66, 69–70, 75, 90–91, 109, 132, 215; being and nonbeing of time, 13–14, 21; time as movement and nonmovement, 22, 25, 36, 40, 62, 175; uninterrupted continuance, 68, 73, 100
arrivant, 208–9. *See also* Derrida
Augustine, 14, 39, 90, 110, 143, 190, 215; distentio animi, 54; recitation of a psalm, 31, 33–34, 37, 53; thick present, 29, 56, 215; threefold present, 27, 29, 54–56, 67, 215; time and motion, 22, 25, 40, 175; time of the soul and time of the world, 24, 75, 121, 216
Austen, Jane, 15

Bakhtin, M. M., 39, 42, 56, 57, 74; background animating dialogue, 64, 65; chivalric romance, 36, 62, 71; chronotope, 27, 41; dialogism, 16; epic past, 34–35, 61; heteroglossia, 25; incorporated genres, 37, 48, 53; polyglossia, 106; refraction, 64
Baldick, Chris, 69, 74, 75, 80, 100
Bannett, Eve Tavor, 137
Bayer–Berenbaum, Lynda, 40, 46–47, 60–61, 67, 69, 82, 91, 116

Beattie, James, 36
Beckford, William, 54
Bernstein, Sarah, 207–8
Blumberg, Jane, 135
Braddon, Mary Elizabeth: *Lady Audley's Secret*, 26, 29, 168–73, 185–95, 201, 209–14, 216
Brooks, Peter, 74, 163, 179–80, 217
Bruce, Donald Williams, 57
Bucke, Charles, 66
Buckle, Henry Thomas, 170
Buffon, Comte de, 23, 26
Burke, Edmund, 14–16, 22, 29, 47, 92, 97, 127, 163, 216; inheritance, 13, 172, 200–201, 213, 216–17; order, symmetry, coherence, 15, 69, 104, 147, 151; sublime, 82–84; "sure principle of transmission," 13, 20, 24, 42, 166, 184, 186, 211; transmission of property and/or values, 13, 20, 42, 61, 73, 76, 122–23, 129, 135, 151, 165. Works: *A Philosophical Enquiry into the Origin of our Ideas of the Sublime and Beautiful*, 53; *Reflections on the Revolution in France*, 13, 14, 27, 34, 63, 213
Burnet, Thomas, 33
Byron, Lord (George Gordon), 22, 119, 133, 139, 155, 156

Cantor, Paul A., 134–35, 159
Castle, Terry, 46, 47, 52, 57, 62
Chambers, Robert, 26
Child Custody Act, 168
chronos, 135–41
Clery, E. J., 50
coherence, 182–83, 209; generational, 15, 17, 24, 69, 70, 72, 76, 77, 97, 104, 216–17; narratological, 15, 20, 24, 70, 72, 75, 81, 97, 100, 108, 111, 169, 172, 179, 180, 184, 209, 216

Coleridge, Samuel Taylor, 18, 119, 139, 145, 157
Collingwood, R. G., 20
Collins, Wilkie, 19, 170, 171; *The Woman in White*, 19, 20, 29, 30, 168–85, 194, 195, 201, 203, 208–14, 216
Collins, William, 36
coverture, 172, 174, 208
Crystal Palace Exhibition, 171
Cvetkovich, Ann, 180, 193

Dacre, Charlotte, 17
Dallas, E. S., 182
Daly, Nicholas, 167, 168, 177–78, 188
Darwin, Charles, 22, 26–27, 165, 166, 180, 184, 191, 208, 214, 217
Darwin, Erasmus, 26, 120
Davy, Sir Humphry, 119
degeneration, 22, 30, 166–67, 208, 213, 216, 217
DeLamotte, Eugenia C., 104
Deleuze, Gilles, 46, 52, 175, 186
Derrida, Jacques, 13, 20, 69–70, 132, 207, 208
Dickens, Charles, 18, 167, 170, 171, 182, 215
Dinshaw, Caroline, 48
discordant concordance, 31, 45, 59, 113
dissociation of sensibility, 26, 31
divorce, 167, 195–96, 200
doppelgänger, 44, 46, 57, 196

Ehlers, Leigh A., 103, 111
Eliot, George, 166
Ellis, Kate Ferguson, 60
embedded genres, 27. *See also* Bakhtin
emplotment, 15, 30, 51, 104–13, 133–34
evolutionary theory, 22–23, 26, 27, 30, 165–67, 169, 208, 216
explained supernatural, 18, 50, 51. *See also* supernatural explained

fabula, 51, 179
fantastic, 18, 49, 58, 128
Fisch, Audrey A., 133
Flaxman, Rhoda L., 39
Fowler, Kathleen, 74, 99, 100, 111, 115
Franci, Giovanna, 134

French Revolution, 14, 20, 24, 26–28, 31–32, 34, 63, 64, 165, 215, 217

Garrick, David, 14
generational succession, 14, 22, 24, 42, 68, 72, 73, 151, 216
Genette, Gérard, 43, 49, 52, 98, 114, 134, 145, 156
geschichte, 24–25

Gibbon, Edward, 14
Godwin, William, 15–16, 22, 72, 91, 96, 111, 119, 127, 207; perfectibility, 15, 126, 139, 166–67, 185; *St. Leon*, 72, 91, 96, 125, 127, 130–32, 153, 203, 209
Gothic, 15–24, 34, 40–43, 54, 57, 59, 60, 63, 78, 99, 104, 125, 129, 171, 189; cusp, 33, 63, 121; devices or conventions, 17, 32, 48, 69, 107, 112, 115, 126, 136, 170
Guattari, Félix, 175

Harrison, John, 71
Hawking, Stephen, 113
Haynie, Aeron, 187
Hazlitt, William, 66
Heidegger, Martin, 21, 86, 137, 157, 162, 167; Care, 94, 139, 151; *Dasein*, 83, 162, 211; "now–saying," 29, 81, 96, 116–17, 142, 188, 190, 215; public time, 53, 167–68; repetition, 45–46, 52–53; "vulgar understanding of time," 54, 81
Heisenberg, Werner, 181
Heller, Tamar, 168
higher criticism, 166
Hoeveler, Diane Long, 17, 119
Horace, 14
Howard, Jacqueline, 16
Hume, Robert, 53
Hunt, Leigh, 119
Huygens, Christiaan, 71, 188

I AM, 144–45, 158, 163
industrialization, 26, 28, 70, 84–85, 216
inheritance, 61, 73, 79, 122, 124–25, 129, 135, 151, 213; matrilineal, 60, 73, 185–86. *See also* primogeniture
insanity, 106, 172–73, 181, 185–88, 193, 201

James, Henry, 19, 170, 174, 192

kairos, 135, 158–64
Kant, Immanuel, 23, 26
Kendrick, Walter M., 178–80, 182
Kent, Christopher, 170
Kermode, Frank, 28, 31, 68, 70, 71,
   86–87, 110, 111, 123, 135, 211, 217
Kilgour, Maggie, 120
Koselleck, Reinhart, 24–25, 31, 56
Kramer, Dale, 76, 110, 115

Lamarck, Jean–Baptiste de, 165–66
Landes, David S., 71
Ledwon, Lenora, 174
Lewis, Matthew, 17, 18, 54
Loesberg, Jonathan, 174
Lomax, William, 152
Luke, Hugh J., 142
Lyell, Sir Charles, 26, 166, 191

MacAndrew, Elizabeth, 49
MacDonald, D. L., 39, 40, 62
MacKenzie, Scott, 58, 59
Mansel, H. L., 19, 170, 174
Married Women's Property Act, 168
Matrimonial Causes Act, 167, 168,
   195–96, 200
Maturin, Charles Robert, 18, 51, 54,
   157; *Melmoth the Wanderer,* 28, 68–
   117, 128, 142, 156, 171, 178–79,
   183, 190, 212, 216
Matus, Jill, 186
Maunder, Andrew, 173, 204
mechanism, 30, 81–85, 91, 95, 117,
   171–72, 190, 209
Mellor, Anne, 162
Miles, Robert, 14, 26, 33, 34, 39, 46,
   63, 67, 121
Milton, John, 36, 63
mimesis₁, 110, 158
mimesis₂, 110, 113, 158, 183
mimesis₃, 110, 113, 158
Moers, Ellen, 16
muthos, 110

Nayder, Lillian, 174
Nellist, Brian, 149
Newton, Sir Isaac, 23
Norton, Caroline, 171
Norton, Rictor, 60, 63
Null, Jack, 78, 98

O'Dea, Gregory, 124, 155
Oliphant, Margaret, 168, 171, 203, 214
Oost, Regina B., 110

Peckham, Morse, 184
Pope, Alexander, 133, 139, 150
primogeniture, 20, 73
public time, 13, 29, 40, 62, 72, 88, 137–
   39, 147, 152, 167–68, 172, 176, 178,
   185, 193–94, 215–16. *See also under*
   Heidegger
Punter, David, 17, 34, 47, 62, 103, 111

Radcliffe, Ann, 16, 18, 53, 88, 104,
   140, 146, 148. Works: *The Castles of
   Athlin and Dunbayne,* 32; *The Italian,* 20, 32, 63; *The Mysteries of
   Udolpho,* 15, 16, 27, 29, 31–67, 69,
   90, 98, 116, 131, 136, 139, 149, 156,
   181, 190, 197, 207, 213, 216; *The
   Romance of the Forest,* 32, 63
Rance, Nicholas, 193
Reade, Charles, 171
Reeve, Clara, 16, 20, 48
Reform Bill, 168
revenant, 207, 209. *See also* Derrida
Ricoeur, Paul, 31, 56, 65–67, 88, 113,
   147–49, 158, 166, 183, 215; bridging
   human and astronomical universes,
   36, 195, 216; bridging memory and
   historical past, 13, 14, 21, 184, 189,
   216, 217; circle of narrativity, 28, 69,
   71, 109–10, 163, 177, 211, 216–17;
   repetition, 45–46. *See also* mimesis
Robinson, Henry Crabbe, 66

Sage, Victor, 106–7, 114
Scott, Sir Walter, 51
sensation fiction/sensation novel, 17,
   18, 19, 20, 24, 165–214, 216
sensibility, 16, 33, 50, 64
Shakespeare, William, 36, 63
Shelley, Mary, 22, 28, 51, 54, 118–64.
   Works: *Falkner,* 120; *The Fortunes of
   Perkin Warbeck,* 120, 121, 125;
   Frankenstein, 103, 120–21, 125,
   132, 133, 138, 156; *The Last Man,*
   22, 28, 29, 119, 120–23, 133–64,
   183, 216; *Lodore,* 120; tales, 121,
   123–33, 216; *Valperga,* 120, 124
Shelley, Percy B., 43, 118, 119, 122–
   23, 155

Sherman, Stuart, 117, 188
Showalter, Elaine, 193
Siddons, Sarah, 14
sjužet, 51, 179
Spark, Muriel, 136, 139, 141–42
Stafford, Fiona J., 23, 118, 123, 125, 135
standard time, 26, 167, 216
Stern, Rebecca, 167, 184
Sterrenburg, Lee, 155
Strauss, David Friedrich, 166
Sturm und Drang, 17
sublimity, 33, 37, 40–43, 53, 56. *See also under* Burke
supernatural explained, 18, 51, 140. *See also* explained supernatural
Sutherland, J. A., 178, 182

Talfourd, Thomas Noon, 63
Taylor, Jenny Bourne, 185, 193
Tennyson, Alfred Lord, 36, 166
Thelwall, John, 64
Thomas, Ronald R., 165, 171
Thoms, Peter, 179
Thomson, James, 36

Todorov, Tzvetan, 18, 49, 58, 128, 179
Trollope, Anthony, 171, 182

uncanniness, 18, 28, 44, 45, 49, 197, 208
Ussher, James, 22–23
usurpation, 16, 17, 20, 24, 35, 48, 73, 124–26, 129, 170

Walpole, Horace, 16, 18, 20, 32, 40, 48, 54
Wandering Jew, 72, 91, 131
Watt, Ian P., 40, 42, 56
Wells, H. G., 134
White, Hayden, 14–15, 20, 51, 105, 133–34
Whitrow, G. J., 114
Wollstonecraft, Mary, 119
Wood, Ellen (Mrs Henry); *East Lynne,* 29, 168–73, 195–214, 216
Wordsworth, William, 142, 151. Works: *Lyrical Ballads,* 18; "Tintern Abbey," 45–46, 154
Wuthering Heights, 20